perspectives

Race and Crime

20.00

perspectives

Race and Crime

Academic Editors

Robert L. Bing III
University of Texas at Arlington

Alejandro del Carmen
University of Texas at Arlington

coursewise
publishing
inc.

Bellevue • Boulder • Dubuque • Madison • St. Paul

Our mission at **Coursewise** is to help students make connections—linking theory to practice and the classroom to the outside world. Learners are motivated to synthesize ideas when course materials are placed in a context they recognize. By providing gateways to contemporary and enduring issues, **Coursewise** publications will expand students' awareness of and context for the course subject.

For more information on **Coursewise,** visit us at our web site: http://www.coursewise.com

To order an examination copy:
Houghton Mifflin Sixth Floor Media 800-565-6247 (voice) / 800-565-6236 (fax)

Coursewise Publishing Editorial Staff

Thomas Doran, ceo/publisher: Environmental Science/Geography/Journalism/Marketing/Speech
Edgar Laube, publisher: Political Science/Psychology/Sociology
Linda Meehan Avenarius, publisher: **Courselinks™**
Sue Pulvermacher-Alt, publisher: Education/Health/Gender Studies
Victoria Putman, publisher: Anthropology/Philosophy/Religion
Tom Romaniak, publisher: Business/Criminal Justice/Economics
Kathleen Schmitt, publishing assistant
Gail Hodge, executive producer

Coursewise Publishing Production Staff

Lori A. Blosch, permissions coordinator
Mary Monner, production coordinator
Victoria Putman, production manager

Cover photo: Copyright © 1997 T. Teshigawara/Panoramic Images, Chicago, IL. All Rights Reserved.

Interior design and cover design by Jeff Storm

Library of Congress Catalog Card Number: 99-067121

ISBN 0-618-02580-4

Printed in the United States of America by Coursewise Publishing, Inc.
7 North Pinckney Street, Suite 346, Madison, WI 53703

10 9 8 7 6 5 4 3 2 1

from the
Publisher

Tom Romaniak

Coursewise Publishing

Several years ago, a character on a TV situation comedy stated in frustration, "I'm a white male at the only time in history that it doesn't pay to be a white male." As a white male myself, I know that, in some respects, the character is right. In these politically correct times, white males are probably the only group that you make fun of without sounding insensitive.

Yet, when I dig deep into this issue, I realize that being a white male does offer me some advantages. Generally speaking, I am not the subject of racist comments or attitudes. Strangers are more likely to approach me because I am white. Opportunity knocks on my door without passing me by. Those in our society who are not "pale males" do not necessarily receive the advantages bestowed on me.

Most successful minorities have had to work harder than their "pale male" counterparts to achieve the same level of success. They not only have to prove mastery of a certain skill set, they also must overcome racist attitudes and perceptions that lead to mistrust.

One of those perceptions that leads to mistrust is that minorities are more likely to be criminal. This perception is based on arrest records, jail populations, and our laws. Law enforcement officials are more likely to stop minorities than whites. Minorities make up a disproportionate share of our jail populations.

How do I know this? I have read the articles and the research presented in this volume. I have talked with Bob Bing and Alex del Carmen—the Academic Editors of this volume. Through this reading and these conversations, I know that minorities face an uphill battle in our society today. They must work harder to stay out of the criminal justice system and work even harder still to achieve the level of success that is more commonly achieved by "pale males."

Bob Bing and Alex del Carmen, both minorities, are passionate about issues of race and crime. They agreed to work on this volume only after securing full editorial authority to determine which articles would make the final publication. They wanted to make sure that this reader fairly represented the issues of race and crime, without worrying about a publisher's political correctness.

I thank them for all of the work and passion that they put into this volume. I also thank them for causing me to stop, think about, and be thankful for the opportunities I have, and to be mindful of the unnecessary obstacles that others face. Hopefully, with this new knowledge, I can work to even the playing field.

I welcome your thoughts and opinions about this volume and the corresponding **Courselinks**™ site for Race and Crime, where you will find additional information and resources. And by all means, email me to tell me your experience.

Tom Romaniak
tomr@coursewise.com

Robert L. Bing III

from the
Academic Editors

Robert L. Bing III
University of Texas at Arlington

Alejandro del Carmen
University of Texas at Arlington

Interest in the issue of race and crime stems from personal experiences, empirical research, and concerns about the criminal justice system. Much of the research on race and crime has been grounded in theories that have a "middle-class" bias—namely, an underlying assumption that crime is largely an African American phenomenon. The criminal justice system also reflects this bias. Law enforcement agencies, courts, and corrections often make decisions based on race or on racial and ethnic stereotypes. The point here is that race is a critical component of the race and crime issue, and requires additional exploration, discussion, and critical thinking. Part of the problem, it seems, has been a reluctance to address the real issues. Classrooms and students are uncharacteristically silent on the issue of race and crime—specifically, they are uncomfortable discussing race. We hope that this reader will provide a forum for intellectual debate and discussion.

One harsh reality is that the levels of offending, rates of arrests, and numbers of incarcerations are higher for blacks than for any other group in American society. This reality should raise questions about race and crime, racism, and disproportionality and structured inequalities in American society. While some individuals argue that discrimination and stereotypes have little to do with the overrepresentation of blacks in the American criminal justice system, we challenge you to immerse yourself in the literature contained in this reader and reach your own conclusions.

We have made a concerted effort to identify some of the best readings on race and crime in the academic and popular literature. This reader has six sections. Section 1 examines the social construction of black crime. The readings discuss conceptual and definitional issues as they relate to race and crime, and also make the case that the study of race and crime is critical. Near the end of this section is a reading about the politicized nature of crime and the implications therein. Section 2 looks more closely at crime causation and race. The readings ask and answer the question: What are the realities with regard to black crime? Section 3 explores society's response to crime—in particular, the criminal justice system's response to black crime, as well as legislation regarding hate crimes. Sections 4 and 5 present readings about the judicial system and incarceration. Here, jurors' roles are discussed in detail, and you learn the realities of and reasons for the overrepresentation of blacks in American penal institutions. Section 6 examines black criminal victimization. One point that you glean rather quickly is that African Americans are victims of crime. Rarely will you be offered the perspectives presented in this section.

Alejandro del Carmen

In sum, we believe that this reader is the best collection of articles on race and crime available. Our challenge to you is simple: Read and absorb this material, and see for yourself the realities of race and crime.

Robert L. Bing III is an associate professor of criminology and criminal justice and is director of the criminology and criminal justice program at the University of Texas at Arlington. He received his bachelor's degree from the College of the Holy Cross and his master's and doctorate from Florida State University. His research interests include race and crime, corrections, plea bargaining, and criminal justice education; he has also authored many articles on a range of topics. Dr. Bing enjoys music, reading, tennis, and quality time with his wife and daughter.

Alejandro del Carmen is an assistant professor of criminology and criminal justice at the University of Texas at Arlington. He received his bachelor's degree from Florida International University and his master's and doctorate from Florida State University. Dr. del Carmen has taught several courses, including criminal justice, criminology, corrections, law, and victimology. He and his wife, Denise, have a child, Gabriel, and a baby girl on her way. Outside academic work, Dr. del Carmen enjoys listening to Frank Sinatra.

Dedications

A special acknowledgment to my wife, Cynthia I. Bing; she has given so much of herself. My participation in this project depended on her support. I also offer a special thanks to my daughter, Melissa M. Bing, who has brightened my world. Last, but not least, I dedicate this book to the loving memory of my mother, Thelbert H. Bing. She has always been a source of inspiration, courage, and knowledge. . . . To all three generations, I am eternally grateful for their love, support, and encouragement.

To Denise, Gabriel, and Gemma, and to my parents, Alejandro and Maria Cristina, for their support, courage, and love. They constantly inspire me to be a better human being.

WiseGuide Introduction

Critical Thinking and Bumper Stickers

The bumper sticker said: Question Authority. This is a simple directive that goes straight to the heart of critical thinking. The issue is not whether the authority is right or wrong; it's the questioning process that's important. Questioning helps you develop awareness and a clearer sense of what you think. That's critical thinking.

Critical thinking is a new label for an old approach to learning—that of challenging all ideas, hypotheses, and assumptions. In the physical and life sciences, systematic questioning and testing methods (known as the scientific method) help verify information, and objectivity is the benchmark on which all knowledge is pursued. In the social sciences, however, where the goal is to study people and their behavior, things get fuzzy. It's one thing for the chemistry experiment to work out as predicted, or for the petri dish to yield a certain result. It's quite another matter, however, in the social sciences, where the subject is ourselves. Objectivity is harder to achieve.

Although you'll hear critical thinking defined in many different ways, it really boils down to analyzing the ideas and messages that you receive. What are you being asked to think or believe? Does it make sense, objectively? Using the same facts and considerations, could you reasonably come up with a different conclusion? And, why does this matter in the first place? As the bumper sticker urged, question authority. Authority can be a textbook, a politician, a boss, a big sister, or an ad on television. Whatever the message, learning to question it appropriately is a habit that will serve you well for a lifetime. And in the meantime, thinking critically will certainly help you be course wise.

Question Authority

Getting Connected

This reader is a tool for connected learning. This means that the readings and other learning aids explained here will help you to link classroom theory to real-world issues. They will help you to think critically and to make long-lasting learning connections. Feedback from both instructors and students has helped us to develop some suggestions on how you can wisely use this connected learning tool.

WiseGuide Pedagogy

A wise reader is better able to be a critical reader. Therefore, we want to help you get wise about the articles in this reader. Each section of *Perspectives* has three tools to help you: the WiseGuide Intro, the WiseGuide Wrap-Up, and the Putting It in *Perspectives* review form.

WiseGuide Intro

In the WiseGuide Intro, the Academic Editors introduce the section, give you an overview of the topics covered, and explain why particular articles were selected and what's important about them.

Also in the WiseGuide Intro, you'll find several key points or learning objectives that highlight the most important things to remember from this section. These will help you to focus your study of section topics.

WiseGuide Intro

At the end of the WiseGuide Intro, you'll find questions designed to stimulate critical thinking. Wise students will keep these questions in mind as they read an article (we repeat the questions at the start of the articles as a reminder). When you finish each article, check your understanding. Can you answer the questions? If not, go back and reread the article. The Academic Editors have written sample responses for many of the questions, and you'll find these online at the **Courselinks**™ site for this course. More about **Courselinks** in a minute. . . .

WiseGuide Wrap-Up

Be course wise and develop a thorough understanding of the topics covered in this course. The WiseGuide Wrap-Up at the end of each section will help you do just that with concluding comments or summary points that repeat what's most important to understand from the section you just read.

In addition, we try to get you wired up by providing a list of select Internet resources—what we call R.E.A.L. web sites because they're **R**elevant, **E**nhanced, **A**pproved, and **L**inked. The information at these web sites will enhance your understanding of a topic. (Remember to use your Passport and start at http://www.courselinks.com so that if any of these sites have changed, you'll have the latest link.)

Putting It in *Perspectives* Review Form

At the end of the book is the Putting It in *Perspectives* review form. Your instructor may ask you to complete this form as an assignment or for extra credit. If nothing else, consider doing it on your own to help you critically think about the reading.

Prompts at the end of each article encourage you to complete this review form. Feel free to copy the form and use it as needed.

The Courselinks™ Site

http://www.courselinks.com

The **Courselinks** Passport is your ticket to a wonderful world of integrated web resources designed to help you with your course work. These resources are found at the **Courselinks** site for your course area. This is where the readings in this book and the key topics of your course are linked to an exciting array of online learning tools. Here you will find carefully selected readings, web links, quizzes, worksheets, and more, tailored to your course and approved as connected learning tools. The ever-changing, always interesting **Courselinks** site features a number of carefully integrated resources designed to help you be course wise. These include:

- **R.E.A.L. Sites** At the core of a **Courselinks** site is the list of R.E.A.L. sites. This is a select group of web sites for studying, not surfing. Like the readings in this book, these sites have been selected, reviewed, and approved by the Academic Editor and the Editorial Board. The R.E.A.L. sites are arranged by topic and are annotated with short descriptions and key words to make them easier for you to use for reference or research. With R.E.A.L. sites, you're studying approved resources within seconds—and not wasting precious time surfing unproven sites.

- **Editor's Choice** Here you'll find updates on news related to your course, with links to the actual online sources. This is also where we'll tell you about changes to the site and about online events.

- **Course Overview** This is a general description of the typical course in this area of study. While your instructor will provide specific course objectives, this overview helps you place the course in a generic context and offers you an additional reference point.

- **www.orksheet** Focus your trip to a R.E.A.L. site with the www.orksheet. Each of the 10 to 15 questions will prompt you to take in the best that site has to offer. Use this tool for self-study, or if required, email it to your instructor.

- **Course Quiz** The questions on this self-scoring quiz are related to articles in the reader, information at R.E.A.L. sites, and other course topics, and will help you pinpoint areas you need to study. Only you will know your score—it's an easy, risk-free way to keep pace!

- **Topic Key** The online Topic Key is a listing of the main topics in your course, and it correlates with the Topic Key that appears in this reader. This handy reference tool also links directly to those R.E.A.L. sites that are especially appropriate to each topic, bringing you integrated online resources within seconds!

- **Message Center** Share your ideas with fellow students and instructors, in your class or in classes around the world, by using the Message Center. There are links to both a real-time chat room and a message forum, which are accessible all day, every day. Watch for scheduled CourseChat events throughout the semester.

- **Student Lounge** Drop by the Student Lounge, a virtual "hangout" with links to professional associations in your course area, online article review forms, and site feedback forms. Take a look around the Student Lounge and give us your feedback. We're open to remodeling the Lounge per your suggestions.

Building Better Perspectives!

Please tell us what you think of this *Perspectives* volume so we can improve the next one. Here's how you can help:

1. Visit our **Coursewise** site at: http://www.coursewise.com

2. Click on *Perspectives*. Then select the Building Better *Perspectives* Form for your book.

3. Forms and instructions for submission are available online.

Tell us what you think—did the readings and online materials help you make some learning connections? Were some materials more helpful than others? Thanks in advance for helping us build better *Perspectives.*

Student Internships

If you enjoy evaluating these articles or would like to help us evaluate the **Courselinks** site for this course, check out the **Coursewise** Student Internship Program. For more information, visit:

http://www.coursewise.com/intern.html

Brief Contents

Contents

At **Coursewise**, we're publishing connected learning tools. That means that the book you are holding is only a part of this publication. You'll also want to harness the integrated resources that **Coursewise** has developed at the fun and highly useful **Courselinks**™ web site for *Race and Crime*. If you purchased this book new, use the Passport that was shrink-wrapped to this volume to obtain site access. If you purchased a used copy of this book, then you need to buy a stand-alone Passport. If your bookstore doesn't stock Passports to **Courselinks** sites, visit http://www.courselinks.com for ordering information.

section

1

The Social Construction of Black Crime

section 2

Causes of Crime: Does Race Matter?

section
3

Society's Response to Crime

section 4

Justice's Blindfold: A Myth or a Reality?

section 5

Incapacitation: A Color and Class Perspective

section
6

The Face of Victims:
A Racial Analysis

Topic Key

This Topic Key is an important tool for learning. It will help you integrate this reader into your course studies. Listed below, in alphabetical order, are important topics covered in this volume. Below each topic, you'll find the reading numbers and titles, and R.E.A.L. web site addresses, relating to that topic. Note that the Topic Key might not include every topic your instructor chooses to emphasize. If you don't find the topic you're looking for in the Topic Key, check the index or the online topic key at the **Courselinks**™ site.

African Americans
8   Races Worry about Crime and Values, Disagree on Government
11   Understanding Violence among Young African American Males: An Afrocentric Perspective
15   The Coca Cola Bottle Theory: A Look at the Twentieth Century Effect of Exigency on Policing Strategies in the African American Community

National Criminal Justice Reference Service
http://www.ncjrs.org/corrhome.htm

Black Criminality
1   Thoughts on Race, Crime, and Criminal Justice: A Black Perspective
2   The Argument for Studying Race and Crime
6   Politicizing Black-on-Black Crime: A Critique of Terminological Preference
10   Race and Crime: An International Dilemma
12   Explaining the Black Homicide Rate
22   A Shocking Look at Blacks and Crime

Criminological Theory
http://home.ici.net/~ddemelo/crime/crimetheory.html

Explanations of Criminal Behavior
http://www.uaa.alaska.edu/just/just110/crime2.html

Corrections
13   The Wrong Men on Death Row
14   Death at Midnight...Hope at Sunrise
21   Differences in the Background and Criminal Justice Characteristics of Young Black, White, and Hispanic Male Federal Prison Inmates
25   Extra Credit

The American Correctional Association
http://www.corrections.com/aca/

The American Jail Association
http://www.corrections.com/aja/

National Criminal Justice Reference Service
http://www.ncjrs.org/corrhome.htm

Courts
16   Differential Punishing of African Americans and Whites Who Possess Drugs: A Just Policy or a Continuation of the Past?
17   Where Did Black Jurors Go? A Theoretical Synthesis of Racial Disenfranchisement in the Jury System and Jury Selection
18   "Driving While Black" and All Other Traffic Offenses: The Supreme Court and Pretextual Traffic Stops
19   The Impact of Federal Sentencing Reforms on African Americans
20   Ethics and Justice: Playing the Race Card

U.S. Supreme Court Multimedia Database
http://oyez.nwu.edu/

United States Sentencing Commission
http://www.ussc.gov/

The Sentencing Project
http://www.sentencingproject.org/

Demographics
5   Beyond a Multiracial America: Racial Demographics and Crime in the United States Today
9   The Political Economy and Urban Racial Tensions

Race and Racism
http://www.users.interport.net/~heugene/race_racism.html

Racetalks Initiatives
http://www.law.upenn.edu/racetalk/

Drugs
16   Differential Punishing of African Americans and Whites Who Possess Drugs: A Just Policy or a Continuation of the Past?
24   Racial Politics, Racial Disparities, and the War on Crime

Race and Racism in American Law
http://www.udayton.edu/~race/

Fear of Crime
27   Measuring Concern about Crime: Some Inter-Racial Comparisons
28   Fear of Crime among Black Elderly
29   Criminal Victimization among Black Americans

The Black World Today
http://www.tbwt.com/

Hate Crimes
3   The Social Construction of a Hate Crime Epidemic
23   Into the Heart of Darkness

Explanations of Criminal Behavior
http://www.uaa.alaska.edu/just/just110/crime2.html

Race and Racism
http://www.users.interport.net/~heugene/race_racism.html

Racial Discrimination
7   Disparate Impact and Disparate Treatment Theory: Conceptual Forms of Employment Discrimination in Law Enforcement
24   Racial Politics, Racial Disparities, and the War on Crime

Race and Racism in American Law
http://www.udayton.edu/~race/

PBS Online Newshour Race Relations
http://www.pbs.org/newshour/bb/race_relations/race_relations.html

Crime Times
http://www.crime-times.org/

Victimization
4   Predicting Crime Story Salience: The Effects of Crime, Victim, and Defendant Characteristics
26   Trends in California Homicide, 1970 to 1993

National Institute of Justice
http://www.ojp.usdoj.gov/nij/victdocs.htm

Office for Victims of Crime
http://www.ojp.usdoj.gov/ovc/

section 1

The Social Construction of Black Crime

Learning Objectives

After studying this section, you will know

- the complexities surrounding black criminality.

- the relationship between race and criminological research.

- that American society is more intolerant of hate crimes today.

- that the number of victims affected by a crime is the best predictor of the space and attention provided to newspaper crime stories.

- that the field of criminology has been slow to adjust to the reality that the racial colors of the U.S. population encompass more than black and white.

- that myths of crime associated with race are created and reinforced through the criminal justice process and the media.

- that the phrase "black-on-black" crime is overutilized.

- that minority members proceed through their career paths more quickly than majority members.

 **WiseGuide Intro**

Race and crime has been the topic of attention for many years. At the core of interest with this topic have been conceptualization and definitional issues. One of many issues pertains to what constitutes black crime. Another pertains to the phrase "black-on-black" crime, relative to use of the term "white-on-white" crime. When you compare/contrast use of these terms, the modal category here is "black-on-black" crime. Rarely does one see the phrase "white-on-white" crime.

How do we trace the evolution of societal interest in black crime? What factors, in society, are responsible for the evolution of crime? One tangible explanation seems to pertain to use of data collected by the Department of Justice. These data show that, with respect to Part One offenses, a disproportionate number are committed by poor people and visible minorities.

There is the potential, however, for misleading analysis and representation of information. One is reminded of the media—several years ago. *Time* magazine darkened the skin of O.J. Simpson in its coverage. Some have argued that *Time* achieved the goal of making Simpson appear evil, sinister, and guilty with this darker image. The media, then, assume some responsibility for the social construction of crime in American society. While the media have done away with the identification of race in the reporting of crime stories, they still tend to treat acts of violence (among blacks) as routine events, in contrast to acts of violent crimes committed by whites.

Other contributing factors include the history of racism and segregation in American society, the reliance on stereotypes, the marginalization of people of color, and the inability of academics to agree on critical issues in the construction of race. There are, indeed, other issues to consider—in the case of interracial marriages and their offspring. What color or race are these individuals? Does skin color determine identification of race? A new paradigm must be established in which to view issues specific to race. Simply put, the issues of who is black and what is meant by the terms *race* and *ethnicity* remain serious social science questions.

The status of an individual does not change the perception of race, and people continue to act based on stereotypes. African Americans with high levels of achievement may be seen as aberrations, yet they remain black! In the classroom, in the hospital, in the cockpit of a commercial jet, observations about skin color may supplant issues specific to competence. The point here is that race matters—it is an important topic that cannot be dismissed.

You should also be alerted to the fact that the dynamics with race preclude easy explanations; it is an important topic yet potentially volatile in the eyes of the public, academics, politicians, and students. In all, the expectation is that the readings in this section will provide exposure to issues specific to the social construction of race, employment opportunities, disparate treatment, the role of the government, and the ways in which stereotypes contribute to the race issue.

? Questions ?

Reading 1. Discuss what is meant by "free-floating" anger.

Reading 2. Why is it important to study race and crime?

Reading 3. Is the United States currently experiencing a hate crime epidemic?

Reading 4. What are the most important variables that affect the amount of space and attention provided to newspaper crime stories?

Reading 5. Describe how the criminological field has adjusted to the changing racial and ethnic composition of the U.S. population.

Reading 6. Identify some of the problems that emanate from the use of the phrase "black-on-black" crime.

Reading 7. How have law enforcement employers measured up to the goal of promoting representation of minority members in high-level administrative positions?

Discuss what is meant by "free-floating" anger.

Thoughts on Race, Crime, and Criminal Justice:

A Black Perspective

Alejandro del Carmen

*Assistant Professor of Criminology and
Criminal Justice
University of Texas at Arlington*

Robert L. Bing III

*Associate Professor of Criminology and
Criminal Justice
University of Texas at Arlington*

Abstract

*This article raises critical issues about
race and crime. Definitional and conceptual issues are addressed in the context of
understanding black criminality.
Questions about so-called black-on-black
crime are also raised. The etiology of
crime in black communities is offered
through an integrated approach, with
economic discrimination at the core of
this complex relationship. The latter part
of the article pertains to contradictions in
society and our criminal justice system.
The reader is challenged to stop failed
practices of the past and to advocate for
meaningful changes, through effective
polices and an investment in competent
and honest personnel.*

Black Crime or Crime?

Crime is both a legal and social reality. It can be regarded as the conduct
that violates the written law or conduct that is perceived by society as
threatening. Why, then, do we differ-
entiate between white crimes and
black crimes? Why do we read about
black-on-black crime? How frequently do we hear the phrase
"white-on-white crime"? Could it be
that crime in America is politicized?
It is clear that use of the phrase sets
the tone and helps to conjure of images of blacks as predators and victims. When Americans think of
crime, do they think black? Could it
also be that in the minds of the
American public the word *crime* is
commensurate with race? In this
case, crime emerges as a social construct based on stereotypes and fears
of victimization. Although we [the
authors] are both law abiding individuals, it is clear to us that judgments are made about us on the basis
of race and ethnicity daily. Each day,
we are reminded of our race and ethnicity, based on interactions with the
white majority. While driving, we are
concerned about police stops. In department stores, we are watched
closely. At concerts, our behaviors are
monitored with apparent intimidation. Our educational accomplishments do not abate this suspicion;
what matters is race and color. The
concern is with minority or black
crime. We ask, if most crimes are intraracial and if most are committed
by whites, why the preoccupation
with black crime? It is partly due to
the high rates of offending by minority populations. On the other hand,
are there other motivations and biases at work? One consequence of
this mentality is the marginalization
of people of color by assigning negative attributes, based on stereotypes
and arrest rates.

Why Do Blacks Commit Crimes?

If we only knew the answer to this
perennial question! Is there a subculture of violence? Is there a *black* gene
that predisposes blacks to high rates
of offending and acts of violence? Are
racism, discrimination, and structural
conditions in American society major
factors? Why do blacks kill blacks or
whites, for that matter? If there is discrimination and racism, why do
blacks commit crimes against their
own people? The answer to these and
other questions, we believe, requires
the integration of several theories.
Economic discrimination is surely
one factor, explaining property-
related crimes. What about violent
crimes? Part of the answer, we believe, lies in an anger, frustration,
self-hatred hypothesis. This is sometimes referred to as "free-floating"
anger—that is, acts of aggression that
stem unpredictably from low thresh-
olds of tolerance in our daily lives as
well as an inability to manage conflicts (Prothrow-Stith, 1991). And,
while discrimination and racial bias
are variables in this complicated
equation, we are careful to note that

these variables are not always present. The integration of theories would also include the impact of capitalism, with its adherence to egoism, breed, and greed. Strain and the dysfunction between culturally prescribed goals and structural means might also be a part of some integrated approach toward understanding the etiology of crimes committed by African Americans. Some of the solutions would come easily, if there were less suspicion, more trust, and less hypocrisy.

Understanding the Problem

The problem of black criminality is enormous. It is an undeniable problem that permeates most of American society. The solution to the problems are not novel ideas, rather notions abandoned in lieu of prison construction, lengthy sentences, and unfair sentencing guidelines, resulting in disparities. We maintain that education is the best approach and constitutes what we refer to as primary prevention. Interestingly, The Sentencing Project has established that there are more black men in prison than there are black men in institutions of higher education. This trend needs to be reversed.

Confounding the education problem has been integration and busing of kids to different neighborhoods. The argument has been made by prominent scholars and activists that black kids in integrated schools have not benefited from better facilities and more resources in suburban schools. These students, activists argue, may not get the nurturing necessary to succeed in school or life. Some, therefore, have called for single-race schools, especially for black males. The position of some is that the role models and nurturing absent at some suburban (or white) schools can be implemented. It, however, remains to be seen if this is workable or constitutional. Returning to the issue of busing, there are some who maintain that busing black youth from their neighborhoods in urban areas to suburban communities may also have the unanticipated effect of promoting criminality in

black neighborhoods. The point is made that some African American youth lose an important identification with their own neighborhoods, resulting in friction and disorganization (c.f., Hagedorn, 1988).

Valiant efforts by whites and others are met with suspicion. The black-white dichotomy, plus the success of other minority groups, has increased the level of tension in some black neighborhoods. As one of many examples, blacks view police patrol with suspicion and distrust. The trust factor or absence thereof, can be understood only by recognizing the history of minority police relations. There may be a tendency to view patrolling of black neighborhoods as a negative factor. One analogy here is the police stop for speeding, where some motorists may lament the fact that there are "bigger fish to fry." Others surely ask: "Why aren't you addressing real crimes?" The point that we want to make here is that some minority group members may see patrol efforts through different lenses, as largely unproductive or as an irritant (that aggravates old wounds). For the student of crime, it is important to know that this mentality is a reality. The challenge, it seems, is to overcome this resistance and not to be discouraged by it.

It seems that the hypocrisy of our laws as well as our institutions results in unlawful decisions. It is difficult, for example, to take code enforcement seriously if individuals know that police or city officials are aware of industry polluting a major river with deadly chemicals, yet punitive actions against that industry do not occur. Further, young black men and women who witness the struggle of their parents may have firsthand experience with their deferred dreams; these individuals may make conscious decisions not to struggle—to do things differently, and sometimes "doing things differently" involves criminal behavior. We call these behaviors rational responses to advance in a fiercely competitive world. As another example, society must understand that, when individuals have been assigned low status in American society, there may be a predisposition to

violence. Simply put, individuals who have very little are willing to take greater risks.

The Mis-education of the American Student

Life in America is replete with fallacies. One fallacy is that, in American society, if you struggle and work hard and delay gratification, there will be benefits. Another is that there is advocacy and fairness in our criminal justice system. Blacks argue racism; whites maintain that they are fair and should not be held accountable for the conduct of their ancestors. Blacks may rationalize or neutralize their conduct by arguing racism or discrimination; whites, meanwhile, do not recognize that their world is one of privilege and are frequently unable to fully appreciate the plight of disadvantaged youth. There are laws forbidding landlords from advertising for white or black tenants. On the other hand, the law permits white men to advertise for special personal relationships with black females or vice versa. There is underrepresentation of blacks in the judiciary and overrepresentation of black Americans in the nation's penal colonies. Harvard Law School admitted black men before it opened its doors to women. Today, there are more women in law school than at any time in our nation's history. Affirmative action programs are under assault—we are less concerned about quality and integrity of personnel than we are about profit and money. Our criminal justice system is, at times, criminogenic; we process offenders without concern for outcome. Legal representation is driven by profit, and there are questions about the adequacy and availability of counsel for indigent offenders. In one state, an offense is a felony; in another, the offense is a misdemeanor. Oliver Wendell Holmes is quoted as saying, "There is nothing logical about the law. The law is at best illogical." Our point here is that the profound hypocrisy in our society as well as our system of justice needs to be addressed. The system lacks credibility and is seen as a game to be played and manipulated.

Concluding Remarks

It is evident from the preceding discussion that views on the causes of crime are dependant on one's reality. Although education is proposed as an effective method to close the gap on these distinct views, it is important to mention that cultural sensitivity needs to be at the core of this process. One's education needs to go beyond the intellectual understanding that blacks and other minorities are oppressed. How can one ever know the depth of the tears shed by a black woman as she holds, in her motherly arms, her child for the last time? How can one learn in a textbook the sounds of a hungry baby as she cries desperately for food? How can one, who enjoys the benefit of having a house, ever know the feeling of being homeless? In order to understand black crime, one must go beyond the intellectual conceptualization that minorities are oppressed in the system of justice—one must understand the feelings of a black man when walking into a public setting where eyes seem to wonder what his "next move" will be; one must understand the anger of some when a black man drives a "good" car; one must understand what it is like to be black! This same principle can be applied to other minorities—Hispanics, for instance, also have a complex reality where their accent is equivalent to the color of a black person. Both represent the core of oppression. The challenge here is to change the system, to look for contradictions in our way of life, to advocate for meaningful change and not remain a guardian of the past. The issue of race and crime is complex, and solutions require that we speak openly and honestly about identification of the problems to implement major changes. It is only through a complete understanding of the cultural, ethnic, and racial uniqueness of minorities that we can begin to fully comprehend the complexities involving their criminal participation. It is our hope that this article will result in meaningful dialogue, resulting in changes in our system of justice.

References

Georges-Abeyie, Daniel. 1984. *The Criminal Justice System and Blacks*. New York: Clark Boardman, Ltd.

Hagedorn, John M. 1988. *People and Folks*. Chicago: Lake View Press.

Prothrow-Stith, Deborah. 1991. *Deadly Consequences*. New York: HarperCollins Publishers.

 Article Review Form at end of book.

Why is it important to study race and crime?

The Argument for Studying Race and Crime

Gary LaFree

University of New Mexico

Katheryn K. Russell

University of Maryland

All roads in American criminology eventually lead to issues of race; the directness of the route varies, however. Unlike the other topic areas for this special issue, race always has been a part of criminology and criminal justice research. The centrality of its position in criminology, however, has changed greatly over time. We begin this essay with a brief history of research on race and crime in American criminology. We then provide an argument for including race in criminology research, and identify some of the key concepts and questions that should be considered in courses highlighting race and crime issues.[1]

Race and Criminology Research in the United States

Edwin Sutherland's well-known description of criminology as "the study of the making of laws, the breaking of laws and reactions to the breaking of laws" (Sutherland and Cressey 1978:3) defines what are

Order of authors is alphabetical. The first author would like to thank the Harry Frank Guggenheim Foundation for its generous support of this project.

probably the two major subareas of criminology: criminal etiology ("the breaking of laws") and the sociology of law ("the making of laws" and "reactions to the breaking of laws"). Criminal etiology leads us to studies of the causes of crime; the sociology of law emphasizes the operation of the legal system.

Etiology may be divided further into individual and social/cultural perspectives. Individual perspectives assume that crime is caused by characteristics within the individual such as body type, intelligence, or hereditary defects. Social/cultural perspectives assume that crime has social or social psychological causes.

Because African-Americans have long been overrepresented in the criminal justice system, concerns about race issues are related closely to these theoretical categories. If the proper focus of criminology is etiology, researchers must explain why blacks commit a disproportionate amount of crime; if the proper focus of criminology is the sociology of law, researchers must explain why a disproportionate number of blacks are arrested, prosecuted, and convicted.

Moreover, for those who agree that etiology is an appropriate concern of criminology, individual and social explanations have very different implications for race issues. Individual explanations emphasize inherent physical deficiencies that are difficult to change through public policy. Arguing that African-Americans (or members of any other

group) are more likely to commit crime and that the reasons for this are biological or psychological can raise serious difficulties for democratic systems. By contrast, social explanations are presumed to imply that persons are amenable to change through public policy; thus such explanations may be less controversial.

This last point is important and should not be minimized. It would be easier if the job of science were simply to uncover truth, with no need to worry about the political and social effects of our research. Yet, the implications of incorporating differences by race into our studies of criminal etiology can have serious consequences. In fact, human beings have an ugly and disturbing tendency to justify every manner of atrocity against particular racial or ethnic minority groups on the basis of perceived differences in their behavior. The American slave trade, the politics of Nazi Germany, apartheid in South Africa, and "ethnic cleansing" in Bosnia-Herzegovina are familiar examples.

In short, we should not take lightly the issue of highlighting race in studies of crime and justice. Nonetheless, we argue that the benefits of examining race in our research outweigh the costs. To put our argument in context, we consider next how race issues have interacted with the theoretical categories introduced above. To do so, we divide the treatment of race in American criminology into four main periods.

"The Argument for Studying Race and Crime," Gary LaFree and Katheryn K. Russell. *Journal of Criminal Justice Education,* Vol. 4, No. 2, Fall 1993. Reprinted by permission.

The Birth of American Criminology, 1890–1919

Crime research first appeared in the United States in the late 1800s. Most of these early works were vulgarized versions of Charles Darwin's theory of evolution, which exerted tremendous influence on both scientific and popular thought in Europe and the United States during this period (Parsons 1909; C. Wright 1899). The first complete American criminology textbook, however, was not published until after World War I (Parmelee 1918). During this early stage of American criminology, research focused mainly on etiology; the major etiological explanations assumed that offenders were distinguished by genetic or other physiological deficiencies.

In view of widespread discrimination against African-Americans, it was almost a foregone conclusion that these explanations would be applied to blacks. A review by Brearley (1932), for example, concludes that the disproportionate rate of homicide among blacks is due to "their [blacks'] peculiar genetically-determined temperament" as well as "excessive emotionality" (111–16). Yet, biological theories did not go unchallenged, even in this early period. Thus at the turn of the century, W.E.B. DuBois ([1899] 1988) confronted biological theories of crime with an empirical analysis of white and black offenders in Philadelphia:

[T]he causes for the present condition of the Negro: slavery and emancipation with their attendant phenomena of ignorance, lack of discipline, and moral weakness; immigration with its increased competition and moral influence. . . [and] the environment in which [the] Negro finds himself—the world of custom and thought in which he must live and work, the physical surrounding of house and home and ward, the moral encouragements and discouragements which he encounters (Myers and Simms 1988:24–25).

Mainstream Academic Criminology, 1920–1959

North American criminology took a decidedly different turn in the 1920s. That period produced a wide variety of social and cultural explanations of crime, including such influential classics as Shaw and McKay's (1942) social disorganization theory, Sutherland's (1939) differential association theory, and Merton's (1938) anomie theory. Research during this period relied mostly on crime data collected from police or other official agents.

The main source for official crime data in the United States has long been the Uniform Crime Reports (UCR), first collected by the Federal Bureau of Investigation in 1930. From its inception, UCR data showed that arrest rates for African-Americans were much higher than those for whites. Yet the validity of the UCR data for drawing conclusions about crime rates—particularly crime rates by race—has been debated intensely ever since UCR data collection began (e.g., Gove, Hughes, and Geerken 1985; President's Commission 1967; Warner 1931). Although many technical issues are present, most of the criticisms can be reduced to concerns about reporting by citizens or by police.

Both of these concerns have important implications for conclusions about crime trends by race. For example, if nonminority members are more likely than minority group members to report crimes to police, conclusions about crime rates by race will be erroneous. Similarly, if police arrest decisions are influenced by race, conclusions about crime in different racial groups will be invalid.

Because criminology focused on etiology during this second period, researchers naturally considered explanations for the disproportionate number of African-Americans snared by the legal system and reported in official data. This situation caused theoretical difficulties for mainstream criminology. For example, social disorganization theorists of the "Chicago school" (e.g., Shaw et al. 1929) argued that immigrant groups moved constantly through the most disorganized, highest-crime areas of cities. As these groups established a solid footing in the economy, they (or their children) moved to more prosperous, less disorganized areas. It became increasingly clear, however, that blacks' urban experiences were different from those of other ethnic and racial groups with regard to social mobility; thus social disorganization theory lacked an adequate explanation.

This fact led Sellin ([1930] 1988) to theorize that although blacks were arrested, convicted, and committed to prison more frequently than whites, "there are specific factors which seriously distort [these rates] for Negroes without affecting these rates for whites in a similar manner" (Myers and Simms (1988:75). According to Sellin, these factors included the discriminatory treatment faced by blacks in the criminal justice system. Sellin's work anticipated the move toward conflict and labeling approaches, which are the hallmark of the next period.

Sociology of Law Perspectives, 1960–1974

Beginning in the 1960s, the traditional emphasis of criminology on etiology was challenged seriously on several theoretical fronts (e.g., Becker 1963; Chambliss and Seidman 1971; Quinney 1973). Although these challenges differ in many ways, they all share the assumption that the most important task of criminology is not to study etiology, but rather to study the creation and application of law. During this period a great many studies of differential legal processing were conducted.

With regard to race, the research completed during this third period of criminological history is a mirror image of the two previous periods. In the first two periods, etiological research (either individual or social) was conducted almost to the exclusion of work on the sociology of law. Beginning in the 1960s, however, sociology of law perspectives became increasingly dominant. There was a virtual explosion of research on the differential treatment of African-Americans and other racial minorities by the legal system (e.g., Bullock 1961; Judson et al. 1969; Partington 1965). At the same time, few criminologists during this third period undertook research on etiological differences by race; those who did so (e.g., Moynihan 1965; Rainwater 1966) often were criticized sharply.

If official data are the hallmark of mainstream criminology, the self-report crime survey is associated most closely with this period (Akers

1964; Erickson and Empey 1963; Short and Nye 1957). Results from self-report surveys strongly supported the sociology of law theorists' expectations with regard to race: they demonstrated that crime rates for African-Americans were much closer to whites' crime rates than was suggested by UCR data. This conclusion helped to justify research that focused on official decision making rather than on etiology.

Toward a Theoretical Synthesis, 1975 to the Present

Beginning in the mid-1970s, criminological thinking entered a fourth period. This period is marked by its eclecticism: both individual and social etiology and sociology of law approaches are generating a great deal of research. As evidence of renewed interest in etiological theories, we can point to recent research on deterrence (Sherman and Berk 1984; Tittle 1980), social control (Hagan, Simpson, and Gillis 1987; Meier 1982), crime victimization (Cohen and Felson 1979; Cohen, Felson, and Land 1980), differential association (Matsueda and Heimer 1987), social disorganization (Bursik 1988; Sampson 1987), economic inequality, poverty, and stress (Blau and Blau 1982; Hawkins 1990; Messner 1989), and a variety of biological and psychological factors (Hirschi and Hindelang 1977; Wilson and Herrnstein 1985). Sociology of law research on sources of race discrimination in legal processing also has continued apace (e.g., Georges-Abeyie 1984; LaFree 1989; Mann 1993; Zatz 1984).

One of the developments that has led to a renewed interest in etiology in this most recent period has been the collection, since 1973, of national survey data on victimization. The availability of such information has provided researchers with an important new source of data for testing the validity of UCR statistics on crime and race. The results of these tests have increased confidence in the quality of UCR data in two important ways. First, the National Crime Survey (NCS) asks people who have been victimized whether they reported the crime to police. Analyses of these data (e.g., Skogan 1984) show little variation in reporting by

race. Thus if blacks' arrest rates are higher than whites', it is probably not because blacks call the police less often than whites when they are victimized.

Second, the NCS data are collected independently of the police and the legal system. Thus, if NCS offending rates by race are similar to arrest rates from the UCR, the similarity suggests that police arrest decisions are influenced less by race than by other considerations. Indeed, systematic comparisons of crime rates by race for the UCR and the NCS show remarkable correspondence. For example, Hindelang (1978:100) found that the percentage of robbery offenders reported as blacks by victims in the NCS was identical to the percentage of blacks among UCR arrests for robbery. In a detailed follow-up study, Hindelang (1981) found that even for burglaries—where the offender is seen only in 6 percent of the NCS cases—UCR arrest statistics correspond very closely to NCS figures on the offenders' race (also see, Curtis 1974:20). Many researchers now think that differences between race and crime estimates from the UCR and from self-report surveys exist largely because self-report surveys overemphasize less serious forms of crime and juvenile delinquency (Elliott and Ageton 1980).

The Argument for Studying Race and Crime

Evidence of justice and fair treatment is critical to the legitimacy of any society. The role of criminology in studying differential treatment by race is decisive, and such study should continue. Fundamental are questions about differential arrest, conviction, and sentencing patterns, studies of institutional racism, and comparisons between ethnic and racial groups in terms of criminal justice processing.

Criminology, however, also should continue to study etiological issues as they relate to race. In fact, the arguments for studying etiology and race at this particular point in U.S. history are particularly compelling. Perhaps the most obvious justification for etiological approaches that study race differences is the depth of the criminal justice

crisis facing African-Americans in the United States today. Although blacks represent only 12 percent of the U.S. population, they now account for 64 percent of robbery arrests, 55 percent of homicide arrests, and 32 percent of burglary arrests (Federal Bureau of Investigation 1989). This means that Blacks' arrest rates for robbery are more than 11 times higher than rates for nonblacks, which include Hispanics, Asian-Americans, Native Americans, whites, and everyone else. These grim statistics are reproduced in the nation's prisons, jails, probation departments, and county morgues. Black males born in the United States today now face a one-in-five lifetime chance of serving a sentence in an adult state prison (Bureau of Justice Statistics 1985a:5). Our failure to study the connection between race and crime has not made race-related crime problems go away.

According to William J. Wilson (1984), a major reason for moving away from studies of differential crime rates by race, beginning in the 1960s, was to avoid negative associations between race and crime: blacks already were disadvantaged by the economy and the society. Thus, to imply that crime problems were more serious for blacks than for others seemed to be double victimization. Yet, it is also the case that no group has suffered more than African-Americans by our failure to understand and control street crime. In fact, homicide has become the leading cause of death among black men age 15 to 24 (U.S. Centers for Disease Control 1990). If current trends continue (Bureau of Justice Statistics 1985b:8), one in every 21 African-American young men now living will die from murder. And in the great majority of these cases, their assailants also will be black.

Apart from the pressing policy issues, studying crime rates by race also has theoretical and research advantages. By examining the different experiences of black and of white Americans, sometimes we can interpret much more clearly how our theories operate. During the administrations of Ronald Reagan and George Bush, for example, incarceration rates reached unprecedented levels in the United States. In the mid-1970s, the United States was admitting about 50,000 new inmates to federal and state prisons each year. A decade later, this figure had quadrupled to 200,000 new inmates a year (Langan 1991). By 1990, the United States had the highest incarceration rate in the world (426 prisoners per 100,000 population), followed by South Africa (336 per 100,000) and the Soviet Union (268 per 100,000) (Mauer 1991).

These statistics, troubling enough when considered for the whole nation, become truly frightening when considered separately for African-Americans. In 1930, blacks made up less than 25 percent of prison admissions in the United States; by 1950 the proportion had increased slightly to 30 percent. Today African-Americans account for about half of all state and federal prisoners. In fact, in the United States nearly 25 percent of all black men age 20–29 are currently in prison, on probation, or on parole (Langan 1991). In this country, substantially more black men are in the correctional system (610,000) than in colleges and universities (436,000) (Langan 1991). When we look separately at crime and punishment rates for blacks and for whites, the implications of our current policies on imprisonment take on a very different tone. We must question the logic of any social control system that affects nearly one-quarter of the young men in a particular racial group.

In addition to the policy and theoretical justifications for including race in our research and teaching, there is also an important research justification. In the absence of objective empirical research on crime rates by race, often we are forced to rely on racial stereotypes. One of the most egregious examples of this was the use of the Willie Horton story in George Bush's 1988 presidential election campaign.

Willie Horton is a black man who was furloughed from his murder sentence in a Massachusetts state prison in 1976. While on furlough, Horton raped a white Maryland woman and stabbed her fiance. The Bush campaign made the Massachusetts prison furlough program a central issue in its contest against Democratic candidate and Massachusetts governor Michael Dukakis. The Horton story was cited by Mr. Bush in campaign speeches,

shown in television commercials, and featured in fliers distributed by Republic state committees. A 1988 story in the *New York Times* concluded that the Horton advertising campaign was "highly effective in damaging Mr. Dukakis's image and left the Democrats scrambling for ways to respond" (New York Times, October 24, 1988). Clearly, our decision to exclude crime differences by race as an area of research does not mean that the public no longer will be influenced by racial stereotypes about crime.

For all of these reasons, we must face the problem of race and crime directly, forthrightly and with the most objective evidence we can muster collectively. Ignoring connections between race and crime has not made them go away. In the next section we consider some of the important issues regarding race that should be addressed in criminology and criminal justice courses.

Central Concepts, Scholars, and Research

The subordinate status of race in criminology research is symbolized by the small number of criminology and criminal justice doctoral programs that offer courses in this area. Just over one-third (7/18) of these programs include a course on race and crime in their curriculum.[2] Although all criminology courses— from juvenile delinquency to corporate crime—should incorporate a discussion of race, this is not the general practice. Perhaps the growing number of course offerings on race and crime will help to move race into the criminology mainstream.

In addition to the theoretical issues discussed above, three other issues are integral to a discussion of race and crime: the definitional, the legal historical, and the practical. The concepts discussed below are important because traditionally they have been at the heart of the race and crime discussion and/or because they help to establish a context for such a discussion. We now present an outline of central concepts, key scholars, and scholarship for the study of race and crime. We also provide a short reading list of introductory literature on this topic (see appendix).*

*The appendix does not appear in this publication.

Definitional Issues
Race and Ethnicity

An important, though often neglected issue in most discussions of race and crime is how "race" is defined. Definitions of race are critical because in turn they define classifications of offenders and victims, and thus influence conclusions about the link between race and crime. A number of researchers have observed that "race" is a term without objective definition. According to Georges-Abeyie,

[T]he most common racial identifiers, and thus definitions of race, often rely on biological characteristics socially and culturally prescribed as the overt physical characteristics of given ethnic and racial groups (1984:9).

Difficulties created by the absence of a uniform definition of race are compounded by the data collection practices of government agencies and programs. For example, both the U.S. Census Bureau[3] and the National Crime Survey (U.S. Department of Justice 1992a:119) allow respondents to provide data on their racial origin. Neither organization applies uniform criteria (e.g., mother's race) or requires external verification. Likewise, the Uniform Crime Reports (UCR) do not provide law enforcement officials with standard guidelines for coding racial origin (U.S. Department of Justice 1984:58).[4]

The problems of classification are equally difficult for non-black minority groups. For example, the category "Hispanic" usually combines groups such as Puerto Ricans, Mexicans, and Cubans; these groups have very different cultural attributes (Mann 1993:11). Moreover, depending on the classification methods employed, "Hispanics" may be classified as white, nonwhite, or other.[5]

Although most official classifications include a "black" category, other classification issues exist. The ambiguity surrounding the definition of "black" is based historically on the "one drop" rule. According to this rule, which developed during slavery, a black is "any person with *any* known African black ancestry" (Davis 1991:5). Although the "one drop" rule is no longer recognized legally, many persons of mixed parentage (e.g., a black parent and a white parent) assume a black racial identity. How are racially based crime rates affected by mixed-ancestry respondents who classify themselves as black? In 1918 the U.S. Census Bureau estimated that at least 75 percent of all American blacks were racially mixed (Davis 1991:57); therefore, this question is not academic hairsplitting.

The above discussion raises a number of concerns. The classification practices of official data gatherers, combined with historical definitions of race, have had a direct impact on the study of crime. What explains the survival of the "one drop" rule in the United States? Further, why does it apply only to one racial minority group? Also, should separate categories be created for those who now are designated "Hispanic"? Questions like these must be examined since they impact our study of race and crime.

Finally, although the terms *race* and *ethnicity* often are used interchangeably, ethnicity generally is defined as describing a group's cultural affiliations (Mann 1993:13). It also has been defined as the "intersection of race, culture, and place of origin" (Georges-Abeyie 1984:11). For example, the UCR Handbook discusses ethnicity as a culture-based, not a race-based concept (U.S. Department of Justice 1984:58).

"Street" Crime and "Suite" Crime

A discussion of street crime and suite crime should be preceded by a look at how crime is defined. Criminologists adopt different definitions of crime according to their ideological assumptions (Vold and Bernard 1986:9). Both conservative and liberal criminologists are likely to define crime as an act or omission that violates the law according to societal norms, but liberal criminologists go one step further and question how realistic those societal norms are (Georges-Abeyie 1984:6). An understanding of these varied perspectives provides students with the insight that crime is not a static concept: "The hidden biases contained within these orientations need to be examined in order to understand the significance of race and eth-

nicity to more general notions concerning criminal propensity and victimization" (Georges-Abeyie 1984:5).

In a discussion of racial minorities and crime, some analysis of crime type is imperative. Most criminology and criminal justice courses focus on UCR "index" offenses,[6] or "street" crime. To avoid a distorted perception of racial minorities and crime, it is important to make clear that index offenses are *not* the most prevalent type of crime[7] and that the UCR does not include all types of harm to society. Mann elaborates:

Although Part II crimes [e.g., assault, embezzlement] are the most prevalent, the FBI Index offenses are the crimes of most concern to the general public and social scientists. Other crimes, such as organized crime, computer crimes, and other "white collar" crimes, particularly those committed by corporations (e.g., hazardous wastes, price fixing) and professional such as medical doctors, lawyers, and accountants (e.g., fee splitting), and many occupational crimes (e.g., false advertising, bogus auto and appliance repairs), are not identified in the UCR despite the billions of dollars in losses involved and physical and mental injuries incurred by victims and their families (1993:27).

In a discussion that outlines the social and political realities behind the definition of crime, students receive the opportunity to examine those offenses which society deems most serious. At the same time they learn that other behaviors also violate the law and cause harm to society.

Legal History

A discussion of the role of race and crime requires a discussion of the history and legal context in which the American criminal justice system has developed. From the time the U.S. Constitution was adopted, the law has been used to control racially and ethnically undesirable populations (Bailey 1991; Bell 1980). Examples of this legally sanctioned control include slavery, black codes, Jim Crow laws, the Chinese Exclusion Act, the Indian Removal Act, and the internment of Japanese-Americans during World War II. This history suggests that "the nexus between racism and law [could] not be much more direct" (Burns 1990:115). The desire to control racial and ethnic minority groups

rests on a belief in racial superiority (Bell 1980) and has been labeled "nativist xenophobia" (Bailey 1991:12). Therefore, a contemporary analysis of the relationship between race and crime requires a look at history. As Bailey observes, "[T]o fully comprehend the context in which legal decisions are made, and in order to evaluate the presence or absence of racial or ethnic biases, it is necessary to understand the historical origins of processes and attitudes that impinge upon current decision making mechanisms" (1991:10).

A historical look at how the race and crime relationship has developed will provide students several benefits: 1) it will create a foundation for discussing the history of race relations in the United States, 2) it provides a context for discussing the legal ramifications of this history and, 3) it allows students to critically examine how theory has developed in this area. In sum, a study of legal history will help students understand why clear analyses of race and crime have been for too long peripheral to the discipline of criminology.

Practical Issues

Much of the discussion that focuses on race and crime is directed at the operation of the criminal justice system. In analyzing the impact of race on the criminal justice system, one generally examines the role of racial minorities in the system as offenders, victims, or professionals. Research focusing on offenders has sparked the most debate. Specifically, the debate centers on whether the criminal justice system discriminates against racial minorities and/or whether racial minorities simply offend at a disproportionate rate (LaFree, Drass, and O'Day 1992; MacLean and Milovanovic 1990). Further, the discipline is divided on how this hypothesis should be tested empirically, on the value of single-stage versus multistage analysis, and on how to compare studies that use different methods (Kleck 1985). Equally important, but often overlooked is the subject of victims. Analyses of the role of race and the criminal justice system have only recently expanded to include a look at victims.

A course on race and crime should address and ultimately put to rest the prevailing myth that whites are more likely than blacks to be victimized by violent crime (U.S. Department of Justice 1992a). Further, attempting to provide a multi-level analysis of the impact of race, the discussion should also include a look at the impact that minority professionals have had on the criminal justice system. This would include an examination of law enforcement officials, judges, lawyers and correctional officers (Georges-Abeyie 1984; B. Wright 1987).

Our discussion outlines areas that should be considered in a course highlighting race and crime. It is particularly important to address the topics outlined under definitional issues (race and ethnicity; street crime and suite crime) and legal history. An overview of these areas presents the student with a broader perspective on the relationship between race and crime. For example, students are provided with a context for analyzing research findings through a discussion of how race is categorized according to official measures. Further, an outline of the distinction between race and ethnicity allows students to assess the impact and the value of considering culture as a means of classifying both official and unofficial measurers of delinquency.

Conclusion

This article has provided an overview of the role race has played in the development of criminological thought. It is clear from this overview that race has consistently been at the core of this evolution. While the race variable has been utilized widely in empirical analyses, it has received only peripheral attention as a concept in criminological theory. While there are undoubtedly a number of reasons that race has not been examined as carefully as other variables, the unfortunate result has been that it has been virtually ignored in criminal justice education. We have argued that the longstanding, omnipresent strain of race within criminology warrants a shift in emphasis.

To help facilitate this, we have outlined several concepts which should be part of any look at the relationship between race and crime.

Specifically, there are a number of issues which should be discussed, including how race and crime are to be defined. Further, there needs to be a historical examination of how the legal system in general, and the criminal justice system in particular have developed in light of racial issues. All told, this will provide students with a framework for developing a better understanding of the relationship between race and crime.

Notes

1. This essay concentrates mostly on differences between whites and African-Americans. African-Americans, the largest racial minority group in the United States, are at the forefront of concerns within the discipline about the appropriateness of studying race. Many of the issues we raise here, however, also are relevant to other racial and ethnic minority groups.

2. Eighteen doctoral programs in criminology/criminal justice were surveyed in April 1993 (ACJS 1991). Program chairs or representatives were asked whether their department offered a class on race and crime (or on minorities and crime). The seven programs that offered such courses were Bowling Green, Florida State, Michigan State, Pennsylvania State, SUNY-Albany, the University of Delaware, and the University of Maryland. Other programs surveyed were Arizona State University, Claremont College, Indiana University of Pennsylvania, John Jay College of Criminal Justice, Ohio State University, Rutgers University, Sam Houston State University, the University of California at Berkeley, the University of California at Irvine, Washington State University, and Western Michigan University.

3. Conversation with Stan Rolark, Senior Statistician, U.S. Bureau of the Census, Racial Statistics Division (April 28, 1993).

4. The Uniform Crime Reporting handbook does not state how law enforcement officials should determine whether an arrestee falls into one racial category or another.

5. The U.S. Census Bureau currently recognizes five racial categories: American Indian or Alaskan Native, Asian or Pacific Islander, black, white, and "other." Hispanics are classified as "other."

6. The UCR index offenses are non-negligent homicide, forcible rape, robbery, aggravated assault, burglary, larceny, auto theft, and arson.

7. According to UCR arrest data for 1991 index offenses accounted for 25 percent of the total offenses reported to police (U.S. Department of Justice 1992b:231).

References

Academy of Criminal Justice Sciences (1991) "ACJS Guide to Graduate Programs in Criminal Justice and Criminology 1989–1990." Cincinnati: Anderson.

Akers, R.L. (1964) "Socioeconomic Status and Delinquent Behavior: A Re-Test." *Journal of Research in Crime and Delinquency* (January):38–46.

Bailey, F. (1991) "Law, Justice, and 'Americans': An Historical Overview." In M. Lynch and B. Patterson (eds.), *Race and Criminal Justice*, pp. 10–21. New York: Harrow and Heston.

Barak, G. (1991) "Cultural Literacy and a Multicultural Inquiry into the Study of Crime and Justice." *Journal of Criminal Justice Education* 2(2):173–92.

Becker, H.S. (1963) *Outsiders: Studies in the Sociology of Deviance.* New York: Free Press.

Bell, D. (1980) *Race, Racism and American Law.* Boston: Little, Brown.

Blau, J. and P. Blau (1982) "The Cost of Inequality: Metropolitan Structure and Violent Crime." *American Sociological Review* 47:114–29.

Brearley, H.C. (1932) *Homicide in the United States.* Chapel Hill: University of North Carolina Press.

Bullock, H. (1962) "Significance of the Racial Factor in the Length of Prison Sentences." *Journal of Criminal Law, Criminology, and Police Science* 52:411.

Bureau of Justice Statistics (1985a) *The Prevalence of Imprisonment: Department of Justice Special Report.* Washington, DC: U.S. Government Printing Office.

———. (1985b) *The Risk of Violent Crime: Department of Justice Special Report.* Washington, DC: U.S. Government Printing Office.

Burns, H. (1990) "Law and Race in Early America." In D. Kairys (ed.) *The Politics of Law*, pp. 115–20. New York: Pantheon.

Bursik, R.J., Jr. (1988) "Social Disorganization and Theories of Crime and Delinquency: Problems and Prospects." *Criminology* 26:519–52.

Chambliss, W.J. and R. Seidman (1971) *Law, Order and Power.* Reading, MA: Addison-Wesley.

Cohen, L.E. and M. Felson (1979) "Social Change and Crime Rate Trends: A Routine Activity Approach." *American Sociological Review* 44:588–607.

Cohen, L.E., M. Felson and K.C. Land (1980) "Property Crime Rates in the United States: A Macrodynamic Analysis 1947–1977 with *Ex Ante* Forecasts for the Mid-1980s." *American Journal of Sociology* 86:90–118.

Curtis, L.A. (1974) *Criminal Violence.* Lexington, MA: Health.

Davis, F.J. (1991) *Who is Black?* University Park: Pennsylvania State University Press.

DuBois, W.E.B. (1899) *The Philadelphia Negro.* Philadelphia: University of Pennsylvania.

Elliott, D.S. and S.S. Ageton (1980) "Reconciling Race and Class Differences in Self-Reported and Official Estimates of Delinquency." *American Sociological Review* 45:95–110.

Erickson, M.L. and L.T. Empey (1963) "Court Records, Undetected Delinquency and Decision Making." *Journal of Criminal Law, Criminology and Police Science* 54:456–69.

Federal Bureau of Investigation (1989) "Crime in the United States." *Uniform Crime Reports*. Washington, DC: U.S. Government Printing Office.

Georges-Abeyie, D., ed. (1984) "Definitional Issues: Race, Ethnicity, and Official Crime/Victimization Statistics." In D. Georges-Abeyie (ed.), *The Criminal Justice System and Blacks*, pp. 5–19. New York: Clark Boardman.

Gove, W.R., M. Hughes, and M. Geerken (1985) "Are Uniform Crime Reports a Valid Indicator of the Index Crime? An Affirmative Answer with Minor Qualifications." *Criminology* 23:451–501.

Hagan, J., J. Simpson, and A.R. Gillis (1987) "Class in the Household: A Power-Control Theory of Gender and Delinquency." *American Journal of Sociology* 92:788–816.

Hawkins, D. (1990) "Explaining the Black Homicide Rate." *Journal of Interpersonal Violence* 151–63.

Hindelang, M.J. (1978) "Race and Involvement in Crime." *American Sociological Review* 43:93–109.

———. (1981) "Variation in Rates of Offending." *American Sociological Review* 46:461–74.

Hirschi, T. and M.J. Hindelang (1977) "Intelligence and Delinquency: A Revisionist Review." *American Sociological Review* 42:571–87.

Judson, C.J., J.J. Pandell, J.B. Owens, J.L. McIntosh, and D.L. Matschullat (1969) "A Study of the California Penalty Jury in First Degree Murder Cases." *Stanford Law Review* 21:1297–1431.

Kleck, G. (1985) "Life Support for Ailing Hypotheses." *Law and Human Behavior* 9:(3)271–85.

LaFree, G. (1989) *Rape and Criminal Justice. The Social Construction of Sexual Assault.* Belmont, CA: Wadsworth.

LaFree, G., K. Drass, and P. O'Day (1992) "Race and Crime in Postwar America: Determinants of African-American and White Rates, 1957–1988." *Criminology* 30:157–88.

Langan, P.A. (1991) *Race and Prisoners Admitted to State and Federal Institutions 1926–1986.* U.S. Department of Justice. Washington, DC: U.S. Government Printing Office.

MacLean, B. and D. Milovanovic (1990) *Racism, Empiricism and Criminal Justice* Vancouver: Collective Press.

Mann, C. (1993) *Unequal Justice.* Bloomington: Indiana University Press.

Matsueda, R. and K. Heimer (1987) "Race, Family Structure, and Delinquency: A Test of Differential Association and Social Control Theories." *American Sociological Review* 52:826–40.

Mauer, M. (1990) "Young Black Men and the Criminal Justice System: A Growing National Problem." Washington, DC: The Sentencing Project.

———. (1991) "Americans Behind Bars: A Comparison of International Rates of Incarceration." Washington, DC: The Sentencing Project.

Meier, R.F. (1982) "Perspectives on the Concept of Social Control." *Annual Review of Sociology* 8:35–55.

Merton, R.K. (1938) "Social Structure and Anomie." *American Sociological Review* 3:672–82.

Messner, S.F. (1989) "Economic Discrimination and Societal Homicide Rates: Further Evidence on the Cost of Inequality." *American Sociological Review* 54:597–611.

Moyonihan, D.P. (1965) *The Negro Family: The Case for National Action.* Washington, DC: U.S. Department of Labor.

Myers, S. and M. Simms, eds. (1988) *The Economics of Race and Crime.* New Brunswick, NJ: Transaction Press.

New York Times, "Foes Accuse Bush Campaign of Inflaming Racial Tensions." October 24, 1988, Section A, p. 1; Section B, p. 5.

Parmelee, M.F. (1918) *Criminology.* New York: Macmillian.

Parsons, P. (1909) *Responsibility for Crime.* New York: Columbia University Press.

Partington, D.H. (1965) "The Incidence of the Death Penalty for Rape in Virginia." *Washington and Lee Law Review* 22:43–75.

President's Commission on Law Enforcement and Administration of Justice (1967) *The Challenge of Crime in a Free Society.* Washington, DC: U.S. Government Printing Office.

Quinney, R. (1973) *Critique of Legal Order.* Boston: Little, Brown.

Rainwater, L. (1966) "Crucible of Identity: The Negro Lower-Class Family." *Daedalus* 95:176–216.

Russell, K.K. (1992) "Development of a Black Criminology and the Role of the Black Criminologist." *Justice Quarterly* 9(4):667–83.

Sampson, R.J. (1987) "Urban Black Violence: The Effect of Male Joblessness and Family Disruption." *American Journal of Sociology* 93:348–82.

Sellin, T. ([1930]/1988) "The Negro and the Problem of Law Observance and Administration in the Light of Social Research." In S. Myers and M. Simms (eds.), *The Economics of Race and Crime*, pp. 71–80. New Brunswick, NJ: Transaction.

Shaw, C.R. and H.D. McKay (1942) *Juvenile Delinquency and Urban Areas.* Chicago: University of Chicago Press.

Shaw, C., H.D. McKay, R. Zorbaugh, and L.S. Cottrell, Jr. (1929) *Delinquency Areas.* Chicago: University of Chicago Press.

Sherman, L.W. and R.A. Berk (1984) "The Specific Deterrent Effects of Arrest for Domestic Assault." *American Sociological Review* 49:261–72.

Short, J.F., Jr. and F.I. Nye (1957) "Reported Behavior as a Criterion of Deviant Behavior." *Social Problems* 5:207–13.

Skogan, W.G. (1984) "Reporting Crime to the Police: The Status of World Research." *Journal of Research in Crime and Delinquency* 21:113–37.

Sutherland, E.H. (1939) *Principles of Criminology.* 3rd ed. Philadelphia: Lippincott.

Sutherland, E.H. and D.R. Cressey (1978) *Criminology*, 10th ed. Philadelphia: Lippincott.

Tittle, C.R. (1980) *Sanctions and Social Deviance.* New York: Praeger.

U.S. Centers for Disease Control (1990) "Homicide among Young Black Males— United States, 1978–1987." *Morbidity and Mortality Weekly Report* 39:869–73.

U.S. Department of Justice (1984) *Uniform Crime Reporting Handbook.* Washington, DC: U.S. Government Printing Office.

———. (1992a) "Criminal Victimization in the United States, 1991." Washington, DC: U.S. Government Printing Office.

———. (1992b) "Crime in the United States, 1991." Washington, DC: U.S. Government Printing Office.

Vold, G. and T. Bernard (1986) *Theoretical Criminology.* New York: Oxford University Press.

Warner, S.B. (1931) "Crimes Known to the Police—An Index of Crime." *Harvard Law Review* 45:307–34.

Wilson, J.Q. and R. Herrnstein (1985) *Crime and Human Nature.* New York: Simon and Schuster.

Wilson, W.J. (1984) "The Urban Underclass." In L.W. Dunbar (ed.), *Minority Report*, pp. 75–117. New York: Pantheon.

———. (1987) *The Truly Disadvantaged.* Chicago: University of Chicago Press.

Wright, B. (1987) *Black Robes, White Justice.* Brown: Little, Brown.

Wright, C.D. (1899) *Outline of Practical Sociology.* New York: Longmans Green.

Young, V. and A. Sutton (1991) "Excluded: The Current Status of African-American Scholars in the Field of Criminology and Criminal Justice." *Journal of Research on Crime and Delinquency* 28(1):101–16.

Zatz, M. (1984) "Race, Ethnicity and Determinate Sentencing." *Criminology* 22(2):147–71.

Article Review Form at end of book.

Is the United States currently experiencing a hate crime epidemic?

The Social Construction of a Hate Crime Epidemic

James B. Jacobs

Professor of Law and Director, Center for Research in Crime & Justice, New York University. J.D. University of Chicago, 1973; Ph.D. University of Chicago, 1975.

Jessica S. Henry

Fellow, Center For Research in Crime & Justice, NYU School of Law. B.A. Bucknell, 1990; J.D. NYU School of Law, 1995.

I. Introduction

Although definitions vary from state to state, "hate crime" generally means a crime against persons or property motivated in whole or in part by racial, ethnic, religious, gender, sexual orientation and other prejudices.[1] Politicians, journalists, interest groups, and some criminologists insist that the United States is experiencing an across-the-board hate crime "epidemic." The use of the epidemic metaphor is meant to dramatize a sharply accelerating hate crime rate. Assertions that a hate crime epidemic exists are almost always accompanied by recommendations for new "hate crime laws" that increase minimum and/or maximum punishment for offenders.

This article attempts to deconstruct the claim that the United States is experiencing a hate crime epidemic. Drawing on the "social construction of reality" perspective,[2] we attempt to show how the "reality" of a hate crime epidemic has come to prevail. First, we examine the hate crime epidemic hypothesis and identify its proponents, including advocacy groups, the media, academics, and politicians. Second, we examine the hate crime data collection efforts of the Anti-Defamation League (ADL), the Southern Poverty Law Center's Klanwatch Project (Klanwatch) and the FBI; figures from these groups are widely used to confirm the existence of the hate crime epidemic. Third, we demonstrate the political and subjective nature of counting hate crimes. Fourth, we offer some contrarian observations on the status of hate crimes.

II. Construction of the Hate Crime Epidemic Hypothesis

Many commentators assert that the rates of all types of hate crimes taken individually and together have reached epidemic levels. In this section, we consider how the hate crime epidemic has been constructed. We first consider the epidemic metaphor. Then we show how some advocacy groups have used the metaphor to dramatize their groups' plight. Finally, we focus on the roles of the media, politicians, and scholars in fostering the belief that a hate crime epidemic exists.

A. "Epidemic"?

According to Webster's dictionary, an "epidemic" is a phenomenon "affecting or tending to affect many individuals within a population, community or region at the same time; excessive, prevalent; contagious."[3] The Atlanta-based Center for Disease Control and Prevention says "an epidemic occurs when the incidence of a condition is higher than normal or higher than what health officials expect."[4] Proponents of social problems, believing that the more serious their problem, the more persuasive their demand for action, have appropriated the term "epidemic" to mobilize public attention and government resources. Calling a social problem an "epidemic" implies the existence of a crisis, a calamity that *demands* immediate political and social action.[5]

Hate crime is so often referred to as an "epidemic" that one might well believe that there is a solid foundation of facts documenting that this social problem is out of control and getting worse. To take just a few examples: Steven Spielberg, the movie producer, told the U.S. Senate

Reprinted by special permission of Northwestern University School of Law. *Journal of Criminal Law and Criminology*, Vol. 86, Issue 2, 1996.

Judiciary Committee that "hate crimes are an epidemic curable only through education";[6] Leo McCarthy, Lieutenant Governor of California, declared that "[t]here is an epidemic of hate crimes and hate violence rising in California";[7] Mississippi State Senator Bill Minor warned, "this is the type of crime that easily spreads like an epidemic";[8] a journalist for the *San Francisco Chronicle* declared that "hate-motivated violence is spreading across the United States in 'epidemic' proportions."[9]

B. Hate Crime Epidemic Proponents

The leading proponents of a hate crime epidemic thesis are advocacy groups representing gays and lesbians, Jews and blacks; advocates for women, Asian-Americans, and the disabled also have demanded explicit inclusion in hate crime legislation.[10] By calling attention to the criminal victimization of their members, these advocates may hope to mobilize law enforcement resources on behalf of their members, and, more broadly, to make out a moral and political claim in furtherance of their groups' agenda of social and political goals.

The existence of a hate crime "epidemic" may be functional for groups like the ADL and Klanwatch. These organizations are committed to preventing and eradicating all bias against those whom they represent as well as obtaining symbolic and material support for their constituents. Whatever the actual number of hate crimes, these groups' assertion of a hate crime *epidemic* effectively gains them political support. A group uses the term "epidemic" to "focus public attention and resources and create social and behavioral changes."[11]

Spokespersons for gays and lesbians probably have been the most persistent proponents of the hate crime epidemic hypothesis. Kevin Berrill, Director of the National Gay and Lesbian Task Force (NGLTF), asserts that "[t]he problem [of bias crime] is alarmingly pervasive. The real message is not whether the numbers are up or down, but rather that we have an epidemic on our hands, one that is in dire need of a remedy."[12] Similarly, Michael Petreli, a spokesperson for Gay and Lesbian

Americans, stated: "[a]nytime there's a murder of a gay or lesbian person, I am concerned because our group . . . believes there is an epidemic of this kind of anti-gay violence."[13] After the NGLTF issued its 1993 survey report, a spokesperson for the NGLTF said that "all the anecdotal evidence tells us this is still an out-of-control epidemic."[14] Ironically, the NGLTF survey report actually stated that violence against gays and lesbians had *decreased* by 14% in the six cities surveyed.[15] Despite this decline, NGLTF spokesperson Tanya L. Domi told a House of Representatives Committee that "[a]nti-gay violence plainly remains at epidemic proportions."[16]

Some women's advocacy groups claim that violence against women constitutes the largest category of hate crime. According to Molly Yard, then-President of NOW, "[w]hen one realizes that rape and wife abuse are the most commonly reported violent crimes in America, it becomes clear that the vast majority of violent crime victims in this country are women. There is widespread agreement among feminists that these crimes against women are motivated by hatred [of women]."[17] Similarly, a *Scholastic Update* article titled "War on Women" explains: "[a]ccording to statistics from law enforcement and women's advocacy groups, crimes of violence against women are rampant, and they've been increasing for more than a decade."[18]

Asian-American advocacy groups lobbying for passage of the federal Hate Crime Statistics Act claimed that Asian-Americans were experiencing increased hate violence.[19] In a letter to the Senate, the National Democratic Council of Asian and Pacific Americans stated: "[o]ur members in California, Texas, Massachusetts and New York are aware of an increase in violent crimes against Asian and Pacific-Americans, most frequently new arrivals from Southeast Asia and Korean-Americans, often elderly."[20] Likewise, Karen G. Kwong of the Asian American Bar Association of the Greater Bay Area wrote:". . . [w]e believe that in California, as well as throughout the nation, there has been an increase in crimes committed against Asians and other mi-

norities which are motivated by racial, ethnic, or religious prejudice."[21] William Yoshino of the Japanese American Citizens League stated: "[we] believe there has been a dramatic upward trend in violence toward Asians since 1980."[22]

These spokespersons and organizations, among others, have successfully created the widespread belief that hate-motivated crimes based on race, religion, ethnicity, gender, sexual preference, and disability are overwhelming the United States. This "reality" has provided the foundation for political and legislative "findings" and has spawned a growing body of hate crime law and jurisprudence.

C. The Media's Role

The media have accepted, reinforced, and amplified the image of a nation engulfed by hate crime. A LEXIS search of news articles from 1993 to 1995 revealed fifty-six stories referring to the "epidemic of hate crime."[23]

Headlines like the following are typical: "A Cancer of Hatred Afflicts America";[24] "Rise in Hate Crimes Signals Alarming Resurgence of Bigotry";[25] "Black-on-White Hate Crimes Rising";[26] "[A]cross the nation hate crimes . . . are on the increase after years of steady decline"[27]; and "[t]hroughout the country, there are increasing numbers of shootings, assaults, murders and vandalism that are motivated by bias and hatred."[28] The alarming state of inter-group relations is "news" while inter-group cooperation is not. A *Newsday* headline states "Bias Crimes Flare Up in City's Heat";[29] a full five paragraphs later we find out that "the number of bias-related incidents in the city *dropped* in the first half of this year from the same period last year."[30]

Not surprisingly, U.S. hate crime has achieved international notoriety. The Xinhua General Overseas News Service distributed an article stating "[t]he United States is seeing a surge of hate crimes motivated by race, religion and sexual bias according to a *Boston Globe* survey."[31] The article further reports increases in nearly every major city in the United States. When FBI Director Louis Freeh released the results of the second Hate Crime Statistics Report during a speech in Germany, he told his hosts that hate crime murders are at least as common in the United States as in Germany, which at the time was said to be experiencing a wave of violence against "foreigners."[32] The media seem almost enthusiastic in presuming the worst about the state of inter-group relationships in American society. For example, a Florida newspaper presented a horrifying attack on an African-American tourist as "a dramatic example of the growing problem of hate crime,"[33] but the writer provided no basis for the assertion that there is a "growing problem of hate."[34]

Sometimes the media may even be responsible for triggering hate crimes. When two African-American children in New York City reported that several whites had sprayed them with white shoe polish, the media gave the incident endless publicity. The week after the alleged attack, sixty-one bias incidents were reported.[35] When, weeks later, the New York Police Department effectively abandoned the investigation amid speculation that the original accusation was fabricated, the media hardly covered the story.[36]

D. Scholarly Perspectives

Perhaps most disturbing, criminal justice scholars have accepted the hate crime epidemic hypothesis with hardly a raised eyebrow. While few books focusing on hate crimes have been published, the overwhelming majority of them lend their support to the social construction of hate crime as an epidemic. In *The Rising Tide of Bigotry and Bloodshed: Hate Crimes*,[37] Jack Levin and Jack McDevitt, two of the leading scholars on hate crimes, claim that America is experiencing a "rising tide" of hate crimes that will get worse in the next decade. This prediction is based upon a review of highly publicized incidents and reports of advocacy groups like the ADL, Klanwatch, and the National Institute Against Prejudice and Violence. A large portion of the book is devoted to detailed descriptions of particular horrific hate crimes.

The authors base their bleak prediction of increasing hate crimes on economic decline having led to so-cial-psychological malaise. Levin and McDevitt believe that "resentment" is at the root of most hate crime offenses. They argue that as Americans are forced to cope with dwindling economic opportunities, they will blame others for taking opportunities away from them. This resentment and frustration, coupled with extant biases and stereotypes, expresses itself through hate crimes; in other words, angry competition over a shrinking economic pie.[38] This explanation is not based on any empirical studies but on the authors' social speculation. The most significant problem with the authors' speculation is the absence of any data on the hate crime rate. In short, the authors may have created a theory in search of a problem.

In *Bias Crime: American Law Enforcement and Legal Responses*,[39] a variety of authors explain how law enforcement agencies have dealt with hate crimes, and advocate improved data collection by the states and federal government. All of the essays assume that hate crimes need to be dealt with and punished as a separate category of crime. Several of the authors express alarm about the prevalence of hate crimes. Joan Weiss, executive director of the Justice Research and Statistics Association, acknowledges that the extent of the problem is unknown, but then claims that "[t]he problem is so pervasive that, even without accurate data, we know that thousands upon thousands of incidents occur throughout the country every year."[40] In another essay, Allen Sapp, Richard Holden, and Michael Wiggins begin by stating, "[i]n recent years, bias-motivated activities directed at members of minority groups have occurred with increasing frequency. The escalating rate of these crimes is proving to be a major source of concern. . . ."[41]

In *Hate Crimes: Confronting Violence Against Lesbians and Gay Men*,[42] various authors focus on violence against homosexuals, beginning with the premise that such attacks, while not a new problem, have increased dramatically. A large portion of the book presents anecdotal evidence of an increase in anti-gay hate crimes, highlighting individual brutal incidents. The authors state that surveys of victimization among gays and lesbians may not present an accurate picture of the magnitude of the anti-gay hate crimes due to both an unwillingness by some individuals to "come out" and possible under-reporting of incidents.

The most inflammatory of the recent books on hate crimes is Alphonso Pinkney's *Lest We Forget: White Hate Crimes*.[43] Pinkney argues that the conservative political climate during the 1980s permitted an atmosphere of hostility against minorities to thrive. Pinkney states, "[t]he most alarming trend was the resurgence of overt racist behavior. . . . [R]acial behavior was rampant."[44] In one chapter, titled "Recent Surge of Racial Violence," Pinkney points the finger of blame at then-President Ronald Reagan: "the point is that Ronald Reagan set the tone and created the environment in which acts of racial violence thrived. . . . Thus, the widespread physical attacks on blacks and other minorities went unchecked."[45] The bulk of the book is devoted to describing highly publicized incidents of violence, some of which were not clearly attributable to racism. For example, Pinkney characterized the Bernhard Goetz case, in which Goetz, a white man, shot four black youths who were trying to rob him, as an example of racial violence. Goetz was acquitted. Similarly, when New York City police shot a mentally unstable black woman as she lunged at another police officer with a knife, Pinkney labeled the incident race-based violence. Pinkney's book is not really about hate crimes, nor does it support the existence of an epidemic of anti-black hate crimes. Indeed, only a few of the incidents covered in the book could uncontroversially be characterized as hate crimes.

A search in WESTLAW's academic journals files found thirty-one articles published between 1992 and 1995 that contained the phrases "hate crime" and "epidemic."[46] Not one of these articles doubts the existence of an across-the-board hate crime epidemic. To the contrary, a hate crime epidemic is assumed and frequently cited as justification for new substantive laws, enhanced sentences, and increased enforcement.

Like journalists who write about hate crimes, the academic commentators selectively apply data that do not support "the facts" they claim to establish. For example, Professor Abraham Abramovsky, in a 1992 law journal article advocating more laws to combat bias crime, claims an "urgency of the escalating problem [of bias crime]."[47] He asserts that "categories of bias crime are rapidly growing along with the reported number of instances."[48] Yet, the proliferation of bias crime categories does not mean more *instances* of bias crimes. Rather, increased categories of crime indicates the willingness of law makers to accommodate more advocacy groups' demands.

Professor Abramovsky expresses alarm that, according to the New York Police Department's statistics for the first four months of 1990, there was a twelve percent increase in the number of bias-related crimes over the same period in 1989.[49] He explains that "the most alarming statistic is that in 1990 the number of bias-related attacks on Asians almost doubled from the number reported in 1989."[50] A footnote provides the detail: "there were 11 bias crimes reported against Asians during the first four months of 1990, compared with 22 reports *in all* of 1989."[51] Is a total of eleven bias incidents against Asian-Americans truly "alarming" in a city with a 1990 Asian-American population of 512,719[52] and with a total of 710,222 FBI index crimes?[53] In the final analysis, the total number of anti-Asian attacks for 1990 was the same as the 1989 figure.[54]

Eleven reported bias crimes in the first four months of 1990 might reflect random crime fluctuations, the prolific criminality of a single offender or of a clique of teenagers, the energies of one police officer or enhanced data collection efficiency. Abramovsky acknowledges the latter possibility, but cites a National Institute Against Prejudice and Violence (NIAPV) study that "reported a steady increase in hate crimes in the last two years from the majority of agencies who collect such data."[55] This begs the question. As efficiency in bias data collection increases, whether by police or by non-governmental organizations (and often in conjunction with each other), and more public attention focuses on the issue, absolute numbers of recorded bias incidents will necessarily increase. Moreover, can comparisons of data over a two-year period really be considered a trend?[56]

Student law review authors have enthusiastically embraced the existence of a hate crime epidemic. One writer in the *Harvard Law Review* states, "[i]n recent years, violence, threats, and vandalism committed because of the race, religion, sexual orientation, or other such characteristics of the victim have increased at an alarming rate."[57] The author explains that Congress passed a Hate Crime Bill in 1990 and that the FBI reported 4,558 hate crimes in 1991.[58] Where the author finds the "increase," let alone the cause for "alarm," is not explained; apparently it is so obvious that it ought simply to be assumed. Another *Harvard Law Review* Note informs us that "[t]he Howard Beach incident highlights an alarming trend of increasing racial violence against minorities in the United States."[59] The support for the existence of such a "trend" was testimony at a 1981 House Judiciary Committee Hearing[60]—*five years prior* to the Howard Beach incident.[61]

E. Politicians and Symbolic Politics

Politicians have enthusiastically climbed aboard the hate crime epidemic bandwagon. Denouncing hate crime and passing sentencing enhancement laws provides elected officials with an opportunity to decry bigotry. Politicians can propose anti-hate legislation as a cheap, quick-fix solution that sends powerful symbolic messages to important groups of constituents.[62] Recognizing the political and symbolic importance of legislation, politicians embrace anti-bias laws, routinely citing advocacy groups' statements and statistics.[63] Senator Alan Cranston (D. Cal.), sponsor of the federal Hate Crime Statistics Act, referred extensively to the 1987 NGLTF statistics: "the number of hate crimes increased substantially, . . . representing a 42% increase from 1986."[64] Co-sponsor John Kerry (D. Mass.) similarly explained:

Hearings which have been held in the House Judiciary Committee indicate that there is a serious problem in America with hate crimes of all types, including violence against Blacks, Hispanics, Asians-Americans, Jews, Arab-Americans and gays. A recent report by the National Gay and Lesbian Task Force [asserts] that hate crimes directed against gays and lesbians are increasing. Legislation is needed to address the serious problem of anti-gay violence.[65]

The claim of "epidemic" levels of violence led to the passage of the 1994 Violence Against Women Act (VAWA).[66] One section of a NOW Legal Defense and Education Fund statement to Congress on VAWA was titled "The Epidemic of Violent Crime Against Women."[67] After citing statistics about violence against women, often based on congressional testimony by other advocacy groups,[68] the NOW statement concluded that "legislation is needed today to protect citizens from an epidemic of gender-based violence."[69]

Politicians seem more concerned with making symbolic statements against widely disfavored prejudices than in formulating specific remedies to carefully defined problems. In an open letter dated August 16, 1991 to members of the New York State legislature, New York's then-Governor Mario Cuomo stated, "as government, our single most effective weapon is the law. I implore you to support the Bias Related Violence and Intimidation Act I have proposed, and make it clear to the people of this state that behavior based on bias will not be ignored or tolerated."[70] In the aftermath of the Bensonhurst riots, then-New York State Attorney General Robert Abrams said that the proposed Bias Related Violence and Intimidation Act "would send a message that hate crimes will be severely punished."[71] When former Governor Jim Florio signed New Jersey's ethnic intimidation bill into law, he declared, "[t]his legislation does more than punish . . . . It says something about who we are, and about the ideals to which this state is committed."[72] Similarly, the U.S. Senate Report on the federal Hate Crimes Reporting Statute declared that "the very effort by the legislative branch to require the Justice Department to collect this information would send an additional important signal to victimized groups everywhere that the U.S. government is concerned about this kind of crime."[73]

III. Sources of Data

One must examine the sources of hate crime data in order to understand how the hate crime epidemic hypothesis has been constructed. Some advocacy groups, such as the ADL, collect data and generate statistics to support their claims that those whom they represent are experiencing an epidemic of bias-motivated victimization. These statistics are used to confirm the "reality" of hate crime. While it is beyond the scope of this Article to critique every advocacy group's hate crime data collection and reporting procedures, we focus on the ADL's data collection methods—by far the most established and sophisticated non-governmental data collection effort. We next examine Klanwatch's hate crime data. Finally, we critique the FBI's recent data collection initiative pursuant to the 1990 Hate Crime Statistics Act.

A. The ADL's Data

Since 1979, the ADL has compiled and published an annual audit of "overt acts or expressions" of anti-Jewish bigotry or hostility.[74] The anti-semitic overt acts or expressions included in the report are not necessarily crimes. They include non-criminal verbal harassment and the distribution of anti-semitic literature, such as neo-Nazi literature and anti-semitic materials, to Jews and non-Jews, in public places.[75] Thus, on its face, one cannot rely on the ADL audit as an indicator of hate *crime*.

The ADL data collection method also contains a great deal of subjectivity. The ADL compiles its statistics from data provided by its twenty-eight regional offices. Each regional office relies upon victim and community group reports, newspaper articles, and local law enforcement agencies for its information.

Individuals and community groups who believe they have been the victims of an anti-semitic incident may call the ADL office. A person at the ADL fills out a standard form, which includes the name of the victim and a description of the incident, and the victim may be encouraged to contact the police. The ADL will then look for newspaper coverage of the

incident and attempt to determine whether similar incidents, if any, suggest a pattern. If the incident is an isolated, non-criminal event, like an anti-semitic message left on an answering machine, the ADL officer will listen to the message, and confirm it as "harassment" for purposes of the audit. The ADL attempts to confirm all reports.

The ADL also must determine whether an incident brought to its attention constitutes "an act or expression of anti-semitism." For example, the organization has decided that a stone thrown through a synagogue window, even without any markings or other verbal expression of anti-semitism, evidences hostility towards a Jewish institution. The Annual Audit then includes this act, even though (as the ADL itself acknowledges) one child could have thrown the stone at another and simply missed.[76]

Thus, the ADL Audit will necessarily be dominated by "low-end" incidents such as anti-semitic comments, literature and graffiti. The ADL reviews any crime that occurs at a Jewish institution for anti-semitic overtones, regardless of whether the police classify the incident as bias-related. The 1993 ADL Audit of Anti-Semitic Incidents lists a "representative sampling" of incidents of anti-semitic harassment. For example, in Connecticut, a high school hockey coach yelled an anti-semitic slur, "Get the Jew Boy," at an opposing player. In Georgia, a business owner accused a Jewish woman who questioned the price increase of service of "trying to Jew me down." In Massachusetts, "Jew!" was yelled by a man in a passing truck at a Jewish mourner leaving a cemetery.[77]

Once an act has been reported and classified as an anti-semitic incident, the ADL attempts to verify it. Validating and investigating property damage is easier to confirm than anonymous reports of personal harassment. Without additional follow-up of reports by unidentified complainants, the ADL states that it *may* not be possible to include these incidents in its Annual Audit.[78] However, "may" is not "must"; some unidentified, unverified reports "may" be included in the ADL's Audit.

The ADL's dependence upon newspaper stories regarding anti-semitic incidents also poses problems. Newspapers vary enormously in their coverage of anti-semitic incidents (especially minor incidents) and in the reliability of their reporting. The propensity to report or not to report bias incidents may have little, if anything, to do with the actual frequency of hate crimes. Perhaps a small town newspaper is more apt to report such incidents because there is less news to report than in a larger urban center. On the other hand, some newspapers in urban centers may have a sizeable readership concerned about anti-semitism. Conversely, a newspaper may not deem such behavior as newsworthy in an area where such conduct or expression is routine. Obviously, we lack any data on the criteria and procedures which journalists employ in confirming claims of hate-crime victimization. We do know, however, that a hate crime is more newsworthy than an "ordinary" crime.[79]

According to its own personnel, the ADL does not purport to be the "end all, be all" provider of anti-semitic statistics.[80] Yet, organizations such as Klanwatch and the Gay and Lesbian Anti-Violence Project have followed the ADL's data collection model, and numerous states have based their anti-bias laws on ADL Guidelines.[81]

B. Klanwatch's Hate Crime Statistics

An article by Klanwatch, a project of the Southern Poverty Law Center, illustrates how the hate crime epidemic has been constructed on the basis of dubious statistics. In the article "Campus Hate Crime Rages in 1992,"[82] Klanwatch claims that there is a "raging hate epidemic" on college campuses. Two types of data are offered to support this claim. First, Klanwatch cites a 1990 report by the NIAPV which states that "25% of minority students will become victims of violence based on prejudice. And 25% of those students will be revictimized, according to a survey conducted by the NIAPV at the University of Maryland at Baltimore."[83] Second, the article reports that the "New York

State Governor's Task Force on Bias-Related Violence survey of 2,823 junior and senior high school students found respondents to be biased against gay and lesbian students."[84]

Klanwatch's conclusion that there is a "raging hate epidemic" on college campuses is questionable. First, Klanwatch does not explain the origin of the NIAPV's twenty-five percent figure. What qualifies as an act of violence? How is a perpetrator identified and his or her prejudice confirmed? Furthermore, the reported NIAPV finding of twenty-five percent conflicts with other data sources. The 1992 National Crime Victimization Survey Report, produced by the Department of Justice, found only 32.1 crimes of violence per 1,000 persons age twelve and over for all Americans.[85] And, while higher, there were still only 50.4 crimes of violence per 1,000 black persons age twelve and over.[86] The FBI statistics on campus crimes for 1990 at the University of Maryland in Baltimore County shows that of its 9,868 students, only twelve incidents of violent crime were reported; of 4,563 students at University of Maryland at Baltimore City, twenty-five incidents of violence were reported.[87]

Klanwatch also fails to explain the link between the New York State Governor's Task Force finding of *biased feelings* among high school students and *acts* of hate on college campuses. The same types of questions remain unanswered: How many students responded to the survey? What qualifies as "bias against gay and lesbian students"? Is personal feeling without action "bias"?

C. The FBI Numbers

The 1990 Hate Crime Statistics Act mandated the collection of hate crime data by the United States Department of Justice.[88] Passage of the Act itself was predicated on the uncritical acceptance of a hate crime epidemic in the United States. Sponsors favored a data collection effort to confirm what they already claimed to know: hate crime is rampant in every category. The FBI was assigned the task of promulgating guidelines on the collection of hate crime data. Local police departments were requested to follow the guidelines in preparing their regular crime reports for the FBI's Uniform Crime Reports.

In releasing the first data collected under the Act, then-FBI Director William Sessions stated: "[w]hile these initial data are limited, . . . they give us our first assessment of the nature of crime motivated by bias in our society."[89] However, it is questionable whether this "assessment" provides any useful information. Only thirty-two state police departments submitted *any data*. Only 2,771 agencies,[90] of the 12,805 law enforcement agencies nationwide reporting to the FBI,[91] participated in the data collection effort; of these, seventy-three percent of the reporting departments reported *no hate crime incidences*.[92] Even among the participating agencies, data collection methodology varied dramatically from state to state, and municipality to municipality.[93] In fact, for 1991 only 4,558 hate crime incidents involving 4,755 incidents were reported *for the entire country*.[94] "Intimidation," the most frequently reported offense, accounted for one-third of all hate crime offenses against property and accounted for 27.4% of reported hate crimes.[95]

Despite the spotty nature of the FBI collection effort, and the small number of hate crimes it revealed, the media seized upon these data as confirmation of a hate crime epidemic. A *Houston Chronicle* editorial stated: "[t]he specter of hate is unfortunately alive and well in the United States . . . . The national report reveals a grim picture."[96] The *Philadelphia Inquirer* announced that the FBI and anti-bigotry groups report an alarming rise in hate crimes.[97] Since this was the first report, it is unclear how the newspaper was able to discern a "rise." *USA Today* simply stated that "no one needs a government report to know such [hate crime] offenses are rising."[98]

The FBI statistics did not square with the much more alarmist reports put forward by advocacy groups for the same time period. For example, the FBI reported that 425 hate crimes nationwide were motivated by sexual-orientation bias. For the same period, the Gay and Lesbian Anti-Violence Project reported 592 bias incidents based on sexual orientation in New York City alone.[99] Similarly, while the FBI for 1991 reported twelve "hate" murders based upon all federally-recognized prejudices,[100] Klanwatch reported twenty-seven murders motivated by bias.[101]

Ironically, this statistical divergence led some of the groups which campaigned most vigorously for the passage of the Hate Crime Statistics Act to denounce the whole federal data collection project. Klanwatch, among the most ardent campaigners for the passage of the federal law, dismissed the first FBI statistics as "inadequate and nearly worthless."[102] The second FBI report did not fare much better.[103]

IV. The Problem with Hate Crime Statistics

The collection of hate crime statistics raises unique problems. The first problem is to define "hate crime." The second problem is to establish a reliable means for determining when a perpetrator's bias should transform an ordinary crime into a hate crime. The third problem is to decide which prejudices are relevant to counting hate crimes.

A. Defining the Hate Crime's Bias Element

Bias or prejudice is not easily defined. The *International Encyclopedia of the Human Sciences* offers this guidance: "[P]rejudice is not a unitary phenomenon . . . . [I]t will take varying forms in different individuals."[104] If what constitutes prejudice seems vague, the scope of prejudice is virtually limitless. Some commentators argue that racism, sexism, homophobia, etc. are structural and pervasive influences in American cultural life.[105] If they are correct, then it may be impossible to point to any interactions between members of different groups unaffected by prejudice, at least to some extent. According to the federal Hate Crime Statistics Act, an ordinary crime becomes a hate crime when "motivated, in whole or in part, by the offender's bias against a race, religion, ethnic/national origin, group, or sexual orientation group."[106] The FBI defines ethnic prejudice as "[a] preformed negative opinion or attitude toward a group of persons of the same race or national origin who share common or similar traits, languages, customs, and traditions (e.g., Arabs, Hispanics, etc.)."[107] Under this definition, practically any crime committed by a member of one group against a member of another could qualify as a hate crime.

B. Motiviation

There are serious problems in determining when a crime is motivated in whole, *or in part*, by bias. In addition to grave First Amendment issues which are beyond the scope of this paper,[108] determining motivation is a complex, frequently impossible, endeavor. Some, probably the majority, of hate crime offenders are not apprehended; their motivation must be inferred.[109] Even if apprehended, offenders will not provide insight into their motivations. In this situation, and in the situation where offenders are not caught, the coding of hate crimes depends upon information provided by the victim or inferred from the crime scene. Yet, the victim may be mistaken, hold personal biases that affect his or her judgment, be overly sensitive, have misperceived the incident, or simply be unreliable. While there will undoubtedly be some clear cases, many cases will be explicable in terms of a number of different motivations.

Consider a fight that occurs over a parking space, during the course of which a racial epithet is used. While obtaining a parking spot "motivates" the fight, under some statutory constructions the fight could be classified as a bias incident, subjecting the epithet utterer to a harsher criminal sanction.[110] A much more complex problem would be presented by attempting to count the number of bias crimes that occurred, for example, during the L.A. riots in the aftermath of the Rodney King trial. Does all the property damage committed by African-Americans against Korean-owned stores count as bias crime?

C. Which Prejudices Count?

Subjectivity also pervades the determination of which prejudices transform an ordinary crime into a hate crime. For example, whether to include sexual orientation in hate crime

bills has stirred controversy in Congress and in some states.[111] Given the sordid history of anti-gay violence, the exclusion of violence against gays and lesbians from any hate crime bill illustrates the point that the definition of hate crime is necessarily a political determination.[112]

Labelling and paying special attention to crimes motivated by certain biases arguably belittles crimes motivated by other biases that do not receive the same recognition. Are legislators delegitimating the victimization of workers who are targets of assaults because of pro- or anti-union biases or of Planned Parenthood employees who are threatened and attacked by violent anti-abortionists?[113]

Which *predicate* crimes count as hate crimes (when motivated by bias) is a legislative determination that also shapes the perceived size and scope of the hate crime epidemic.[114] For example, the Hate Crime Statistics Act of 1990 originally enumerated for data collection eight predicate crimes when motivated by certain biases: "murder, non-negligent manslaughter, forcible rape, aggravated assault, simple assault, intimidation, arson, and destruction, damage or vandalism of property."[115] Exercising Congressionally-authorized discretion, the Attorney General added robbery, burglary, and motor vehicle theft.[116] However, certain crimes were not included. One might wonder, for example, why kidnapping, if motivated by bias, does not count as a hate crime?

The political act of classifying whether or not a crime will be counted as hate crime determines the size of the problem. If hate graffiti counts, then the hate crime rate will be formidable indeed. If only violent crimes motivated by bias are counted, then the hate crime rate will be considerably lower.

V. Telling a Different Story with the Same Data

It is impossible to prove the null hypothesis: there is no hate crime epidemic. Even if we were to take on this quixotic task, "proof" would require the use of the same statistics criticized in this article. Nevertheless, these same data can be used to tell a very different story than

that which prevails in the media, government, and the legal academy.

We could, for example, point out that the Uniform Crime Report was able to identify only a small number of hate crimes. Similarly, the NYC Police Department, which has had a Bias Crime Unit for almost fifteen years,[117] reported 440 bias *incidents* in 1994;[118] a relatively small number for a city which records 710,000 felony arrests each year.

There are sharply conflicting views of the same situations. While a 1991 Klanwatch report stated that the number of white supremacist groups had increased significantly, the Georgia Bureau of Investigation reported "membership of white supremacist groups in Georgia had been pretty stable over the past few years" and that there were doubts whether "there had been any increase in the number of groups in such states."[119]

If it is true that "[t]he more people hear about hate crimes . . . the more likely they are to report such incidents to the ADL or the police,"[120] then why hasn't the number of reported hate crimes vastly increased? Even if we accept the inevitability of underreporting, an epidemic of hate crime would mean that more people are affected. If more people are affected, there should be a significant increase in the number of people reporting these crimes. Yet there hasn't been, at least according to both the FBI and the NYPD.

Does it make sense to say that 4,588 reported hate crimes constitutes an epidemic when more than 14,872,883 index crimes were reported to the FBI in 1991?[121] Should an epidemic be inferred from less than .039% of all reported crimes? In fact, the total number of hate crimes (most of which fall into the less serious crime categories) represents only a minute fraction of reported crimes. It is impossible to conclude that these numbers represent a *trend* one way or the other.

VI. Ahistoricism

The socially constructed claim that hate crime has reached epidemic proportions flies in the face of history. It requires a certain amount of amnesia to state that "[n]ot since the days when the [Ku Klux] Klan regularly lynched people at the turn of the century. . . have we had anything like we have today,"[122] or to state that "black students today face a level of hatred, prejudice and ignorance comparable to that of the days of Bull Connor, Lester Maddox and Orval Faubus."[123] It is far beyond the scope of this Article to provide a comprehensive history of racial and ethnic violence, much less anti-religious violence, anti-homosexual violence, and anti-gender violence in the United States; such a history would require nothing less than a multi-volume treatise. Suffice it to say, however, that the claim that the country is now experiencing unprecedented levels of violence in all these categories borders on the preposterous.

A. Native Americans

Almost from the moment European settlers arrived in this country, Native Americans were the target of bigotry and hatred. Viewed as savages, they were routinely removed from their land by force. The nineteenth century was punctuated with atrocities against Native Americans, and unfortunately, by "atrocities" we are not referring to name calling and racist leaflets. Department of War documents from the early 1800s reveal that the United States, in an effort to exterminate Native Americans, distributed blankets infected with the smallpox virus.[124] During the 1820s, in North Carolina, Georgia, and other southern states, the Cherokees were rounded up by the U.S. military and force-marched to Oklahoma. During this 3,000 mile march, known as the "Trail of Tears," hundreds of Cherokees died either at the hands of their military escorts, or from starvation and exposure.

In Arizona and New Mexico, settlers and officials of the Catholic church attacked Navajo camps, kidnapping women and children to use as slaves. During the 1850s and 1860s, the U.S. military hunted down and killed Navajos in a carefully orchestrated campaign. They surrendered after their peach orchards and crops were burned. The Navajos also were subjected to a forced march, known as "The Long Walk," to Bosque Redondo, a remote military outpost in southeastern New Mexico. Those unable to keep up were shot. During the four years of imprisonment at Bosque Redondo, nearly half the Navajo population died.

In the late 1800s, several counties in Arizona and New Mexico offered bounties for Indian scalps—$500 for male scalps and $250 for women and children. A *New York Times* article, titled "Arizona and New Mexico Settlers Propose to Destroy the Savages," reported that citizens were organizing "in armed bodies for the purpose of going on a real old-fashioned Indian hunt."[125]

B. Blacks, Lynchings and the Klan

Lynching has a long history in the United States. It was first used after the Revolutionary War by vigilante patriots against loyalists and criminals. In the American West during the 1800s, cattle and horse thieves, murderers, claim jumpers, Hispanics, and Native Americans were common targets of lynch mobs.[126] Lynching, however, reached its pinnacle with the Klan's terrorism of blacks from the post-Civil War era well into the twentieth century.[127]

From 1882 to 1968, 4,743 people were lynched; the vast majority were black.[128] During the peak lynching years, 1889–1918, the five most active lynching states were Georgia (360), Mississippi (350), Louisiana (264), Texas (263), and Alabama (244).[129] In 1892, 200 lynchings occurred in a single year.[130] These numbers include only the recorded lynchings; one can only speculate on the number of blacks whose deaths at the hand of lynch mobs went unreported. Many hundreds more blacks were injured and killed during race riots in the late nineteenth and early twentieth century. In March of 1871, a riot erupted in Meridian, Mississippi during the trial of three blacks accused of making "incendiary speeches." An argument escalated into a shooting spree in which twenty-five to thirty blacks were killed by rioters.[131] Blacks who escaped the rioters unharmed took to the woods to hide, and the three blacks on trial were taken from the courthouse by Klansmen and hanged.[132] The early part of the twentieth century saw anti-black riots, often led by the Klan, in Chicago, Tulsa, Memphis, and Washington, D.C.[133]

The Ku Klux Klan, formed in 1865, terrorized southern blacks during the post-Civil War period to such a degree that many blacks went into semi-permanent hiding. According to David Chalmers, author of *Hooded Americanism: The History of the Ku Klux Klan,*

Unless there were federal troops at hand, the safest thing for Negroes to do was to hide during periods of Klan activity or after outbreaks of violence. It was reported that in some regions of South Carolina, more than a majority of the Negroes slept in the woods during the Klan's active winter of 1870–71.[134]

In the 1920s, Klan membership soared into the millions. At its peak, it is estimated that four to five million people all across the country were members of the Klan.[135] The Klan targeted not only blacks, but recent immigrants, Catholics, Jews, and communists.[136] (By contrast, Klan members today are estimated at approximately 5,000 nationwide.)

C. Nativism: A Politics of Hatred

Beginning in the 1820s and extending into the twentieth century, a mainstream political movement developed that was based on hatred of Catholics, Jews, and recent immigrants, primarily Irish, Italians, and Germans. Nativist leaders were not simply a fringe element on the American scene. They were elected to political office and published widely-read anti-Catholic and anti-immigrant newspapers. During the 1820–30s, the movement was called "nativism"; it then metamorphosed into the "Know Nothing Party." Later in the century it went by the name of American Protective Association (APA). In the twentieth century, it was again called nativism.

The rhetoric of the nativists encouraged hatred. Catholic churches were burned. Gangs and mobs attacked priests and immigrants in Massachusetts, Maine, Maryland, New Jersey, New York, and

Pennsylvania.[137] In the 1840s, Philadelphia was the scene of sporadic rioting over the course of three months.

> Nativists and Irishmen, Protestants and Catholics clashed in fistfights and knifefights. They exchanged gunfire. They menaced each other with cannons, ready to be loaded with stacks of shot, powder, nails, chains, "anything" as one observer put it, that could be used "to kill and maim the foe." . . . [S]ome thirty people were killed, hundreds wounded, dozens of homes burned out.[138]

Anti-immigrant and anti-Catholic violence flourished into the twentieth century. Anti-semitism became a force to be reckoned with and was rampant in all areas of American life. Newspaper classified advertisements for employment, housing, and vacation rentals openly declared that Jews were not acceptable.[139] Ironically, one of the most virulent American anti-semites of the first half of the twentieth century was a Catholic priest, Charles Coughlin. Father Coughlin's church had been the target of many Klan-orchestrated cross burnings. During the late 1920s, Coughlin began broadcasting his sermons on radio. Once the Great Depression hit, Coughlin began focusing on economic and social issues. An avowed enemy of the New Deal, Coughlin founded the National Union for Social Justice (NUSJ). By 1936, NUSJ recruited over five million members. His radio broadcasts, which boasted an audience of at least ten million listeners, were peppered with anti-semitic attacks; he praised Nazi Germany and the Third Reich. His anti-semitic message appealed to nativism's past victims, Irish and German Catholics. Young followers of Father Coughlin bragged about attacking Jews in Boston and New York.

Anti-semitism even reached the highest levels of the federal government. President Roosevelt's Assistant Secretary of State in the early 1940s, Breckenridge Long, was a nativist and an anti-semite. He wrote, "large numbers of Jews from Russia and Poland are entirely unfit to become citizens of this country . . . . [T]hey are lawless, scheming, defiant. . . just the same as the criminal Jews who crowd our police court dockets in New York."[140]

D. Others

We believe that the same ahistoricism that characterizes recent pronouncements of unprecedented violence against ethnic and racial groups affects claims about prejudice-motivate violence against women, gays, and lesbians. Until recently, however, gays and lesbians feared to openly affirm or demonstrate their sexual orientation. Now it is routine. Violence against women has always been high, but we know of no reason to believe that it is higher now than earlier in the century, when women all too often had no where to go to report their victimization.

VII. Conclusion

Professor Abramovsky asserts that, "no one seriously questions the severity of the problem [of bias crime]."[141] We do. The uncritical acceptance of a hate crime epidemic is unfortunate. It distorts discourse about the allocation of scarce resources both within and without the criminal justice system. Further, this pessimistic and alarmist portrayal of a divided conflict-ridden community may create a self-fulfilling prophecy and exacerbate societal divisions.[142]

Minority groups may have good reasons for claiming the U.S. is in the throes of an epidemic. An "epidemic" demands attention, remedial actions, resources, and reparations. The electronic and print media also have reasons to support the existence of a rampant hate crime epidemic. Crime sells—so does racism, sexism, and homophobia. Garden variety crime has become mundane. The law and order drama has to be revitalized if it is to command attention.

History may show that modern society has actually experienced a reduction in violent crime against marginal groups. It is hardly necessary to point out our nation's history of bias: Native Americans were brutally murdered as the West was conquered; the blood and sweat of Chinese and other immigrant workers stain the expanses of railroad tracks across the midwest; lynchings of blacks were once common; violence against various European immigrants and Jews was a fact of life. Clearly, violence motivated by racism, xenophobia, anti-semitism and other biases is not new.

Perhaps what is new is greater intolerance of prejudice. The conclusion that hate crime has reached epidemic proportions today simply evinces the fact that bias crime is now much less acceptable and that victimized groups have a special social and political status. While it is possible to understand how and why the picture of a "hate crime epidemic" has come to dominate the American imagination, it is doubtful that this picture depicts reality.

Notes

1. The federal government and most states do not include gender bias in their definition of hate crimes. Some states, like New York, do not include sexual orientation bias. "Other prejudices" which some states include, at least for purposes of collecting data, are physical or mental handicap, age, economic or social status. *See, e.g.,* Or. Rev. Stat. § 181.550 (1993). For an excellent review of state hate crime statutes, see Lu-in Wang, Hate Crimes Law (1995).
2. *See* Peter L. Berger, *The Social Construction of Reality: A Treatise in the Sociology of Knowledge* (1990); Hans H. Gerth & C. Wrights Mills, *The Power Elite* (1957).
3. *Webster's Ninth New Collegiate Dictionary* (1989).
4. See Eric Zorn, An Outbreak of Epidemics, *Atlanta Const.*, Mar. 28, 1994, at A11.
5. Id.
6. Jake Batsell, Spielberg Speaks Out Against Hate Crimes; FBI Data Show Report on Rise in Arizona, Ariz. Republic. June 29, 1994, at A11 (quoting Spielberg's testimony to the Senate Judiciary Subcommittee).
7. Bills Introduced to Combat Hate Crimes, *UPI*, Mar. 22, 1993, available in *Lexis* News Library, UPSTAT File (quoting Lt. Gov. Leo McCarthy of California).
8. Gina Holland, Mississippi Ills Require Hate Crimes Bill, Backers Maintain, *Com. Appeal*, Jan. 7, 1994, at 1B (quoting Sen. Bill Minor).
9. Suzanne Espinosa, Black-on-White Hate Crimes Rising, *S.F. Chron.*, Nov. 17, 1993, at A10.
10. See James B. Jacobs, The Emergence and Implications of American Hate Crime Jurisprudence, 22 *Isr. Y.B. on Hum. Rts.* 113, 116–18 (1993) [hereinafter *Isr. Y.B.*].
11. Eric Zorn, A Trend That's . . . Well, Epidemic, *Chi. Trib.*, Mar. 23, 1994, at N1 (citing Ward Cates, Center for Disease Control).

12. Walt Albro, Report: Anti-Gay Violence Shows Dramatic Increase, *UPI*, Mar. 19, 1992.

13. Advocacy Group Urges Police to Consider Anti-Gay Motive, *Gannett News Service*, Oct. 11, 1994 (statement of Michael Petreli).

14. Survey Finds Decrease in Anti-Gay Violence, *N.Y. Times*, Mar. 9, 1994, at A13 (statement of David M. Smith).

15. Id.

16. House Appropriations/Commerce, Justice, State, the Judiciary, and Related Agencies FY 95 Commerce, Justice and State Appropriations (May 3, 1994) (testimony of Tanya L. Domi, Legislative Director of the National Gay and Lesbian Task Force on behalf of the American Jewish Committee, Anti-Defamation League and the People for the American Way Action Fund).

17. Hate Crime Statistics Act of 1988: Hearing Before the Subcommittee on the Constitution of the Committee on the Judiciary United States Senate, 100th Cong., 2d Sess. 263–64 (1988) (testimony of Molly Yard, then-President of NOW) [hereinafter Senate Hearing].

     In addition, Ms. Yard argued that "when crimes such as homicide, assault, robbery, burglary, theft, arson, vandalism, trespass and threats are committed against women, they should be evaluated in terms of 'hate' motivation for purposes of categorization." Id. at 264.

18. Lauren Tarshis, The War on Women, 124 *Scholastic Update* 14, Apr. 3, 1992.

19. See Note, Racial Violence Against Asian Americans, 106 *Harv. L. Rev.* 1926 (1993).

20. Senate Hearing, supra note 17, at 261 (letter to Senator Paul Simon from Susan C. Lee).

21. Senate Hearing, supra note 17, at 246 (letter to Senator Paul Simon from Karen G. Kwong).

22. Senate Hearing, supra note 17, at 84 (testimony of William Yoshino, Midwestern Regional Director, Japanese American Citizens League).

23. This search was conducted in the Lexis "NEWS" library, "CURNEWS" file as of April 1995.

24. Spencer Rumsey, A Cancer of Hatred Afflicts America, *Newsday*, May 27, 1993, at 129.

25. Benjamin J. Hubbard, Commentary on Tolerance, *L.A. Times*, Apr. 4, 1993, at B9.

26. Espinosa, supra note 9, at A10.

27. Claire Safran, They Burn Churches, Don't They? *Women's Day*, Nov. 21, 1989, at 68.

28. Civil Rights Commission to Hold Forum on Hate Crimes in Detroit, *U.S. Newswire*, July 15, 1991.

29. William Douglas, Bias Crime Flare Up in City's Heat, *Newsday*, July 21, 1991, at 19.

30. Id. (emphasis added).

31. Survey Finds Rising Hate Crimes in U.S., *Xinhua Gen. Overseas News Service*, July 30, 1990.

32. Karen D'Souza, Hate Crime Rise: Hostility or Awareness, *Phoenix Gazette*, June 29, 1994, at B8.

33. Tom Scherberger & Sue Carlton, A Quiet Life Suddenly Shattered by Hatred, *St. Petersburg Times*, Jan. 16, 1993, at 1A.

34. Admittedly, one can find stories downplaying the prevalence of hate crimes. For example, a headline in *The Atlanta Constitution* boasted of Atlanta (as it gears up to host the 1996 Olympics): "Hate Crimes Becoming More Rare, Police Say." This article quoted a Gwinnett County police sergeant who proudly proclaimed that "in 1992 we had almost [no hate crimes and cult activity]." Gail Hagans, King Week '93 Hate Crime Becoming More Rare, Police Say, *Atlanta Const.*, Jan. 18, 1993, at J1. Interestingly, Larry Pelligrini, President of the ACLU Georgia's Lesbian and Gay Rights Chapter, says the ACLU in 1991 received 93 reports of hate crimes in the Atlanta area alone. Kathy Scruggs, Police Insensitive, Activists Say Handcuff Man Case, Crime Report Cited, *Atlanta Const.*, Mar. 1, 1992, at D5.

35. This is not unusual: "[e]xperts say that the surge in cases is actually a predictable phenomenon that has occurred several times in recent years on the heels of a particularly shocking bias attack that attracted wide publicity." Lynda Richardson, 61 Acts of Bias: One Fuse Lights Many Different Explosions, *N.Y. Times*, Jan. 28, 1992, at B1.

36. James B. Jacobs, Rethinking the War Against Hate Crimes: A New York City Perspective, 11 *Crim. Just. Ethics* 55, 58, (Summer/Fall 1992) [hereinafter *Crim. Just. Ethics*].

37. Jack Levin & Jack McDevitt, *The Rising Tide of Bigotry and Bloodshed: Hate Crimes* (1993).

38. Id. at 45–63.

39. *Bias Crimes: American Law Enforcement and Legal Responses* 6–7 (Robert J. Kelly ed., 1993).

40. Joan C. Weiss, Ethnoviolence: Impact Upon and Response of Victims and the Community, in *Bias Crime*, supra note 39, at 179 (emphasis added).

41. Allen D. Sapp, Richard N. Holden & Michael E. Wiggins, Value and Belief Systems of Right-Wing Extremists: Rationale and Motivation of Bias-Motivated Crimes, in *Bias Crimes*, supra note 39, at 105.

42. *Hate Crimes: Confronting Violence Against Lesbians and Gay Men* (Gregory M. Herek & Kevin T. Berrill eds., 1992).

43. Alphonso Pinkney, *Lest We Forget: White Hate Crimes* 20 (1994).

44. Id.

45. Id. at 27.

46. The search was run on 11/19/94 in Westlaw's "MAG-ASAP" file.

47. Abraham Abramovsky, Bias Crime: A Call for Alternative Responses, 19 *Fordham Urb. L.J.* 875, 876 (1992).

48. Id.

49. Id. at 882.

50. Id. at 883.

51. Id. at 883 n.56 (emphasis added).

52. See Bureau of the Census, U.S. Dep't of Com., 1990 CPH-3-245H (1990); Census of Population and Housing, Population and Housing Characteristics for Census Tracts and Block Numbering Areas, New York-Northern New Jersey-Long Island, NY-NJ-CT CMSA, New York, NY PMSA 505–07 tbl. 5 (1991) (this number represents all counted Asian and Pacific Islander persons in the city of New York, based on a summation of individuals in Bronx County, Kings County, New York County, Queens County, and Richmond County).

53. Fed. Bureau of Investigation, U.S. Dep't of Just., Crime in the U.S.: 1990, *Uniform Crime Rep.*, at 101 tbl. 6 (1991) [hereinafter *Uniform Crime Rep.: 1990*]. Crime Index Offenses include the violent crimes of murder, non-negligent manslaughter, forcible rape, robbery, and aggravated assault as well as the property crimes of burglary, larceny-theft, motor vehicle theft, and arson. Id.

54. NYPD Bias Incident Investigating Unit, Incident Report (Mar. 20, 1991).

55. Abramovsky, supra note 47, at 884.

56. Several books on the subject of hate crime are predicted on the existence of a hate crime epidemic. See, e.g., Levin & McDevitt, supra note 37, at ix.

57. Note, Hate is Not Speech: A Constitutional Defense of Penalty Enhancement for Hate Crimes, 106 *Harv. L. Rev.* 1314 (1993).

58. Id. at 1314 n.1.

59. Note, Combatting Racial Violence: A Legislative Proposal, 101 *Harv. L. Rev.* 1270 (1988).

60. Id. at 1270 n.2 (citing Racially Motivated Violence: Hearing Before the Subcomm. on Criminal Justice of the House Comm. on the Judiciary, 97th Cong., 1st Sess. 77 (1983) (testimony of Mary F. Berry)).

61. On December 20, 1986, a group of white youths assaulted three black men with baseball bats in Howard Beach, a neighborhood of Queens. Jeffery K. Parker, Gang of Whites Attacks 3 Blacks in Queens, *Wash. Post*, Dec. 21, 1986, at A17. As one of the black men fled the scene, he was accidentally struck and killed by an automobile. Id. A total of six youths were convicted of various charges related to the incident. Three Youths Convicted in Howard Beach Case, *Jet*, Aug. 8, 1988, at 33.

62. James B. Jacobs, Implementing Hate Crime Legislation Symbolism and Crime Control, *Ann Surv. Am. L.* 541 (1992/1993) [hereinafter *Ann. Surv. Am. L.*]

63. See Jacobs, Isr. Yb., supra note 10, at 136–38.
64. Senate Hearing, supra note 17, at 248.
65. Id. at 253 (statement of Senator John Kerry).
66. 28 U.S.C. § 1445 (1994).
67. The Violence Against Women Act of 1993: Hearings on H.R. 1133 Before the Subcomm. of Civil and Constitutional Rights, 139 Cong. Rec. H10363 (daily ed. Nov. 20, 1993) (NOW Legal Defense and Education Fund on the Violence Against Women Act of 1993: H.R. 1133) [hereinafter NOW Statement].
68. Id.; see also supra notes 10–22 and accompanying text.
69. NOW Statement, supra note 67.
70. Letter from Mario M. Cuomo, Governor of the State of New York, to the New York Legislature (Aug. 16, 1991).
71. Letter from Robert Abrams, Attorney General of the State of New York, to New York Senate Majority Leader Ralph Marion (Oct. 12, 1989).
72. Larry Levinson, Florio Signs Bias Bill, UPI, Aug. 8, 1990, available in Lexis, Nexis library, UPSTAT file.
73. S. Rep. No. 21, 101st Cong., 1st Sess. 3 (1989). See also James B. Jacobs & Barry Eisler, The Hate Crimes Statistics Act of 1990, 29 Crim. Law Bull. 99 (1993).
74. Anti-Defamation League, 1992 Audit of Anti-Semitic Incidents 24 (on file with the author).
75. Id. at 27.
76. Id.
77. ADL Audit of Anti-Semitic Incidents for 1993. U.S. Newswire, Feb. 16, 1995.
78. Id. at 28 (emphasis added).
79. Steven Chermak, Victims in the News: Crime and the American News Media 54 (1995) (ranking hate crimes as the fourth most newsworthy crime).
80. Telephone interview with Gail Gams, Anti-Defamation League (Sept. 28, 1993).
81. Over half of all states in the United States have based one or more sections of their hate statutes on the ADL model. For a chart of the states that have followed the ADL hate crime data collections model, see Robert J. Kelly, Jess Maghan & Woodrow Tennat, Hate Crimes: Victimizing the Stigmatized, in Bias Crime, supra note 39, at 45–46.
82. Klanwatch Intelligence Report, Feb. 1993, at 1.
83. Id.
84. Id. at 2.
85. Bureau of Just. Stat., U.S. Dep't of Just., Criminal Victimization in the U.S.: 1992, at 22 tbl. 3—Victimization Rates for Persons Age 12 and Over, By Type of Crime and Sex of Victims (1992).
86. Id. at 24 tbl. 6—Victimization Rates For Persons Age 12 and Over, By Type of Crime and Race of Victims.
87. Uniform Crime Rep.: 1990, supra note 53, at 122 tbl. 7—Number of Offenses Known to the Police, Universities and College Campuses, 1990.

88. Hate Crime Statistics Act, Pub. L. 100–275, 104 Stat. 140 (1990). The first FBI report was released in January 1993. See also Jacobs & Eisler, supra note 73.
89. U.S. Dep't of Just., FBI Press Release, Jan. 1, 1993 [hereinafter FBI Press Release] (on file with the author).
90. Id.
91. Fed. Bureau of Investigation, U.S. Dep't of Just., Crime in the U.S.: 1991, Uniform Crime Rep., at 295 tbl. 74 (1992) [hereinafter Uniform Crime Rep.: 1991].
92. FBI Press Release, supra note 89.
93. The 1990 FBI Resource Book (pre-hate crime bill) compares 11 states' hate data collection methods. In some states, data collection was voluntary, in others it was mandated. Some states provided additional resources for data collection, while others hoped to stretch existing resources to encompass hate crime reporting. In addition, some states applied a much broader definition of what qualifies as a hate crime than others.
94. FBI Press Release, supra note 89.
95. Id. The most frequently reported bias was racial. Id.
96. First-Time FBI Report Reveals Prevalence of Malice, Hous. Chron., Jan. 11, 1993, at 12.
97. Monica Rhor & Sabrina Walters, "A Meanness Afoot" Gives Push to Update Hate Crime Laws, Phil., Inq., Jan. 25, 1993, at S1.
98. Dan Lovely & Richard Vega, A Death in Coral Springs: We Came Here For Freedom . . . We Live In Hell, USA Today, Jan. 10, 1993, at 4.
99. Anti-Violence Project: 1992 Report at 3 (on file with the author).
100. FBI Press Release, supra note 89.
101. In 1991, there were approximately 23,000 non-negligent homicides nationwide. Homicide statistics are considered the most reliable crime statistics because murders are almost always reported. However, counting hate crime murders is highly unreliable because of the difficulty of determining the motives (in whole or in part) of the perpetrators, approximately 40% of whom are never even caught.
102. Klanwatch Director Dan Welch, Klanwatch Intelligence Report, Feb. 1993, at 5.
103. The second FBI report, released by FBI Director Freeh while he was in Berlin on June 29, 1994, did not attract nearly as much media attention as did the first report. In fact, the media seemed much more interested in the Congressional testimony about hate crime that Steven Spielberg gave that same day than in the 7,654 hate crimes reported by the FBI for 1993. Crim. Just. Information Services, Uniform Crime Rep., Hate Crime—1993 (June 1994).
104. Otto Klineberg, 12 Prejudice: The Concept, International Encyclopedia of the Social Sciences 444 (David L. Sills ed., 1968).

105. "To the extent this [common American] cultural belief system has influenced all of us, we are all racists." Charles R. Lawrence III, The Id, The Ego and Equal Protection: Reckoning with Unconscious Racism, 39 Stan. L. Rev. 317, 322 (1987).
106. Fed. Bureau of Investigation, Uniform Crime Rep., Hate Crime Data Collection Guidelines 4 (1990).
107. Id. at 5.
108. For an excellent discussion of these First Amendment Issues, see Susan Gellman, Sticks and Stones Can Put You In Jail, But Can Words Increase Your Sentence? Constitutional and Policy Dilemmas of Ethnic Intimidation Laws, 39 UCLA L. Rev. 333 (1991).
109. According to the FBI, 42% of all hate crime offenders are never arrested. Hate Crime—1993, supra note 103, at 1.
110. Alternatively, should an attack that is aimed at a person who is incorrectly perceived to be a member of a certain group be considered a hate crime? For example, in Laguna Beach, CA, a heterosexual man was brutally attacked by two men who incorrectly perceived him to be gay. The two attackers pled guilty to all charges, including the commission of a hate crime. While the motivation for the attack was hatred for gays, the attack was factually perpetrated against a non-gay man.
111. Within the Hate Crime Statistics Act of 1990, which collects data for sexual orientation bias, an apparent non sequitur included to appease Senator Jesse Helms professes support for "American family values" and disclaims any intent to promote homosexuality. See Jacobs & Eisler, supra note 73, at 102. See also Joseph M. Fernandez, Recent Developments, Bringing Hate Crime Into Focus, 26 Harv. C.R.-C.L. L. Rev. 261, 276–281 (1991).
    In Arizona, sexual orientation was (at least temporarily) dropped from a pending hate crime bill. See Hate Crime Bill: Justice Dies in a Desk Drawer, Ariz. Republic, Feb. 16, 1995, at B6 ("Sexual orientation was not included in the [Arizona hate crime] bill. [State Senator] Smith made no secret that the bill would go absolutely nowhere with a mention of gays and lesbians."). Id.
112. See Jacobs, Ann. Serv. Am. L., supra note 62, at 544–45.
113. On December 31, 1994, a gunman attacked two abortion clinics in Brookline, Massachusetts, killing two receptionists and wounding five other people. These are not the first deaths or assaults against people providing abortion services.
114. See Jacobs & Eisler, supra note 73, at 102–105.
115. Fed. Bureau of Investigation, Uniform Crime Rep., Hate Crime Data Collection Guidelines 1 (1991).

116. These categories were created to coincide with crimes already listed in the UCR so as to facilitate data collection efforts.

117. See Jacobs, *Crim. Just. Ethics*, supra note 36, at 55.

118. Audit of Anti-Semitic Incidents, Anti-Defamation League, at 19, app. A (1994).

119. Ronald Smothers, Hate Groups Seen Growing as Neo-Nazis Draw Young, *N.Y. Times*, Feb. 19, 1992, at A14.

120. Jacob Sullum, How Perilous are Hate Crimes? *Sacramento Bee*, Dec. 6, 1992, at F1.

121. *Uniform Crime Rep.*; 1991, supra note 91, at 5.

122. Racially Motivated Violence, Hearings Before the Subcommittee on Criminal Justice of the House Committee on the Judiciary, 100th Congr., 2d Sess. 14 (1988) (statement of the Rev. C. T. Vivian, Chairman of the Board, Center for Democratic Renewal).

123. Richard Bernstein, *Dictatorship of Virtue: How The Battle Over Multiculturalism Is Reshaping Our Schools, Our Country, Our Lives* 199 (1995) (quoting statement of John Slaughter, President of Occidental College).

124. Angie Debo, *History of the Indians of the United States* (1972).

125. Lewis H. Carlson & George A. Colburn, *In Their Place: White America Defines Her Minorities, 1850–1950*, at 24 (1972).

126. Walter T. Howard, *Lynchings: Extra-Legal Violence in Florida during the 1930s*, at 17 (1995).

127. Claudine L. Ferrell, *Nightmare & Dream: Anti-Lynching In Congress 1917–1922*, at 92 (1986).

128. Howard, supra note 126, at 18.

129. Id.

130. Ferrell, supra note 127, at 91.

131. Everette Swinney, *Suppressing the Ku Klux Klan: The Enforcement of the Reconstruction Amendments 1870–1877*, at 145 (1987).

132. David M. Chalmers, *Hooded Americanism: The History of the Ku Klux Klan* 14 (1987).

133. Ferrell, supra note 127, at 92.

134. Chalmers, supra note 132, at 14.

135. Anti-Defamation League, Hate Groups in America: A Record of Bigotry and Violence (1988).

136. Id. at 110–111.

137. David H. Bennett, *The Party Of Fear: The American Far Right from Nativism to the Militia Movement* 37–39 (1995).

138. Id. at 56.

139. Carlson & Colburn, supra note 125, at 279.

140. Id. at 269.

141. Abramovsky, supra note 47, at 913.

142. See James B. Jacobs, Should Hate Be a Crime?, 113 *Pub. Interest* 3 (1993).

 Article Review Form at end of book.

What are the most important variables that affect the amount of space and attention provided to newspaper crime stories?

Predicting Crime Story Salience:

The Effects of Crime, Victim, and Defendant Characteristics

Steven Chermak

Department of Criminal Justice
Indiana University
Bloomington, Indiana 47405

Introduction

The amount of research examining the presentation of crime in the news media has grown dramatically. Marsh (1989), for example, documented the increased interest in this topic by analyzing the research published since 1893. He concluded that the number of studies published between 1960 and 1986 more than doubled the total number of studies published between 1893 and 1959 (Marsh, 1989:508). Research interest continues to grow. Since 1986, seventeen content studies have been published, focusing on the crimes, victims, and defendants presented in the news (see appendix).

This study attempts to build on this body of research. Multiple regression is used to compare how crime, victim, and defendant characteristics affect the amount of space provided to crime stories. Few studies have used multivariate statistical techniques to generate knowledge about the media's presentation of crime, and no study has documented the important crime incident charac-teristics in a sample that includes all types of crime stories. This study also examines whether crime is presented similarly in newspapers located in cities with different rates of crime.

Research on the Presentation of Crime in the News Media

Existing research examining how crime is presented in the news media has made several important contributions. Research indicates that crime is an important news topic, accounting for at least 25 percent of the total news space available (Graber, 1980:26). Research also shows that serious personal crimes, especially murders, are high priority news items (Cohen, 1975: Chermak, 1994, 1995; Ericson, Baranek, and Chan, 1991; Graber, 1980; Humphries, 1981; Sheley and Ashkins, 1981; Skogan and Maxfield, 1981). White-collar and property crimes are less likely to be presented (Chermak, 1994, 1995; Evans and Lundman, 1983: Graber, 1980; Jerin and Fields, 1995). Some research concludes that drug offenses are rarely presented in the news (Graber, 1980), although other research indicates that coverage has increased (Chermak, 1994, 1995; Jerin and Fields, 1995).

Other research has identified the victim and defendant characteristics frequently presented in the news. Each of these studies report percentile rankings, assuming that a specific characteristic is important when a high percentage of stories contain that item. Victims are typically portrayed as young or elderly, White, and male (Chermak, 1995; Entman, 1990, 1992, 1994; Graber, 1980; Humphries, 1981; Mawby and Brown, 1984). Defendants are usually presented as African American and female (Barlow, Barlow, and Chiricos, 1995; Entman, 1990, 1992, 1994). Occupation is only presented when it is noteworthy, such as when the victim is a police officer (Chermak, 1995; Surette, 1989).

A wealth of information on the presentation of crime in the news is available, but some important gaps remain. First, the extant research generally neglects to include content from various sized cities. The studies that make these comparisons found that newspapers in all cities overemphasize violent crime (Cohen, 1975; Graber, 1980; Skogan and Maxfield, 1981; Windhauser, Seiter, and Winfree, 1990; Lotz, 1991). Most of these studies did not examine cities with crime rates that varied significantly. Cities were selected for the present study in a way that allowed for a larger variation in city size and crime rate than has been typically employed in past research.

Second, few studies have examined how characteristics of crime incidents affect the salience of crime stories. The existing body of content research provides a good sense of the characteristics that influence whether crimes are selected for coverage. Not much is known about how these characteristics affect the amount of "play" provided to crime stories. Does the seriousness of the event affect the amount of space received? Do characteristics of the victim or defendant affect story placement? A refined understanding of the importance of crime, victim, and defendant characteristics can be achieved by examining the relative size of crime stories.

Third, content research has not used multivariate statistical technique to generate knowledge about the presentation of crime in the news. Most content research relies on word or theme counts to generate conclusions. Of the thirty-six studies published focusing on the presentation of crime content in the news media since 1975, only three used multivariate techniques (see appendix*).[1] These three studies are discussed below.

Two of these studies focused on the media's presentation of homicide (Johnstone, Hawkins, and Michener, 1994; Wilbanks, 1984). Johnstone, Hawkins, and Michener (1994) examined the presentation of homicide in two Chicago newspapers (The *Tribune* and *Sun-Times*) and used logistic regression to examine how several victim, defendant, and incident characteristics affected a dichotomous report-no report measure and a prominence score of minimal, moderate, and major attention.

The strongest predictor of whether a story was reported and its prominence was the number of victims murdered. Other significant predictors were the number of offenders and whether an unusual method was used to complete a murder. These researchers also found that murders of African American and Hispanic victims were less likely to be reported, and that murders of women and chil-

*The appendix does not appear in this publication.

dren were more likely to be presented. Murders committed by female offenders did not have an influence on the presentation of homicide.

Wilbanks (1984) examined the presentation of homicide in Miami. Using regression to identify the variables influencing how a homicide was presented, he found that the best predictor of the number of articles and the number of column inches provided to a story was when multiple victims were killed in an incident. More articles were written about homicides involving innocent victims, and less were written about homicides involving Hispanic victims.

The third study using multivariate statistical techniques contrasted the images of victims by type of offense and sex of offender (Fishman and Weimann, 1985). Using log linear analysis, this research indicated that victims were more likely to be presented for the seriousness of the offense rather than for the sex of the offender. Victims were more likely to be presented favorably when a story included an offender who was male or the offense was less serious, but were presented negatively when the offender was female or the crime committed was serious.

This study attempts to fill these gaps in the literature by using multivariate statistical techniques to examine the presentation of crime in newspapers from various sized cities. Data are presented in three sections. First, the sample, the coding of the variables, and analytic procedure are discussed in the research methodology section. Second, the results from several analyses on the presentation of crime are provided in the findings section. Third, the implications of the results, and suggestions for future research are provided in the discussion section.

Research Methodology

Content analysis was used to collect data on the characteristics of crimes, victims, and defendants presented in crime stories. Data were collected from six newspapers (the *Detroit News*, the *Dallas Morning News*, the *San Francisco Chronicle*, the *Cleveland Plain Dealer*, the *Albany Times Union*, and the *Buffalo News*). Each organiza-

tion is a popular news outlet concerned primarily with local news.

These news organizations were selected from the generation of a list of cities that had at least one newspaper with a circulation of 50,000. These cities were then placed into a medium, large, or extra large category depending on city population and crime rate. Two newspapers from each category were selected.

The analyses that follow are of the crime, victim, and defendant characteristics presented in specific incident stories. These stories cover the details of a crime event, discussing who, what, where, and how. Crime stories presented every fifth day during the first six months of 1990 were included in the sample, although stories smaller than three column inches were excluded. The total number of specific incident stories is 1,557.

Table 1 provides descriptive statistics for the dependent and independent variables. Two dependent variables are investigated in this study. The first is the size of the story. Newspaper stories were measured in inches. The mean newspaper story size is nearly twelve inches. It may be possible that the six newspapers sampled varied greatly in the total number of inches available for the presentation of news. Since the size variable was not measured as the proportion of total space available for crime, the results are presented in two additional ways to strengthen the reliability of the results.

First, an attention score is used as a second dependent measurement (Budd, 1964). The attention score is a measure of prominence; each crime story is assigned a value between zero and five. A newspaper story received one point for each of the following criteria: (1) the story had a headline of two column inches or more in width; (2) the story carried a headline more than half the number of columns of a page: (3) the story began above the fold (top half) of the page; (4) the story occupied at least three quarters of a column; or (5) the article appeared on page one. The newspaper attention score mean is 1.52.

Second, the results of an analysis of the Dallas–Detroit, Cleveland–San Francisco, and Albany–Buffalo

Table 1 Mean and Standard Deviation of Variables

Variables	Mean	SD	n
Dependent			
Attention score	1.52	.99	1,557
Size	11.76	9.04	1,557
Independent			
Crime variables			
Murder	.31	.46	1,503
Other violent	.20	.40	
Victimless	.15	.35	
Economic	.11	.32	
Misdemeanor	.06	.30	
Other crimes	.10	.30	
Property[a]			
Number of crimes	2.87	2.03	1,354
Weapon	.30	.46	1,557
Home	.32	.47	943
Street	.29	.46	
Other location	.10	.30	
Public building[a]			
Defendant variables			
Female	.10	.30	1,373
Male[a]			
Young	.05	.21	942
Old	.44	.50	
Middle age[a]			
Professional	.49	.50	681
Criminal justice	.26	.44	
Student	.06	.25	
Low status	.05	.21	
Other occupation	.07	.25	
Blue collar[a]			
Prior record	.08	.27	1,423
Victim variables			
Female	.33	.47	898
Business	.09	.29	
Male[a]			
Child	.15	.36	539
Youth	.10	.30	
Old	.29	.45	
Middle age[a]			
Professional	.24	.43	329
Criminal justice	.33	.47	
Student	.18	.38	
Low status	.08	.27	
Other occupation	.05	.22	
Blue collar[a]			
Number of victims	2.80	2.06	960

[a]Reference category

media are presented. The newspapers examined in each category should be similar in the total amount of news space available because of similarities in circulation.

The effects of four crime variables are examined. The first variable is type of offense. The first crime mentioned in each story was coded then placed into one of seven offense categories: murder (includes manslaughter); other violent offenses (i.e., rape, assault, and robbery); property offenses (i.e., burglary, larceny); economic crimes (i.e., embezzlement, fraud, and extortion); victimless crimes (drugs, prostitution, and gambling); misdemeanors; and other crimes (includes an assortment of infrequently cited crimes such as bias related crimes, driving while intoxicated, and perjury). Six dummy variables were created; the property crime category will be used as the reference category.

The second crime variable is the number of crimes mentioned in a story. The number of crimes was recoded into one of eight categories. Five or fewer crimes were discussed in 84 percent of the stories. The first five categories of the number of crimes variable account for stories mentioning one, two, three, four, or five crimes, respectively. If six to ten crimes were mentioned, it was given the number six; eleven to twenty crimes were given seven; and twenty to one hundred were given the number eight. This coding is based on the assumption that the number of crimes that can be discussed is limited.[2]

Weapon is the third crime variable and it is coded as a dummy variable. Zero indicates that a weapon was not mentioned, while a code of one includes stories where some weapon (i.e., gun, knife, club) was mentioned. Finally, the offense location is also binary coded, resulting in three dummy variables. The four location categories are public building (school, shopping center, tavern), street, private residence (victim's or defendant's home), and other locations. The public building category will serve as the reference category.

Sex, age, status, and prior record of the defendant are coded as dummy variables. Gender is coded one for females and zero for males, allowing for the determination of the effect of being female, compared with being male, on the size and attention provided to crime stories. The defendant's age is coded into two dummy variables with the effects of defendant young (up to sixteen years old), and defendant old (over thirty-five years old) being compared to defendant middle-aged (seventeen to thirty-five years old). These categories should be more useful than treating age as a continuous variable. One-year increments in age may have little effect on space concerns, but differences in groups should be important. It is hypothesized that crimes committed by children and older adults should receive significantly more space than crimes committed by middle-aged adults.

The status of the defendant is measured by various indicators, including occupation. The occupation categories are professional (includes executives and politicians), blue collar, criminal justice personnel (police officers, judges), and an other occupation category. The fifth category is defendants of low status, including unemployed defendants and defendants incarcerated or serving a community sentence when committing another offense. The final category includes stories that stress that the defendant is a student. The status variable is coded into five dummy variables: professional, criminal justice, student, low status, and other occupations. Blue-collar workers serve as the reference category.

Prior record is also coded as a dummy variable. Zero indicates that prior record was not mentioned in a story, while a code of one indicates that the defendant's prior record was mentioned. Race is not included in the discussion because there were too few cases where race is identified for the results to be meaningful because it is rarely mentioned in newspaper crime stories (Campbell, 1995).[3]

The coding of the victim variables is similar to the defendant coding. The status of the victim is dummy coded into the same categories mentioned above, and the number of victims is coded the same as the number of crimes variable.

Two victim characteristics are coded differently. First, the victim's sex is coded into two dummy variables. The effects on story size and prominence of being female and of being a business (e.g., store, bank) are compared with being male. Approximately 9 percent of the stories discussed the victimization of a business rather than the victimization of an individual.

The second difference in coding is victim age. Age of the victim is coded into four categories rather than three. The middle-aged and old categories are the same as mentioned above. The youth variable, however, is broken down into two categories:

child (one to seven years old) and youth (eight to sixteen years old). These categories are used to capture whether young child victims have a significant effect on the space and attention provided to crime stories. The child, youth, and old age categories are dummy coded with the middle-aged category serving as the reference category.

Existing research examining the factors that affect news selection decisions supports the conclusion that certain characteristics should influence the amount of space and attention provided to an incident. Incident characteristics that are extraordinary, compared to official statistics on crime, should be provided more space and attention. Of the crime variables of interest, the variables measuring seriousness should have a significant effect on the space and attention provided to a crime story. It is hypothesized that stories discussing murder, multiple crimes, and multiple victims will be provided more space and attention. Stories about young child victims should be provided more space and attention. A defendant's status should also affect the importance of a crime story. Stories about high status defendants (criminal justice personnel and professionals) should be provided more space and attention, and crime stories discussing low status individuals should be provided less space and attention. To determine the effects of crime, victim, and defendant characteristics on the salience of crime stories, crime stories must be rendered equivalent on all rival explanations. This requires the use of multiple regression.

Multiple regression is one approach that can be used to examine the relationship among variables. Regression attempts to explain the variation of a dependent measurement by examining its relationship to a set of independent variables (Hardy, 1993:1). This statistical technique makes possible the prediction of the effect that a change in an independent variable (e.g., number of crimes) would have on a dependent variable (size or attention of a crime story), controlling for other independent variables. Most of the variables examined in the following analyses are dummy coded. Thus, the regres-

sion coefficients for the independent variables translate into the change in size or attention provided to crime stories, compared to a reference category. For example, the coefficients for type of offense translate into the change in attention or column inches of stories about each offense category, compared to the property crime reference category.

Findings

Table 2 shows the results from the analyses examining the important crime, victim, and defendant variables. The results examining most of the control variables are not presented because these variables had little influence on the space and attention provided to crime stories. The weapon, location, victim sex, and victim status variables did not influence the space and attention provided to crime stories. Contrary to what was hypothesized, both the victim age and defendant status variable did not have an influence.

The first four columns of Table 2 present the effects of type of offense, defendant's age, defendant's sex, and number of victims on the attention and size of a crime story. The last four columns provide the effects of type of offense, defendant's age, defendant's sex, and the number of crimes variables. These analyses were run as separate equations because of the similarities between the number of crimes and number of victims measures.

The results provide some support for the conclusion that the seriousness of the offense contributes significantly to the presentation of crime in the news. Controlling for the type of offense reported and the defendant's age and sex, the number of victims and the number of crimes have a significant effect on the space and attention provided to crime stories. Murder stories received significantly more attention and space compared to property offenses when the number of crimes variable is included. The results also indicate that stories discussing drugs, prostitution, and gambling receive more attention than stories examining property offenses. Stories discussing the crimes of older adults (over thirty-five) receive significantly more attention and

Table 2 Regression of Attention and Size on Crime, Defendant, and Victim Variables

Variables	Attention		Size		Attention		Size	
	b	*B*	*b*	*B*	*b*	*B*	*b*	*B*
Number of victims	.07****	.15	.74****	.24	X	X	X	X
Number of crimes	X	X	X	X	.04***	.09	.33***	.10
Type of offense								
Murder	.19	.10	1.2	.11	.34***	18	2.4***	.18
Other violent	.02	.01	.09	.007	.09	.05	–.17	–.01
Victimless	.70***	.12	2.5	.07	.26*	.10	1.4	.07
Economic	.32	.07	1.8	.06	.20	.06	1.2	.06
Misdemeanor	–.02	–.005	.22	.01	.06	.02	.81	.03
Other crimes	–.27	–.06	–.74	–.03	–.02	–.005	.61	.03
Property[a]								
Defendant age								
Young	.01	.003	1.1	.04	.02	.005	1.8*	.06
Old	.09	.05	.96**	.08	.13**	.07	1.8****	.14
Middle age[a]								
Defendant sex								
Female	.16	.05	2.3***	.13	.13	.04	1.5**	.07
Male[a]								
(Constant)	1.11****		6.77****		1.04****		7.28****	
	$F = 4.04$****		$F = 7.27$****		3.21****		5.47****	
	$R^2 = .06$		$R^2 = .11$		$R^2 = .04$		$R^2 = .06$	
	adj.$R^2 = .05$		adj.$R^2 = .10$		adj.$R^2 = 03$		adj.$R^2 = .05$	
	$N = 617$		$N = 596$		$N = 843$		$N = 841$	

*$t<.10$. **$t<.05$. ***$t<.01$. ****$t<.001$.

[a]Reference category

space than stories discussing the crimes of younger adults. Crimes committed by female defendants received significantly more space than the crimes committed by male defendants. The other offense variables and the child defendant variable did not have an effect on the space and attention provided to crime stories.

Table 3 refines the analysis reported in Table 2 by providing the results for different sized cities. It was thought that because reporters have access to very different types of crimes when covering crimes in larger cities, victim and defendant characteristics would have more of an impact on the salience of crime stories. The type of offense should be more important in cities where reporters do not have as much access to serious, violent crimes. The first four columns of Table 3 provide the unstandardized and standardized coefficients when crime stories presented in the Dallas and Detroit media are considered, the middle four columns provide results for the Cleveland and San Francisco newspapers, and the last four columns provide results for the Albany and Buffalo newspapers.

The number of victims affected by an incident was the best predictor of the attention and space provided to crime stories in all media organizations examined. The effects for type of offense, defendant's sex, and defendant's age are mixed. For example, the victimless crime offense category has a significant effect on the attention of crime stories in Dallas–Detroit, but not in Cleveland–San Francisco and Albany–Buffalo. Moreover, it did not have any influence on the size of the crime stories. The murder offense category and the old defendant variable significantly affected only the size provided to crime stories in the media from smaller cities. Female defendants received significantly more attention and space in the Cleveland–San Francisco media, but not in Dallas–Detroit or Albany–Buffalo.

Discussion

Studies using content analysis are often criticized because of their inability to account for the actual decision making that occurs to produce crime stories. Researchers argue that the inferences made from content analysis are weak unless the presentation of crime is coupled to an examination of the news production process (Ericson, Baranek, and Chan, 1991). This coupling requires the reliance on various research methodologies, such as observations, interviews, and content analysis. Space constraints prevent the use of several methodologies for this study. Although linking media content images to news process data is important, the data presented here have some value for understanding the

Table 3 · Regression of Attention and Size in Different Cities

Variable	Dallas–Detroit				Cleveland–San Francisco				Albany–Buffalo			
	Attention		Size		Attention		Size		Attention		Size	
	b	B	b	B	b	B	b	B	b	B	b	B
Number of victims	.08**	.17	1.1****	.35	.08***	.17	1.1****	.25	.11***	.20	.89****	.24
Murder	.24	.11	.80	.06	.30	.16	1.1	.07	.08	.05	3.5**	.26
Other violent	.21	.09	.38	.03	.22	.10	−1.2	−.07	−.23	−.11	.41	.03
Victimless	2.1***	.27	6.8	.09	.59*	.10	2.7	.06	−.06	−.01	1.7	.04
Economic	.43	.06	−.78	−.02	.29	.07	2.2	.06	.46	.10	.49	.01
Misdemeanor	−.66	−.12	−2.0	−.06	.09	.01	−3.0	−.04	.17	.04	3.9*	.14
Other crimes	.17	.03	−.03	−.001	−.51	−.08	−2.2	−.04	−.47	−.13	−.22	−.01
Property[a]												
Defendant age												
Young	.20	.05	1.1	.05	−.06*	−.02	3.5	.10	.02	.007	1.2	.04
Old	.02	.01	.32	.02	.04	.03	1.2	.07	.17	.08	2.0**	.14
Middle age[a]												
Defendant sex												
Female	−.27	−.08	.96	.05	.48***	.17	2.6*	.11	.11	.04	.30	.01
Male[a]												
(Constant)	1.32****		8.06****		.959****		7.14****		1.01****		4.83****	
	$F = 2.19$***		$F = 2.35$***		$F = 2.16$**		$F = 3.00$****		$F = 2.56$***		$F = 4.05$****	
	$R^2 = .13$		$R^2 = .14$		$R^2 = .08$		$R^2 = .11$		$R^2 = .12$		$R^2 = .17$	
	adj. $R^2 = .07$		adj. $R^2 = .08$		adj. $R^2 = .04$		adj. $R^2 = .07$		adj. $R^2 = .07$		adj. $R^2 = .13$	
	$N = 159$		$N = 153$		$N = 252$		$N = 248$		$N = 208$		$N = 202$	

*$t < .10$. **$t < .05$. ***$t < .01$. ****$t < .001$.

[a]Reference category

newsworthiness of crime events. This research makes several contributions to the extant research and raises some additional concerns that will need to be addressed in the future.

First, this study illustrated that the data analysis possibilities for content analysis are great. Access to content data has grown dramatically with innovations in media technology. Both television and newspaper news content can easily be downloaded from the World Wide Web or electronic data bases. This access provides the opportunity to apply statistical methods to answer important substantive and methodological questions. Thus far, however, researchers have not explored the data analysis possibilities of content analysis.

Second, this research has identified several variables that seem to be particularly newsworthy. The number of victims consistently explained the greatest amount of variation in story attention and length in all cities. These results are consistent with past research (Johnstone, Hawkins, and Michener, 1994). The type of crime committed, however, is not as important as might have been expected when examining research relying on percentage counts. The effects of homicide were low when the number of victims variable was included in an equation. These results point to an interesting conclusion regarding the news value of murder. Although murder accounts for a large proportion of the crimes selected for presentation in the news, murders may not necessarily be given large amounts of attention or space. This indicates that other factors must combine with murder before an incident becomes an important crime story.

Third, although this research filled several gaps in the extant research, a couple of issues still need to be addressed. It will be important to follow the "life course" of crime stories in future research to more accurately determine what variables drive reporter decision making. For example, reporters are provided several opportunities to revisit a crime incident as a case progresses through the criminal justice system. The characteristics of crime incidents discussed at several stages may more accurately reflect the variables that affect a reporter's decision making. These images may be more likely to influence public opinion because the likelihood of recall increases when the media provides several stories about a specific case.

Another issue is a consideration of interaction effects. Some victim or defendant characteristics may be important for specific types of offenses, or when combined with other demographic characteristics. Occupation may affect what crimes get presented to the public, although it may not affect salience because the offense committed by someone working in a newsworthy occupation may not be serious. A judge arrested for murder would be an important news story in any city, but it is also a rare event. A judge charged with drunk driving, which is much more likely to occur, will probably get some coverage in the news. This offense is not serious enough in most cities to secure a significant amount of space. Future research will have to examine the interaction of specific independent variables to better understand what is important about crime in the news.

Fourth, it is important to recognize that the sample includes crimes actually presented in the media. The stories about the crimes that are in the sample are more important than the vast majority because most are not given coverage. The extant research relying on percentage counts documents clearly the characteristics most likely to be presented in the news. Thus, the extant research provides information on the factors that affect what crimes are selected for presentation. What is interesting about the findings is that, of the crimes considered to be worthy of some coverage, most of the variables considered do not have a significant impact on the amount of "play" provided to an incident. One would expect to find that stories that receive significant amounts of space would be the most likely to affect public opinion or criminal justice decision making. What may be important is not the overall presentation of crime, but whether specific high profile cases affect these processes. Content research has yet to provide a clear understanding of the factors that need to be present in order for an event to be sensational.

It is important to realize that news results from a process. The complexity of this process may be difficult to capture in a regression equation, but has been demonstrated using other methodologies (Ericson, Baranek, and Chan, 1989; Fishman, 1980; Gans, 1979). The motivation of officials to provide information to reporters, the willingness of victims or other individuals to subject themselves to questioning by reporters, whether a crime incident can be tied to similar events, and whether it is a slow news day could all affect the amount of space provided to a story. Future research will have to use a combination of methodologies to link how the news production process combines with characteristics of an incident to determine what crimes become celebrated, what crimes get placed on the front page, and what crimes are relegated to the back sections of a newspaper. This research should include an examination of news content using multivariate statistics.

Notes

1. In an examination of several Canadian media organizations, Ericson, Baranak, and Chan (1991) used discriminant analysis to determine how the presentation of crime varies by medium and market. This study was not discussed within the text because of the focus on these areas. It is an important study because it illustrates other statistical applications available to the content researcher.

2. Several analyses were run allowing the crime variable to remain as the actual number of crimes mentioned. The results were not different. and the change in the coefficients was small.

3. The race of the defendant could only be identified in 20 percent of the stories, and the race of the victim could only be identified in 8 percent. Race was able to be identified in those stories that included a picture of the victim or defendant for these stories. Several regression analyses were run examining the effects of race of victim and race of the defendant. The amount of attention and space given to stories that included a picture of African American victims and an other race category (Hispanic, Asian) was compared to the salience of stories that included a picture of a White victim. Similar comparisons were made when the race of the defendant was identified. The race of the victim and the race of the defendant did not have a significant effect on either dependent measure. In addition, neither race variable decreased the predictive ability of the important variables discussed in the findings section.

References

Ammons, L., Dimick, J., and Pilotta, J. J. (1982). Crime news reporting in a Black weekly. *Journalism Quarterly* 59:310–13.

Antunes, G. E., and Hurley, P. A. (1977). The representation of criminal events in Houston's two daily newspapers. *Journalism Quarterly* 54:756–60.

Barlow, M. H., Barlow. D. E., and Chiricos, T. G. (1995). Economic conditions and ideologies of crime in the media: A content analysis of crime news. *Crime and Delinquency* 41(1):3–19.

Budd, R. W. (1964). Attention score: A device for measuring news' play. *Journalism Quarterly* 41(2):259–62.

Campbell, C. (1995). *Race, myth and the news*. Thousand Oaks, CA: Sage Publications.

Chermak, S. M. (1994). Body count news: How crime is presented in the news media. *Justice Quarterly* 11(4):561–82.

Chermak, S. M. (1995). *Victims in the news: Crime and the American news media*. Boulder, CO: Westview Press.

Cohen, S. (1975). A comparison of crime coverage in Detroit and Atlanta newspapers. *Journalism Quarterly* 52(4):726–34.

Davis, R. (1994). *Decisions and images: The Supreme Court and the press*. Englewood Cliffs, NJ: Prentice Hall.

Ditton, J., and Duffy, J. (1983). Bias in the newspaper reporting of crime news. *British Journal of Criminology* 23(2):159–65.

Entman, R. M. (1990). Modem racism and images of Blacks in local television news. *Critical Studies in Mass Communication* 7:332–45.

Entman, R. M. (1992). Blacks in the news: Television, modem racism, and cultural change. *Journalism Quarterly* 69(2):341–61.

Entman, R. M. (1994). Representation and reality in the portrayal of Blacks on network television news. *Journalism Quarterly* 71(3):509–20.

Ericson, R. V., Baranek, P. M., and Chan, J. B. L. (1989). *Negotiating control: A study of news sources*. Toronto: University of Toronto Press.

Ericson, R. V., Baranek, P. M., and Chan, J. B. L. (1991). *Representing order: Crime, law, and justice in the news media*. Toronto: University of Toronto Press.

Evans, S. S., and Lundman, R. J. (1983). Newspaper coverage of corporate price-fixing: A replication. *Criminology* 21(4):529–41.

Fedler, F., and Jordan, D. (1981). How emphasis on people affects coverage of crime. *Journalism Quarterly* 474–78.

Fishman, M. (1980). *Manufacturing the news*. Austin. TX: University of Texas Press.

Fishman, G., and Weimann, G. (1985). Presenting the victim: Sex-based bias in press reports on crime. *Justice Quarterly* 2(4):491–503.

Gans, H. J. (1979). *Deciding what's news: A study of CBS Evening News, Newsweek and Time*. New York: Pantheon Books.

Graber, D. (1979). Is crime news coverage excessive? *Journal of Communication* Summer:81–92.

Graber, D. (1980). *Crime news and the public*. New York: Praeger Publishers.

Hardy, M. A. (1993). *Regression with dummy variables*. Newbury Park, CA: Sage Publications.

Humphries, D. (1981). Serious crime, news coverage, and ideology: A content analysis of crime coverage in a metropolitan paper. *Crime and Delinquency* 27(2):191–205.

Jacob, H., and Lineberry, R. (1982). *Crime on urban agendas.* Evanston, IL: Northwestern University, Center for Urban Affairs and Policy Research.

Jerin, R. A., and Fields, C. B. (1995). Murder and mayhem in *USA Today:* A quantitative analysis of the national reporting of states' news. In *Media, process and the social construction of crime: Studies of newsmaking criminology,* ed. G. Barak, New York: Garland Publishing, Inc.

Johnstone, J. W. C., Hawkins, D. F., and Michener, A. (1994). Homicide reporting in Chicago dailies. *Journalism Quarterly* 71(4):860–72.

Jones, E. T. (1976). The press as metropolitan monitor. *Public Opinion Quarterly* 40(2):239–44.

Lotz, R. E. (1991). *Crime and the American press.* New York: Praeger Publishing.

Marsh, H. L. (1989). Newspaper crime coverage in the U.S.: 1893–1988. *Criminal Justice Abstracts* 506–14.

Mawby, R. I. and Brown, J. (1984). Newspaper images of the victim: A British study. *Victimology: An International Journal* 9(1):82–94.

Meyer, J. C. (1975). Newspaper reporting of crime and justice: Analysis of an assumed difference. *Journalism Quarterly* 52(4):731–34.

Randall, D. M. (1987a). The portrayal of business malfeasance in the elite and general public media. *Social Science Quarterly* 68(2):281–93.

Randall, D. M. (1987b). The portrayal of corporate crime in network television news. *Journalism Quarterly* 64:150–53.

Randall, D. M., Lee-Sammons, L., and Hagner, P. R. (1988). Common versus elite crime coverage in network news. *Social Science Quarterly* 69(4):910–29.

Schlesinger, P., Tumber, H., and Murdock, G. (1991). The media politics of crime and criminal justice. *British Journal of Sociology* 42(3):397–420.

Sheley, J. F., and Ashkins, C. D. (1981). Crime, crime news and crime views. *Public Opinion Quarterly* 45:492–506.

Sherizen, S. (1978). Social creation of crime news: All the news fitted to print. In *Deviance and the mass media,* ed. C. Winick. Beverly Hills, CA: Sage Publications.

Skogan, W. G., and Maxfield, M. G. (1981). *Coping with crime: Individual and neighborhood reactions.* Beverly Hills, CA: Sage Publications.

Smith, S. J. (1984). Crime in the news. *British Journal of Criminology* 24(3):289–95.

Surette, R. (1989). Media trials. *Journal of Criminal Justice* 17(4):293–308.

Wilbanks, W. (1984). *Murder in Miami: An analysis of homicide patterns and trends in Dade County, Florida, 1917–1983.* New York: University Press of America.

Windhauser, J. W., Seiter, J., and Winfree, L. T. (1990). Crime news in the Louisiana Press. 1980 v. 1985. *Journalism Quarterly* 67:72–78.

 Article Review Form at end of book.

Describe how the criminological field has adjusted to the changing racial and ethnic composition of the U.S. population.

Beyond a Multiracial America:

Racial Demographics and Crime in the United States Today

Kathleen O. Korgen, Ph.D., and Patricia M. Odell, Ph.D.

Most Americans realize that the racial and ethnic face of the United States is in the process of dramatic change. No longer can an analysis of race relations in the United States focus merely on black and white Americans. According to Census Bureau projections, Hispanics will become the largest minority group in the United States by the year 2013, while Asian Americans have doubled their numbers in the last decade of the twentieth century. By the midpoint of the twenty-first century, one out of three Americans will be either Hispanic or Asian (U.S. Bureau of the Census, 1995; Yetman, 1999).

However the field of criminology has been painfully slow to adjust to the reality that the racial colors of the U.S. population encompass more than black and white. In fact, many criminology textbooks used in college courses still refer solely to African Americans when discussing racial minorities and the criminal justice system (e.g., Barlow, 1993; Siegel, 1998). Criminological articles scarcely have a better record. The Criminal Justice Abstracts (CJA) from 1968–1997 reveal a lag in race and

ethnic studies that move beyond African Americans. The CJA listings for works on race and crime during those years contain 479 on blacks, compared with only 177 on Hispanics, 32 on Native Americans, and 22 on Asians. Studies on the death penalty indicate even more starkly the overall concentration on black-white issues. Sixty-one out of sixty-five publications from 1968 to 1997 cited by the Criminal Justice Abstracts focus only on a comparison between blacks and whites. The other four citations are for studies that concentrated on Hispanics.

Clearly, criminologists are only starting to come to grips with a multiracial rather than a merely biracial United States. Still further racial intricacy looms on the horizon, however. Ready or not, criminologists must now also adjust to the increasing complexity of racial categorizations.

Designated racial classifications have never offered clear-cut distinctions between unified racial groups in U.S. society. For instance, for the past century, anyone with any African heritage was consigned to the black racial category through the "one drop rule." Of course, "black" is not the only racial assignation, which subsumes individuals from a great variety of racial backgrounds.

Indeed, most racial categories in the Census and other collections of descriptive data, such as the Bureau of Criminal Justice statistics, share this flaw. For example, increasing numbers of Americans who have one distant Native American relative choose to define themselves as Native American. Meanwhile, "Hispanic" is an *ethnic* category that groups Spanish-speaking persons of all races.

Today, a dramatic transformation in racial classifications is underway in the United States. The new means of categorization will profoundly influence how crimes are classified according to race. As noted above, the traditional monoracial classification of Americans has always favored simplicity over accuracy. Today's greater attempts at accuracy are sure to complicate matters.

Many mixed race Americans, traditionally classified as members of a single (minority) race, now demand the creation of a multiracial category. This is not a trivial demand, since persons of mixed race descent are now both a numerically and politically powerful force in the United States. According to the U.S. Census Bureau, while mixed race births constituted only 1.8 percent of all births

Kathleen O. Korgen and Patricia M. Odell, "Beyond a Multiracial America: Racial Demographics and Crime in the United States Today." Reprinted by permission.

in 1975, they accounted for 4.6 percent of births in 1995, and the percentage is increasing. This mixed race "baby boom" and the refusal of these Americans to force themselves into monoracial racial categories weakens the foundation of the traditional racial structure in the United States.

Until today, criminologists, as well as most other social scientists, have covered up the existence of Americans of more than one racial background by assigning them to a monoracial category. Soon this will no longer be possible. The Office of Management and Budget (OMB) has taken the first step in dismantling the traditional monoracial classification system by directing the U.S. Bureau of the Census to allow mixed race Americans to check all boxes that apply to their racial background in the Census 2000. Meanwhile, the movement to establish an umbrella multiracial category continues to grow.

The acknowledgment of multiracial persons raises new questions as to the validity of traditional racial classifications and new challenges for social scientists. Criminologists, who gather and analyze demographic data under the auspices of that increasingly outdated monoracial system, must now find a way to recognize a rapidly increasing mixed race population. Just as they begin to acknowledge racial and ethnic diversity beyond black and white, criminologists must now also distinguish mixed as well as monoracial Americans if they are to effectively study the influence of race in our criminal justice system.

Sources

Barlow, Hugh. *Introduction to Criminology*, 6th ed. New York: HarperCollins College Publishers, 1993.

Criminal Justice Abstracts 1968–1997.

Siegel, Larry J. *Criminology*, 6th ed. New York: Wadsworth Publishing Company, 1998.

U.S. Bureau of the Census. *Current Population Reports*, Series p25–1092. Washington, D.C.: U.S. Government Printing Office, 1995.

Yetman, Norman R. *Majority and Minority*. Needham Heights, MA: Allyn and Bacon, 1999, p. 432.

 Article Review Form at end of book.

tal Arrests, Distribution by Race, 1988*

harged	Total Arrests					Percent Distribution				
	Total	White	Black	American Indian or Alaskan Native	Asian or Pacific Islander	Total	White	Black	American Indian or Alaskan Native	Asian or Pacific Islander
	11,224,528	7,559,138	1,459,177	113,777	92,436	100.0	67.3	30.8	1.0	0.8
egligent er	17,944	7,567	10,118	120	139	100.0	42.2	56.4	0.7	0.8
	30,470	15,768	14,209	253	240	100.0	51.7	46.6	0.8	0.8
	133,683	45,437	86,832	483	931	100.0	34.0	65.0	0.4	0.7
ssault	353,868	203,457	144,574	3,155	2,682	100.0	57.5	40.9	0.9	0.8
	355,913	235,043	114,901	2,918	3,051	100.0	66.0	32.3	0.8	0.9
	1,252,117	806,752	417,442	12,899	15,024	100.0	64.4	33.3	1.0	1.2
theft	182,634	101,260	77,594	1,456	2,324	100.0	55.4	42.5	0.8	1.3
	14,631	10,839	3,591	112	89	100.0	74.1	24.5	0.8	0.6
	535,965	272,229	255,733	4,011	3,992	100.0	50.8	47.7	0.7	0.7
he	1,805,295	1,153,894	613,528	17,385	20,488	100.0	63.9	34.0	1.0	1.1
total	2,341,260	1,426,123	869,261	21,396	24,480	100.0	60.9	37.1	0.9	1.0
s	770,687	475,488	281,237	8,112	5,850	100.0	61.7	36.5	1.1	0.8
g	80,746	51,661	28,022	412	651	100.0	64.0	34.7	0.5	0.8
	289,752	193,247	94,597	910	998	100.0	66.7	32.6	0.3	0.3
t ty; iving,	12,998	8,501	4,337	43	117	100.0	65.4	33.4	0.3	0.9
	141,378	78,164	61,598	680	936	100.0	55.3	43.6	0.5	0.7
	247,169	182,678	60,177	2,293	2,021	100.0	73.9	24.3	0.9	0.8
rying, etc.	180,337	101,522	76,264	788	1,763	100.0	56.3	42.3	0.4	1.0
nd ized vice except e	88,526	50,862	36,391	476	797	100.0	57.5	41.1	0.5	0.9
ution olations	83,342	63,643	18,270	798	631	100.0	76.4	21.9	1.0	0.8
	1,074,345	613,680	452,574	3,407	4,564	100.0	57.1	42.1	0.3	0.4
	17,148	8,154	7,846	33	1,115	100.0	47.6	45.8	0.2	6.5
nst family	58,166	37,671	18,435	589	1,471	100.0	64.8	31.7	1.0	2.5
e	1,314,556	1,171,282	119,684	13,910	9,680	100.0	89.1	9.1	1.1	0.7
	501,732	439,416	47,883	11,005	3,428	100.0	87.6	9.5	2.2	0.7
	666,566	530,926	118,312	15,518	1,810	100.0	79.7	17.7	2.3	0.3
nduct	644,992	405,800	229,286	7,282	2,624	100.0	62.9	35.5	1.1	0.4
	29,557	16,876	12,070	519	92	100.0	57.1	40.8	1.8	0.3
ases fic)	2,472,917	1,544,864	878,860	23,398	25,795	100.0	62.5	35.5	0.9	1.0
	13,847	6,085	7,656	49	57	100.0	43.9	55.3	0.4	0.4
oitering s	64,922	47,246	15,896	546	1,234	100.0	72.8	24.5	0.8	1.9
	129,585	105,129	20,521	1,613	2,322	100.0	81.1	15.8	1.2	1.8

9. Uniform Crime Reports. Washington, D.C.: U.S. Government Printing Office.

Identify some of the problems that emanate from the use of the phrase "black-on-black" crime.

Politicizing Black-on-Black Crime:

A Critique of Terminological Preference

Robert L. Bing III, Ph.D.

*Associate Professor
Criminology and Criminal Justice Program
Department of Sociology and Anthropology
University of Texas at Arlington*

Abstract

This article argues that the phrase black-on-black crime is being over utilized. The phrase black-on-black crime perpetuates negative images of African-Americans. Problems emanating from use of the phrase black-on-black crime and the need for conceptual clarity are presented. The issues of terminological preference, ethnicity and race are addressed along with a discussion of negative policy implications and recommendations for movement beyond race-oriented research on crime.

Introduction

Much attention has been devoted to black-on-black crime (e.g., Headley, 1983; Pouissant, 1983; Mitchell and Daniels, 1989). Many newspapers and scholarly publications have addressed this topic (e.g., Mitchell and Daniels, 1989; Mauer, 1990). It is not unusual to see in the written press or to hear through the electronic media stories depicting the evils of living in the black community. The headlines (in major metropolitan newspapers) and special issues (in sociological and criminological journals) have occurred with such frequency that some individuals now associate black people with criminality. Simply put, it has become fashionable to discern between crime and black-on-black crime. Rarely, does one read or hear about white crime or white-on-white crime. This is troubling when one considers that most crimes, including serious violent crimes, are committed by and against whites as well as blacks (United States Department of Justice, 1989). The prevalence of crime among whites is documented in the *Sourcebook of Criminal Justice Statistics*, (1988). This publication, for example, shows that in 1987, whites were charged with over 60 percent of the index crimes, while blacks were charged with just under 40 percent of the index crimes in 1987. Why, then, do we persist in characterizing crime in the black community as black-on-black, when crime in the United States is a very white problem as well?

This article has several objectives; they include de-politicization of the phrase black-on-black crime as well as an examination of the conceptual problems surrounding the issue of race and ethnicity. The issue of race and ethnicity, in particular, needs dialogue among researchers who might otherwise overlook their important distinctions (see, e.g., Georges-Abeyie, 1989).

The Issue of Color

This society is very color conscious. Before assessing the character and integrity of a person, we usually acknowledge skin color. As a college professor, my students see me first as a black person, then as a college professor. Similarly, when a law enforcement officer observes a black man on the street—this observation may be due to gender and reasonable suspicion, but race invariably plays a role in the surveillance effect (e.g., Wilbanks, 1987; Cole, 1990).

Concomitantly, our criminological textbooks are inundated with references to individuals on the basis of race. For example, in Gwynn Nettler's *Killing One Another* (1982), the issue of race and criminality is very apparent—the subject index has a category for blacks, but no category for whites. Nettler (1982:60) states: Black people suffer from a

"Politicizing Black-on-Black Crime: A Critique of Terminological Preference," Robert L. Bing III. *The Journal of Research on Minority Affairs.* Reprinted by permission.

disproportionately high crime rate that victimizes principally their own minority. The disproportion is more striking in attacks against persons than in offenses against property. Black rates of arrest and convictions for aggravated assault, robbery, rape, murder . . . exceed those of the American population in general . . . Similarly, Wilbanks controversial *The Myth of A Racist Criminal Justice System* is replete with statements about black criminality. He uses several studies purporting to show that the higher frequency of crime in the black community explains why blacks are disproportionately represented in the criminal justice system. Nettler and Wilbanks are not alone; other textbooks also assign special categories for blacks (e.g., Nettler, 1982; Vetter and Territo, 1984). The implication of this special treatment is that blacks are very different from their white counterparts.

Presumably as a result of this peculiar treatment and specific categorization on the basis of race, it is a known fact that some police departments train their recruits in the handling of alleged black crime, while only a small percentage are trained to respond to corporate or white collar crimes (McLaughlin, 1990). The identification of race with crime is so pervasive that off duty black police officers may be advised to remain in their cars if they observe a crime in progress or to telephone the activity to a uniformed police officer, on the assumption that few would believe (in light of inflammatory coverage about black criminality) that a black man or woman in plain clothes was a police officer (Alex, 1969; McLaughlin, 1990). This advice is consistent with the negative perceptions already perpetuated by the media and academics.

Negative Connotations

An editorial in the St. Louis *Post-Dispatch* (1990), titled, *Black Criminals, Black Victims* corresponds with Nettler's observation that blacks are responsible for a disproportionate number of crimes. This revelation, however, is not consistent with the notion that most blacks commit crimes—it only means that blacks commit a disproportionate number

of crimes. Authors and researchers should be certain to distinguish between the term disproportionate number of crimes and most crimes. The *Post-Dispatch* article, responding to the release of a local study of black-on-black crime goes on to say, It's bad enough that these youngsters have no respect for their own lives; its worse that they are willing to place the lives of innocent bystanders in jeopardy. The *Post-Dispatch* article deserves critical observation because it creates the impression that most blacks, rather than whites lead a life of crime. There have been a litany of studies focusing on black-on-black crime, ranging from Washington, D.C. to Kansas City, Missouri to the coastal cities of California. Frequently, there is a negative assessment of the crime problem, especially for black males. In a study about black-on-black crime, Shirley Wilson (1989) writes, "Unfortunately, the situation with which we are confronted today is a growing trend, particularly on the part of young black males . . ." While this statement may be true, it serves to obscure more recent developments regarding race and crime in the United States. For example, in 1970, black males were 12 times more likely to be arrested for murder than whites. By 1985, this ratio had dropped to 5:1. One consequence of the black-on-black crime focus, then, is the neglect of rising crime rates among whites (Sourcebook of Criminal Justice Statistics, 1988). Continuing the focus on black-on-black crime results in the implication that the crime phenomenon is purely or mainly a *black thing.*

Terminological preference may be a hallmark of academe, nonetheless, there is a need to use the phrase black-on-black crime responsibly. As it stands, there is a possibility that the phrase black-on-black crime will be used to absolve society of any responsibility for the plight of poor people and visible minorities (e.g., black men). Perhaps, the frequency of crime in black communities will result in misconceptions about the roots of crime. The phrase resurrects images believed abandoned years ago, specifically, that blacks live in a subculture of violence. However, this perspective does not take into consideration the pathological impact of slavery and oppression (cf., Fanon,

1963; Poussaint, 1983). Nor does it acknowledge the relationship between slavery and self-hatred (Fanon, 1963). Shortly after, Menacham Amir published, *Patterns in Forcible Rape* (1971). He hinted that the act of rape, particularly in predominantly black communities, was victim-precipitated. Amir also states (1971:339):

Although the number of forcible rapes tended to increase during the summer months, there was no significant association either with the season or with the month of the year. While *Negro intramural rapes were spread all over the year, white intramural events showed a more consistent increase during the summer,* which was found to be the season when multiple rapes were most apt to occur.

One may infer from this quotation that acts of violence are indigenous to the black culture. More importantly, it is precisely this belief (long refuted) that resurfaces now that the phrase black on black crime is in vogue.

Political Abuses and Self-Serving Agendas

The more recent literature that focuses on black-on-black crime (e.g., Mitchell and Daniels, 1987) carries with it the potential for abuse and grave misunderstandings. Headlines reading *BLACK-ON-BLACK CRIME* or simply, *BLACKS AND CRIME* serve only to perpetuate the myth that blacks commit more crimes than their white counterparts. Individuals of informed or reasonable persuasion may be able to penetrate beyond the headlines and understand that the frequency of crime within the black community is a complex issue with many causal factors (cf., Wilson, 1987). On the other hand, others (especially those with a hidden agenda) may seize the moment to use the term to their advantage. Clearly, unless there are disclaimers about the phrase black-on-black crime, an uninformed population of both black and white individuals may begin to genuinely believe that being black is tantamount to being violent. It could arguably unfold as a self-fulfilling prophecy.

In the same vein, there are other negative consequences of focusing on black-on-black crime. Black-on-black crime implies that

acts of criminal violence do not occur with great frequency in the white community. Table 1 points toward the prevalence of crime among both blacks and whites.

It illustrates how an exclusive focus on black offending distracts from the rates of offending among whites—who accounted for 45% of all murder arrests, over one-third of all robbery arrests, over one-half of all rape arrests and over 60%, of all arrests on drug charges. In addition, the crime of arson (at 69% for Anglo-Americans) is clearly a white phenomenon, yet, no one publicly refers to arson as a white crime. Table 1 shows that whites account for at least 2 out of every 3 arrests. Similarly, data published in the most recent issue of the Uniform Crime Report (1991) reveals percentage increases for white Americans in every category of part one crimes. Succinctly put, crime in the U.S. is a very white problem, yet, we continue to read reports, scholarly articles, books and newspaper headlines titled black-on-black crime.

Other Problems

One, in the war on drugs, federal agents are relying increasingly on drug courier profiles. While agents deny that race is a factor, according to Lisa Belkin of *The New York Times* (1990), many stops are invariably based upon race. Belkin argues that in several case-studies, many black men and women are stopped on the basis of race and not behavior as the courts have required. The unintentional or deliberate use of the phrase, *black-on-black* crime may have the effect of further intensifying police harassment of blacks (see, e.g., Wright, 1987). This type of police harassment recently manifested itself in the streets of Los Angeles.

Second, some criminal justice personnel or politicians may use the phrase, black-on-black crime in a different context. It may not be uncommon for ultra-conservatives (i.e., David Duke) to make inaccurate or self-serving inferences about race and crime. Specifically, these individuals may conclude that the crime problem is indigenous to the black community, and therefore, cannot be affected by public policies such as increased job training. In addition, the equation

of blacks with criminality could be used to justify increased police patrol as a means of controlling the black community, fostering in the most negative way a big brother mentality! Third, the phrase, black on black crime may be used to verify or confirm stereotypical images. In an essay titled Encountering A Stereotype, Gregory Freeman of *The St. Louis Post-Dispatch* (1990) writes of his experiences in a downtown drugstore.

In the store I happened to approach an elderly white woman. She clutched her purse defensively as she feared that I might take it from her . . . The woman didn't cringe when someone got near her. But for some reason I made her nervous. I can't say for sure why. But I can say I was the only black person in the store.

He then offers a number of examples about white jewelers who are reluctant to open their doors to blacks and white cab drivers who intentionally discriminate against blacks for fear of being victimized. The point to be made here is that academics and practitioners alike must be sensitive to the various ways the phrase black-on-black crime can be abused or misinterpreted.

Conceptual Issues

Georges-Abeyie (1984:5) introduces another concern for those intrigued with the black crime phenomenon.

Before minority criminality or criminal victimization can be discussed rationally, the political, social, and cultural biases hidden in crime definitions must be identified. Few would argue that the prevailing schools of thought—the conservative, liberal, radical, critical perspectives—color definitional issues and interpretations of criminals and criminality. The hidden biases contained within these orientations need to be examined in order to understand the significance of race and ethnicity to more general notions of criminal propensity and victimization.

The issue of who is black and what is meant by race and ethnicity deserve clarification. In *Ebony* magazine (March 1990), the issue of race and ethnicity re-surfaces in an essay titled, *Who's Black and Who's Not? New Ethnicity Raises Provocative Questions About Racial Identity. Ebony* magazine suggests that there are blacks with white features and indi-

Table I

Offense

Total

Murder, nor
manslaugh
Forcible rap
Robbery
Aggravated
Burglary
Larceny-the
Motor vehic
Arson

Violent crim
Property cri

Crime Index

Other assau
Forgery and
counterfeit
Fraud
Embezzleme
Stolen prop
buying, rec
possessing
Vandalism
Weapons: ca
possessing
Prostitution
commerci
Sex offenses
forcible ra
and prost
Drug abuse
Gambling
Offenses ag
and childr
Driving und
the influe

Liquor laws
Drunkennes
Disorderly c
Vagrancy
All other off
(except n
Suspicion
Curfew and
law violatio
Runaways

*Source: FBI,

with the blackness of Willie Horton. The Willie Horton case was a racist slur against African-Americans—because it reaffirmed the significance of race in our society for both gullible white and black Americans. Consistent with the Bush campaign, Pinderhughes (1989:8) finds that:

Social systems . . . maintain stability by identifying certain persons or behaviors as deviant. In defining what is not acceptable, the system uses deviance to separate the normal from the abnormal, thus reinforcing boundaries within the system . . . these societal processes—stereotyping, discrimination, prejudice, labeling—employ projection upon another.

Such was the effect of the Bush campaign and the potential for continued abuse remains. We must strive toward an accurate portrayal of black crime. Studies of crime must be kept in perspective, particularly in light of frequent headlines regarding black on black crime. Researchers engaged in the study of crime should also guard against the over representation of ethnic minorities, especially where random sampling is not possible. Misinterpretations may mask the negative impact of racism, sexism and residential isolation as contributing factors in the black crime scare (cf., Duster, 1987; Wilson, 1987).

References

Alex, Nicholas. *Black in Blue*. New York: Apple-Century-Crofts, Inc. 1969.

Amir, Menachem. *Patterns in Forcible Rape*. Chicago: The University of Chicago Press, 1971.

Cole, George. *The American System of Criminal Justice*. Belmont: Brooks-Cole Publishing Company, 1989.

Belkin, Lisa. Airport Anti-Drug Nets Snare Many People Fitting Profiles, *The New York Times*, March, 20, 1990.

Duster, Troy. Crime, Youth Unemployment, and the Black Urban Underclass, 33(2) *Crime and Delinquency* 1987.

Fanon, Frantz. *The Wretched of the Earth*. New York: Grove Press, Inc., 1963.

Georges-Abeyie, Daniel. Definitional Issues: Race, Ethnicity, and Official Crime/Victimization Statistics, in Georges-Abeyie (ed.), *Criminal Justice System and Blacks*. New York: Clark Boardman Company, Ltd., 1984.

Georges-Abeyie, Daniel. Race, Ethnicity, and Spatial Dynamic: Toward a Realistic Study of Black Crime, Crime Victimization, and Criminal Processing of Blacks, 16(4) *Social Justice* 1989.

Gould, Stephen Jay. Why We Should Not Name Races—A Biological View, in *Ever Since Darwin*. New York: W.W. Norton & Company, 1989.

Headley, Bernard. *Black on Black Crime: The Myth and the Reality*. 20 *Crime and Social Justice* 1983.

Jamieson, K. and T. Flanagan (eds). *Sourcebook of Criminal Justice Statistics—1988*. U.S. Department of Justice, Bureau of Justice Statistics. Washington,D.C.: United States Government Printing Office, 1989.

Mauer, Marc. *Young Black Men and the Criminal Justice System: A Growing National Problem*. Washington: The Sentencing Project, February 1990 (unpublished).

McLaughlin, Vance. Written correspondence with Vance McLaughlin, Director of Training, Savannah Police Department, Savannah, GA (March 1990).

Mitchell, Mark and Stacey Daniels. Black on Black Homicide: Kansas City's Response 104 (6) *Public Health Reports* 1989.

Montagu-Ashley. *The Concept of Race*. New York: Free Press of Glencoe, 1964.

Montagu-Ashley. *On Being Human*. New York: H. Schuman, 1950.

Nettler, Gwynn. *Killing One Another*. Cincinnati: Anderson Publishing Company, 1982.

Norment, Lynn. Who's Black and Who's Not? *Ebony* March 134–138,1990.

Pinderhughes, Elaine. *Understanding Race, Ethnicity, and Power* New York: The Free Press, 1989.

Pouissant, Alvin. Black-on-Black Homicide 8 *Victimology*, 1983.

Sanders, W. and T. Pinhey. *The Conduct of Social Research* New York: CBS Publishing, 1983.

U.S. Department of Justice, Bureau of Statistics, *Annual Report, Fiscal 1986*. Washington, D.C.: U.S. Government Printing Office,1987.

U.S. Department of Justice, Bureau of Justice Statistics. *Bulletin* October 1986.

U.S. Department of Justice. *Crime in the United States*. Washington, D.C.: U.S. Government Printing Office, 1987.

U.S. Department of Justice. *Crime in the United States*. Washington, D.C.: U.S. Government Printing Office, 1989.

Wilbanks, William. *The Myth of a Racist Criminal Justice System*. Belmont: Wadsworth Publishing Company, 1987.

Wilson, William Julius. *The Truly Disadvantage: The Inner City, the Underclass, and Public Policy*. Chicago: The University of Chicago Press, 1987.

Wolfgang, Marvin. Victim-Precipitated Criminal Homicide, *Journal of Criminal Law, Criminology, and Police Science* vol 48:1–11, 1957.

Wolfgang, M. Patterns in Criminal Homicide. New York: Wiley, Press, 1958.

Wolfgang, M. and F. Ferracuti. *The Subculture of Violence: Towards An Integrated Theory in Criminology*. Beverly Hills, CA: Sage Publishing, 1982.

Wright, Bruce. *Black Robes, White Justice: Why Our Justice System Doesn't Work For Blacks*. Secaucus: Lyle Stuart Inc., 1987.

Vetter, Harold and Leonard Territo. *Crime and Justice in America*. St. Paul: West Publishing Company, 1984.

Black Criminals, Black Victims. *St. Louis-Post Dispatch*, February 12, 1990.

Encountering A Stereotype. *St. Louis-Post Dispatch*, January 26, 1990.

Article Review Form at end of book.

How have law enforcement employers measured up to the goal of promoting representation of minority members in high-level administrative positions?

Disparate Impact and Disparate Treatment Theories:

Conceptual Forms of Employment Discrimination in Law Enforcement

O. Elmer Polk

University of Texas at Arlington

It has been said that "justice is blind"! The differential treatment of various groups in the employment market, however, has not led all members of all societal groups to believe the blindfold is intact concerning the issue of employment discrimination. This quantitative, legal study traces the legal evolution of ethnically based employment discrimination in America and the emergence of differing theoretic perspectives. Disparate impact and disparate treatment theories are described and their primary propositions are compared. A model is developed to test disparate impact theory based on the outcomes of employment practices in law enforcement. Findings are both encouraging and discouraging in that the results show minority members proceeding through their career paths more quickly than majority members but also show that law enforcement employers have failed to attain representative levels of diversity in higher-level administrative positions.

Introduction

From the 1896 U.S. Supreme Court decision in *Plessey v. Ferguson* to *Brown v. Board of Education* in 1954, the separate but equal doctrine was firmly entrenched in American society. The Brown decision attempted to end school desegregation at "all deliberate speed," and this nonspecific guideline endured until the passage of the Civil Rights Act of 1964, which required schools to desegregate "at once" (Abraham,1987,181). The demise of legally sanctioned segregation brought numerous issues to the courts and governmental agencies related to affording constitutional guarantees of equal protection to all citizens regardless of race. It also brought to the white population a greater awareness of race-based differentials in such areas as consumer spending (Caplovitz, 1967), housing markets (Carney, 1972), poverty, crime, employment, and income (Silberman, 1978). The employment arena was found to be the setting of many inequalities by the courts, and

a significant body of law developed addressing discriminatory issues and theories.

Equal Employment Opportunity Law

The basic principles of equal employment opportunity law were established by the U.S. Supreme Court in *Griggs v. Duke Power Company* (1971). Duke Power Company required all employees to have a high school diploma and successful scores on written intelligence and mechanical comprehension tests. A class action suit was filed by black employees alleging that the education and testing preconditions of employment violated protections of the Civil Rights Act of 1964. The Court held that the employer was prohibited from requiring the preconditions because both requirements disqualified blacks at a substantially higher rate than whites, and any precondition that disqualifies minorities disproportionately is illegal, regardless of the employer's intent, unless the employer can show selection standards to be a bona fide occupational qualification that is a business necessity.

After *Griggs*, several Supreme Court decisions clarified grounds on which cases could be successfully brought to court on discrimination claims. In *Wards Cove Packing v. Atonio* (1989), the Court restricted the ability of plaintiffs to prevail on discrimination issues by shifting the burden of proof of alleged discrimination to the worker (Martin, 1991). In *Wards Cove Packing,* the Court held that if the absence of minorities holding skilled positions is due to a dearth of qualified nonwhite applicants then the selection methods in question cannot be said to have a disparate impact on nonwhites. The Court further held that a statistical showing of racial imbalance between the skilled jobs and the nonskilled jobs was insufficient to establish a prima facie case of discrimination. The proper comparison should be between the racial composition of at-issue jobs and the racial composition of the relevant job market. Therefore, workers who do not possess required job skills are not part of the relevant job market.

Griggs and *Wards Cove* are examples of the difficulty of defining discrimination. Black's Law Dictionary defines discrimination as the "unfair treatment or denial of normal privileges to persons because of their race, age, nationality, or religion" or "a failure to treat all persons equally where no reasonable distinction can be found between those favored and those not favored" (Black, 1989, 420). Statutory law governing race discrimination is taken primarily from Title VII of the Civil Rights Act of 1964,§703(a)(1) and states that

It shall be an unlawful employment practice for an employer to fail or refuse to hire or to discharge any individual, or otherwise discriminate against any individual with respect to compensation, terms, conditions, or privileges of employment, because of such individual's race, color, religion, or national origin (42 U.S.C. §2000 e-2).

The procedural interpretation of the above definition defines fairness and equality as concepts of equal treatment in employment decision making. The substantive interpretation views fairness and equality as stemming from the substantive outcome of organizational practices (Edelman et al., 1991). Procedural equality does not guarantee substantive equality because of its failure to address past discrimination that contributes to present inequality.

Legal Theories of Employment Discrimination

The theories most frequently followed by the courts are disparate treatment and disparate impact (Paetzold & Willborn, 1996; Youngblood, 1990). Disparate treatment cases arise when an employer treats some people less favorably than others similarly situated because of race, color, religion, sex, or national origin. The differential treatment is purposeful, and intent to discriminate may be inferred to the employer (Hadley, 1990). The Supreme Court in *McDonnell Douglas v. Green* (1973) specified the general requirements for a plaintiff to present a prima facie case of disparate treatment discrimination. The employee must allege to be a member of a protected group and that an adverse personnel action or decision was taken against him or her because of the protected trait. A comparison is made between the employee and others similarly situated who are not members of the same protected group. It is necessary to show adverse treatment of the employee and, if possible, others of the same protected group.

Establishing the prima facie case is important because it gives the plaintiff the opportunity to present circumstantial evidence of discriminatory intent. The Supreme Court in *Texas Department of Community Affairs v. Burdine* (1981) defined a prima facie case as a "legally mandatory rebuttable assumption" (Hadley, 1990; Youngblood, 1990). When the prima facie case is established, it may be presumed that, unless there are alternative explanations, the adverse action taken by the employer was probably precipitated by discriminatory motives. If the plaintiff establishes a prima facie case, the burden of production shifts to the employer, who must present a nondiscriminatory reason for its decision (*Furnco*

Construction Company v. Waters, 1979; *Texas Department of Community Affairs v. Burdine,* 1981).

In disparate impact cases, discrimination does not have to be intended to be unlawful. If an employment practice has a disparate impact on a member of a protected group, there is a basis for inferring discrimination. Disparate impact occurs when facially neutral employment practices fall more harshly on one group than another and cannot be justified by business necessity (Civil Rights Act of 1991; *International Brotherhood of Teamsters v. U.S.,* 1977).

In 1971, The Supreme Court held in *Griggs* that Title VII of the Civil Rights Act of 1964 prohibits employment practices with discriminatory effects and those that are intended to discriminate. This created disparate impact theory, which focuses on objective and subjective criteria, tests, or other barriers to employment which discriminate against members of protected groups. The legal requirements for disparate impact were specified in *Griggs,* but there has been confusion over their application.

The decision in *Wards Cove* shifted the burden of proof requirements established in Griggs by stating that a worker who contends that an employer's practices have a "disparate impact" on women and minorities must disprove an employer's assertion that the practices serve a legitimate business purpose. The Civil Rights Act of 1991 served to generally restore the standards for disparate impact to what they were prior to *Wards Cove,* and the burden of proof now falls on the plaintiff to show that the employer uses a particular employment practice that results in a statistically disparate impact on protected groups.

Once the prima facie case of disparity is made by the plaintiff, the burden shifts to the employer to show that the questioned employment practices do not cause disparate impact or that the practice is job-related and a business necessity. The plaintiffs may also show that an alternative practice was proposed which would not have disparate impact which the employer refused to accept. The employer then has the burden of showing that the alternative could not be used because of business necessity.

The evidence of discrimination in disparate impact cases usually focus on statistical disparities rather than specific cases. The decision concerning whether an employment practice causes significant disparity is best decided by following the 80 percent guideline utilized by the Equal Employment Opportunity Commission (EEOC). Some courts use a standard deviation test to determine whether the disparity is two or three standard deviations from the mean. Two deviations show disparity and three show gross disparity. The 80 percent rule, however, is used in the majority of cases and in all investigations by the EEOC.

The new civil rights act restored the guidelines of discrimination suits to what they were prior to *Wards Cove,* but it did not address the comparison bases to be used in determining disparity. Thus, the holdings in *Wards Cove* remain in effect. In *Dothard v. Rawlinson* (1977), the Court allowed the comparison to be between the affected group and the general population. In *New York City Transit Authority v. Beazer* (1979), the Court accepted measures indicating the racial composition of otherwise qualified applicants for at-issue jobs. *In Wards Cove,* the Court held that the proper comparison is between the racial composition in the qualified population in the relevant job market and the racial composition of the at-issue jobs. The Court acknowledged that if the proper statistics could not be obtained then alternatives such as those in *Beazer* and *Dothard* could be used.

Affirmative Action

There are two basic interpretations of equal employment opportunity law. The procedural interpretation (disparate treatment) is concerned with the equal treatment of everyone in employment decisions. The substantive interpretation (disparate impact) is concerned with the outcome of agency practices. The former approach considers affirmative action to be inconsistent with Title VII of the Civil Rights Act of 1964 because it gives preferences to minorities or women. Thus, employers are making race- or gender-based employment decisions, which are prohibited by Title VII. The latter approach considers affirmative action to be required under Title VII because the effects of past discrimination will continue unless an affirmative effort is made by employers to facilitate the incorporation of previously underrepresented groups into the labor force at all levels (Edelman et al., 1991). The procedural approach fails to remedy past discrimination, and the substantive approach may cause some instances of reverse discrimination (McConnell, 1983).

Opponents of affirmative action claim that it is unconstitutional because it is violative of the Equal Protection Clause of the Fourteenth Amendment and is not amenable to rectification by court order (Feagins, 1990; Loury, 1985). Furthermore, it is illegal in that it violates the statutory provisions of Title VII and is destructive because it creates resentment by the effected majority (Feagins, 1990). Proponents of affirmative action maintain that equal treatment of those with different starting points perpetuates the inequality which presently exists and will continue until the vestiges of past discrimination are alleviated (Schwartz, 1984). Justice Powell wrote in *Wygant v. Jackson Board of Education* (1986) that, as part of this nation's dedication to eradicating racial discrimination, innocent persons may be called upon to bear some of the burden of the remedy. In our political system, the majority rules but the rights of minorities must be protected, even if some members of the majority are temporarily disadvantaged (Welch, 1990).

Affirmative action issues were clarified in 1989 by the Court in *City of Richmond v. J.A. Croson Company,* where the Court left no doubt that any race-based classification would be subjected to the strictest judicial scrutiny. The focus of the Court was changed in this case from broad considerations of social class issues to an emphasis on the individual. Generalized past discrimination does not justify affirmative action, and the Court indicated that the use of numerical quota requirements would be viewed as a per se violation of the mandate to tailor carefully any racial classification.

Much has been written on the differing philosophies fueling the affirmative action controversy and how to tailor affirmative action to meet current legal requirements. Comparatively, little scientific research has been conducted on the effectiveness of such programs in eradicating discrimination. Two representative studies show that the programs are helpful. Lewis (1989) found that affirmative action has significantly increased the representation of blacks in law enforcement. Martin (1991) researched the effect of affirmative action on women in policing and found that the hiring of females had been significantly improved, but not their promotions. Both Lewis and Martin reported significant increases in the frequencies of the protected groups in their studies.

Methodology

This study examines a large sample of law-enforcement officers to examine whether the propositions of disparate impact theory can be supported in law-enforcement employment and whether law-enforcment employers are engaging in discriminatory practices. Analyses address the following issues:

1. Minority members in a sample who have been the victims of discrimination will have achieved a lower level of employment success than whites in the sample, as shown by disparate rates of representation in the rank structure and they will not progress through their career paths commensurately with whites.

2. Those law-enforcement agencies utilizing discriminatory practices will fail to achieve compliance with the 80 percent rule of the EEOC.

This study uses secondary, cross-sectional, individual-level data from the Texas Career Paths Project conducted jointly by Sam Houston State University and the Texas Commission on Law Enforcement Officer Standards and Education

Identify some of the problems that emanate from the use of the phrase "black-on-black" crime.

Politicizing Black-on-Black Crime:

A Critique of Terminological Preference

Robert L. Bing III, Ph.D.

*Associate Professor
Criminology and Criminal Justice Program
Department of Sociology and Anthropology
University of Texas at Arlington*

Abstract

This article argues that the phrase black-on-black crime is being over utilized. The phrase black-on-black crime perpetuates negative images of African-Americans. Problems emanating from use of the phrase black-on-black crime and the need for conceptual clarity are presented. The issues of terminological preference, ethnicity and race are addressed along with a discussion of negative policy implications and recommendations for movement beyond race-oriented research on crime.

Introduction

Much attention has been devoted to black-on-black crime (e.g., Headley, 1983; Pouissant, 1983; Mitchell and Daniels, 1989). Many newspapers and scholarly publications have addressed this topic (e.g., Mitchell and Daniels, 1989; Mauer, 1990). It is not unusual to see in the written press or to hear through the electronic media stories depicting the evils of living in the black community. The headlines (in major metropolitan newspapers) and special issues (in sociological and criminological journals) have occurred with such frequency that some individuals now associate black people with criminality. Simply put, it has become fashionable to discern between crime and black-on-black crime. Rarely, does one read or hear about white crime or white-on-white crime. This is troubling when one considers that most crimes, including serious violent crimes, are committed by and against whites as well as blacks (United States Department of Justice, 1989). The prevalence of crime among whites is documented in the *Sourcebook of Criminal Justice Statistics*, (1988). This publication, for example, shows that in 1987, whites were charged with over 60 percent of the index crimes, while blacks were charged with just under 40 percent of the index crimes in 1987. Why, then, do we persist in characterizing crime in the black community as black-on-black, when crime in the United States is a very white problem as well?

This article has several objectives; they include de-politicization of the phrase black-on-black crime as well as an examination of the conceptual problems surrounding the issue of race and ethnicity. The issue of race and ethnicity, in particular, needs dialogue among researchers who might otherwise overlook their important distinctions (see, e.g., Georges-Abeyie, 1989).

The Issue of Color

This society is very color conscious. Before assessing the character and integrity of a person, we usually acknowledge skin color. As a college professor, my students see me first as a black person, then as a college professor. Similarly, when a law enforcement officer observes a black man on the street—this observation may be due to gender and reasonable suspicion, but race invariably plays a role in the surveillance effect (e.g., Wilbanks, 1987; Cole, 1990).

Concomitantly, our criminological textbooks are inundated with references to individuals on the basis of race. For example, in Gwynn Nettler's *Killing One Another* (1982), the issue of race and criminality is very apparent—the subject index has a category for blacks, but no category for whites. Nettler (1982:60) states: Black people suffer from a

disproportionately high crime rate that victimizes principally their own minority. The disproportion is more striking in attacks against persons than in offenses against property. Black rates of arrest and convictions for aggravated assault, robbery, rape, murder . . . exceed those of the American population in general . . . Similarly, Wilbanks controversial *The Myth of A Racist Criminal Justice System* is replete with statements about black criminality. He uses several studies purporting to show that the higher frequency of crime in the black community explains why blacks are disproportionately represented in the criminal justice system. Nettler and Wilbanks are not alone; other textbooks also assign special categories for blacks (e.g., Nettler, 1982; Vetter and Territo, 1984). The implication of this special treatment is that blacks are very different from their white counterparts.

Presumably as a result of this peculiar treatment and specific categorization on the basis of race, it is a known fact that some police departments train their recruits in the handling of alleged black crime, while only a small percentage are trained to respond to corporate or white collar crimes (McLaughlin, 1990). The identification of race with crime is so pervasive that off duty black police officers may be advised to remain in their cars if they observe a crime in progress or to telephone the activity to a uniformed police officer, on the assumption that few would believe (in light of inflammatory coverage about black criminality) that a black man or woman in plain clothes was a police officer (Alex, 1969; McLaughlin, 1990). This advice is consistent with the negative perceptions already perpetuated by the media and academics.

Negative Connotations

An editorial in the St. Louis *Post-Dispatch* (1990), titled, *Black Criminals, Black Victims* corresponds with Nettler's observation that blacks are responsible for a disproportionate number of crimes. This revelation, however, is not consistent with the notion that most blacks commit crimes—it only means that blacks commit a disproportionate number

of crimes. Authors and researchers should be certain to distinguish between the term disproportionate number of crimes and most crimes. The *Post-Dispatch* article, responding to the release of a local study of black-on-black crime goes on to say, It's bad enough that these youngsters have no respect for their own lives; its worse that they are willing to place the lives of innocent bystanders in jeopardy. The *Post-Dispatch* article deserves critical observation because it creates the impression that most blacks, rather than whites lead a life of crime. There have been a litany of studies focusing on black-on-black crime, ranging from Washington, D.C. to Kansas City, Missouri to the coastal cities of California. Frequently, there is a negative assessment of the crime problem, especially for black males. In a study about black-on-black crime, Shirley Wilson (1989) writes, "Unfortunately, the situation with which we are confronted today is a growing trend, particularly on the part of young black males . . ." While this statement may be true, it serves to obscure more recent developments regarding race and crime in the United States. For example, in 1970, black males were 12 times more likely to be arrested for murder than whites. By 1985, this ratio had dropped to 5:1. One consequence of the black-on-black crime focus, then, is the neglect of rising crime rates among whites (Sourcebook of Criminal Justice Statistics, 1988). Continuing the focus on black-on-black crime results in the implication that the crime phenomenon is purely or mainly a *black thing*.

Terminological preference may be a hallmark of academe, nonetheless, there is a need to use the phrase black-on-black crime responsibly. As it stands, there is a possibility that the phrase black-on-black crime will be used to absolve society of any responsibility for the plight of poor people and visible minorities (e.g., black men). Perhaps, the frequency of crime in black communities will result in misconceptions about the roots of crime. The phrase resurrects images believed abandoned years ago, specifically, that blacks live in a subculture of violence. However, this perspective does not take into consideration the pathological impact of slavery and oppression (cf., Fanon,

1963; Poussaint, 1983). Nor does it acknowledge the relationship between slavery and self-hatred (Fanon, 1963). Shortly after, Menacham Amir published, *Patterns in Forcible Rape* (1971). He hinted that the act of rape, particularly in predominantly black communities, was victim-precipitated. Amir also states (1971:339):

Although the number of forcible rapes tended to increase during the summer months, there was no significant association either with the season or with the month of the year. While *Negro intramural rapes were spread all over the year, white intramural events showed a more consistent increase during the summer,* which was found to be the season when multiple rapes were most apt to occur.

One may infer from this quotation that acts of violence are indigenous to the black culture. More importantly, it is precisely this belief (long refuted) that resurfaces now that the phrase black on black crime is in vogue.

Political Abuses and Self-Serving Agendas

The more recent literature that focuses on black-on-black crime (e.g., Mitchell and Daniels, 1987) carries with it the potential for abuse and grave misunderstandings. Headlines reading *BLACK-ON-BLACK CRIME* or simply, *BLACKS AND CRIME* serve only to perpetuate the myth that blacks commit more crimes than their white counterparts. Individuals of informed or reasonable persuasion may be able to penetrate beyond the headlines and understand that the frequency of crime within the black community is a complex issue with many causal factors (cf., Wilson, 1987). On the other hand, others (especially those with a hidden agenda) may seize the moment to use the term to their advantage. Clearly, unless there are disclaimers about the phrase black-on-black crime, an uninformed population of both black and white individuals may begin to genuinely believe that being black is tantamount to being violent. It could arguably unfold as a self-fulfilling prophecy.

In the same vein, there are other negative consequences of focusing on black-on-black crime. Black-on-black crime implies that

acts of criminal violence do not occur with great frequency in the white community. Table 1 points toward the prevalence of crime among both blacks and whites.

It illustrates how an exclusive focus on black offending distracts from the rates of offending among whites—who accounted for 45% of all murder arrests, over one-third of all robbery arrests, over one-half of all rape arrests and over 60%, of all arrests on drug charges. In addition, the crime of arson (at 69% for Anglo-Americans) is clearly a white phenomenon, yet, no one publicly refers to arson as a white crime. Table 1 shows that whites account for at least 2 out of every 3 arrests. Similarly, data published in the most recent issue of the Uniform Crime Report (1991) reveals percentage increases for white Americans in every category of part one crimes. Succinctly put, crime in the U.S. is a very white problem, yet, we continue to read reports, scholarly articles, books and newspaper headlines titled black-on-black crime.

Other Problems

One, in the war on drugs, federal agents are relying increasingly on drug courier profiles. While agents deny that race is a factor, according to Lisa Belkin of *The New York Times* (1990), many stops are invariably based upon race. Belkin argues that in several case-studies, many black men and women are stopped on the basis of race and not behavior as the courts have required. The unintentional or deliberate use of the phrase, *black-on-black* crime may have the effect of further intensifying police harassment of blacks (see, e.g., Wright, 1987). This type of police harassment recently manifested itself in the streets of Los Angeles.

Second, some criminal justice personnel or politicians may use the phrase, black-on-black crime in a different context. It may not be uncommon for ultra-conservatives (i.e., David Duke) to make inaccurate or self-serving inferences about race and crime. Specifically, these individuals may conclude that the crime problem is indigenous to the black community, and therefore, cannot be affected by public policies such as increased job training. In addition, the equation

of blacks with criminality could be used to justify increased police patrol as a means of controlling the black community, fostering in the most negative way a big brother mentality! Third, the phrase, black on black crime may be used to verify or confirm stereotypical images. In an essay titled Encountering A Stereotype, Gregory Freeman of *The St. Louis Post-Dispatch* (1990) writes of his experiences in a downtown drugstore.

In the store I happened to approach an elderly white woman. She clutched her purse defensively as she feared that I might take it from her . . . The woman didn't cringe when someone got near her. But for some reason I made her nervous. I can't say for sure why. But I can say I was the only black person in the store.

He then offers a number of examples about white jewelers who are reluctant to open their doors to blacks and white cab drivers who intentionally discriminate against blacks for fear of being victimized. The point to be made here is that academics and practitioners alike must be sensitive to the various ways the phrase black-on-black crime can be abused or misinterpreted.

Conceptual Issues

Georges-Abeyie (1984:5) introduces another concern for those intrigued with the black crime phenomenon.

Before minority criminality or criminal victimization can be discussed rationally, the political, social, and cultural biases hidden in crime definitions must be identified. Few would argue that the prevailing schools of thought—the conservative, liberal, radical, critical perspectives—color definitional issues and interpretations of criminals and criminality. The hidden biases contained within these orientations need to be examined in order to understand the significance of race and ethnicity to more general notions of criminal propensity and victimization.

The issue of who is black and what is meant by race and ethnicity deserve clarification. In *Ebony* magazine (March 1990), the issue of race and ethnicity re-surfaces in an essay titled, *Who's Black and Who's Not? New Ethnicity Raises Provocative Questions About Racial Identity. Ebony* magazine suggests that there are blacks with white features and indi-

viduals who are the progeny of interracial marriages who do not think of themselves as black. Lynn Norment of *Ebony* (1990:134) writes:

. . . As we embark upon the 90's, we are finding that more and more individuals— mostly young women who just a few years ago definitely would have considered themselves black are now calling themselves otherwise.

This revelation, no matter how seemingly small, should be acknowledged by academics, practitioners and researchers. Stated differently, the study and subsequent categorization of criminal activity on the basis of race is complicated by interracial marriages. Another example may involve the categorization of Hispanics. How, for instance, does one code information about Hispanics who have white skin versus those with black skin? These few examples point toward the complexity of attempting to compare and contrast rates of offending on the basis of race.

Stephen Gould (1989) raises questions about the wisdom of categorizing human beings on the basis of race. He argues that despite the efforts of many (cf., Montagu-Ashley, 1964) there remains the bias of placing human beings into subcategories, a practice that should be discouraged. He maintains that attempts to compartmentalize people on the basis of race represent an outmoded approach to the study of human behavior, society and culture. Criminologists should borrow from the wisdom of Gould and de-emphasize categorization of criminality on the basis of race.

Conclusion

While, there can be little doubt that blacks commit a disproportionate number of many part one offenses, and are in turn, disproportionately victimized by crimes involving physical contact, the need for conceptual clarity and carefully phrased terms is apparent. Black-on-black crime has become highly politicized. This should not be surprising, since both crime and race have always been heavily politicized in American society. Each election year some candidates use the crime issue to advantage. In 1988, Vice President George Bush exploited the crime issue

Table 1 — Total Arrests, Distribution by Race, 1988*

Offense Charged	Total Arrests					Percent Distribution				
	Total	White	Black	American Indian or Alaskan Native	Asian or Pacific Islander	Total	White	Black	American Indian or Alaskan Native	Asian or Pacific Islander
Total	11,224,528	7,559,138	1,459,177	113,777	92,436	100.0	67.3	30.8	1.0	0.8
Murder, nonnegligent manslaughter	17,944	7,567	10,118	120	139	100.0	42.2	56.4	0.7	0.8
Forcible rape	30,470	15,768	14,209	253	240	100.0	51.7	46.6	0.8	0.8
Robbery	133,683	45,437	86,832	483	931	100.0	34.0	65.0	0.4	0.7
Aggravated assault	353,868	203,457	144,574	3,155	2,682	100.0	57.5	40.9	0.9	0.8
Burglary	355,913	235,043	114,901	2,918	3,051	100.0	66.0	32.3	0.8	0.9
Larceny-theft	1,252,117	806,752	417,442	12,899	15,024	100.0	64.4	33.3	1.0	1.2
Motor vehicle theft	182,634	101,260	77,594	1,456	2,324	100.0	55.4	42.5	0.8	1.3
Arson	14,631	10,839	3,591	112	89	100.0	74.1	24.5	0.8	0.6
Violent crime	535,965	272,229	255,733	4,011	3,992	100.0	50.8	47.7	0.7	0.7
Property crime	1,805,295	1,153,894	613,528	17,385	20,488	100.0	63.9	34.0	1.0	1.1
Crime Index total	2,341,260	1,426,123	869,261	21,396	24,480	100.0	60.9	37.1	0.9	1.0
Other assaults	770,687	475,488	281,237	8,112	5,850	100.0	61.7	36.5	1.1	0.8
Forgery and counterfeiting	80,746	51,661	28,022	412	651	100.0	64.0	34.7	0.5	0.8
Fraud	289,752	193,247	94,597	910	998	100.0	66.7	32.6	0.3	0.3
Embezzlement	12,998	8,501	4,337	43	117	100.0	65.4	33.4	0.3	0.9
Stolen property; buying, receiving, possessing	141,378	78,164	61,598	680	936	100.0	55.3	43.6	0.5	0.7
Vandalism	247,169	182,678	60,177	2,293	2,021	100.0	73.9	24.3	0.9	0.8
Weapons: carrying, possessing, etc.	180,337	101,522	76,264	788	1,763	100.0	56.3	42.3	0.4	1.0
Prostitution and commercialized vice	88,526	50,862	36,391	476	797	100.0	57.5	41.1	0.5	0.9
Sex offenses (except forcible rape and prostitution	83,342	63,643	18,270	798	631	100.0	76.4	21.9	1.0	0.8
Drug abuse violations	1,074,345	613,800	452,574	3,407	4,564	100.0	57.1	42.1	0.3	0.4
Gambling	17,148	8,154	7,846	33	1,115	100.0	47.6	45.8	0.2	6.5
Offenses against family and children	58,166	37,671	18,435	589	1,471	100.0	64.8	31.7	1.0	2.5
Driving under the influence	1,314,556	1,171,282	119,684	13,910	9,680	100.0	89.1	9.1	1.1	0.7
Liquor laws	501,732	439,416	47,883	11,005	3,428	100.0	87.6	9.5	2.2	0.7
Drunkenness	666,566	530,926	118,312	15,518	1,810	100.0	79.7	17.7	2.3	0.3
Disorderly conduct	644,992	405,800	229,286	7,282	2,624	100.0	62.9	35.5	1.1	0.4
Vagrancy	29,557	16,876	12,070	519	92	100.0	57.1	40.8	1.8	0.3
All other offenses (except traffic)	2,472,917	1,544,864	878,860	23,398	25,795	100.0	62.5	35.5	0.9	1.0
Suspicion	13,847	6,085	7,656	49	57	100.0	43.9	55.3	0.4	0.4
Curfew and loitering law violations	64,922	47,246	15,896	546	1,234	100.0	72.8	24.5	0.8	1.9
Runaways	129,585	105,129	20,521	1,613	2,322	100.0	81.1	15.8	1.2	1.8

*Source: FBI. 1989. Uniform Crime Reports. Washington, D.C.: U.S. Government Printing Office.

with the blackness of Willie Horton. The Willie Horton case was a racist slur against African-Americans—because it reaffirmed the significance of race in our society for both gullible white and black Americans. Consistent with the Bush campaign, Pinderhughes (1989:8) finds that:

Social systems . . . maintain stability by identifying certain persons or behaviors as deviant. In defining what is not acceptable, the system uses deviance to separate the normal from the abnormal, thus reinforcing boundaries within the system . . . these societal processes—stereotyping, discrimination, prejudice, labeling—employ projection upon another.

Such was the effect of the Bush campaign and the potential for continued abuse remains. We must strive toward an accurate portrayal of black crime. Studies of crime must be kept in perspective, particularly in light of frequent headlines regarding black on black crime. Researchers engaged in the study of crime should also guard against the over representation of ethnic minorities, especially where random sampling is not possible. Misinterpretations may mask the negative impact of racism, sexism and residential isolation as contributing factors in the black crime scare (cf., Duster, 1987; Wilson, 1987).

References

Alex, Nicholas. *Black in Blue.* New York: Apple-Century-Crofts, Inc. 1969.

Amir, Menachem. *Patterns in Forcible Rape.* Chicago: The University of Chicago Press, 1971.

Cole, George. *The American System of Criminal Justice.* Belmont: Brooks-Cole Publishing Company, 1989.

Belkin, Lisa. Airport Anti-Drug Nets Snare Many People Fitting Profiles, *The New York Times,* March, 20, 1990.

Duster, Troy. Crime, Youth Unemployment, and the Black Urban Underclass, 33(2) *Crime and Delinquency* 1987.

Fanon, Frantz. *The Wretched of the Earth.* New York: Grove Press, Inc., 1963.

Georges-Abeyie, Daniel. Definitional Issues: Race, Ethnicity, and Official Crime/ Victimization Statistics, in Georges-Abeyie (ed.), *Criminal Justice System and Blacks.* New York: Clark Boardman Company, Ltd., 1984.

Georges-Abeyie, Daniel. Race, Ethnicity, and Spatial Dynamic: Toward a Realistic Study of Black Crime, Crime Victimization, and Criminal Processing of Blacks, 16(4) *Social Justice* 1989.

Gould, Stephen Jay. Why We Should Not Name Races—A Biological View, in *Ever Since Darwin.* New York: W.W. Norton & Company, 1989.

Headley, Bernard. *Black on Black Crime: The Myth and the Reality.* 20 *Crime and Social Justice* 1983.

Jamieson, K. and T. Flanagan (eds). *Sourcebook of Criminal Justice Statistics—1988.* U.S. Department of Justice, Bureau of Justice Statistics. Washington,D.C.: United States Government Printing Office, 1989.

Mauer, Marc. *Young Black Men and the Criminal Justice System: A Growing National Problem.* Washington: The Sentencing Project, February 1990 (unpublished).

McLaughlin, Vance. Written correspondence with Vance McLaughlin, Director of Training, Savannah Police Department, Savannah, GA (March 1990).

Mitchell, Mark and Stacey Daniels. Black on Black Homicide: Kansas City's Response 104 (6) *Public Health Reports* 1989.

Montagu-Ashley. *The Concept of Race.* New York: Free Press of Glencoe, 1964.

Montagu-Ashley. *On Being Human.* New York: H. Schuman, 1950.

Nettler, Gwynn. *Killing One Another.* Cincinnati: Anderson Publishing Company, 1982.

Norment, Lynn. Who's Black and Who's Not? *Ebony* March 134–138,1990.

Pinderhughes, Elaine. *Understanding Race, Ethnicity, and Power* New York: The Free Press, 1989.

Pouissant, Alvin. Black-on-Black Homicide 8 *Victimology,* 1983.

Sanders, W. and T. Pinhey. *The Conduct of Social Research* New York: CBS Publishing, 1983.

U.S. Department of Justice, Bureau of Statistics, *Annual Report, Fiscal 1986.* Washington, D.C.: U.S. Government Printing Office,1987.

U.S. Department of Justice, Bureau of Justice Statistics. *Bulletin* October 1986.

U.S. Department of Justice. *Crime in the United States.* Washington, D.C.: U.S. Government Printing Office, 1987.

U.S. Department of Justice. *Crime in the United States.* Washington, D.C.: U.S. Government Printing Office, 1989.

Wilbanks, William. *The Myth of a Racist Criminal Justice System.* Belmont: Wadsworth Publishing Company, 1987.

Wilson, William Julius. *The Truly Disadvantage: The Inner City, the Underclass, and Public Policy.* Chicago: The University of Chicago Press, 1987.

Wolfgang, Marvin. Victim-Precipitated Criminal Homicide, *Journal of Criminal Law, Criminology, and Police Science* vol 48:1–11, 1957.

Wolfgang, M. Patterns in Criminal Homicide. New York: Wiley, Press, 1958.

Wolfgang, M. and F. Ferracuti. *The Subculture of Violence: Towards An Integrated Theory in Criminology.* Beverly Hills, CA: Sage Publishing, 1982.

Wright, Bruce. *Black Robes, White Justice: Why Our Justice System Doesn't Work For Blacks.* Secaucus: Lyle Stuart Inc., 1987.

Vetter, Harold and Leonard Territo. *Crime and Justice in America.* St. Paul: West Publishing Company, 1984.

Black Criminals, Black Victims. *St. Louis-Post Dispatch,* February 12, 1990.

Encountering A Stereotype. *St. Louis-Post Dispatch,* January 26, 1990.

 Article Review Form at end of book.

How have law enforcement employers measured up to the goal of promoting representation of minority members in high-level administrative positions?

Disparate Impact and Disparate Treatment Theories:

Conceptual Forms of Employment Discrimination in Law Enforcement

O. Elmer Polk

University of Texas at Arlington

It has been said that "justice is blind"! The differential treatment of various groups in the employment market, however, has not led all members of all societal groups to believe the blindfold is intact concerning the issue of employment discrimination. This quantitative, legal study traces the legal evolution of ethnically based employment discrimination in America and the emergence of differing theoretic perspectives. Disparate impact and disparate treatment theories are described and their primary propositions are compared. A model is developed to test disparate impact theory based on the outcomes of employment practices in law enforcement. Findings are both encouraging and discouraging in that the results show minority members proceeding through their career paths more quickly than majority members but also show that law enforcement employers have failed to attain representative levels of diversity in higher-level administrative positions.

Introduction

From the 1896 U.S. Supreme Court decision in *Plessey v. Ferguson* to *Brown v. Board of Education* in 1954, the separate but equal doctrine was firmly entrenched in American society. The Brown decision attempted to end school desegregation at "all deliberate speed," and this nonspecific guideline endured until the passage of the Civil Rights Act of 1964, which required schools to desegregate "at once" (Abraham,1987,181). The demise of legally sanctioned segregation brought numerous issues to the courts and governmental agencies related to affording constitutional guarantees of equal protection to all citizens regardless of race. It also brought to the white population a greater awareness of race-based differentials in such areas as consumer spending (Caplovitz, 1967), housing markets (Carney, 1972), poverty, crime, employment, and income (Silberman, 1978). The employment arena was found to be the setting of many inequalities by the courts, and

a significant body of law developed addressing discriminatory issues and theories.

Equal Employment Opportunity Law

The basic principles of equal employment opportunity law were established by the U.S. Supreme Court in *Griggs v. Duke Power Company* (1971). Duke Power Company required all employees to have a high school diploma and successful scores on written intelligence and mechanical comprehension tests. A class action suit was filed by black employees alleging that the education and testing preconditions of employment violated protections of the Civil Rights Act of 1964. The Court held that the employer was prohibited from requiring the preconditions because both requirements disqualified blacks at a substantially higher rate than whites, and any precondition that disqualifies minorities disproportionately is illegal, regardless of the employer's intent, unless the employer can show

selection standards to be a bona fide occupational qualification that is a business necessity.

After *Griggs,* several Supreme Court decisions clarified grounds on which cases could be successfully brought to court on discrimination claims. In *Wards Cove Packing v. Atonio* (1989), the Court restricted the ability of plaintiffs to prevail on discrimination issues by shifting the burden of proof of alleged discrimination to the worker (Martin, 1991). In *Wards Cove Packing,* the Court held that if the absence of minorities holding skilled positions is due to a dearth of qualified nonwhite applicants then the selection methods in question cannot be said to have a disparate impact on nonwhites. The Court further held that a statistical showing of racial imbalance between the skilled jobs and the nonskilled jobs was insufficient to establish a prima facie case of discrimination. The proper comparison should be between the racial composition of at-issue jobs and the racial composition of the relevant job market. Therefore, workers who do not possess required job skills are not part of the relevant job market.

Griggs and *Wards Cove* are examples of the difficulty of defining discrimination. Black's Law Dictionary defines discrimination as the "unfair treatment or denial of normal privileges to persons because of their race, age, nationality, or religion" or "a failure to treat all persons equally where no reasonable distinction can be found between those favored and those not favored" (Black, 1989, 420). Statutory law governing race discrimination is taken primarily from Title VII of the Civil Rights Act of 1964,§703(a)(1) and states that

It shall be an unlawful employment practice for an employer to fail or refuse to hire or to discharge any individual, or otherwise discriminate against any individual with respect to compensation, terms, conditions, or privileges of employment, because of such individual's race, color, religion, or national origin (42 U.S.C. §2000 e-2).

The procedural interpretation of the above definition defines fairness and equality as concepts of equal treatment in employment decision making. The substantive interpretation views fairness and equality as stemming from the substantive outcome of organizational practices (Edelman et al., 1991). Procedural equality does not guarantee substantive equality because of its failure to address past discrimination that contributes to present inequality.

Legal Theories of Employment Discrimination

The theories most frequently followed by the courts are disparate treatment and disparate impact (Paetzold & Willborn, 1996; Youngblood, 1990). Disparate treatment cases arise when an employer treats some people less favorably than others similarly situated because of race, color, religion, sex, or national origin. The differential treatment is purposeful, and intent to discriminate may be inferred to the employer (Hadley, 1990). The Supreme Court in *McDonnell Douglas v. Green* (1973) specified the general requirements for a plaintiff to present a prima facie case of disparate treatment discrimination. The employee must allege to be a member of a protected group and that an adverse personnel action or decision was taken against him or her because of the protected trait. A comparison is made between the employee and others similarly situated who are not members of the same protected group. It is necessary to show adverse treatment of the employee and, if possible, others of the same protected group.

Establishing the prima facie case is important because it gives the plaintiff the opportunity to present circumstantial evidence of discriminatory intent. The Supreme Court in *Texas Department of Community Affairs v. Burdine* (1981) defined a prima facie case as a "legally mandatory rebuttable assumption" (Hadley, 1990; Youngblood, 1990). When the prima facie case is established, it may be presumed that, unless there are alternative explanations, the adverse action taken by the employer was probably precipitated by discriminatory motives. If the plaintiff establishes a prima facie case, the burden of production shifts to the employer, who must present a nondiscriminatory reason for its decision (*Furnco Construction Company v. Waters,* 1979; *Texas Department of Community Affairs v. Burdine,* 1981).

In disparate impact cases, discrimination does not have to be intended to be unlawful. If an employment practice has a disparate impact on a member of a protected group, there is a basis for inferring discrimination. Disparate impact occurs when facially neutral employment practices fall more harshly on one group than another and cannot be justified by business necessity (Civil Rights Act of 1991; *International Brotherhood of Teamsters v. U.S.,* 1977).

In 1971, The Supreme Court held in *Griggs* that Title VII of the Civil Rights Act of 1964 prohibits employment practices with discriminatory effects and those that are intended to discriminate. This created disparate impact theory, which focuses on objective and subjective criteria, tests, or other barriers to employment which discriminate against members of protected groups. The legal requirements for disparate impact were specified in *Griggs,* but there has been confusion over their application.

The decision in *Wards Cove* shifted the burden of proof requirements established in Griggs by stating that a worker who contends that an employer's practices have a "disparate impact" on women and minorities must disprove an employer's assertion that the practices serve a legitimate business purpose. The Civil Rights Act of 1991 served to generally restore the standards for disparate impact to what they were prior to *Wards Cove,* and the burden of proof now falls on the plaintiff to show that the employer uses a particular employment practice that results in a statistically disparate impact on protected groups.

Once the prima facie case of disparity is made by the plaintiff, the burden shifts to the employer to show that the questioned employment practices do not cause disparate impact or that the practice is job-related and a business necessity. The plaintiffs may also show that an alternative practice was proposed which would not have disparate impact which the employer refused to accept. The employer then has the

burden of showing that the alternative could not be used because of business necessity.

The evidence of discrimination in disparate impact cases usually focus on statistical disparities rather than specific cases. The decision concerning whether an employment practice causes significant disparity is best decided by following the 80 percent guideline utilized by the Equal Employment Opportunity Commission (EEOC). Some courts use a standard deviation test to determine whether the disparity is two or three standard deviations from the mean. Two deviations show disparity and three show gross disparity. The 80 percent rule, however, is used in the majority of cases and in all investigations by the EEOC.

The new civil rights act restored the guidelines of discrimination suits to what they were prior to *Wards Cove*, but it did not address the comparison bases to be used in determining disparity. Thus, the holdings in *Wards Cove* remain in effect. In *Dothard v. Rawlinson* (1977), the Court allowed the comparison to be between the affected group and the general population. In *New York City Transit Authority v. Beazer* (1979), the Court accepted measures indicating the racial composition of otherwise qualified applicants for at-issue jobs. *In Wards Cove,* the Court held that the proper comparison is between the racial composition in the relevant job market and the racial composition of the at-issue jobs. The Court acknowledged that if the proper statistics could not be obtained then alternatives such as those in *Beazer* and *Dothard* could be used.

Affirmative Action

There are two basic interpretations of equal employment opportunity law. The procedural interpretation (disparate treatment) is concerned with the equal treatment of everyone in employment decisions. The substantive interpretation (disparate impact) is concerned with the outcome of agency practices. The former approach considers affirmative action to be inconsistent with Title VII of the Civil Rights Act of 1964 because it gives preferences to minorities or

women. Thus, employers are making race- or gender-based employment decisions, which are prohibited by Title VII. The latter approach considers affirmative action to be required under Title VII because the effects of past discrimination will continue unless an affirmative effort is made by employers to facilitate the incorporation of previously underrepresented groups into the labor force at all levels (Edelman et al., 1991). The procedural approach fails to remedy past discrimination, and the substantive approach may cause some instances of reverse discrimination (McConnell, 1983).

Opponents of affirmative action claim that it is unconstitutional because it is violative of the Equal Protection Clause of the Fourteenth Amendment and is not amenable to rectification by court order (Feagins, 1990; Loury, 1985). Furthermore, it is illegal in that it violates the statutory provisions of Title VII and is destructive because it creates resentment by the effected majority (Feagins, 1990). Proponents of affirmative action maintain that equal treatment of those with different starting points perpetuates the inequality which presently exists and will continue until the vestiges of past discrimination are alleviated (Schwartz, 1984). Justice Powell wrote in *Wygant v. Jackson Board of Education* (1986) that, as part of this nation's dedication to eradicating racial discrimination, innocent persons may be called upon to bear some of the burden of the remedy. In our political system, the majority rules but the rights of minorities must be protected, even if some members of the majority are temporarily disadvantaged (Welch, 1990).

Affirmative action issues were clarified in 1989 by the Court in *City of Richmond v. J.A. Croson Company,* where the Court left no doubt that any race-based classification would be subjected to the strictest judicial scrutiny. The focus of the Court was changed in this case from broad considerations of social class issues to an emphasis on the individual. Generalized past discrimination does not justify affirmative action, and the Court indicated that the use of numerical quota requirements would be viewed as a per se violation of the

mandate to tailor carefully any racial classification.

Much has been written on the differing philosophies fueling the affirmative action controversy and how to tailor affirmative action to meet current legal requirements. Comparatively, little scientific research has been conducted on the effectiveness of such programs in eradicating discrimination. Two representative studies show that the programs are helpful. Lewis (1989) found that affirmative action has significantly increased the representation of blacks in law enforcement. Martin (1991) researched the effect of affirmative action on women in policing and found that the hiring of females had been significantly improved, but not their promotions. Both Lewis and Martin reported significant increases in the frequencies of the protected groups in their studies.

Methodology

This study examines a large sample of law-enforcement officers to examine whether the propositions of disparate impact theory can be supported in law-enforcement employment and whether law-enforcment employers are engaging in discriminatory practices. Analyses address the following issues:

1. Minority members in a sample who have been the victims of discrimination will have achieved a lower level of employment success than whites in the sample, as shown by disparate rates of representation in the rank structure and they will not progress through their career paths commensurately with whites.

2. Those law-enforcement agencies utilizing discriminatory practices will fail to achieve compliance with the 80 percent rule of the EEOC.

This study uses secondary, cross-sectional, individual-level data from the Texas Career Paths Project conducted jointly by Sam Houston State University and the Texas Commission on Law Enforcement Officer Standards and Education

Table 1 Rank Diversity in Advanced or Specialized Positions (N = 5323)

Rank	Total	White		Hispanic		Black		Other	
Chief	62	54	(87.1%)	5	(8.1%)	3	(4.8%)	0	
Captain	166	148	(89.2%)	13	(7.8%)	1	(0.6%)	4	(2.4%)
Lieutenant	464	400	(86.0%)	40	(8.6%)	13	(2.8%)	9	(1.9%)
Sergeant	1,140	911	(79.9%)	128	(11.2%)	51	(4.5%)	26	(2.3%)
Corporal	626	512	(81.8%)	36	(5.8%)	58	(9.3%)	13	(2.1%)
Detective	673	406	(60.3%)	206	(30.6%)	33	(4.9%)	12	(1.8%)
Patrol	1,821	1,298	(71.2%)	330	(18.1%)	141	(7.7%)	32	(1.8%)
Other	371	254	(68.5%)	53	(14.3%)	54	(14.6%)	2	(0.5%)

(TCLEOSE). There are 30 departments in the sample having 7,122 advanced or specialized positions. The return rates ranged from 31 to 100 percent, with an aggregate rate of 75 percent.

Findings and Results

Lack of representative percentages of personnel by race in various law enforcement positions have been attributed to many causes, including the lower test scores by minorities on written examinations (Stahl & Staufenberger, 1974) and the results of past discriminatory practices (Feagins, 1990). The consequences of perceptions of discrimination can be serious, as evidenced in the 1991 Rodney King case (Cannon, 1993) and the recent New York City Amadou Diallo case, where several police officers shot him repeatedly (Jet, 1999). Several studies have documented the minority underrepresentation in police personnel and have detailed the problems caused in crime clearance rates, community relations, use of force, and assignment patterns (Stark, 1972; Wilson, 1968). Table 1 shows the representation of minorities in each rank. Blacks and Hispanics are under represented in the management; 4.8 percent of all blacks and 7.1 percent of all Hispanics served in management-level ranks, compared with 15.1 percent of all whites. Minorities have higher representation in the other category, which usually has less social status.

Diversity Issues in Length of Assignment

Table 2 shows the mean of years in each assignment by the various ethnic groups. Blacks moved through assignment periods faster than all others in assignments 1, 4, 5, 6, and 10. Hispanics moved faster than all others in assignments 3 and 9. Respondents in the other ethnic category moved fastest in assignments 2, 6, 7, and 8. Blacks moved slower than any group in assignment 7. Hispanics moved slowest in assignments 5, 6 and 8. Whites moved the slowest of all groups in assignments 1, 2, 4, 9, and 10. Members of the other category moved slowest in assignment 3. Computing the mean of the mean amount of time spent in each assignment showed blacks moved through their career paths more quickly than any other ethnic group, spending an average of 2.63 years per assignment prior to promotion or transfer. Hispanics were the next quickest group, spending an average of 2.86 years per assignment, while members of the other category were third quickest, spending 2.87 years per assignment. Whites were the slowest group, spending an average of 3.08 years in each assignment.

In summary, the analysis of length of assignment produced findings that blacks proceed through their career paths more quickly than any other ethnic group. Hispanics are the next fastest group, followed by members of the other category. Whites proceed more slowly than any other group, and white males

were the slowest subgroup. The differences between ethnic groups were statistically significant at the .05 level during the first four assignments, which included 4,078 respondents.

Whether these findings show legal race discrimination depends on several legal theories, methods of establishing comparison bases, and evidentiary standards of showing a prima facie case.

Disparate Impact Analysis Model

Four major characteristics from court cases and statutory provisions can be summarized in a model for analysis of disparate impact. (1) The plaintiff challenges an existing employment practice as discriminatory and files suit, (2) the plaintiff incurs the burden of showing a prima facie case of discrimination, (3) after the prima facie case is established, the employer incurs the burden of production in showing the business necessity of the challenged employment practice, (4) the comparison base is between the racial composition of at-issue jobs and the racial composition of the qualified pool of applicants in the relevant job market (EEOC requires that minorities be selected at a rate of 80 percent or more of the rate at which majority applicants are chosen).

For purposes of this study, it is stipulated that a job applicant with standing in the relevant court of jurisdiction challenges an existing employment practice concerning the

Table 2 Length of Assignment by Ethnicity

Total Sample (N = 5323)	Black	Hispanic	White	Other
Assignment 1	4.64	5.08	5.36	4.67
Assignment 2	3.62	3.59	4.21	3.50
Assignment 3	3.20	3.08	3.61	3.71
Assignment 4	2.04	2.83	3.25	2.36
Assignment 5	2.58	3.08	2.87	2.88
Assignment 6	2.69	2.73	2.70	2.63
Assignment 7	2.23	2.21	2.22	1.77
Assignment 8	2.20	2.42	2.25	1.46
Assignment 9	1.87	1.76	2.23	*
Assignment 10	1.25	1.82	2.18	*
mean=	2.63	2.86	3.08	2.87
Mean years of present education	14.77	13.96	14.39	14.80
Mean years of total experience	11.92	13.68	16.02	14.93

*No respondents in the other category were in assignments 9 and 10.

Note: The means for males plus females do not equal total means in the total sample due to inclusion of missing gender cases in the total sample.

department's promotional procedures. The comparison base is between the group comprising existing advanced or specialized officers and all existing officers employed by the agencies. Thus, prima facie discrimination will be determined by comparison of the selection rate of minorities and whites. The selection rate of the minorities must be 80 percent of the selection rate for whites. The model will be applied to length of assignment to determine if there is disparity by ethnicity in the amount of time taken to progress through career paths. It is emphasized that establishing a prima facie case does not necessarily constitute a finding of discrimination.

Results of the Disparate Impact Model

The information in Table 3 compares the selection rates of respondents in four individual departments and in the total sample. Department #1 achieved enviable results. No disparity was found in its selection procedures. It far surpassed the 80 percent rule requiring minorities to be selected at a rate that is 80 percent or better of the majority selection rate. As shown in the table, Department 1 has achieved a high degree of representativeness for all ethnic categories. It also achieved near perfect equality for mean time in assignment by eth-

nicity. The department demonstrates that equality can be accomplished. However, the other three departments incurred varying degrees of difficulty with disparity. Department 2 showed weakness in the number of blacks selected, but the disparity could be alleviated by promoting 2 more blacks. The disparity progressively worsened. Department 3 would have to promote 9 Hispanics and 10 blacks to alleviate disparity; Department 4 would have to promote 19 Hispanics and 10 blacks; and the total sample would have to promote 176 blacks to alleviate disparity statewide.

The model in Table 3 is based on *Wards Cove Packing* provisions, where the comparison is between advanced (at-issue) positions and total officers (qualified labor pool in relevant market). Another interpretation of *Wards Cove* allows the base of comparison to be between the rank being sought (at-issue jobs) and members of the next lower rank (qualified labor pool in the relevant market). It is logical that the later model would produce less disparity in that *Wards Cove* held that it is not discrimination if no minorities are hired due to a "dearth" of qualified applicants. The underrepresentation of minorities in the higher ranks of this study caused a reduction in the degree of disparity using the second model. However, disparate impact is still found in the

total sample on blacks and Hispanics seeking promotion to sergeant, on blacks seeking promotion to lieutenant, and on blacks seeking promotion to captain.

These findings show clearly some of the complexities experienced by law-enforcement administrators. The courts have traditionally considered the statistical composition of higher-level positions in making their decisions. The lack of diversity, however, may be sociological and beyond the control of the administrator. Disparity is found in the rank structure of the total sample, indicating the possibility of discrimination against blacks. An analysis of length of time per assignment, however, shows that blacks proceed through their career paths quicker than any other ethnic group, and no disparity is found in the total sample concerning length of assignment. The career progression is within the control of administrators but rank structure is not, in that minorities may be recruited and still not accept employment with an agency.

Disparate impact theory proposes that minorities may hold lower levels of education due to the continuing effects of past discriminatory practices which barred many minority members from attending schools of their choice. Among study respondents, however, blacks had the highest levels of education and the lowest

Table 3 Analysis of Prima Facie Disparate Impact

Relevant Job Market Compared with At-Issue Jobs*

Dept.	Black		Hispanic		White		Other		Disparity
Dept. 1	89	(24 28%)	599	(163 27%)	882	(248 28%)	2	(2 100%)	No
Dept. 2	23	(3 13%)	32	(9 28%)	129	(30 23%)	0		Yes
Dept. 3	94	(3 3%)	121	(3 2%)	542	(66 12%)	1	(1 100%)	Yes
Dept. 4	178	(2 1%)	478	(12 3%)	2,515	(91 8%)	15	(3 20%)	Yes
Total	3,016	(354 12%)	3,909	(811 21%)	18,279	(3,983 22%)	145	(98 68%)	Yes
Time in Assign.	2.63		2.86		3.08		2.87		No

	Mean Time in Assignment			Mean Education			Experience		
	Blk	**Hisp**	**Wht**	**Blk**	**Hisp**	**Wht**	**Blk**	**Hisp**	**Wht**
Dept. 1	3.50	3.34	3.50	13.92	13.82	13.68	14	15	18
Dept. 2	1.80	3.48	3.82	15.00	13.77	13.70	09	13	15
Dept. 3	1.65	3.63	1.95	14.66	14.00	13.60	05	10	10
Dept. 4	6.50	4.50	5.71	16.00	14.45	14.80	18	19	25
Total	2.63	2.86	3.08	14.77	13.96	14.39	12	14	16

*Analysis conducted on one large police department (1), one other police department (2), one sheriff's office (3), one state law enforcement agency (4), and the total sample (Total).

**Ethnic composition of relevant job market (present total number of officers) provided by TCLEOSE. At-issue job frequencies taken from survey data.

amount of law-enforcement experience, and they progressed through their career paths significantly faster than whites. However, analysis of rank representation by ethnicity shows prima facie disparate impact discrimination in the total sample. It should be noted that, while the higher educational accomplishments of blacks in the sample is encouraging, it may also be explained by the need for blacks to have achieved higher education to gain promotions that were given to others without such educational level and is still not sufficient to increase diversity at the top rank levels.

Implications of Findings

The application of the statistical analyses to a disparate impact model found disparity in some departments and in the total sample. Statistical findings of disparity are important because they can establish a prima facie case of discrimination shifting to the employer the burden of proving that the challenged practice is not discriminatory or is a business necessity.

The data in this study support a conclusion that the only positive indicators of discrimination are beyond the complete control of police man-

agement. *Wards Cove* held that the comparison base is between at-issue jobs and the qualified pool of applicants in the relevant job market. In this study, there are many examples where the qualified pool of applicants contained no minority members; thus, there is no legal discrimination if a majority member is selected.

The sensitivity of police managers to the discrimination issue appears to have been addressed to some extent in the larger departments and in the sheriffs' offices where there is an overrepresentation of blacks in entry-level jobs. Furthermore, all ethnic and gender groups are progressing through their career paths at a faster rate than the majority group. The data do not show whether all police administrators are aggressively recruiting minorities, but it is shown that, in the large departments having the resources to recruit, the overall personnel composition is very close to that of the communities they serve. In smaller agencies where the funding may not be present, the degree of representation is less. Police administrators without the funds to recruit and with nonrepresentative personnel may be discriminatory or may be

frustrated because of the inability beyond administrative control to attract minority applicants.

According to the theory of disparate impact, the effects of past discrimination can be alleviated by providing affirmative action to qualified minority members. The alleviation of the effects of past discrimination operates primarily through affirmative action programs based on goals and timetables. Commonly, those timetables call for the goals to be obtained in fifteen or twenty years. If the theory is correct in its primary premise, then a replication of this study in twenty years should find the level of differential distribution of personnel by race significantly reduced.

List of Authorities

Brown v. Board of Education, 349 U.S. 294 (1954).
City of Richmond v. J.A. Croson Co., 488 U.S. 469 (1989).
Dothard v. Rawlinson, 433 U.S. 321 (1977).
Furnco Construction Co. v. Waters, 438 U.S. 557 (1979).
Griggs v. Duke Power Company, 401 U.S. 424 (1971).
International Brotherhood of Teamsters v. U.S., 431 U.S. 324 (1977).
McDonnell Douglas v. Green, 411 U.S. 807 (1973).

New York City Transit Authority v. Beazer, 440 U.S. 568 (1979).

Plessey v. Ferguson, 163 U.S. 537 (1896).

Texas Department of Community Affairs v. Burdine, 450 U.S. 248 (1981).

Wards Cove Packing v. Atonio, 490 U.S. 642 (1989).

Wygant v. Jackson Board of Education, 476 U.S. 267 (1986).

References

Abraham, H.J. 1987. *The Judiciary*. Dubuque, Iowa: Wm. C. Brown Publishers, 173–199.

Black, H. C. 1989. *Black's Law Dictionary*. St. Paul, Minn.: West Publishing Co.

Cannon, L. 1993. "Jury Selection Begins in Trial of L.A. Officers." *The Washington Post*. February 4, A3.

Caplovitz, D. 1967. *The Poor Pay More*. New York: The Free Press.

Carlson, S. M. 1992. "Trends in Race/Sex Occupational Inequality: Conceptual and Measurement Issues." Social Problems 39: 268–285.

Carney, J. P. 1972. *Nation of Change*. New York: Harper and Row Publishers, Inc.

Edleman et al. 1991. "Legal Ambiguity and the Politics of Compliance: Affirmative Action Officer's Dilemma." *Law and Policy* 13 (1):73–81.

Feagins, Ken. 1990. "Some Current Thoughts on Public Samesin Affirmative Action and Our Segregated Society." *Texas Bar Journal* 4: 1333–1334.

Hadley, Ernest C. 1990. *A Guide to Federal Sector Equal Employment Law and Practice*. New York: Dewey Publications, Inc.

Jet. 1999. "White New York Cops Shot 41 Times and Killed Unarmed Black Man." *Jet* 95 (February 22): 15.

Lewis, W.G. 1989. in Susan E. Martin. 1991. "The Effectiveness of Affirmative Action: The Case of Women in Policing." *Justice Quarterly* 4: 489–503.

Loury, Glen C. 1985. "Beyond Civil Rights." *The New Republic* as quoted in George McKenna and Stanley Feingold. 1989. *Taking Sides*. Guilford, Conn.: Dushkin Publishing Group, Inc.

Martin, S. 1991. "The Effectiveness of Affirmative Action: Women in Policing." *Justice Quarterly* 4: 489–503.

McConnell, D. M. 1983. "Title VII at Twenty—The Unsettled Dilemma of Reverse Discrimination." *Wake Forest Law Review* 3: 1073–1083.

Paetzold, R.L., & Steven L. Willborn. 1996. "Deconstructing Disparate Impact: A View of the Model Through New Lenses." *North Carolina Law Review* 74: 325.

Panken, Peter M. 1992. *Labor and Employment Law Update: Civil Rights Act of 1991*. New York: The American Law Institute.

Schwartz, Herman. 1984. "In Defense of Affirmative Action" in George McKenna and Stanley Feingold. 1989. *Taking Sides*. Guilford, Conn.: Dushkin Publishing Group, Inc.

Silberman, Charles E. 1978. *Criminal Violence: Criminal Justice*. New York: Vintage Books.

Stahl, O. Glenn, and Richard A. Staufenberger. 1974. *Police Personnel Administration*. North Scituate, Mass.: Duxbury Press.

Stark, Rodney. 1972. *Police Riots*. Belmont, Calif.: Wadsworth Publishing Company, Inc.

Welch, Terrence S. 1990. "Affirmative Action Benefits the Entire Nation." *Texas Bar Journal* 4: 1335–1336.

Wilson, James Q. 1968. *Varieties of Police Behavior* as quoted in Rodney Stark. 1972. *Police Riots*. Belmont, Calif.: Wadsworth Publishing Company, Inc.

Youngblood, M.K. 1990. "Title VII: The Theories and Burdens of Employment Discrimination." *Texas Bar Journal* 12: 1323–1325.

 Article Review Form at end of book.

WiseGuide Wrap-Up

- Black Americans are underrepresented in the judiciary and overrepresented in the nation's penal colonies.

- The full articulation between race and crime is essential for research and education in the field of criminology.

- Crime cannot and should not be studied as if there were only two racial categories.

- The phrase "black-on-black" crime is overutilized and often out of context.

R.E.A.L. sites

This list provides a print preview of typical **Coursewise** R.E.A.L. sites. (There are over 100 such sites at the **Courselinks**™ site.) The danger in printing URLs is that web sites can change overnight. As we went to press, these sites were functional using the URLs provided. If you come across one that isn't, please let us know via email to: webmaster@coursewise.com. Use your Passport to access the most current list of R.E.A.L. sites at the **Courselinks** site.

Site name: National Multicultural Institute

URL: http://www.nmci.org/links.htm

Why is it R.E.A.L.? This site provides a virtual tour of the civil rights movement in the United States. In addition, it offers a wide selection of links to several sites that discuss various dimensions of multiculturalism in detail.

Key topics: civil rights, African Americans, Martin Luther King, multiculturalism, diversity training

Try this: What contribution was made to the civil rights of blacks in *Brown vs. Board of Education?* What precipitated the Montgomery Bus Boycott of 1955–1956?

Site name: Race and Racism in American Law

URL: http://www.udayton.edu/~race/

Why is it R.E.A.L? This site offers a discussion on the relationship between race and the American law. It includes statutes, legal cases, and excerpts from law review articles pertaining to race and racism. This site also contains numerous race/law-related links.

Key topics: racial discrimination, drugs, race, law, affirmative action, gender

Try this: What is a minority group? Define *race.* Who made the statement that all men are descendants from Adam, no matter how strange they appear?

Site name: PBS Online Newshour Race Relations

URL: http://www.pbs.org/newshour/bb/race_relations/race_relations.html

Why is it R.E.A.L? This site offers up-to-date information on various aspects of race and racism. Specifically, it contains stories on prison gangs, discrimination, and racism in the judical branch, and covers most issues of the race and crime dilemma.

Key topics: race, crime, politics, violence, civil rights, hate crimes, law, racial discrimination

Try this: Discuss the newly discovered scientific evidence about Thomas Jefferson and Sally Hemings. Discuss some of the complexities surrounding President Truman's historic decision to integrate the military.

section 2

Learning Objectives

After studying this section, you will know

- that both African Americans and whites agree that crime is an important problem that is not being properly addressed and that race relations need improvement.

- that the urban poverty of the ghettos has produced social problems such as crime.

- that it is alleged that Africans have the highest crime rate internationally, while Asians have the least.

- that African American adolescent males and young adults continue to be victims of institutionalized racism and violence.

- that high incidents of violence, especially homicide, can best be examined by racial and economic discrimination.

Causes of Crime: Does Race Matter?

 If we study the history of the United States, we may be left with the impression that America was built on violence. In fact, since the birth of this nation, on both domestic and foreign fronts, there has been a trend of violence by and against the American people. Despite this, at no other time in history have the American people been as concerned about violent episodes on the domestic front as they are today. Recently, school shootings have led to public outcries demanding the control or regulation of handguns, arcade games, and videos. In addition, citizens are increasingly demanding "reasons" to help them explain why humans are capable of committing such atrocities.

The public demand for explanations has found a receptive audience in the academic world, as scholars attempt to better understand the "causes" of violence and criminality. Some of these scholars have suggested that, to better understand criminal behavior, we must examine carefully individuals who commit crimes the most: African Americans and Hispanics. Thus, the major questions here are: What causes crime, and does race matter? One might argue that violence predisposes us to crime, that bigotry results in hate crimes, that capitalism breeds greed, and that greed results in the commission of some offenses. Some argue that crime is a rational response to social inequalities, while others posit the notion that labeling, conflict, and disorganization result in crime. In addition, some emphasize the importance of family and education and argue that, without either, individuals are at greater risk. What is the impact of segregation and the migration of industry from the inner city to suburban America? The point is simply that there are several plausible explanations for crime, especially for the criminal incidents committed by members of minority groups, and that it is critical for students to be familiar with the different perspectives.

In this section, we explore the hypothesis that the loss of family values is a contributing factor in the minority crime causation equation. The theme "family disintegration" is not at the core of our philosophy; it is simply offered as one of many "think pieces" in the reader. We encourage you to recognize that even this hypothesis is tenuous. Other possible factors may cause crime among minority members: One contributing factor is the labeling and use of stereotypes. Another factor may be that aggressive patrolling practices that target minority-populated areas may influence the overrepresentation of blacks and other minorities in the criminal justice system. One of the readings in this section incorporates some of the classical arguments used to explain the rates of crime in American society. It is widely believed that the unemployed and unskilled are at risk for criminal conduct. Restated, the absence of meaningful jobs and unskilled laborers, coupled with despair, may predispose some to theft/robbery or to the selling of drugs as a source of income. In this equation, the loss of industry to suburban areas, leaving behind low-income neighborhoods that are economically depressed, thereby marginalizes a race. Where jobs exist, there is competition within and between minority groups in these neighborhoods. The partial solution, it seems, is that the government needs to invest in cities, by creating opportunities for home ownership and free enterprise zones. These free enterprise zones should be strategically located, providing tax incentives for industry to return to the inner city. It is worth noting that the transformation of our cities has had an impact on crime rates. William Julius Wilson (a black scholar at Harvard) maintains that white and black flight, especially loss of the black middle class to the suburbs, has resulted in the loss of role models and buffers to abate high feelings of despair.

It is important for you, the criminal justice student, to understand that the relationship between race and crime involves the interactions of several theories or perspectives. A study of recent trends may also contribute to a better understanding of this phenomenon. In fact, recent statistics have shown that the income disparity between whites and minority members is wider today than it was years ago. Thus, it is not hard to believe that the "rage" among the black middle class is very real. After reading the articles in this section, you should be left with the understanding that, in today's American society, there are strong economic, cultural, and structural reasons for black criminality and that no one "reason" alone can explain this phenomenon.

? Questions ?

Reading 8. Discuss how blacks and whites differ in opinion regarding the proper method to reduce criminality.

Reading 9. What are some of the problems associated with the high joblessness and declining social organization in inner-city ghetto neighborhoods?

Reading 10. What are some of the explanations given to justify the overrepresentation of blacks in criminal incidents at the national and international levels?

Reading 11. Discuss the alleged violent nature of the 365 years of African involvement in the Americas.

Reading 12. Which explanation offered in the literature on the high rate of homicides among blacks makes the strongest argument? Why?

Discuss how blacks and whites differ in opinion regarding the proper method to reduce criminality.

Races Worry about Crime and Values, Disagree on Government

What emerges from a *Wall Street Journal*/NBC News poll on black and white America is a picture of an America in which blacks and whites agree, at least superficially, on much: the importance of the crime problem, a sense that some but not nearly enough progress has been made in race relations in recent years and a feeling that integration as a goal isn't as important as it once was.

The survey suggests that blacks may be more inclined than whites to agree with the likes of Republicans William Bennett and Dan Quayle on the severity of some social problems. More blacks than whites say that the quality of public schools and the phenomenon of children being raised in single-parent households are very serious problems. The two races are about even—74% of blacks and 70% of whites—in citing welfare dependency as a particularly serious problem, according to the survey, conducted by Democratic pollster Peter Hart and Republican Robert Teeter.

But there is a big gap on the approach society should take toward solving such problems. By significant margins, blacks feel that government should play a substantial role in attacking the economic distress they view as the root of society's problems. Whites are more likely to see the nation's problems as based in moral decline, and to see a far lesser

role for government in solving most of those problems.

A majority of blacks, 53%, say the country's social and economic problems are mainly the result of financial pressures on families. By contrast, a majority of whites, 58%, say those problems are mainly the result of a decline in moral values. (The lowest-income whites are somewhat more inclined to cite financial pressures rather than moral values as the cause of social problems, but still cite that reason less often than blacks do.) And whereas 30 years ago black activism was focused intensely on integrating society, blacks today seem less convinced than whites that their basic problems will be solved simply through more integration.

And to the extent that whites make presumptions about what blacks want government to do, they may have it wrong. Blacks don't seem to want the government to create programs; asked to pick among several possible causes for continuing poverty in America's cities, just 7% cited a lack of government funding and programs. Instead, blacks tend to say the government is responsible for creating jobs and other economic opportunities.

In the survey, 65% of whites and 70% of blacks agreed that there has been some or a lot of progress in easing racial tensions in the past 10 years.

The one area in which there seems to be a striking convergence is in what politicians call social values.

Blacks and whites were in virtual agreement on the severity of problems of drugs and violent crime, with 97% of blacks calling violent crime a very serious or most serious problems, while 92% of whites did so. And while 37% of whites rated the phenomenon of children being raised in single-parent households as a very serious or most serious problems, 55% of blacks said it was.

But the convergence of views breaks down on questions about economics, and there are hints of new thinking all around on the fundamental questions of integration.

In the *Journal*/NBC News survey, blacks clearly showed their belief that government has to play a role in creating jobs. Asked which institution—government, business, community groups or individuals—has the greatest responsibility for creating jobs and strengthening the economy, a solid 67% of blacks cited the government. That sentiment was more pronounced among lower-income blacks but only slightly so. Among blacks making under $30,000 a year, 71% cited government, while 60% of those making more than $30,000 did so.

Across the board, whites were less inclined to cite government's responsibility. Just 41% cited government as the institution with the greatest responsibility for creating jobs and economic strength, while 37% named the business community. Even among the poorest whites, only about half cited the government's responsibility.

In dealing with inner-city problems in particular, blacks are more likely to see the need for government intervention, while whites think private initiatives are more useful. Among blacks, 68% called for a greater emphasis on government spending on education and training programs for the inner cities, while just 36% of whites thought those were the right areas for emphasis. A majority of whites said the better option would be to emphasize "private initiative and personal responsibility by people living in the inner cities."

Rethinking Integration

As blacks and whites ponder the persistence of America's social problems, they seem to agree that broader integration of American society is an important goal. But there also seems to be some rethinking among blacks that perhaps integration shouldn't be as high a priority as building up black economic and social institutions.

Among whites, 70% say that racial integration has been good for society, while a similar share of blacks, 65%, also say that integration has been good. But a slightly larger minority of blacks than whites, 23% to 17%, say racial integration has been bad for society.

Whatever the areas of agreement between blacks and whites on hot-button social issues, the survey suggests one area where perceptions are different. Asked whether blacks or whites are more likely to receive welfare benefits, 47% of whites say blacks are more likely, while 30% of blacks say African-Americans are more likely to receive them.

In reality, both groups are partly right. The number of whites on welfare exceeds the number of blacks. Whites comprise 38.9% of Aid to Families with Dependent Children recipients, slightly above the 37.2% of recipients who are black, according to the Department of Health and Human Services. But because blacks make up just 12.1% of the overall American population, the share of the black population on welfare easily outstrips the white share.

In any event, blacks and white alike seem to have grasped one reality of life in America today: blacks are more likely to be the victims of crime. Crime statistics collected by the Federal Bureau of Investigation indicate that 49.6% of the nations' murder victims in 1992 were black, while 47.2% of the victims were white.

And when asked in the survey who is more likely to be a victim of crime, 53% of blacks said they were; 46% of whites agreed.

 Article Review Form at end of book.

What are some of the problems associated with the high joblessness
and declining social organization in inner-city ghetto neighborhoods?

The Political Economy and Urban Racial Tensions

William Julius Wilson

Recent books such as Andrew
Hacker's *Two Nations* (1992) and
Derrick Bell's *Faces at the Bottom of
the Well* (1992) promote the view
that racial antagonisms are so deep
seated, so primordial that feelings
of pessimism about whether
America can overcome racist sentiments and actions are justified. The
events surrounding the recent rebel-
lion in Los Angeles, the worst race
riot in the nation's history, aggravated these feelings. However, in
this atmosphere of heightened racial
awareness we forget or overlook the
fact that racial antagonisms are
products of situations—economic
situations, political situations, and
social situations.

To understand the manifestation of racial antagonisms during certain periods, is to comprehend, from
both analytic and policy perspectives, the situations that increase and
reduce them. As revealed in the title I
have chosen for this paper ("The

William Julius Wilson was the recipient of
the 1994 Frank E. Seidman Distinguished
Award in Political Economy, based at
Rhodes College. The 1994 Selection
Committee included Kenneth J. Arrow,
James Buchanan, Vernon L. Smith, James
Tobin and Harold F. Williamson, Jr. The
Award Director is Mel G. Grinspan. William
Julius Wilson is Lucy Flower University
Professor of Sociology and Public Policy at
the University of Chicago.

Political Economy and Urban Racial
Tensions"), I shall try to demonstrate
this important point by showing how
the interrelations of political policies
and economic and social processes
directly and indirectly affect racial
tensions in urban America. In the tradition of the Seidman Award, this
paper integrates insights from economics and the other social sciences
not only in the analysis of urban
racial tensions, but in the presentation of policy options as well.

Political Policies, Economic Processes and the City-Suburban Racial Divide

Since 1960, the proportion of whites
inside central cities has decreased
steadily, while the proportion of minorities has increased. In 1960 the nation's population was evenly divided
between cities, suburbs, and rural
areas (Weir 1993). By 1990, both
urban and rural populations had declined, leaving suburbs with nearly
half of the nation's population. The
urban population dipped to 31 percent by 1990. As cities lost population
they became poorer and more minority in their racial and ethnic composition. Thus in the eyes of many in the
dominant white population, the minorities symbolize the ugly urban
scene left behind. Today, the divide

between the suburbs and the city is,
in many respects, a racial divide. For
example, whereas 68 percent of all
the residents in the city of Chicago
were minority in 1990—blacks
(1,074,471), Hispanics (545,852), and
Asian & others (152,487) and whites
(1,056,048)—83 percent of all suburban residents in the Chicago metropolitan area were white. Across the
nation, in 1990, whereas 74 percent of
the dominant white population lived
in suburban and rural areas, a majority of blacks and Latinos resided in
urban areas.

These demographic changes relate to the declining influence of
American cities and provided the
foundation for the New Federalism,
an important political development
that has increased the significance of
race in metropolitan areas. Beginning
in 1980, the federal government dras-
tically reduced its support for basic
urban programs. The Reagan and
Bush administrations sharply cut
spending on direct aid to cities, including general revenue sharing,
urban mass transit, public service
jobs and job training, compensatory
education, social service block grants,
local public works, economic development assistance and urban development action grants. In 1980 the
Federal contribution to city budgets
was 18 percent, by 1990 it had
dropped to 6.4 percent. In addition,
the most recent economic recession
sharply reduced urban revenues that

"The Political Economy and Urban Racial Tension," William Julius Wilson. *American Economist*, Vol. 39, No. 1, 1995. Reprinted by permission.

the cities themselves generated, thereby creating budget deficits that resulted in further cutbacks in basic services and programs, and increases in local taxes (Caraley 1992).

The combination of the New Federalism, which resulted in the sharp cuts in federal aid to local and state governments, and the recession created for many cities, especially the older cities of the East and Mid-West, the worst fiscal and service crisis since the Depression. Cities have become increasingly under-serviced and many have been on the brink of bankruptcy. They have therefore not been in a position to combat effectively three unhealthy social conditions that have emerged or become prominent since 1980: (1) the outbreaks of crack-cocaine addiction and the murders and other violent crimes that have accompanied them; (2) the AIDS epidemic and its escalating public health costs; and (3) the sharp rise in the homeless population not only for individuals, but for whole families as well (Caraley 1990).

Fiscally strapped cities have had to watch in helpless frustration as these problems escalated during the 1980s and made the larger city itself seem like a less attractive place in which to live. Accordingly, many urban residents with the economic means have followed the worn-out path from the central city to the suburbs and other areas, thereby shrinking the tax base and further reducing city revenue.

The growing suburbanization of the population influences the extent to which national politicians will support increased federal aid to large cities and to the poor. Indeed, we can associate the sharp drop in federal support for basic urban programs since 1980 with the declining political influence of cities and the rising influence of electoral coalitions in the suburbs (Weir 1993). Suburbs cast 36 percent of the vote for President in 1968, 48 percent in 1988, and a majority of the vote in the 1992 election.

In each of the three presidential elections prior to the 1992 election, the Democratic presidential candidate scored huge majorities in the large cities only to lose an overwhelming majority of the states where these cities were located. This naked reality is one of the reasons why the successful Clinton Presidential campaign de-signed a careful strategy to capture more support from voters who do not reside in central cities.

However, although there is a clear racial divide between the central city and the suburbs, racial tensions in the metropolitan areas continue to be concentrated in the central city. They affect the relations and patterns of interaction between blacks, other minorities, and the whites who remain, especially lower income whites.

Racial Tensions in the Central City

Like inner-city minorities, lower-income whites have felt the full impact of the urban fiscal crisis in the United States. Moreover, lower-income whites are more constrained by financial exigencies to remain in the central city than their middle-class counterparts and thereby suffer the strains of crime, higher taxes, poorer services, and inferior public schools. Furthermore, unlike the more affluent whites who choose to remain in the wealthier sections of the central city, they cannot easily escape the problems of deteriorating public schools by sending their children to private schools, and this problem has grown with the sharp decline in urban parochial schools in the United States.

Many of these people originally bought relatively inexpensive homes near their industrial jobs. Because of the deconcentration of industry, the racially changing neighborhood bordering their communities, the problems of neighborhood crime, and the surplus of central-city housing created by the population shift to the suburbs, housing values in their neighborhoods have failed to keep pace with those in the suburbs. As the industries that employ them become suburbanized, a growing number of lower-income whites in our central cities find that not only are they trapped in their neighborhoods because of the high costs of suburban housing, but they are physically removed from job opportunities as well. This situation increases the potential for racial tension as they compete with blacks and the rapidly growing Latino population for access to and control of the remaining decent schools, housing, and neighborhoods in the fiscally strained central city.

Thus the racial struggle for power and privilege in the central city is essentially a struggle between the have-nots; it is a struggle over access to and control of decent housing and decent neighborhoods, as exposed by the black-white friction over attempts to integrate the working-class ethnic neighborhoods of Marquette Park on Chicago's South Side; it is a struggle over access to and control of local public schools, as most dramatically demonstrated in the racial violence that followed attempts to bus black children from the Boston ghettos of Roxbury and Dorchester to the working-class neighborhoods of South Boston and Charlestown in the 1970s; finally, it is a struggle over political control of the central city, as exhibited in cities like Chicago, Newark, Cleveland, and New York in recent years when the race of the mayoralty candidate was the basis for racial antagonism and fear that engulfed the election campaign.

In some cases the conflicts between working-class whites and blacks are expressed in ethnic terms. Thus in a city such as Chicago white working-class ethnics are stressing that their ethnic institutions and unique ways of life are being threatened by black encroachment on their neighborhoods, the increase of black crime, and the growth of black militancy. The emphasis is not simply that blacks pose a threat to whites but that they also pose a threat to, say, the Polish in Gage Park, the Irish in Brighton Park, the Italians in Cicero, or the Serbians, Rumanians, and Croatians in Hegewich. These communities are a few of the many ethnic enclaves in the Chicago area threatened by the possibilities of a black invasion, and their response has been to stress not only the interests of whites but the interests of their specific ethnic group as well. The primary issue is whether neighborhood ethnic churches and private ethnic schools can survive if whites leave their communities in great numbers and move either to other parts of the cities or to the suburbs. The threatened survival of ethnic social clubs and the possible loss of ethnic friends are also crucial issues that contribute to the anxiety in these communities.

Although the focus of much of the racial tension has been on black and white encounters, in many urban neighborhoods incidents of ethnic antagonisms involve Latinos. According to several demographic projections, the Latino population, which in 1990 had exceeded 22 million in the United States, will replace African-Americans as the nation's largest minority group between 1997 and 2005. They already outnumber African-Americans in Houston and Los Angeles and are rapidly approaching the number of blacks in Dallas and New York. In cities as different as Houston, Los Angeles, and Philadelphia "competition between blacks and Hispanic citizens over the drawing of legislative districts and the allotment of seats is intensifying" (Rohter 1993, p. 11). In areas of changing populations, Latino residents increasingly complain that black officials currently in office cannot represent their concerns and interests (Rohter 1993).

The tensions between blacks and Latinos in Miami, as one example, have emerged over competition for jobs and government contracts, the distribution of political power, and claims on public services. It would be a mistake to view the encounters between the two groups solely in racial terms, however. In Dade County there is a tendency for the black Cubans, Dominicans, Puerto Ricans, and Panamanians to define themselves by their language and culture and not by the color of their skin. Indeed, largely because of the willingness of Hispanic whites and Hispanic blacks to live together and mix with Haitians and other Caribbean blacks in neighborhoods relatively free of racial tension, Dade County is experiencing the most rapid desegregation of housing in the nation (Rohter 1993).

On the other hand, native-born, English speaking African-Americans continue to be the most segregated group in Miami. They are concentrated in neighborhoods that represent high levels of joblessness and clearly identifiable pockets of poverty in the northeast section of Dade County (Rohter 1993). Although there has been some movement of higher income groups from these neighborhoods in recent years, the poorer blacks are more likely to be trapped because of the combination of extreme economic marginality and residential segregation.

Race and the New Urban Poverty

The problems faced by blacks in poor segregated communities are even more severe in the older cities of the East and Midwest. Indeed, there is a new poverty in our nation's metropolises that has far ranging consequences for the quality of life in urban areas, including race relations. By the "new urban poverty," I mean poor segregated neighborhoods in which a substantial majority of individual adults are either unemployed or have dropped out of the labor force. For example, in 1990 only one in three adults (35%) ages 16 and over in the twelve Chicago community areas with poverty rates that exceeded 40 percent held a job.[1] Each of these community areas, located on the South and West sides of the city, is overwhelmingly black. We can add to these twelve high jobless areas three additional predominantly black community areas, with rates of poverty of 29, 30 and 36 percent respectively, where only four in ten (42%) adults worked in 1990. Thus, in these fifteen black community areas, representing a total population of 425,125, only 37 percent of all the adults were gainfully employed in 1990. By contrast, 54 percent of the adults in the seventeen other predominantly black community areas in Chicago, with a total population of 545,408, worked in 1990. This was close to the city-wide figure of 57 percent. Finally, except for one largely Asian community area with an employment rate of 46 percent, and one largely Latino community area with an employment rate of 49 percent, a majority of the adults held a job in each of the forty-five other community areas of Chicago.[2]

To repeat, the new urban poverty represents poor segregated neighborhoods in which a substantial majority of the adults are not working. To illustrate the magnitude of the changes that have occurred in inner-city ghetto neighborhoods in recent years, let me take the three Chicago community areas (Douglas, Grand Boulevard and Washington Park) featured in St. Clair Drake and Horace Cayton's classic book entitled *Black Metropolis*, published in 1945. These three community areas, located on the South Side of the city of Chicago, represent the historic core of Chicago's black belt.

A majority of adults were gainfully employed in these three areas in 1950, five years after the publication of *Black Metropolis*, but by 1990 only four in ten in Douglas worked, one in three in Washington Park, and one in four in Grand Boulevard. In 1950, 69 percent of all males 14 and over worked in the Bronzeville neighborhoods of Douglas, Grand Boulevard, and Washington Park, by 1990 only 37 percent of all males 16 and over held jobs in these three neighborhoods.[3]

Upon the publication of the first edition of *Black Metropolis* in 1945, there was much greater class integration in the black community. As Drake and Cayton pointed out, Bronzeville residents had limited success in "sorting themselves out into broad community areas designated as 'lower class' and 'middle class' . . . Instead of middle class areas, Bronzeville tends to have middle-class buildings in all areas, or a few middle class blocks here and there" (pp. 658–660). Though they may have lived on different streets, blacks of all classes in inner-city areas such as Bronzeville lived in the same community and shopped at the same stores. Their children went to the same schools and played in the same parks. Although there was some class antagonism, their neighborhoods were more stable than the inner-city neighborhoods of today; in short, they featured higher levels of social organization.

By 'social organization' I mean the extent to which the residents of a neighborhood are able to maintain effective social control and realize their common values. There are two major dimensions of neighborhood social organization: (1) the prevalence, strength, and interdependence of social networks; and (2) the extent of collective supervision that the residents direct and the personal responsibility they assume in addressing neighborhood problems (Sampson 1992).

Both formal institutions and informal networks reflect social organization. In other words, neighborhood social organization depends on the extent of local friendship ties, the degree of social cohesion, the level of resident participation in formal and informal voluntary associations, the density and stability of formal organizations, and the nature of informal social controls. Neighborhoods that integrate the adults by an extensive set of obligations, expectations, and social networks are in a better position to control and supervise the activities and behavior of children, and monitor developments—e.g., the breaking up of congregations of youth on street corners and the supervision of youth leisure time activities (Sampson 1992).

Neighborhoods plagued with high levels of joblessness are more likely to experience problems of social organization. The two go hand-in-hand. High rates of joblessness trigger other problems in the neighborhood that adversely affect social organization, ranging from crime, gang violence, and drug trafficking to family break-ups and problems in the organization of family life. Consider, for example, the problems of drug trafficking and violent crime. As many studies have revealed, the decline of legitimate employment opportunities among inner-city residents builds up incentives to sell drugs (Fagan 1993). The distribution of crack in a neighborhood attracts individuals involved in violence and other crimes. Violent persons in the crack marketplace help shape its social organization and its impact on the neighborhood. Neighborhoods plagued by high levels of joblessness, insufficient economic opportunities, and high residential mobility are unable to control the volatile drug market and the violent crimes related to it (Fagan 1993, Sampson 1986). As informal controls weaken in such areas, the social processes that regulate behavior change (Sampson 1988).

A more direct relationship between joblessness and violent crime is revealed in recent longitudinal research by Delbert Elliott (1992) of the University of Colorado, a study based on National Youth Survey data from 1976 to 1989, covering ages 11 to 30. As Elliott (1992) points out, the transition from adolescence to adulthood usually results in a sharp drop in most crimes, including serious violent behavior, as individuals take on new adult roles and responsibilities. "Participation in serious violent offending (aggravated assault, forcible rape, and robbery) increases from ages 11 to 12 to ages 15 and 16 then declines dramatically with ad-

vancing age" (Elliott 1992, p. 14). Although black and white males reveal similar age curves, "the negative slope of the age curve for blacks after age 20 is substantially less than that of whites" (p. 15).

The black-white differential in the percentage of males involved in serious violent crime, although almost even at age 11, increases to 3:2 over the remaining years of adolescence, and reaches a differential of nearly 4:1 during the late twenties. However, when Elliott (1992) only compared employed black and white males, he found no significant differences between the two groups in rates of suspension or termination of violent behavior by age 21. Employed black males experienced a precipitous decline in serious violent behavior following their adolescent period. Accordingly, a major reason for the substantial overall racial gap in the termination of violent behavior following the adolescent period is the large proportion of jobless black males, whose serious violent behavior was more likely to extend into adulthood.[4] The new poverty neighborhoods feature a high concentration of jobless males and, as a result, experience rates of violent criminal behavior that exceed those of other urban neighborhoods.

Also, consider the important relationship between joblessness and the organization of family life. Work is not simply a way to make a living and support one's family. It also constitutes the framework for daily behavior and patterns of interaction because of the disciplines and regularities it imposes. Thus in the absence of regular employment, what is lacking is not only a place in which to work and the receipt of regular income, but also a coherent organization of the present, that is, a system of concrete expectations and goals. Regular employment provides the anchor for the temporal and spatial aspects of daily life. In the absence of regular employment, life, including family life, becomes more incoherent. Persistent unemployment and irregular employment hinder rational planning in daily life, the necessary condition of adaptation to an industrial economy (Bourdieu 1965). This problem is most severe for a jobless family in a low employment neighborhood. The

family's lack of rational planning is more likely to be shared and therefore reinforced by other families in the neighborhood. The problems of family organization and neighborhood social organization are mutually reinforcing.

Factors Associated with the Increase in Neighborhood Joblessness and Decline of Social Organization

Although high jobless neighborhoods also feature concentrated poverty, high rates of neighborhood poverty are less likely to trigger problems of social organization if the residents are working. To repeat, in previous years the working poor stood out in neighborhoods like Bronzeville. Today the non-working poor predominate in such neighborhoods. What accounts for the rise in the proportion of jobless adults in inner-city communities such as Bronzeville?

An easy explanation is racial segregation. However, as we shall soon see, a race-specific argument is not sufficient to explain recent changes in neighborhoods like Bronzeville. After all, Bronzeville was just as segregated in 1950 as it is today, yet the level of employment was much higher back then.

Nonetheless, racial segregation does matter. If large segments of the African-American population had not been historically segregated in inner-city ghettos we would not be talking about the new urban poverty. The segregated ghetto is not the result of voluntary or positive decisions of the residents to live there. As Douglas Massey and Nancy Denton (1993) have carefully documented, the segregated ghetto is the product of systematic racial practices such as restrictive covenants, redlining by banks and insurance companies, zoning, panic peddling by real estate agents, and the creation of massive public housing projects in low-income areas. Moreover, urban renewal and forced migration uprooted many urban black communities. Freeway networks built through the hearts of many cities in the 1950s produced the most dramatic changes. Many viable low-income communities were destroyed. Furthermore, discrimination in employment and inferior educational opportunities further restricted black residential mobility.

Segregated ghettos are less conducive to employment and employment preparation than other areas of the city. Segregation in ghettos exacerbates employment problems because it embraces weak informal employment networks, contributes to the social isolation of individuals and families and therefore reduces their chances of acquiring the human capital skills that facilitate mobility in a society. Since no other group in society experiences the degree of segregation, isolation, and poverty concentration as African-Americans, they are far more likely to be at a disadvantage when they have to compete with other groups in society, including other "discriminated against" groups, for resources and privileges.

But, to repeat, neighborhoods like Bronzeville were highly segregated decades ago when employment rates were much higher. Given the existence of segregation, one then has to account for the ways in which other changes in society interact with segregation to produce the recent escalating rates of joblessness and problems of social organization. Several factors stand out.

Prominent among these is the impact of changes in the economy, changes that have had an adverse effect on poor urban blacks, especially black males. In 1950, 69 percent of all males 14 and over worked in the Bronzeville neighborhoods of Douglas, Grand Boulevard, and Washington Park, and in 1960, 64 percent of this group were employed. However, by 1990 only 37 percent of all males 16 and over held jobs in these three neighborhoods.[5]

Thirty and forty years ago, the overwhelming majority of black males were working. Many of them were poor, but they held regular jobs around which their daily family life was organized. When black males looked for work, employers considered whether they had strong backs because they would be working in a factory or in the back room of a shop doing heavy lifting and labor. They faced discrimination and a job ceiling, but they were working. The

work was hard and they were hired. Now, economic restructuring has broken the figurative back of the black working population.

Data from our Urban Poverty and Family Life Study show that 57 percent of Chicago's employed inner-city black fathers (aged 15 and over and without bachelor degrees) who were born between 1950 and 1955 worked in manufacturing industries in 1974. By 1987 that figure fell to 27 percent. Of those born between 1956 and 1960, 52 percent worked in manufacturing industries as late as 1978. By 1987 that figure had declined to 28 percent.[6]

The loss of traditional manufacturing and other blue-collar jobs in Chicago has resulted in increased joblessness among inner-city black males and a concentration in low-wage, high-turnover laborer and service-sector jobs. Embedded in segregated ghetto neighborhoods that are not conducive to employment, inner-city black males fall further behind their white and their Hispanic male counterparts, especially when the labor market is slack. Hispanics "continue to funnel into manufacturing because employers prefer" them "over blacks, and they like to hire by referrals from current employees, which Hispanics can readily furnish, being already embedded in migration networks" (Krogh, p. 12). Inner-city black men grow bitter about and resent their employment prospects and often manifest or express these feelings in their harsh, often dehumanizing, low-wage work settings.

Their attitudes and actions create the widely shared perception that they are undesirable workers. The perception then becomes the basis for employer decisions to deny them employment, especially when the economy is weak and many workers are seeking jobs. The employment woes of inner-city black males gradually grows over the long term not only because employers are turning more to the expanding immigrant and female labor force, but also because the number of jobs that require contact with the public continues to climb. Because of the increasing shift to service industries, employers have a greater need for workers who can effectively serve and relate to the consumer. Our research reveals that they believe that such qualities are lacking

among black males from segregated inner-city neighborhoods.

The position of inner-city black women in the labor market is also problematic. Their high degree of social isolation in poor segregated neighborhoods, as reflected in social networks, reduces their employment prospects. Although our research indicates that employers consider them more desirable as workers than the inner-city black men, their social isolation decreases their ability to develop language and other job-related skills necessary in an economy that rewards employees who can work and communicate effectively with the public.

The increase in the proportion of jobless adults in the inner city is also related to the outmigration of large numbers of employed adults from working and middle-class families. The declining proportion of non-poor families and increasing and prolonged joblessness in the new poverty neighborhoods make it considerably more difficult to sustain basic neighborhood institutions. In the face of increasing joblessness, stores, banks, credit institutions, restaurants, and professional services lose regular and potential patrons. Churches experience dwindling numbers of parishioners and shrinking resources; recreational facilities, block clubs, community groups, and other informal organizations also suffer. As these organizations decline, the means of formal and informal social control in the neighborhood become weaker. Levels of crime and street violence increase as a result, leading to further deterioration of the neighborhood.

As the neighborhood disintegrates, those who are able to leave do so, including many working and middle-class families. The lower population density created by the outmigration exacerbates the problem. Abandoned buildings increase and provide a haven for crack dens and criminal enterprises that establish footholds in the community. Precipitous declines in density also make it more difficult to sustain or develop a sense of community or for people to experience a feeling of safety in numbers. (Jargowsky 1994:18)

The neighborhoods with many black working families stand in sharp contrast to the new poverty areas. Research that we have conducted on the social organization of Chicago neighborhoods reveals that in addition to much lower levels of perceived unemployment than in the poor neighborhoods, black working and middle class neighborhoods also have much higher levels of perceived social control and cohesion, organizational services and social support.

The rise of new poverty neighborhoods represents a movement from, what the historian Allan Spear (1967) has called an institutional ghetto—which duplicates the structure and activities of the larger society, as portrayed in Drake and Cayton's description of Bronzeville—to an unstable ghetto, which lacks the capability to provide basic opportunities, resources, and adequate social controls.

New Poverty Neighborhoods and Urban Racial Tensions

The problems associated with the high joblessness and declining social organization (e.g., individual crime, hustling activities, gang violence) in inner-city ghetto neighborhoods often spill over into other parts of the city, including the ethnic enclaves. The result is not only hostile class antagonisms in the higher income black neighborhoods near these communities, but heightened levels of racial animosity, especially among lower income white ethnic and Latino groups whose communities border or are in proximity to the high jobless neighborhoods.

The problems in the new poverty neighborhoods have also created racial antagonisms among some of the higher income groups in the city. The new poverty in ghetto neighborhoods has sapped the vitality of local business and other institutions, and it has led to fewer and shabbier movie theaters, bowling alleys, restaurants, public parks and playgrounds, and other recreational facilities. Therefore residents of inner-city neighborhoods more often seek leisure activity in other areas of the city, where they come into brief contact with citizens of different racial, ethnic, or class backgrounds. Sharp differences in cultural style and patterns of interaction that reflect the social isolation of neighborhood networks often lead to clashes.

Some behavior of residents in socially isolated inner-city ghetto neighborhoods—e.g., the tendency to enjoy a movie in a communal spirit by carrying on a running conversation with friends and relatives during the movie or reacting in an unrestrained manner to what they see on the screen—offends the sensibilities of or is considered inappropriate by other groups, particularly the black and white middle classes. Their expression of disapproval, either overtly or with subtle hostile glances, tends to trigger belligerent responses from the inner-city ghetto residents who then purposefully intensify the behavior that is the source of middle-class concerns. The white, and even the black middle class, then exercise their option and exit, to use Albert Hirschman's (1970) term, by taking their patronage elsewhere, expressing resentment and experiencing intensified feelings of racial or class antagonisms as they depart.

The areas left behind then become the domain of the inner-city ghetto residents. The more expensive restaurants and other establishments that serve the higher income groups in these areas, having lost their regular patrons, soon close down and are replaced by fast-food chains and other local businesses that cater to the needs or reflect the economic and cultural resources of the new clientele. White and black middle-class citizens, in particular, complain bitterly abut how certain conveniently located areas of the central city have changed following the influx of ghetto residents.

Demagogic Messages

I want to make a final point about economic, political and social situations that have contributed to the rise of racial antagonisms in urban areas. During periods of hard economic times, it is important that political leaders channel the frustrations of citizens in positive or constructive directions. However, for the last few years just the opposite frequently occurred. In a time of heightened economic insecurities, the negative racial rhetoric of some highly visible white and black spokespersons increased racial tensions and channeled frustrations in ways that severely divide the racial groups. During hard economic times people become more receptive to demagogic messages that deflect attention from the real source of their problems. Instead of associating their declining real incomes, increasing job insecurity, growing pessimism about the future which failed economic and political policies, these messages force them to turn on each other—race against race.

As the new urban poverty has sapped the vitality of many inner-city communities, many of these messages associate inner-city crime, family breakdown and welfare receipt with individual shortcomings. Blame the victim arguments resonate with many urban Americans because of their very simplicity. They not only reinforce the salient belief that joblessness and poverty reflect individual inadequacies, but discourage support for new and stronger programs to combat inner-city social dislocations as well.

What Must Be Done?

I have outlined some of the situations that inflate racial antagonisms in cities like Chicago—namely those that involve the interrelation of recent political policies and economic and social processes (including the emergence of the new urban poverty). Let me conclude this paper with some thoughts on social policy that build on this situational perspective.

I believe that it will be difficult to address racial tensions in our cities unless we tackle the problems of shrinking revenue and inadequate social services, and the gradual disappearance of work in certain neighborhoods. The city has become a less desirable place in which to live, and the economic and social gap between the cities and suburbs is growing. The groups left behind compete, often along racial lines, for the declining resources, including the remaining decent schools, housing, and neighborhoods. The rise of the new urban poverty neighborhoods exacerbates the problems. Their high rates of joblessness and social disorganization create problems that not only affect the residents in these neighborhoods but that spill over into other parts of the larger city as well. All of these factors aggravate race relations and elevate racial tensions.

Ideally it would be great if we could restore the federal contribution to the city budget that existed in 1980, and sharply increase the employment base. However, regardless of changes in federal urban policy, the fiscal crisis in the cities would be significantly eased if the employment base could be substantially increased. Indeed, the social dislocations caused by the steady disappearance of work have led to a wide range of urban social problems, including racial tensions. Increased employment would help stabilize the new poverty neighborhood, halt the precipitous decline in density, and ultimately enhance the quality of race relations in urban areas. The employment situation in inner-city ghetto neighborhoods would improve if the United States' economy, which is now experiencing an upturn, could produce low levels of unemployment over a long period of time.

I say this because in slack labor markets employers are—and indeed, can afford to be—more selective in recruiting and in granting promotions. They overemphasize job prerequisites and exaggerate experience. In such an economic climate, disadvantaged minorities suffer disproportionately and the level of employer discrimination rises. In contrast, in a tight labor market, job vacancies are numerous, unemployment is of short duration, and wages are higher. Moreover, in a tight labor market the labor force expands because increased job opportunities not only reduce unemployment but also draw into the labor force those workers who, in periods when the labor market is slack, respond to fading job prospects by dropping out of the labor force altogether. Accordingly, in a tight labor market the status of disadvantaged minorities improves because of lower unemployment, higher wages, and better jobs (Tobin 1965).

Moreover, affirmative action and other anti-bias programs are more successful in tight labor markets than in slack ones. Not only are sufficient positions available for many qualified workers, but also employers, facing a labor shortage, are not as resistant to affirmative action. Furthermore, a favorable economic climate encourages supporters of affirmative action to push such programs because they perceive greater

chances for success. Finally, non-minority workers are less resistant to affirmative action when there are sufficient jobs available because they are less likely to see minorities as a threat to their own employment.

However, a rising tide does not necessarily lift all boats. Special additional steps to rescue many inner-city residents from the throes of joblessness should be considered, even if the economy remains healthy. Such steps might include the creation of job information data banks in the new poverty neighborhoods and subsidized car pools to increase access to suburban jobs. Training or apprenticeship programs that lead to stable employment should also be considered.

Nonetheless, because of their level of training and education, many of the jobs to which the inner-city poor have access are at or below the minimum wage and are not covered by health insurance. However, recent policies created and proposed by the Clinton Administration could make such jobs more attractive. By 1996, the expanded Earned Income Tax Credit will increase the earnings from a minimum-wage job to $7-an-hour. If this benefit is paid on a monthly basis and is combined with health care, the condition of workers in the low-wage sector would improve significantly, and the rate of employment would rise.

Finally, given the situational basis of much of today's racial tensions, I think that there are some immediate and practical steps that the President of the United States can take to help create the atmosphere for serious efforts and programs to improve racial relations. I am referring to the need for strong political and moral leadership to help combat racial antagonisms. In particular, the need to create and strongly emphasize a message that unites, not divides racial groups.

It is important to appreciate that the poor and the working classes of all racial groups struggle to make ends meet, and even the middle class has experienced a decline in its living standard. Indeed, Americans across racial and class boundaries worry about unemployment and job security, declining real wages, escalating medical and housing costs, child care programs, the sharp decline in the quality of public education, and

crime and drug trafficking in their neighborhoods. Given these concerns, perhaps the President ought to advance a new public rhetoric that does two things: focuses on problems that afflict not only the poor, but the working and middle classes as well; and emphasizes integrative programs that contribute to the social and economic improvement of all groups in society, not just the truly disadvantaged segments of the population. In short a public rhetoric that reflects a vision of racial unity.

The President of the United States has the unique capacity to command nationwide attention from the media and the general public, the capacity to get them to consider seriously a vision of racial unity and of where we are and where we should go.

I am talking about a vision that promotes values of racial and intergroup harmony and unity; rejects the commonly held view that race is so divisive in this country that whites, blacks, Latinos, and other ethnic groups cannot work together in a common cause; recognizes that if a message from a political leader is tailored to a white audience, racial minorities draw back, just as whites draw back when a message is tailored to racial minority audiences; realizes that if the message emphasizes issues and programs that concern the families of all racial and ethnic groups, individuals of these various groups will see their mutual interests and join in a multi-racial coalition to move America forward; promotes the idea that Americans across racial and class boundaries have common interests and concerns including concerns about unemployment and job security, declining real wages, escalating medical and housing costs, child care programs, the sharp decline in the quality of public education, and crime and drug trafficking in neighborhoods; sees the application of programs to combat these problems as beneficial to all Americans, not just the truly disadvantaged among us; recognizes that since demographic shifts have decreased the urban white population and sharply increased the proportion of minorities in the cities, the divide between the suburbs and the central city is, in many respects, a racial divide and that it is vitally important, therefore, to emphasize city-suburban cooperation, not separation; and, finally, pushes the idea that all groups, including those in the throes of the new urban poverty, should be able to achieve full membership in society because the problems of economic and social marginality are associated with inequities in the larger society, not with group deficiencies.

If the President were to promote vigorously this vision, efforts designed to address both the causes and symptoms of racial tensions in cities like New York, Chicago, Philadelphia, Miami, and Los Angeles would have a greater chance for success.

Notes

1. The figures on adult employment presented in this paragraph are based on calculations from data provided by the 1990 U.S. Bureau of the Census and the *Local Community Fact Book for Chicago*, 1950. The adult employment rates represent the number of employed individuals (14 and over in 1950 and 16 over in 1990) among the total number of adults in a given area. Those who are not employed include both the individuals who are members of the labor force but are not working and those who have dropped out or are not part of the labor force. Those who are not in the labor force "consists mainly of students, housewives, retired workers, seasonal workers enumerated in an 'off' season who were not looking for work, inmates of institutions, disabled persons, and persons doing only incidental unpaid family work" (*The Chicago Fact Book Consortium*, 1984, p. xxv).

2. A community area is a statistical unit derived by urban sociologists at the University of Chicago for the 1930 census in order to analyze varying conditions within the city of Chicago. These delineations were originally drawn up on the basis of settlement and history of the area, local identification and trade patterns, local institutions, and natural and artificial barriers. Needless to say, there have been major shifts in population and land use since then. But these units remain useful to trace changes over time, and they continue to capture much of the contemporary reality of Chicago neighborhoods.

3. The figures on male employment are based on calculations from data provided by the 1990 U.S. Bureau of the Census and the *Local Community Fact Book for Chicago*, 1950.

4. In Elliott's study 75 percent of the black males who were employed between the ages of 18–20 had terminated their involvement in violent behavior by age

21, compared to only 52 percent of those who were unemployed between the ages of 18–20. Racial differences remained for persons who were not in a marriage/partner relationship or who were unemployed.

5. The figures on male employment are based on calculations from data provided by the 1990 U.S. Bureau of the Census and the *Local Community Fact Book for Chicago*, 1950.

6. For a discussion of these findings, See Marilyn Krogh, *"A Description of the Work Histories of Fathers Living in the Inner-City of Chicago."* Working paper, Center for the Study of Urban Inequality, University of Chicago, 1993. *The Urban Poverty and Family Life Study* (UPFLS) includes a survey of 2,495 households in Chicago's inner-city neighborhoods conducted in 1987 and 1988; a second survey of a subsample of 175 respondents from the larger survey who were reinterviewed solely with open-ended questions on their perceptions of the opportunity structure and life chances; a survey of a stratified random sample of 185 employers, designed to reflect the distribution of employment across industry and firm size in the Chicago metropolitan area, conducted in 1988; and comprehensive ethnographic research, including participant observation research and life-history interviews conducted in 1987 and 1988 by ten research assistants in a representative sample of black, Hispanic and white inner-city neighborhoods.
   The UPFLS was supported by grants from the Ford Foundation, the Rockefeller Foundation, the Joyce Foundation, the Carnegie Corporation, the Lloyd A. Fry Foundation, the William T. Grant Foundation, the Spencer Foundation, the Woods Charitable Fund, the Chicago Community Trust, the Institute for Research on Poverty, and the U.S. Department of Health and Human Services.

Bibliography

Bell, Derrick. 1992. *Faces at the Bottom of the Well: The Permanence of Racism*. New York: Basic Books, 1992.

Caraley, Demetrios. 1992. "Washington Abandons the Cities," *Political Science Quarterly*. 107, Spring.

Drake, St. Clair and Horace Cayton. 1945. *Black Metropolis: A Study of Negro Life in a Northern City*. New York: Harcourt, Brace, Jovanovich, Inc.

Elliot, Delbert S. 1992. "Longitudinal Research in Criminology: Promise and Practice." Paper presented at the NATO Conference on Cross-National Longitudinal Research on Criminal Behavior, Frankfurt, Germany, July 19–25.

Fagan, Jeffrey. 1993. "Drug Selling and Licit Income in Distressed Neighborhoods: The Economic Lives of Street-Level Drug Users and Dealers," in *Drugs, Crime and Social Isolation*, (edited by G. Peterson and A. Harold Washington). Urban Institute Press, 1993.

Hacker, Andrew. 1992. *Two Nations: Black and White, Separate, Hostile and Unequal*. New York: Charles Scribner's Sons.

Hirschman, Albert O. 1970. *Exit, Voice and Loyalty: Responses to Decline in Firms, Organizations, and States*. Cambridge, Mass.: Harvard University Press.

Jargowsky, Paul A. 1994. "Ghetto Poverty Among Blacks in the 1980's." *Journal of Policy Analysis and Management*, Vol. 13, pp. 288–310.

Krogh, Marilyn. 1993. "A Description of the Work Histories of Fathers Living in the Inner-City of Chicago." *Workingpaper*, Center for the Study of Urban Inequality, University of Chicago.

Massey, Douglas S. and Nancy A. Denton. 1993. *American Apartheid: Segregation and the Making of the Underclass*. Cambridge, Mass: Harvard University Press.

Rohter, Larry. 1993. "As Hispanic Presence Grows, So Does Black Anger." *New York Times*, June 20, p. 11.

Sampson, Robert J. 1986. "Crime in Cities: The Effects of Formal and Informal Social Control." *In Communities and Crime*, edited by Albert J. Reiss, Jr., and Michael Tonry (271–310). Chicago: University of Chicago Press.

Sampson, Robert J. 1992. "Integrating Family and Community-Level Dimensions of Social Organization: Delinquency and Crime in the Inner-City of Chicago." Paper presented at the International Workshop: "Integrating Individual and Ecological Aspects on Crime," Stockholm, Sweden, August 31–September 5, 1992.

Sampson, Robert J. and William Julius Wilson. 1993. "Toward a Theory of Race, Crime, and Urban Inequality." In *Crime and Inequality* (eds. John Hagan and Ruth Peterson). Stanford University Press, in press.

Spear, Allan. 1967. *Black Chicago: The Making of a Negro Ghetto*. Chicago: University of Chicago Press.

Tobin, James. 1965. "On Improving the Economic Status of the Negro." *Daedalus* 94:878–898.

Wacquant, Loic J. D. and William Julius Wilson. 1989. "Poverty, Joblessness, and the Social Transformation of the Inner City" in *Welfare Policy for the 1990s* (edited by Phoebe Cottingham and David Ellwood), 70–102. Cambridge: Harvard University Press.

Weir, Margaret. 1993. "Race and Urban Poverty: Comparing Europe and America." Center for American Political Studies, Harvard University, Occasional Paper 93–9, March.

Wilson, William Julius. 1987. *The Truly Disadvantaged: The Inner City, The Underclass, and Public Policy*. Chicago: University of Chicago Press.

 Article Review Form at end of book.

What are some of the explanations given to justify the overrepresentation of blacks in criminal incidents at the national and international levels?

Race and Crime:

An International Dilemma

J. Philippe Rushton

J. Philippe Rushton is professor of psychology at the University of Western Ontario in London, Ontario, Canada. He is the author of Race, Evolution, and Behavior, *recently published by Transaction, on which this article is based.*

In their magisterial *Crime and Human Nature*, J.Q. Wilson and R.J. Herrnstein noted that the Asian underrepresentation in U.S. crime statistics posed a theoretical problem. The solution proposed by criminologists as early as the 1920s was that the Asian "ghetto" protected members from the disruptive tendencies of the outside society. For blacks, however, the ghetto is said to foster crime.

The overrepresentation of blacks in U.S. crime statistics has existed since the turn of the twentieth century. The census of 1910 showed more blacks than whites in jail, in the north as well as in the south. Official figures from the 1930s through the 1950s showed that the number of blacks arrested for crimes of violence in proportion to the number of whites ranged from 6:1 to 16:1. These statistics have not improved in the interim.

Breaching a long taboo, liberals from Bill Clinton to Jesse Jackson have recently made it respectable to theorize about "black-on-black" crime. Conservative magazines like the *National Review* have also begun to discuss aspects of the race/crime link (see "Blacks . . . and Crime,"

May 16, 1994; "How to Cut Crime," May 30, 1994). What is yet to be acknowledged, however, is the international generalizability of the race/crime relationship. The matrix found within the United States, with Asians being most law-abiding, Africans least, and Europeans intermediate, is to be observed in other multiracial countries like Britain, Brazil, and Canada. Moreover, the pattern is revealed in China and the Pacific Rim, Europe and the Middle East, and Africa and the Caribbean. Because the "American dilemma" is global in manifestation, explanations must go well beyond U.S. particulars.

I emphasize at the outset that enormous variability exists within each of the populations on many of the traits to be discussed. Because distributions substantially overlap, with average differences amounting to between 4 and 34 percent, it is highly problematic to generalize from a group average to a particular individual. Nonetheless, as I hope to show, significant racial variation exists, not only in crime but also in other traits that predispose to crime, including testosterone, brain size, temperament, and cognitive ability.

The global nature of the racial pattern in crime is shown in data collated from INTERPOL using the 1984 and 1986 yearbooks. After analyzing information on nearly 100 countries, I reported, in the 1990 issue of the *Canadian Journal of Criminology*, that African and Caribbean countries had double the rate of violent crime (an

aggregate of murder, rape, and serious assault) than did European countries, and three times more than did countries in the Pacific Rim. Averaging over the three crimes and two time periods, the figures per 100,000 population were, respectively, 142, 74, and 43.

I have corroborated these results using the most recent INTERPOL yearbook (1990). The rates of murder, rape, and serious assault per 100,000 population reported for 23 predominantly African countries, 41 Caucasian countries, and 12 Asian countries were: for murder, 13, 5, and 3; for rape, 17, 6, and 3; and for serious assault, 213, 63, and 27. Summing the crimes gave figures per 100,000, respectively, of 243, 74, and 33. The gradient remained robust over contrasts of racially homogeneous countries in northeast Asia, central Europe, and sub-Saharan Africa, or of racially mixed but predominantly black or white/Amerindian countries in the Caribbean and Central America. In short, a stubborn pattern exists worldwide that requires explanation.

Testosterone and the Family

The breakdown of the black family and the strengths of the Asian family are often used to explain the crime pattern within the United States. Learning to follow rules is thought to depend on family socialization. Since the 1965 Moynihan Report documented the high rates of marital dissolution, frequent heading of families by women, and numerous illegitimate births, the figures cited as evidence for the instability of the black family in America have tripled.

A similarly constituted matrifocal black family exists in the Caribbean with father-absent households, lack of paternal certainty, and separate bookkeeping by spouses. The Caribbean pattern, like the American one, is typically attributed to the long legacy of slavery. However, the slavery hypothesis does not fit data from sub-Saharan Africa. After reviewing long-standing African marriage systems in the 1989 issue of *Ethology and Sociobiology,* anthropologist Patricia Draper of Pennsylvania State University concluded: "coupled with low investment parenting is a mating pattern that permits early sexual activity, loose economic and emotional ties between spouses . . . and in many cases the expectation on the part of both spouses that the marriage will end in divorce or separation, followed by the formation of another union."

The African marriage system may partly depend on traits of temperament. Biological variables such as the sex hormone testosterone are implicated in the tendency toward multiple relationships as well as the tendency to commit crime. One study, published in the 1993 issue of *Criminology* by Alan Booth and D. Wayne Osgood, showed clear evidence of a testosterone-crime link based on an analysis of 4,462 U.S. military personnel. Other studies have linked testosterone to an aggressive and impulsive personality, to a lack of empathy, and to sexual behavior. Testosterone levels explain why young men are disproportionately represented in crime statistics relative to young women, and why younger people are more trouble-prone than older people. Testosterone reliably differentiates the sexes and is known to decline with age.

Ethnic differences exist in average level of testosterone. Studies show 3 to 19 percent more testosterone in black college students and military veterans than in their white counterparts. Studies among the Japanese show a correspondingly lower amount of testosterone than among white Americans. Medical research has focused on cancer of the prostate, one determinant of which is testosterone. Black men have higher rates of prostate cancer than do white men who in turn have higher rates than do Oriental men.

Sex hormones also influence reproductive physiology. Whereas the average woman produces 1 egg every 28 days in the middle of the menstrual cycle, some women have shorter cycles and others produce more than one egg; both events translate into greater fecundity including the birth of dizygotic (two-egg) twins. Black women average shorter menstrual cycles than white women and produce a greater frequency of dizygotic twins. The rate per 1,000 births is less than 4 among east Asians, 8 among whites, and 16 or greater among Africans and African-Americans.

Racial differences exist in sexual behavior, as documented by numerous surveys including those carried out by the World Health Organization. Africans, African-Americans and blacks living in Britain are more sexually active, at an earlier age, and with more sexual partners than are Europeans and white Americans, who in turn are more sexually active, at an earlier age, and with more sexual partners than are Asians, Asian-Americans, and Asians living in Britain. Differences in sexual activity translate into consequences. Teenage fertility rates around the world show the racial gradient, as does the pattern of sexually transmitted diseases. World Health Organization Technical Reports and other studies examining the worldwide prevalence of AIDS, syphilis, gonorrhea, herpes, and chlamydia typically find low levels in China and Japan and high levels in Africa, with European countries intermediate. This is also the pattern found within the United States.

International data on personality and temperament show that blacks are less restrained and less quiescent than whites and whites are less restrained and less quiescent than Orientals. With infants and young children observer ratings are the main method employed, whereas with adults the use of standardized tests are more frequent. One study in French-language Quebec examined 825 four- to six-year olds from 66 countries rated by 50 teachers. All the children were in preschool French-language immersion classes for immigrant children. Teachers consistently reported better social adjustment and less hostility-aggression from east Asian than from white than from African-Caribbean children. Another study based on twenty-five countries from around the world showed that east Asians were less extraverted and more anxiety-prone than Europeans who in turn were less outgoing and more restrained than Africans.

Behavior Genetics

Differences between individuals in testosterone and its various metabolites are about 50 percent heritable. More surprising to many are the studies suggesting that criminal tendencies are also heritable. According to American, Danish, and Swedish adoption studies, children who were adopted in infancy were at greater risk for criminal convictions if their biological parents had been convicted than if the adopting parents who raised them had been convicted. In one study of all 14,427 nonfamilial adoptions in Denmark from 1924 to 1947, it was found that siblings and half-siblings adopted separately into different homes were concordant for convictions.

Convergent with this adoption work, twin studies find that identical twins are roughly twice as much alike in their criminal behavior as fraternal twins. In 1986 I reported the results of a study of 576 pairs of adult twins on dispositions to altruism, empathy, nurturance, and aggressiveness, traits which parents are expected to socialize heavily. Yet 50 percent of the variance in both men and women was attributable to genetics. The well-known Minnesota Study of Twins Raised Apart led by Thomas J. Bouchard, Jr., has confirmed the importance of genetic factors to personality traits such as aggressiveness, dominance, and impulsivity. David Rowe at the University of Arizona reviewed much of this literature in his 1994 book *Limits of Family Influence.* He explains how siblings raised together in the same family may differ genetically from each other in delinquency.

Genes code for enzymes, which, under the influence of the environment, lay down tracts in the brains and neurohormonal systems of individuals, thus affecting people's minds and the choices they make about behavioral alternatives. In regard to aggression, for example, people inherit nervous systems that dispose them to anger, irritability, impulsivity, and a lack of conditionability. In general, these factors influence *self-control*, a psychological variable figuring prominently in theories of criminal behavior.

Behavior genetic studies provide information about environmental effects. As described in Rowe's book, the important variables turn out to be within a family, not between families. Factors such as social class, family religion, parental values, and child-rearing styles are not found to have a strong common effect on siblings. Because individual minds channel common environments in separate ways siblings acquire alternative sets of information. Although siblings resemble each other in their exposure to violent television programs, it is the more aggressive one who identifies with aggressive characters and who views aggressive consequences as positive.

Within-family studies show that intelligence and temperament separate siblings in proneness to delinquency. It is not difficult to imagine how an intellectually less able and temperamentally more impulsive sibling seeks out a social environment different from his or her more able and less impulsive sibling. Within the constraints allowed by the total spectrum of cultural alternatives, people create environments maximally compatible with their genotypes. Genetic similarity explains the tendency for trouble-prone personalities to seek each other out for friendship and marriage.

One objection sometimes made to genetic theories of crime is the finding that crime rates fluctuate with social conditions. Generational changes in crime, however, are expected by genetic theories. As environments become less impeding and more equal, the genetic contribution to individual difference variation necessarily becomes larger. Over the last 50 years, for example, there has been an increase in the genetic contribution to both academic attainment and longevity as harmful environmental effects have been mitigated and more equal opportunities created. Thus, easing social constraints on underlying "at risk" genotypes leads to an increase in criminal behavior.

Intelligence

The role of low cognitive ability in disposing a child to delinquency is established even within the same family where a less able sibling is observed to engage in more deviant behavior than an advantaged sibling. Problem behaviors begin early in life and manifest themselves as an unwillingness or inability to follow family rules. Later, drug abuse, early onset of sexual activity, and more clearly defined illegal acts make up the broad-based syndrome predicted by low intelligence.

Racial differences exist in average IQ-test scores and again the pattern extends well beyond the United States. The global literature on IQ was reviewed by Richard Lynn in the 1991 issue of *Mankind Quarterly*. Caucasoids of North America, Europe, and Australia generally obtained mean IQs of around 100. Mongoloids from both North America and the Pacific Rim obtained slightly higher means, in the range of 101 to 111. Africans from south of the Sahara, African-Americans, and African-Caribbeans (including those living in Britain) obtained mean IQs ranging from 70 to 90.

The question remains of whether test scores are valid measures of group differences in mental ability. Basically, the answer hinges on whether the tests are culture-bound. Doubts linger in many quarters, although a large body of technical work has disposed of this problem among those with psychometric expertise, as shown in the book of surveys by Snyderman and Rothman. This is because the tests show similar patterns of internal item consistency and predictive validity for all groups, and the same differences are to be found on relatively culture-free tests.

Novel data about speed of decision making show that the racial differences in mental ability are pervasive. Cross-cultural investigations of reaction times have been done on nine- to twelve-year olds from six countries. In these elementary tasks, children must decide which of several lights is on, or stands out from others, and move a hand to press a button. All children can perform the tasks in less than one second, but more intelligent children, as measured by traditional IQ tests, perform the task faster than do less intelligent children. Richard Lynn found Oriental children from Hong Kong and Japan to be faster in decision time than white children from Britain and Ireland who were faster than black children from Africa. Arthur Jensen has reported the same three-way pattern in California.

Brain Size

The relation between mental ability and brain size has been established in studies using magnetic resonance imaging, which, *in vivo*, construct three-dimensional pictures of the brain and confirm correlations reported since the turn of the century measuring head perimeter. The brain size/cognitive ability correlations range from about 0.10 to 0.40. Moreover, racial differences are found in brain size. It has often been held that racial differences in brain size, established in the nineteenth century, disappear when corrections are made for body size and other variables such as bias. However, modern studies confirm nineteenth-century findings.

Three main procedures have been used to estimate brain size: (a) weighing wet brains at autopsy; (b) measuring the volume of empty skulls using filler; and (c) measuring external head size and estimating volume. Data from all three sources triangulate on the conclusion that, after statistical corrections are made for body size, east Asians average about 17 cm^3 (1 cubic inch) more cranial capacity than whites who average about 80 cm^3 (5 cubic inches) more than blacks. Ho and colleagues at the Medical College of Wisconsin analyzed brain autopsy data on 1,261 American subjects aged 25 to 80 after excluding obviously damaged brains and reported, in the 1980 issue of *Archives of Pathology and Laboratory Medicine,* that, after controlling for age and body size, white men averaged 100 grams more brain weight than black men, and white women averaged 100 grams more brain weight than black women. With endocranial volume, Beals and colleagues computerized the world database of up to 20,000 crania and published their results in the 1984 issue of *Current Anthropology.* Sex-combined brain cases differed by continental area with populations from Asia averaging 1,415 cm^3, those from Europe averaging 1,362 cm^3, and those from Africa averaging 1,268 cm^3.

Using external head measurements I have found, after corrections are made for body size, that east Asians consistently average a larger brain than do Caucasians or Africans. Three of these studies were published in the journal *Intelligence.* In a 1991 study, from data compiled by the U.S. space agency NASA, military samples from Asia averaged 14 cm^3 more cranial capacity than those from Europe. In a stratified random sample of 6,325 U.S. Army personnel measured in 1988 for fitting helmets, I found that Asian-Americans averaged 36 cm^3 more than European-Americans who averaged 21 cm^3 more than African-Americans. Most recently, I analyzed data from tens of thousands of men and women aged 25 to 45 collated by the International Labour Office in Geneva and found that Asians averaged 10 cm^3 more than Europeans and 66 cm^3 more than Africans.

Racial differences in brain size and IQ show up early in life. Data from the national Collaborative Perinatal Project on 19,000 black children and 17,000 white children show that black children have a smaller head perimeter at birth and, although they are born shorter in stature and lighter in weight, by age seven "catch-up growth" leads them to be larger in body size than white children, but still smaller in head perimeter. Head perimeter at birth correlated with IQ at age seven in both the black and the white children.

Origins of Race Differences

Racial differences exist at a more profound level than is normally considered. Why do Europeans average so consistently between Africans and Asians in crime, family system, sexual behavior, testosterone level, intelligence, and brain size? It is almost certain that genetics and evolution have a role to play. Transracial adoption studies indicate genetic influence. Studies of Korean and Vietnamese children adopted into white American and white Belgian homes showed that, although as babies many had been hospitalized for malnutrition, they grew to excel in academic ability with IQs ten points higher than their adoptive national norms. By contrast, Sandra Scarr and her colleagues at Minnesota found that at age 17, black and mixed-race children adopted into white middle-class families performed at a lower level than the white siblings with whom they were raised. Adopted white children had an average IQ of 106, an average aptitude based on national norms at the 59th percentile, and a class rank at the 54th percentile; mixed-race children had an average IQ of 99, an aptitude at the 53rd percentile, and a class rank at the 40th percentile; and black children had an average IQ of 89, an aptitude at the 42nd percentile, and a class rank at the 36th percentile.

No known environmental variable can explain the inverse relation across the three races between gamete production (two-egg twinning) and brain size. The only known explanation for this trade-off is life-history theory. A life-history is a genetically organized suite of characters that evolved in a coordinated manner so as to allocate energy to survival, growth, and reproduction. There is, in short, a trade-off between parental effort, including paternal investment, and mating effort, a distinction Patricia Draper referred to as one between "cads" and "dads."

Evolutionary hypotheses have been made for why Asians have the largest brains and the most parenting investment strategy. The currently accepted view of human origins, the "African Eve" theory, posits a beginning in Africa some 200,000 years ago, an exodus through the Middle East with an African/non-African split about 110,000 years ago, and a Caucasoid/Mongoloid split about 40,000 years ago. Evolutionary selection pressures are different in the hot savanna where Africans evolved than in the cold arctic where Asians evolved.

The evidence shows that the further north the populations migrated out of Africa, the more they encountered the cognitively demanding problems of gathering and storing food, gaining shelter, making clothes, and raising children successfully during prolonged winters. The evolutionary sequence fits with and helps to explain how and why the variables cluster. As the original African populations evolved into Caucasoids and Mongoloids, they did so in the direction of larger brains and lower levels of sex hormone, with concomitant reductions in aggression and sexual potency and increases in forward planning and family stability.

Despite the vast body of evidence now accumulating for important genetic and behavioral differences among the three great macro-races, there is much reluctance to accept that the differences in crime are deeply rooted. Perhaps one must sympathize with fears aroused by race research. But all theories of human nature can be used to generate abusive policies. And a rejection of the genetic basis for racial variation in behavior is not only poor scholarship, it may be injurious to unique individuals and to complexly structured societies. Moreover, it should be emphasized that probably no more than about 50 percent of the variance among races is genetic, with the remaining 50 percent due to the environment. Even genetic effects are necessarily mediated by neuroendocrine and psychosocial mechanisms, thus allowing opportunity for benign intervention and the alleviation of suffering.

 **Article Review Form at end of book.**

Discuss the alleged violent nature of the 365 years of African involvement in the Americas.

Understanding Violence among Young African American Males:

An Afrocentric Perspective

Anthony E. O. King

Anthony E. O. King, Ph.D., is an associate professor in the School of Social Work at the University of Alabama. His research focuses on African American family life, male-female relationships, and human services for incarcerated African American males.

African American teenagers are 3 to 5 times more likely than European-American youth to be murder victims (U.S. Department of Justice, 1991). They are also more likely to be victims of robbery and aggravated assult (U.S. Department of Justice, 1991). Moreover, African American teenagers commit about 80% of the violent crimes perpetrated against African Americans between the ages of 12 and 19, and 90% of the time the offenders and the victims are males (U.S. Department of Justice, 1991).

The homicide rate for 12- to 15-year-old African American males is 5 times the rate for European American teenagers and 3 times the rate for African American females (U.S. Department of Justice, 1991). These trends are not new. African American males of all ages have had one of the highest, if not the highest, homicide rate in the nation for almost 100 years. What appears to be unique about the present situation is the ex-

tensive involvement of adolescent and young adult African American males in violent activities. Nevertheless, statistically speaking, violence has always been one of the leading public health problems for African American male adolescents and young adults.

Throughout the last decade, the media have drawn attention to the number of violent crimes committed by adolescents and young adults, especially young African American males. Television networks, newspapers, and popular magazines have devoted a considerable amount of air time and print space to covering tragic stories of teen homicides, murders, and rapes. As a result, Americans are more aware of violent crimes committed by African American teenagers and young adults than at any other time in the history of the United States.

Major television networks also have aired discussions and debates between national scholars and politicians regarding the causes and solutions to this seemingly senseless violence. These discussions never explore how chattel slavery, institutional racism, and intransigent poverty and economic deprivation have contributed to the violence observed in many African American

communities. In my opinion, this is similar to trying to explain how batter becomes cake without examining the role that flour, eggs, and milk play in the baking process.

Chattel slavery, institutional racism, and poverty are the three most salient and pervasive features of the African experience in the United States. Thus, to fully understand the nature and etiology of contemporary violence among African American males, one has to examine the relationship between these unique social, economic, and historical features of the African American male experience and the violence that currently permeates the neighborhoods of so many African American communities (Akbar, 1989).

Contrary to traditional European and European American social science theory, the violent behaviors exhibited by many young African American males were practically nonexistent in Africa prior to the Atlantic slave trade (Bohannan, 1960; Brearley, 1932; Curtis, 1975, Jackson, 1990, Silberman, 1978). If this is true, then how might we explain the intraethnic and intragender violence that has been so much a part of the African American male experience?

Anthony E. O. King, *Journal of Black Studies*, Vol. 28, No. 1, September 1997, pp. 79–96. Copyright © 1997 by Sage Publications, Inc. Reprinted by permission of Sage Publications, Inc.

I have attempted to answer this question by exploring the problem from an Afrocentric perspective. In other words, I have examined this problem from the historical, cultural, and social vantage point of the African American community, because the social, economic, and historical experiences of African Americans are unlike those of any other ethnic and cultural group in this country. No other group was enslaved for 225 years in this country. No other group was systematically denied their basic human, social, and economic rights for almost 325 years. No other group has experienced the poverty and economic deprivation that African Americans have experienced. Finally, no other group has been, and continues to be, victimized by institutionalized discriminatory practices and policies in every arena of American life solely on the basis of an immutable attribute such as skin color.

The Afrocentric paradigm overcomes Eurocentric social science theories' inability to adequately and fairly explain the worldview, culture, psychology, and behaviors of African Americans. During the past 25 years, African American psychologists, historians, and social scientists have used this perspective to gain a greater understanding of the African American experience and to explore the efficacy of a variety of strategies and interventions designed to ameliorate the various social problems that plague millions of African Americans (Asante, 1980, 1987; Azibo, 1989; Baldwin, 1976; Myers, 1988; Nobles, 1982; Phillips, 1990).

The ultimate goal of this article is to present a culturally relevant and historically valid conceptual framework for understanding intraethnic and intragender violence among young African American males. The absence of, and need for, an interdisciplinary paradigm has been acknowledged by other scholars (Comer, 1985). More important, I hope that the analysis presented here will lead to the development and implementation of programs and services that will reduce this problem and prevent another generation of African American males from waging war on themselves and their communities.

The Violent History of American Society

The United States is the most violent nation in the history of the modern world! More important, social workers and public health professionals must understand that the violence that characterizes modern American life did not begin with the birth of rap, latchkey children, so-called broken homes, MTV, or crack cocaine. The seeds of violence were planted into the moral and social character of this nation with the brutal and inhumane enslavement of millions of Africans on land that was violently and maliciously stolen from Native Americans (Bealer, 1972; Brown, 1970; Williams, 1966).

The Violence of American Slavery

The 365 years of African enslavement in the Americas was the most violent period in the history of the modern world. To provide European colonial powers with the inexpensive labor needed to expand their budding capitalistic empires, 40 million (some estimates are as high as 150 million) African men, women, and children were kidnapped and enslaved throughout North, Central, and South America (Jackson, 1990).

The mortality rate among African people during the enslavement period was incredible. One out of every three Africans captured during slave raids died on the march to the coast, and another one third perished at sea long before they reached their final destination (Jackson, 1990). These deaths, coupled with the ethnic conflicts spawned by the Atlantic slave trade, cost the lives of an estimated 100 million African men, women, and children (Jackson, 1990). Simply stated, the enslavement of African people throughout the New World was the single most violent and brutal act ever committed against any group of people in the history of the world. The slave system that developed in the United States was equally deadly and violent.

The American system of enslavement was the most violent and inhumane form of slavery that the modern world has ever known. The Constitution of the United States treated African people as property and denied them their humanity in both custom and law (Franklin, 1956). Africans were brought to the United States in chains, under the most horrible conditions, and forced to work without compensation for more than 220 years. For the most part, they enjoyed no greater civil or social rights in most states than those granted farm animals. No institutionalized provision was made for them to earn their freedom. Their enslavement was perpetual in theory and under the best of circumstances manumission occurred only at the whim of the people who owned them. Every conceivable effort was made to degrade and dehumanize enslaved Africans. More important, the violence perpetrated against Africans during the enslavement period in the United States was designed to strip them of their cultural and human dignity, and literally transform them into docile, childlike creatures who could be worked like farm animals and if necessary disciplined similarly (Huggins, 1990; Lester, 1968).

The basic social stratification system of the United States was built on the belief that African people were descendants of subhuman groups, incapable of "civilized" behavior and devoid of a history worthy of repeating (Magubane, 1989). Every major social institution in this country conspired to create a nation in which African people were considered genetically, socially, and politically inferior to even the most immoral and uncivilized European American. The types of violent acts committed against the enslaved African community reflected these attitudes. The specific types of violence committed against African males, however, were particularly vicious and abhorrent.

Violence Against Enslaved African Males

From the moment they arrived in the Americas, male Africans were treated more violently and with greater brutality than any other segment of the enslaved African community. African males, both boys and men, were treated worse than girls and women because they represented a direct challenge to the supremacy and hegemony of the European American male (Hall, 1981). No form of physical punishment was spared or considered too savage if it was effective in controlling the enslaved African male (Huggins, 1990). As a consequence, unmerciful beatings, lynchings, and the mutilation of various body parts, particularly the male genitalia, were all routine disciplinary measures used to punish enslaved African males.

To enhance the psychological effects of these cruel and inhumane disciplinary methods, European Americans would castrate or lynch enslaved African males and then publicly burn their semilifeless bodies for everyone to see (Mellon, 1988). Enslaved African boys, as well as their mothers and sisters, were frequently forced to watch their brothers, uncles, fathers, and grandfathers tortured to death by mobs of bloodthirsty men, women, and children (Huggins, 1990; Lester, 1968; Mellon, 1988).

These public events were also designed to influence the behavior of the European American community. For the most part, they served to reinforce the widely held belief among all European Americans that African people had no basic human rights that "White" people had to respect (*Scott v. Samford, Russell, and Emerson,* 1857). Moreover, these sadistic sideshows contributed to the legitimization of physical violence as an acceptable means for controlling African males in the United States. It is important to point out that the barbarous assault on the humanity of African males did not stop when slavery ended in 1865.

Violence Against African American Males after Enslavement

After enslavement ended, little changed for African American males. Although they were no longer considered property, they were not treated as full citizens by any level of government or the European American community. When they tried to assert their rights to national citizenship guaranteed by the Fourteenth and Fifteenth Amendments, European Americans responded with amazing violence and animus.

If an African American male demanded to be paid prevailing wages for his labor or argued his right to earn a living based solely on his willingness to work and sacrifice, all levels of government and nearly every sector of the larger society stood ready to oppose him with any means necessary (Rosengarten, 1974). Often, this confrontation resulted in African American males literally being beaten to death by either law enforcement personnel, mobs of hostile citizens, or both. During the late 19th century and the first three decades of the 20th century, thousands of African American males were murdered and many more were horribly disfigured and crippled for simply demanding to be treated as social, civil, and political equals (Fishel & Quarles, 1970; Myrdal, 1944; Williams & Williams, 1972; Wintersmith, 1974).

Between 1885 and 1921, 4,096 lynchings were recorded in the United States, an average of 113 per year, or roughly 9.5 per month for 36 years (Fishel & Quarles, 1970). About 80% of the individuals lynched were African American males (Hughes, 1962). Most of the victims had been accused but not officially charged with raping a "White" female, a crime rarely substantiated (Hughes, 1962). In addition, within a 3-year span (1918–1921), 28 African Americans, mostly males, were publicly burned by mobs (Fishel & Quarles, 1970). It was not unusual for African American male children, adolescents, or teenagers to be lynched or burned alive. For example, between 1918 and 1919, six children were either lynched or burned alive in the United States (Hughes, 1962).

The lynching of African American males caused massive celebrations on the part of many European Americans, especially in the border and southern states. Hughes (1962) described one of those celebrations in the following manner:

A mob near Valdosta, Georgia, frustrated at not finding the man they sought for murdering a plantation owner, lynched three innocent Negroes instead; the pregnant wife of one of the three wailed at her husband's death so loudly that the mob seized her and burned her alive, too.

As the flames enveloped Mary Turner's body, her unborn child fell to the ground and was trampled underfoot; white parents held their children up to watch. (p. 37).

These horrible murders were well publicized in newspapers, not necessarily to condemn them but to provide those citizens unable to attend with the juicy facts surrounding the destruction of another "uppity" or "crazed" African/African American. Newspapers "usually reported lynchings in detail, including how long it took the victim to lose consciousness, how the spectators scrambled to view the charred remains, and how the women and children enjoyed it" (Wintersmith, 1974, p. 38).

Moreover, between 1865 and 1940, race riots initiated and carried out by European Americans (18 major riots between 1915 and 1919) led to the deaths of over 500 African Americans (Staples, 1982; Williams & Williams, 1972). Local, state, and federal law enforcement and judiciary officials rarely intervened (Franklin, 1956; Hughes, 1962; Myrdal, 1944). They often were willing participants in these bloodbaths.

Police Brutality and Capital Punishment

Much to the surprise of most Americans, police brutality against African American males did not begin with the Rodney King beating in Los Angeles. African American males of every age and social and economic class are aware that the most insignificant encounter with law enforcement officers can lead to a violent encounter, which, in turn, could lead to a severe beating or even death. Police brutality against African American males has a long history (Fosdick, 1972).

According to Staples (1982), "it is no surprise to find that for the years 1920–1932, out of 479 blacks killed by white persons in the South, 54 percent were slain by white police officers" (p. 44). In addition, a Police Foundation study found that "75 percent of the civilians killed by police in seven cities between 1973–74 were black males" (p. 44). Moreover, this study concluded that most of the shootings "did not appear to have served any compelling purpose" and "fell into a middle ground" where it was difficult to determine if the shooting was justified or not" (p. 44).

As the Rodney King case illustrates, city and county law enforcement agencies have continued to wage a violent, brutal, and most important, illegal war against African American males. Everyday, in every major city in this nation, African American males are shot, beaten, and murdered while in the custody of law enforcement officers. As in the past, their deaths are rarely the unfortunate outcome of sane nondiscriminatory policing.

The court systems of this nation also have demonstrated a willingness to use judiciary authority to impose capital punishment (the ultimate form of state-sponsored violence) disproportionately on African American males. Between 1930 and 1988, 50% of the prisoners executed under civil authority in the United States were African American males (U.S. Department of Justice, 1990). Moreover, 89% (405) of the 455 Americans executed for rape during this same period were African American males, even though more than half of the individuals arrested for rape in this country are White males (U.S. Department of Justice, 1989, 1990). As of May 30, 1990, 40% of the prisoners under sentence of death in the United States are African American males (U.S. Department of Justice, 1990). Surprisingly, the overwhelming majority of these men are not on death row for killing African Americans. Death sentences and executions appear to be reserved primarily for individuals convicted of killing Whites (Staples, 1982).

In an analysis of first degree indictments for murder in Florida counties between 1972 and 1978, it was found that, overall, 17 percent of the black men who murdered whites were given the death penalty, compared to 3 percent whose victims were black. White defendants were more apt than blacks to win acquittal, be judged incompetent to stand trial or get their cases dismissed while blacks were much more likely to face trial and be found guilty. A bias against men was also evident as only 1.6 percent of female murder defendants drew the death penalty as opposed to 12 percent of the men. (Staples, 1982, p. 49)

Rarely are African American males sentenced to death for raping and murdering African Americans, in spite of the fact that in 1988, 87% of their murder and nonnegligent manslaughter victims were African American (U.S. Department of Justice, 1990). In the following comment, sociologist Robert Staples (1982) summarized the findings from a study that examined the relationship between the race of the victim and the sentence of the offender:

Between 1973 and 1977, it was reported that only 6 percent of those arrested for homicide were blacks who killed whites but these blacks constituted 40 percent of the convicts on death row. Just 5 percent were blacks who killed other blacks. (Staples, 1982, p. 49)

This legal and extralegal violence against African American males has led to the devaluation of their lives and a systematic and pervasive disregard for their basic humanity. This attitude is a salient and fundamental feature of American society (Hawkins, 1987). However, the history of violence against African American males fails to explain the carnage currently taking place in the African American community. Social, economic, educational, and political deprivation and oppression also contribute to the excessive amounts of violence perpetrated by and against African American male adolescents and adults. Living under these conditions, coupled with violence waged against them through racism and discrimination, undermines many African American males' psychosocial development, sense of hope, and self-worth. In addition, these debilitating circumstances deny African American males the opportunities to develop the social and practical competencies required to prosper in a decidedly Eurocentric, racist, and competitive society.

The Impact of Racial Discrimination and Poverty on African American Males

By the time most African American males are 10 to 13 years old, they have already witnessed the doors of

opportunity slam shut on the dreams of literally hundreds of African American men in their communities. Millions of young African American boys learn very early in life that the lives of incredible numbers of adult African American males are punctuated by frequent bouts of unemployment, poverty, ill health, and misery. They also notice that adult African American males die about 14 years before European American women, 9.5 years before African American women, and almost 8 years before European American males (U.S. Bureau of the Census, 1992).

The high mortality rates among African American males also leave many adolescent and teenage males without sufficient numbers of adult males willing or able to teach them how to successfully navigate the minefields of American racism, economic dislocation, and violence. Furthermore, the aforementioned problems create a shortage of African American males who can and will provide the guidance, love, and nurturing necessary to help many African American boys and teenagers overcome the pessimism, fear, anger, and fatalism that often surrounds them.

African American boys and teenagers are as intelligent and perceptive as any other group of boys and young men in this country. They know that if they cannot dribble a basketball, hit a baseball, or sack a quarterback, this country has little use for them, and more important, comparatively little encouragement and assistance will be forthcoming to help them achieve outside of sports. Furthermore, African American boys understand that if they cannot dance or sing, or do stand-up comedy, their chances of ever achieving economic stability and security will be 10 times as difficult as for their European American counterparts, and under the worst circumstances slim to none.

In the midst of the hopelessness that frequently permeates the lives of many African American youths lie powerful malt liquors, ice, heroin, and crack cocaine; each equally capable of shielding a young mind from the painful reality of the day-to-day struggle to survive and thrive in a hostile environment. To make matters worse, television and movie theaters spew forth programs, films, and images that glorify wealth and materialism. The conspicuous consumption, irresponsible sexual behaviors, and gratuitous violence depicted in the media undermine the development of a culturally and socially appropriate value system in millions of African American boys, adolescents, and young adults. Not being able to enjoy the pimp or straight lifestyles contributes to the despair and frustration that African American adolescents and young adult males display. It is exceedingly difficult to grow up African and poor in a racist and affluent society.

Striving to mature under these social conditions often leads to unimaginable levels of confusion, personal frustration, and emotional pain. More important, these conditions destroy, albeit ever so slowly, the moral character and conscience of many young men and boys. The emotional upheaval that they endure all too often leads to an obvious sense of personal devaluation, degradation, and a disrespect for their lives and the lives of their peers. The relatively low value placed on the lives of African American male teenagers and young adults by the larger society makes it even easier for emotionally overwhelmed adolescents and teenagers to grab a gun, a knife, or a bat and use their peers as human depositories for all the pain and frustration in their lives.

Poverty and racism, however, are only two of the major causal factors that have led to the high rates of violent behaviors exhibited by male African American teenagers and young adults. This nation's obsession with violence, which forms the general context in which African American boys and young adults live, also plays a major role in this tragic scenario.

The Violent Nature of Contemporary American Society

The United States is a society that glorifies violent behavior. It is one of the few nations in the world in which violence and the taking of another human being's life is considered an event suitable for prime-time enter-

tainment and amusement. Moreover, this society glamorizes war and the concept of war more than any other society in modern history. Almost every human activity in this country is reduced to the paradigm of war, in which a violent and physically aggressive mentality is valued and rewarded. Some of this country's most popular sports—such as football, hockey, and boxing—rely heavily on the warrior mentality and the athlete's willingness and ability to inflict punishment and pain on his opponent. Even basketball, a sport traditionally known for its grace and style, has degenerated to a point where it has begun to resemble a cross between touch football and roller derby.

It is not surprising that a significant number of African American boys and adolescents strive to become professional boxers. What other group of males have so few options in life that they are willing to risk life and limb for a few dollars and a little "respect"? Violence in the United States is a commodity that can be advertised, sold, and encouraged, because all Americans, especially males, are socialized to accept violence as "normal" behavior, particularly when it is perpetrated by males.

In the past, sports, particularly basketball and football, served as an effective diversion for the frustration and anger of millions of alienated African American boys. Sports also served as a means by which a poor adolescent or young adult could dribble, pitch, or run his way out of the ghetto. During the last decade and a half, however, these games have lost their ability to capture the attention of many African American male youths. Most have realized that only a handful of African American males will become successful professional athletes and enjoy the riches and acclaim accorded Magic Johnson or Michael Jordan.

It is also important to remember that children learn how to cope with frustration, disappointment, and anger from adults, the media, and the larger society. Thus, African American boys and teenagers learn to resolve their disagreements and handle unpleasant feelings in a violent manner from the adults they know personally or the adult role

models they observe in the media. Hence, it is both ironic and sad that the adults in this country are wringing their hands over teen violence, when, between 1979 and 1988, arrests for violent crimes among individuals under the age of 18 decreased 7.5%, whereas the rate for individuals 18 and over increased 33.2%. (U.S. Department of Justice, 1990).

Until the last decade or so, the African American community was far more capable of protecting most of its young males from the most devastating social and psychological effects of institutional racism, economic deprivation, and inadequate education. However, recent national and international events have severely weakened the African American community's ability to perform this vital role. Two particular events or factors have served the role of the proverbial "straw" that breaks the camel's back—the dramatic decline in the American economic system coupled with the exponential growth in the number of firearms and potent mood-altering drugs. Both have overwhelmed the African American community's ability to protect its children, especially young males, from the most destructive effects of poverty, unemployment, institutionalized racial discrimination, and overburdened female-headed households.

Hopelessness, low self-worth, lack of purpose, and a pernicious case of anomie have invaded the hearts and minds of a significant segment of an entire generation of African American males. These feelings and attitudes have left millions of African American adolescent and young adult males in a state of role and identity confusion unparalleled in African American history. This disorientation, in turn, has made them more vulnerable than at any period in this nation's history to the most negative and self-destructive values and ideals of popular American culture.

Conclusions and Recommendations

In summary, three specific historical, economic, and social factors and five personal characteristics best explain why African American male teenagers and young adults tend to engage in violent acts more often than most non-African American youths.

Historical, Economic, and Social Factors

First, African American adolescent males and young adults continue to be the victims of institutionalized racism and violence. Second, the African American community has lost much of its ability to protect its children from the most destructive effects of economic stagnation and deprivation, the illegal drug trade, and the proliferation of dangerous firearms. As a result, millions of African American boys and teenagers are forced to live under social and economic conditions that undermine their moral, social, and spiritual growth and development. Third, these adolescents and young adults are forced to grow up in a society that glorifies violence and rewards physically aggressive behavior. These general conditions have led to the development of five self-destructive attitudes, perceptions, or psychosocial states among large numbers of young African American males.

Self-Destructive Attitudes, Perceptions, and Psychosocial States

First, many young African American males exhibit behavior symptomatic of low self-worth that is typically caused by the lack of nurturing and self-knowledge. Second, they lack a clear sense of purpose and direction. This disorientation is caused by the absence of sufficient numbers of positive role models who could transmit the culturally appropriate values and knowledge required to understand their responsibilities and obligations in life.

Third, too many African American males lack the social, educational, and vocational competencies required to thrive in a hostile local environment and a racist broader society. Many young men fail to pursue opportunities to acquire basic literacy skills simply because they lack the confidence required to take the first step toward solving these deficits. The absence of

self-confidence results from a dearth of positive growth-enhancing experiences from which a sense of accomplishment of socially valued tasks could develop.

Fourth, a large segment of the African American male community lacks a sense of "connectedness" with themselves and the broader African American community. Many feel personally alienated and isolated from the perceived values and attitudes of the African American community. They do not feel that there is an important role for them to play in the African American community. Public welfare services and society's acceptance of single-parent, female-headed families has left many African American males without a clue as to their role and function within the African American community. Finally, many young African American male adolescents and adults lack a culturally specific and relevant worldview and ethos that would guide them in their interactions and relationships with other African American males, the African American community, and the larger non-African American society. These adolescents and young adults have been overexposed to the toxic social, physical, and psychosocial conditions inherent in popular American culture (West, 1993). Consequently, they lack a worldview and belief system that would help them overcome the ravages of economic deprivation, institutional racism and discrimination, and the despair and hopelessness that accompany these problems.

Thus, the antisocial and violent behavior that characterizes the lives of hundreds of thousands of African American male adolescents and young adults is a symptom of the extent to which they have become emotionally and socially disconnected from themselves, their cultural and historical heritage, and their communities (Silberman, 1978). Their violent behaviors are cries for nurturing, a culturally relevant and consistent ethos that affirms their humanity, a sense of generalized purpose, and the skills and attitudes required to do more than merely survive in a hostile chaotic society.

Violence prevention programs that seek to end the violence that presently permeates large sections of the African American community

must address the legitimate psychosocial needs of African American male teenagers and young adults. In addition, public health, crime prevention, and other human service professionals, particularly social workers, must develop Afrocentric programs and services that will help African American boys and young adults function as healthy African Americans (Nobles, 1982). Finally, violence prevention programs should pay more attention to incarcerated African American males. Particular attention needs to be paid to African American teenagers and youth who presently occupy 40% of the long-term, state-operated, juvenile facilities across America (U.S. Department of Justice, 1988). These are the young people who will eventually have the greatest influence on teenagers who have yet to shoot, stab, or rob their first victim. If the African American community, social workers, and other human service professionals can help incarcerated African American males develop a sense of hope and self-respect and equip them with the skills required to survive and thrive in a hostile environment, then they will leave adult and juvenile correctional institutions and return to their communities willing and capable of assuming the responsibilities African men have assumed for thousands of years. If we fail them, we fail all Americans of African descent.

References

Akbar, N. (1989). *Chains and images of psychological slavery.* Jersey City, NJ: New Mind Productions.

Asante, M. K. (1980). *Afrocentricity: The theory of social change.* Buffalo, NY: Amulefi.

Asante, M. K. (1987). *The Afrocentric idea.* Philadelphia: Temple University Press.

Azibo, D. (1989). African-centered theses on mental health and a nosology of Black/African personality disorder. *Journal of Black Psychology, 15*(2), 174–214.

Baldwin, J. A. (1976). Black psychology and Black personality. *Black Books Bulletin, 4*(3), 6–11.

Bealer, A. W. (1972). *Only the names remain: The Cherokees and the Trail of Tears.* Boston: Little, Brown.

Bohannan, P. (1960). Patterns of murder and suicide. In P. Bohannan (Ed.), *African homicide and suicide.* Princeton, NJ: Princeton University Press.

Brearley, H. C. (1932). *Homicide in the United States.* Chapel Hill: University of North Carolina Press.

Brown, D. (1970). *Bury my heart at wounded knee: An Indian history of the American West.* New York: Holt, Rinehart & Winston.

Comer, J. P. (1985). Black violence and public policy. In L. A. Curtis (Ed.), *American violence and public policy* (pp. 63–86). New Haven, CT: Yale University Press.

Curtis, L. A. (1975). *Violence, race and culture.* Lexington, MA: Lexington Books.

Fishel, L. H., & Quarles, B. (1970). *The Black American: A documentary history.* Glenview, IL: Scott, Foresman.

Fosdick, R. (1972). *American police systems.* Montclair, NJ: Patterson Smith Reprint Series.

Franklin, J. H. (1956). *From slavery to freedom.* New York: Knopf.

Hall, L. K. (1981). Support systems and coping patterns. In L. E. Gary (Ed.), *Black men* (pp. 159–167). Beverly Hills, CA: Sage.

Hawkins, D. F. (1987). Devalued lives and racial stereotypes: Ideological barriers to the prevention of family violence among Blacks. In R. L. Hampton (Ed.), *Violence in the Black family: Correlates and consequences* (pp. 189–205). Lexington, MA: Lexington Books.

Huggins, N. I. (1990). *Black oddyssey: The African-American ordeal in slavery.* New York: Vintage.

Hughes, L. (1962). *Fight for freedom: The story of the NAACP.* New York: Berkley.

Jackson, J. G. (1990). *Introduction to African civilization.* New York: Carol.

Lester, J. (1968). *To be a slave.* New York: Dell.

Magubahe, B. M. (1989). *The ties that bind: African-American consciousness of Africa.* Trenton, NJ: Africa World Press.

Mellon, J. (Ed.). (1988). *Bullwhip days, the slaves remember: An oral history.* New York: Avon Books.

Myers, L. J. (1988). *Understanding an Afrocentric world view: Introduction to optimal psychology.* Dubuque, IA: Kendall/Hunt.

Myrdal, G. (1944). *An American dilemma.* New York: Harper & Row.

Nobles, W. W. (1982). The reclamation of culture and the right to reconciliation: An Afrocentric perspective on developing and implementing programs for the mentally retarded offender. In A. Harvey & T. Carr (Eds.), *The Black mentally retarded offender: A holistic approach to prevention and rehabilitation.* New York: United Church of Christ Commission for Racial Justice.

Phillips, F. B. (1990). NTU psychotherapy: An Afrocentric approach. *Journal of Black Psychology, 17*(1), 55–74.

Rosengarten, T. (1974). *All God's dangers: The life of Nate Shaw.* New York: Knopf. Scott v. Samford, Russell, and Emerson, 19 U.S. 393 (1857).

Silberman, C. E. (1978). *Criminal violence-criminal justice: Criminals, police, courts, and prisons in America.* New York: Random House.

Staples, R. (1982). *Black masculinity: The Black males roles in American society.* San Francisco: Black Scholar Press.

U.S. Bureau of the Census. (1992). *Statistical abstract of the United States: 1991* (111th ed.). Washington, DC: Government Printing Office.

U.S. Department of Justice, Federal Bureau of Investigation. (1989). *Uniform crime reports 1989: Crime in the United States.* Washington, DC: Government Printing Office.

U.S. Department of Justice, Office of Justice Programs, Bureau of Justice Statistics. (1988). *Survey of youth in Custody, 1987* (NCJ–113365). Washington, DC: Government Printing Office.

U.S. Department of Justice, Office of Justice Programs, Bureau of Justice Statistics. (1990). *Sourcebook of criminal justice statistics—1989* (NCJ–124224). Washington, DC: Government Printing Office.

U.S. Department of Justice, Office of Justice Programs, Bureau of Justice Statistics. (1991). *Teenage victims* (NCJ–128129). Washington, DC: Government Printing Office.

West, C. (1993). *Race matters.* Boston: Beacon.

Williams, E. (1966). *Capitalism & slavery.* New York: Capricorn Books.

Williams, L. E., & Williams, L. E. II. (1972). *Anatomy of four race riots: Racial conflict in Knoxville, Elaine (Arkansas), Tulsa and Chicago, 1919–1921.* Jackson: University and College Press of Mississippi.

Wintersmith, R. F. (1974). *Police and the Black community.* Lexington, MA: Lexington Books.

 Article Review Form at end of book.

Which explanation offered in the literature on the high rate of homicides among blacks makes the strongest argument? Why?

Explaining the Black Homicide Rate

Darnell F. Hawkins

Race has been a correlate of crime for as long as modern social scientists have been examining these variables. The rate of crime, especially homicide, has been and continues to be higher for African Americans than for whites. Are blacks genetically predisposed to violence or is their involvement in such crimes a vestige of slavery and the contemporary aftermath—social prejudice and discrimination? Or, is black crime and violence the result of socioeconomic conditions that have relegated so many African Americans to an underclass status that is nearly impossible to escape? In this reading, Darnell Hawkins asks and answers these questions while critically examining various theoretical explanations of the disproportionate rate of black homicide.

Until recently, explanations of black crime and violence were rooted in the ongoing effects of slavery, inequality, and discrimination. Hawkins refers to these as "external" reasons for black-white crime differences, circumstances residing outside the black community and over which African Americans had little control. Present-day theorists are just as likely, however, to emphasize "internal" conditions as well, those over which the minority community has some control. The social disorganization of black communities and the subculture of violence that some contend is perpetuated in black communities are often cited as more important than the legacy of slavery and discrimination.

Hawkins demonstrates the interaction between traditional external conditions and more contemporary internal circumstances. In so doing, he makes a strong case for the detrimental impact of economic inequality and racial discrimination. He is emphatic in his conclusion that deprivation, whether one is black or white, is linked to high rates of homicide. Discrimination imposes an economic burden on African Americans that is not comparable to that of any other group. In the end, black violence must be understood in the context of both historical legacy and modern socioeconomic conditions.

Numerous attempts have been made to devise theories to explain the etiology of homicide. These include explanations that focus on the psychosocial traits of individual offenders as well as on group and societal characteristics. Ethnic and racial group differences in the rate of homicide have been noted in many societies, as have the effects of racial and ethnic heterogeneity on rates of violence across societies. The comparatively high rate of homicide among American Blacks has been well documented during the last half-century. Nevertheless, relatively few theories of the etiology of homicide specifically address the question of what accounts for racial differences.

In the current discussion the literature of the past 50 years on homicide in the United States is reviewed in an attempt to identify explanations that have been offered for the extremely high rate of homicide among Blacks. Although somewhat cursory, this review reveals significant patterns. First, theory-oriented discussions of this phenomenon were more common at the turn of the century than during recent decades. A notable exception may be the work of a few theorists within the "subculture" tradition. Recent literature consists primarily of quantitative assessments of rate differences. The researchers within this tradition offer few explicit explanations for the Black-White homicide differential.

On the other hand, implicit reasons for racial differences are embedded in the methods used to study homicide in the U.S. In particular, Black-White comparisons in criminology are implicitly etiological, in that they presuppose various ways that race influences group differences. These presuppositions are an integral part of the social scientific view of race relations and social life among Blacks that has persisted for most of the twentieth century.

Many of the ideas central to this implicit theorizing have been the target of increasing criticism and debate during recent years. One major area of disagreement concerns the causal significance of historical and economic factors for the persistence of current levels of sociopathology among American Blacks. Many have questioned the extent to which slavery's legacy and present-day poverty and inequality provide explanations for the current Black-White crime

Darnell F. Hawkins, *Journal of Interpersonal Violence*, Vol. 5, 1990, pp. 151–163. Copyright © 1990 by Sage Publications, Inc. Reprinted by permission of Sage Publications, Inc.

rate differential. We will explore these issues by first examining more closely the nature of the theory that is implicit in Black-White comparisons in American social science.

The Comparison Is the Message

Social data differentiated by race has been routinely collected by governmental agencies and social researchers for many decades. Black-White comparisons have been common in social science research for most of this century. So common has this practice become that researchers frequently collect and analyze such data without any theoretically grounded reason for doing so. Such data have constituted a kind of "moral statistic" during the past, and during recent decades, its collection has been prompted by legal scrutiny of racial discrimination. Social scientists have documented racial differences in values and public opinion: the number of persons living in poverty, raised in single-parent homes, born to teen mothers, or arrested for various criminal acts. Such comparisons have been ubiquitous among both Black and White researchers and observers, making Blacks perhaps the most widely studied racial/ethnic group in the United States (Jaynes and Williams, 1989).

These differences are routinely reported and are a well-known feature of the social landscape as surveyed by social scientists or the mass media. Yet very little theory is brought to bear to explain these differences. Like any other comparisons within social science, racial comparisons are appropriate when past empirical research informs clear hypotheses about reasons for systematic group differences. But many Black-White comparisons in American social research today are made in knee-jerk fashion and without explanation, as if reasons for observed differences were "common knowledge."

It is tempting to dismiss such seemingly atheoretical studies as "mindless empiricism." But dismissing them ignores the real impact that these studies have as theory-laden "moral statistics" and political documents.[1] This article argues that a vast array of presumptions, metatheory, and theory is an integral part of such comparisons. In a society such as the United States, where race and racism have so greatly affected everyday life, these race-related theoretical underpinnings have achieved the status of common knowledge. As "common knowledge," however, they are far from harmless or noncontroversial. Black-White comparisons, although obviously useful, frequently become themselves the "message" (to paraphrase Marshall McLuhan). As silent, implicit theory, this message remains an uncontested but potentially damaging aspect of American race relations and politics.

The implicit conceptualizations and theory evident in Black-White comparisons are best revealed through an examination of the "findings" and "conclusions" that have been reported by American race relations researchers. Among them are the following:

1. When analyzed in the aggregate, most measures of various social phenomena will reveal that Blacks are more "disadvantaged" than Whites.

2. Race has been a significant "causal" factor in the distribution of advantages in the United States.

3. Most Black deficits are attributable to "social" causes. These include the legacy of slavery and oppression and continuing racism and inequality. These causes may also include sociocultural factors not linked directly to slavery and oppression such as African cultural heritage or sociocultural patterns unique to American Blacks that have arisen since the end of slavery.

4. To the extent that Black-White differences are not attributable to "social" causes, genetic differences may explain variance.

In their various forms, these themes underlie most social scientific comparisons of Blacks and Whites in the United States, whether the concern is teenage pregnancy, unemployment, or crime. They are the core of liberal race relations theory and research within the American social sciences (Vander Zanden, 1973, as cited in Pettigrew, 1980, p. xxxi). Let us now turn our attention to the criminological literature and consider the origin and development of these themes in early research on homicide.

Race and Homicide Rates

In comparison to almost all other types of crime, data on homicide have been affected less by problems of reliability and validity. One of the first major social scientific inquiries devoted entirely to the analysis of homicide (Brearley, 1932) reported that the rate among Blacks was more than seven times that for Whites. Official crime and mortality data and a large number of empirical studies conducted since Brearley's have merely documented the persistence of this racial difference. The work of Wolfgang (1958), for example, and numerous follow-up studies in that tradition have been largely data-driven and nontheoretical (Hawkins, 1986). When explicit explanations are offered, they are generally derived from reasons offered by Brearley for the race differences that he observed. Much the same can be said of the significant studies of national homicide patterns by Henry and Short (1954) and Pettigrew and Spier (1962).

In a chapter entitled, "The Negro and Homicide," Brearley (1932) reviewed a range of explanations for the disproportionate incidence of homicide among Blacks that was common during the early twentieth century. He noted that these explanations range from more credible ones to those based on prejudice or hasty generalizations. Among the various explanations outlined in his chapter were the following (pp. 111–116):

1. The West African cultural heritage from which most Black Americans originally came is characterized by a disregard for the sanctity of human life. This disregard was strengthened by the brutal conditions under which Blacks were forced to live in the New World.

2. Because of their peculiar genetically-determined temperament, Blacks lack the power to control themselves in accordance with the requirements of others.

3. Blacks are characterized by excessive emotionality which can be attributed partly to their evolution in climatic conditions characterized by excessive heat.

4. "Their education and training is less; their poverty is greater and consequently their housing and living conditions are more deplorable; there is less provision made for colored defectives; they are in a more or less unstable condition because they have but lately been given freedom and many of them, especially in the cities and the North, are in a new and strange environment; they are discriminated against socially and industrially; they are often abused by the police; and sometimes, at least, not fairly treated by the courts" (p. 115, quoting Reuter, 1927, p. 363).

5. The high homicide rate of Blacks may be more apparent than real. If interracial slayings were eliminated, and a careful study made of comparable groups of Whites and Blacks of the same economic, educational, and social status and the same inability to secure justice except by recourse to violence, approximately equal homicide rates might be found for the two races.

These were the common explanations for Black sociopathology that emerged during the decades immediately following the Civil War. Some were merely popular explanations for the group crime rate differences (within and across races) during this period. Others were popular conceptions specifically of Blacks. A comparison between Brearley's list and that derived from the current literature review reveals that social scientists have rejected the more racist and nonpositivist explanations. But when attempting to explain the high rate of Black homicide, many contemporary researchers have merely repeated more acceptable items from the Brearley listing without major modification or theoretical elaboration. This practice is especially evident in the numerous post-Wolfgang case studies of homicide in selected urban areas (Block, 1975; Bourdouris, 1970;

Lundsgaarde, 1977; Pokorny, 1965; Voss and Hepburn, 1968). Further, implicit in most multicity quantitative analyses is a Brearley-type listing, since measures of poverty, inequality, population density, and so forth, are often included in the multivariate models without sufficient theoretical justification (Blau and Blau, 1982; Messner, 1982, 1983; Messner and Tardiff, 1986). The result is a kind of nonfocused "shopping list" of reasons for the high rate of homicide among Blacks.

This "shopping list" approach to explaining the disproportionate rate of Black homicide—listing a range of sociocultural, historical-structural, economic, social psychological, biological and other factors that may contribute to the high incidence of homicide among Blacks—does not provide the guidance needed to shape policy. During the past several decades, the etiology of crime has been conceptualized most often in terms of multiple factor causation. Researchers typically argue that no single cause of any form of criminal behavior can be isolated, and they make little effort to assess the possible primacy of certain causal factors in comparison to others. But acknowledging the existence of multiple causes does not mean that all causal factors are equally important. Durkheim and other theorists noted that many factors contribute to the etiology of crime, but they also noted the causal primacy of certain factors in comparison to others.

Although little explicit theorizing has addressed the possible primacy of different causal factors in the etiology of Black homicide, recent investigations reveal a major change in the choice of explanations offered. Researchers examining Black-White homicide differences have noticeably shifted in their assumptions about the general "locus of causation." The tendency during recent years has been to emphasize "internal" as opposed to "external" factors. As part of this shift, a few researchers have attacked the now traditional focus on slavery and racial oppression as the major sources of explanation for the Black-White differential. These themes are explored next.

External Versus Internal Causation

The terms "internal" and "external" are useful as a heuristic device as long as they are not taken to imply the existence of mutually exclusive and unrelated phenomena. Many researchers acknowledge that certain "internal" conditions stem directly from various "external" forces. This article uses the terms to describe those causal factors that researchers appear to regard as primary—a distinction similar to the notion of proximate as opposed to less immediate causation in legal reasoning.

From Brearley through Wolfgang and into the 1960s and 1970s, the dominant explanations offered for the high rate of Black homicides were external. Although Brearley listed a number of competing explanations, he himself favored the explanation offered by Reuter (1927), cited earlier. Writing when slavery and the Reconstruction era were not distant memories and racial segregation and oppression were common in both the South and non-South, Brearley stressed the significance of social-structural factors, such as racial oppression. As Pettigrew (1980) has noted, this emphasis was evident in all areas of race relations research during this period.

Wolfgang, too, saw the high rate of Black homicide as primarily the result of the legacy of slavery and postslavery discrimination and oppression. Wolfgang and Ferracuti (1982) labeled as "subculture of violence" those social conditions that were "internal" to the Black community (e.g., social disorganization), and saw them as important contributors to sociopathology. They did, however, see these internal factors as themselves caused largely by external forces, specifically White racism.

As the 20th century wanes, no new explanations for the Black-White homicide differential (or other forms of Black sociopathology) have emerged. The internal colonialist explanations offered by Blauner (1972) has never been systematically applied to the study of crime, although the potential exists for such application. Building on ideas similar to those presented by Fanon (1963, 1967) and Memmi (1967), Blauner viewed Black Americans as a colonized people despite the legal gains of the 1960s. Fanon (1963, 1967) noted the high level of intragroup violence found among colonized peoples, and attributed it to the self-hatred that results from colonialist oppression. Marxist theorists have seldom addressed the question of what accounts for racial differences in levels of violence. Since the late 1970s and early 1980s, however, considerable debate has centered around several important questions, all generated because the rate of violent crime among Blacks has failed to decline significantly during the last half-century (see Lane, 1986).

Increasingly, researchers question the causal significance of the two most commonly cited "external" reasons for Black-White differences—slavery and its legacy, and continued inequality and discrimination. One current argument maintains that many of the most blatant forms of racial discrimination have been alleviated during the past three decades. Some researchers ask: If discrimination contributes to the Black crime rate, why haven't the two phenomena fallen off together? In addition, many researchers have questioned whether poverty explains the patterning of homicide within or across groups. They note the absence of a significant statistical correlation in some studies between area homicide and poverty rates. Some have noted that neither absolute nor relative deprivation alone or together can fully explain the distribution of homicide (Messner, 1982). Although not definitive, these and related research findings buttress arguments that the Black-White homicide differential may not result primarily from such external causes as current Black economic disadvantage. Yet these researchers provide few alternative explanations.

Similarly, many researchers are questioning the viability of the argument that this country's history of slavery affects current Black crime patterns. Even if the effects of slavery can be shown to have contributed to high rates of Black homicide during the early 20th century, these researchers ask how significant are

such effects today—nearly 125 years after slavery's end? The very persistence of Black disadvantage and sociopathology has been used, among other things, to call into question explanations that emphasize the significance of slavery and past oppression. That is, the temporal distance between current social conditions and slavery is said to cast doubt on its role as a major causal factor. The legal reforms of the 1960s have been cited as further evidence of the demise of slavery-produced social institutions and practices in modern American society.

As the traditional liberal explanations for Black sociopathology have been attacked, a group of researchers sometimes identified as Black conservatives has begun to explore other possible external causes. This group has also focused on alleged causes of Black disadvantage that are presumably internal to the Black community. The most prominent among these researchers are Sowell (1981, 1986) and Loury (1985, 1987). Regardless of the merit of their arguments, their major contribution has been to address the question of Black-White difference from a more theoretical perspective. The issues they raise are not new but part of a long line of work carried on by both Black and White researchers since the turn of the century.[2]

One question argued by these investigators regards which phenomenon was the greater contributor to 20th-century Black disadvantage: slavery or the massive rural-South-to-urban-North migration of the turn of the century? Frazier (1957) posed this question and concluded that the migration was a major cause of Black social disorganization and the crime it spawned in the urban North during the first half of this century. Other researchers have noted that migration to urban America was a source of sociopathology not only for Blacks but also for various White ethnic groups entering the country. This argument was a central theme of the Chicago school of sociology (Park, Burgess, and McKenzie, 1928) and was later popularized by Banfield (1970) and Glazer (1971).

This immigrant analogy was used to predict that as Blacks became economically successful, fully socialized urban residents, their rates of so-

ciopathology would drop. Irish Americans are frequently cited as an especially impressive example of such a transformation. After being the target of religious and ethnic prejudice for many decades and being regarded as prone to criminality, they are now said to be model Americans. Greeley (1974, pp. 42–43) and Schaefer (1979, pp. 129–143) showed that by the 1960s and 1970s, the average income earned by Irish Catholics was equal to that earned by most other major ethnic groups, nearly equal to the income of Jewish Americans, and greater than that earned by German Americans. These statistics and those for other ethnic and racial groups, including some more recent non-White immigrants, are often presented in contradistinction to data that document persisting Black disadvantage (Lane, 1986).

These and other attacks on traditional liberal explanations have left researchers without adequate explanations for the persistence of high rates of homicide among Blacks. The recent media coverage of the rapid rise in the homicide rate for the nation's capital has highlighted a paucity of theory and solutions. The current rate of Black homicide is much the same as that observed by Brearley more than 50 years ago. The failure of criminologists and other social scientists to offer explanations for this significant aspect of Black disadvantage represents a failure of both liberal and radical social theory in the United States. Liberal race relations theory is the product of reformist and activist impulses aimed at discounting biological notions of racial difference and ameliorating the social conditions of Black Americans. Given such a legacy, the high rate of crime among Blacks has been problematic—as much a political embarrassment as a topic for scientific scrutiny. Criminologists of a liberal bent have chosen to emphasize and investigate the problems of bias in the administration of justice rather than the problem of disproportionate killing among Blacks. Yet, given the continued political and scientific salience of this social problem, different lines of explanations have been pursued. Many researchers have turned to an emphasis on "internal" factors to account for the high rate of criminal violence among Blacks.

Internal Factors Cited

The Self-Perpetuating Subculture

The concept of a subculture has a long history in sociological research. Subcultural theory of the etiology of homicide was both implicit and explicit in Brearley's 1932 work and that of later researchers, notably Henry and Short (1954), Wolfgang (1958), Wolfgang and Spier (1962), and Lundsgaarde (1977). It has been the preeminent explanation for the etiology of crime for the past 50 years. The concept has been used frequently to explain the behavior of White ethnic groups (including southern Whites), as well as that of non-Whites. Indeed, the idea of a pathological Black subculture is implicit in much social research of the last 100 years. Within criminology, Wolfgang and Ferracuti (1982) formalized this theory into the notion of a subculture of violence.

As the persuasiveness of "external" explanations for Black sociopathology has weakened, many researchers have returned to Wolfgang's "subculture of violence" thesis. They have tended, however, to leave out Wolfgang's consideration of the force of external factors in shaping the subculture. While Wolfgang and Ferracuti have been criticized for failing to give sufficient weight to external factors, more recent theorists rely on a concept of subculture that pays even less attention to the interaction of dominant culture and subculture. Indeed, many recent analysts explicitly argue that slavery and postslavery racism do not explain the Black-White crime differential. History and current economic inequalities are acknowledged, but the Black community is depicted as an isolated, wholly self-perpetuating, pathological subculture (Curtis, 1975; Silberman, 1978). Such a subculture is said to be perpetuated less by White racism than by a lack of self-help among Blacks. This line of arguments has become more persuasive in a post-civil-rights-law era, in which affirmative action programs and much attention to the Black underclass have not conspicuously improved the welfare of the majority of Blacks.

Genes and Violence

The other major internal explanation for both intra- and inter-group crime differentials is that different groups are genetically more or less predisposed to violence. As previously noted, Brearley (1932) mentioned the possibility that constitutional differences between Blacks and Whites may explain their differing levels of homicide. Brearley de-emphasized this explanation, however, in favor of external causes. Notions of genetic differences between the races are obviously part of the implicit theory embedded in modern Black-White comparisons. The demise of liberal and radical perspectives on Black disadvantage opens the door to explicit theory linking social behavior and biological traits.

Wilson and Herrnstein (1985) provided one of the most recent restatements of the genetic/biological theory. They discounted most external explanations, including any version of the subculture of violence theory, as inadequate for explaining the Black-White crime differential. While acknowledging the limitation of all theories, including their own, to completely account for Black-White crime differences, they argued that genetic differences cannot be ignored. Both the research credentials of the authors and the absence of counter arguments have led to much scholarly and public receptiveness to this line of explanation.

Economic Inequality and Discrimination Revisited

How convincing are these alternative explanations for the high rate of homicide among Blacks? Are they supported by empirical research? It is proposed here that we must not abandon the idea that past and present racial discrimination and economic inequality are major contributors to the high rate of homicide among Blacks. The Black-White homicide differential results from the structure of American society, not from genetic or other deficiencies originating with Blacks as a group. Neither the quantitative criminological research on homicide nor any other research has discredited the im-

portance of these factors for understanding both historical and contemporary rates of violence among Blacks.

Indeed, many research findings and other observations argue for a continuing emphasis on inequality and discrimination as significant causal factors. Despite some findings to the contrary, a significant correlation has been shown to exist among societal inequality, discrimination, and homicide (Vold and Bernard, 1986). Deprivation, whether relative or absolute, is linked to high rates of homicide. Among all groups in the United States, regardless of race, homicide is found disproportionately among the lowest socioeconomic groups. Among Blacks, homicide is concentrated among the underclass. Given their methods, researchers have not been able to discount the importance of purely economic inequality (as opposed to its possible subcultural correlates) for explaining comparably high rates of homicide among Blacks, Native Americans, and southern Whites, as well as among many White ethnic immigrants during the years immediately following their entry into the United States.

Indeed, given the clustering of homicide among poor populations within societies with high levels of economic inequality, one can question the appropriateness of the traditional Black-White comparisons found in social research. That is, we must begin to ask such questions as these: What is the appropriate White group for comparison with the Black population? Is it poor Whites? Is it Whites of Southern heritage? Are all non-White populations appropriate comparison groups for understanding the sources of Black disadvantage in the United States? The debate concerning whether race or social class is the best predictor of one's life chances illustrates the need to ponder these questions (Wilson, 1978). Researchers have long noted that comparing the disproportionately lower-income Black population to a more affluent aggregate White population distorts and conceals many differences and similarities between the groups. It is also a comparison that is guided by little concern for theory. We must begin to rethink not only the theory embedded in Black-White comparisons but the importance of accounting for economic inequality in interpreting racial difference. This is an important concern when attempting to explain the rate of Black homicide in the United States.

However, an emphasis on economic inequality does not mean that we should ignore the historical context within which such inequality arose. The effects of historical forces upon current social conditions simply cannot be denied. No other ethnic group to whom Blacks as a group are often unfavorably compared was enslaved en masse and brought to this country by force. An internal colonialist model rather than an immigrant analogy might be most useful for conceptualizing the historical dimensions of Black-White relations in the United States. It is highly likely that slavery set into motion certain structural, social psychological, and economic forces that partly account for the Black-White crime differential, and that greatly affect in many other ways the behavior of both Blacks and Whites in the United States today. These forces may be extremely difficult to operationalize and quantify using positivistic scientific methods. But the difficulty of the task should not make us retreat. On the contrary, the difficulty should spur us to develop ever more refined, sensitive, and powerful research questions and methods in our attempt to articulate the causes and find the solutions to the continuing problem of Black homicide.

Notes

1. As in earlier European societies, crime indices in the United States are used as a measure of societal morality and the condition of the "dangerous class." In the United States, crime committed by Blacks has also been a politically volatile subject. The controversy surrounding the depiction of a Black criminal in the 1988 presidential campaign provides evidence of this phenomenon. Even more recently, the Stuart case in Boston has highlighted this phenomenon.
2. Many trace its origins to the classic debate between Booker T. Washington and W.E.B. Du Bois. Each of these men represented a point of view that was shared by many scholars and public

officials, both Black and White, during the late 1800s and early 1900s. At base, the debate involved questions of the relative importance of legal reform versus self-help as methods for reducing Black social disadvantage. In more recent years, this debate has included the use of an "immigrant analogy" to discuss causes of and remedies for Black deficits. Many of the ideas of Sowell and Loury are shared by such White researchers as Glazer and Moynihan.

References

Banfield, E. 1970. *The Unheavenly City: The Nature and Future of Our Urban Crisis.* Boston: Little, Brown.

Blau, J. R., and Blau, P. M. 1982. "The Cost of Inequality: Metropolitan Structure and Violent Crime" in *American Sociological Review* 47, p. 114–129.

Blauner, R. 1972. *Racial Oppression in America.* New York: Harper & Row.

Block, R. 1975. "Homicide in Chicago: A Nine-Year Study (1965–1973)." *Journal of Criminal Law and Criminology,* 66, 496–510.

Boudouris, J. 1970. *Trends in Homicide, Detroit, 1926–68.* Unpublished doctoral dissertation, Wayne State University, Detroit, Michigan.

Brearly, H. C. 1932 *Homicide in the United States.* Chapel Hill: University of North Carolina Press.

Curtis, L.A. 1975. *Violence, Race and Culture.* Lexington, MA: D.C. Health

Fanon, F. 1963. *The Wretched of the Earth.* New York: Grove.

———. 1967 *Black Skin, White Mask.* New York: Macmillian.

Frazier, E. F. 1957. *The Negro in the United States.* New York: Macmillian.

Glazer, N. 1971. "Black and Ethnic Groups: The Difference, and the Political Difference It Makes" in N. I. Huggins, M. Kilson, & D. M. Fox (Eds.), *Key Issues in the Afro-American Experience* (Vol. 2, 193–211). New York: Harcourt Brace Jovanovich.

Greeley, A. M. 1974. *Ethnicity in the United States: A Preliminary Reconnaissance.* New York: Wiley.

Hawkins, D. F. 1986. *Homicide Among Black Americans.* Lanham, MD: University Press of America.

Henry, A. F., and Short, J. F. 1954. *Suicide and Homicide.* Glencoe, IL: Free Press.

Jaynes, G. D., and Williams, R. M., Jr. (Eds.). 1989. *A Common Destiny: Blacks and American Society.* Washington, D.C.: National Academy Press.

Lane, R. 1986. *Roots of Violence in Black Philadelphia, 1860–1900.* Cambridge, MA: Harvard University Press.

Loury, G. C. 1985. "The Moral Quandary of the Black Community" in *Public Interest* 79, 9–22.

———. 1987. "Matters of Color—Blacks and the Constitutional Order" in *Public Interest* 85, 109–123.

Lundsgaarde, H. P. 1977. *Murder in Space City: A Cultural Analysis of Houston Homicide Patterns.* New York: Oxford University Press.

Memmi, A. 1967. *The Colonizer and the Colonized.* Boston: Beacon.

Messner, S. F. 1982. "Poverty, Inequality, and the Urban Homicide Rate: Some Unexpected Findings" in *Criminology* 20, 103–114.

———. 1983. "Regional Differences in the Economic Correlates of the Urban Homicide Rate: Some Evidence on the Importance of the Cultural Context." *Criminology* 21, 477–488.

Messner, S. F., and Tardiff, K. 1986. "Economic Inequality and Levels of Homicide: An Analysis of Urban Neighborhoods" in *Criminology* 24, 297–318.

Park, R. Burgess, E. W., and McKenzie, R. D. 1928. *The City.* Chicago: University of Chicago Press.

Pettigrew, T. F. (Ed.). 1980. *The Sociology of Race Relations.* New York: Free Press.

Pettigrew, T. F. and Spier, R. B. 1962. "The Ecological Structure of Negro Homicide" in *American Journal of Sociology* 67, 621–629.

Pokorny, A. D. 1965. "A Comparison of Homicide in Two Cities" in *Journal of Criminal Law, Criminology, and Police Science* 56, 479–487.

Reuter, E. G. 1927. *American Race Problems.* New York: Crowell.

Schaefer, R. T. 1979. *Racial and Ethnic Groups.* Boston: Little, Brown.

Silberman, C. E. 1978. *Criminal Violence, Criminal Justice.* New York: Vintage.

Sowell, T. 1981. *Ethnic America.* New York: Basic Books.

———. 1986. *A Conflict of Visions.* New York: William Morrow.

Vander Zanden, J. W. 1973. "Sociological Studies of American Blacks" in *Sociological Quarterly* 14,32.

Vold, G. B., and Bernard, T. J. 1986. *Theoretical Criminolgy.* New York: Oxford University Press.

Voss, H., Hepburn, J. R. 1968. "Patterns in Criminal Homicide in Chicago" in *Journal of Criminal Law, Criminology and Police Science,* 59, 499–508

Wilson, J. Q., and Herrnstein, R. J. 1985. *Crime and Human Nature.* New York: Simon & Schuster.

Wilson, W. J. 1978 *The Declining Significance of Race.* Chicago: University of Chicago Press.

Wolfgang, M. E. 1958. *Patterns in Criminal Homicide.* New York: Wiley.

Wolfgang, M. E., and Ferracuti, F. 1982. *The Subculture of Violence: Towards an Integrated Theory in Criminology.* Beverly Hills, CA: Sage.

Article Review Form at end of book.

WiseGuide Wrap-Up

- Blacks argue that solutions to the crime problem should be approached through governmental intervention.

- African American men and women convicted of crimes receive different sanctions, depending on the color of the crime victims.

- The high incidents of violence, especially homicide, are best examined by racial and economic discrimination.

R.E.A.L. Sites

This list provides a print preview of typical **Coursewise** R.E.A.L. sites. (There are over 100 such sites at the **Courselinks**™ site.) The danger in printing URLs is that web sites can change overnight. As we went to press, these sites were functional using the URLs provided. If you come across one that isn't, please let us know via email to: webmaster@coursewise.com. Use your Passport to access the most current list of R.E.A.L. sites at the **Courselinks** site.

Site name: Criminological Theory

URL: http://home.ici.net/~ddemelo/crime/crimetheory.html

Why is it R.E.A.L.? This site is a good source to find out more about criminological theories. It covers the early as well as the contemporary theories of crime. The visitor is able to read in-depth information about biological, psychological, rational choice, labeling, social control, and conflict theories. The student reading about these theories should keep in mind that some of them are used to explain criminality among members of minority classes.

Key topics: black criminality, born criminal, theories of crime, labeling, subculture, social control, strain, radical

Try this: Describe the underlying premise of social control theories. How do strain theorists explain crime?

Site name: Explanations of Criminal Behavior

URL: http://www.uaa.alaska.edu/just/just110/crime2.html

Why is it R.E.A.L.? This site contains information about the major theories of crime. These theories aim at explaining why crime takes place. The student visiting this site will find a comprehensive outline of the major theories of crime that highlights their main contribution to the criminological literature.

Key topics: theories of crime, left realism, conflict theory, minimal brain dysfunction, twin studies

Try this: What are the two main types of criminological theories? Describe the five modes of adaptation to social strain.

Site name: Crime Times

URL: http://www.crime-times.org/

Why is it R.E.A.L.? This site contains research reviews and information on the biological causes of criminal, violent, and psychopathic behavior. This is of particular interest to the race and crime student, since biological predisposition to criminality has been regarded as insightful by many in the attempt to explain the criminality of minorities. Others claim that this premise is racist and offers many justifications for racism.

Key topics: aggression, biology, psychology, crime, psychopathy, intelligence

Try this: Do genes influence one's predisposition to act aggressively? Is there a link between a low I.Q. and aggressive behavior?

section

3

Learning Objectives

After studying this section, you will know

- that most inmates wrongfully convicted to death row are minority members.

- that police chiefs rank the death penalty as the least effective and least cost-saving method of preventing crime.

- that the U.S. Supreme Court has affected, through judicial decision making, the acts of police aggression toward African Americans.

- that some drug-related laws should be revisited to ensure better treatment of African Americans by the system of justice.

 **WiseGuide Intro**

This section examines the societal response to crime, and some of the issues addressed here overlap with other sections of the reader. We examine the characteristics of those who commit hate crimes, the views of minority members toward law enforcement, the death penalty as a response to crime, and the effectiveness of legislation with regard to crime in American society. Hate crimes are essentially acts of prejudice based on one's race, gender, or ethnicity. Since hate crimes raise levels of suspicion, anger, and hostility within communities, hate crime legislation is seen as one way to address these concerns and to acknowledge that we can be victims in today's world, based on who we are. Hate crime legislation is one of many responses to the bigotry and prejudice that characterize society. Recent shootings, which included hatred against certain people, make the case that our society is riddled with prejudice and that there is the need to identify crimes motivated by hatred. It remains to be seen whether or not hate bills will become effective pieces of legislation.

Another societal response to crime is use of the death penalty for capital crimes. Today, most Americans favor this method of punishment for heinous crimes. The death penalty, however, is hampered by politics, perceptions, and discretion. It seems a penalty that we do not want to enforce, given the number of capital crimes committed, relative to the number of individuals on death row. One of many ironies with regard to capital punishment is that it is reserved for an elite few. The death penalty is prima facie evidence that our system of justice is patently unfair. The lack of adequate representation for indigents accused of capital crimes raises fundamental questions about fairness and equality as a response to crime. Recently, the American Bar Association (ABA) called for a moratorium on capital punishment, raising questions about feckless counsel and gender and race discrimination. Confounding matters here is that our responses to crime sometimes seem grounded in theology—that is, what we believe to be true, instead of the empirical evidence. It is amazing, for example, how bright, well-educated individuals can debate this issue and not be influenced by the data.

Public policy ought to be grounded in scientific research. It is amazing how appropriations for more and more boot camps are made without knowledge of the empirical evidence. The funding is predicated on the illusion of reduced rates of recidivism. The same can be said of the financial burdens government assumes (at the expense of the taxpayer) to build more and more prisons. Even the private prison concept is flawed at several levels and should be questioned: Is there a breach when the government transfers custody to a private unit? Is the net effect of private prisons to skim the best of the worse—to leave the worst of the worse behind in government-run prisons, making our prisons doubly difficult to manage? The societal response to crime ought to be rational and with reasonable expectations. One auspicious beginning would be with the federal sentencing guidelines, where disparities exist between crack cocaine and powder cocaine use.

Other societal responses include greater use of community corrections as an alternative to imprisonment. There is, for instance, a growing body of literature that points toward the punitive nature of probation, especially intensive probation. If intensive and regular probation can be made "dreaded" by offenders, relative to the monotony of prison life, this should be explored. The use of fines, while not discussed in this reader, may be an effective strategy for the public to consider. In all, there are no guarantees that all of these proposals will abate disparate treatment or will address many of the color and class issues that emerge in this book. At best, we self-correct by purging draconian criminal justice policies and wisely investing in our most important resource, people.

As indicated, this section covers topics that are tangential to the other sections. The objective is to expose you to societal/criminal justice policy initiatives. One last idea pertains to the need to think outside of the box and to develop different paradigms—for responding to race and crime issues. Thinking about crime from a broader perspective—as a public health problem—may represent a beginning. Another response to the crime problem might be development and implementation of culturally specific programs for offenders in our state and federal prisons. Recognizing that we have problems and exploring the adequacy of existing programs/policies for the offender as well as society may be ways to break the cycle of failure and to address policy issues specific to race.

? Questions ?

Reading 13. How many death row inmates are found innocent when compared with the number of executions?

Reading 14. How do police chiefs regard the effectiveness of the death penalty?

Reading 15. Identify two relatively recent events that have marked the differences that exist in the way European and African Americans react to policing strategies.

Reading 16. Describe the differential punishments given to blacks in the United States during the period of slavery.

How many death row inmates are found innocent when compared with the number of executions?

The Wrong Men on Death Row

A growing number of bad convictions challenges the death penalty's fairness.

Joseph P. Shapiro

Gary Gauger's voice was flat when he called 911 to report finding his father in a pool of blood. Police arrived at the Illinois farmhouse Gauger shared with his parents and discovered that his mother was dead, too. The 40-year-old son, a quirky ex-hippie organic farmer, became a murder suspect. After all, someone had slashed Ruth and Morrie Gauger's throats just 30 feet from where Gary slept. There were no signs of a struggle or robbery. But what most bothered the cops was the son's reaction: He quietly tended to his tomato plants as they investigated. Eventually, Gauger was sentenced to die by lethal injection—until it became clear police had the wrong guy. His case is not unusual.

After years of debate, most Americans now believe the death penalty is an appropriate punishment for the most repulsive murders. But that support is rooted in an underlying assumption: that the right person is being executed. The most recent list by an antideath-penalty group shows that Gary Gauger is one of 74 men exonerated and freed from death row over the past 25 years—a figure so stark it's causing even some supporters of capital punishment to rethink whether the death penalty can work fairly. Among them is Gerald Kogan, who recently stepped down as chief justice of Florida's Supreme Court. "If one innocent person is executed along the way, then we can no longer justify capital punishment," he says.

Mistaken Convictions

For every 7 executions—486 since 1976—1 other prisoner on death row has been found innocent. And there's concern even more mistaken convictions will follow as record numbers of inmates fill death rows, pressure builds for speedy executions, and fewer attorneys defend prisoners facing execution. Next week, Gauger and scores of others mistakenly condemned will gather at Northwestern University School of Law in Chicago for the National Conference on Wrongful Convictions & the Death Penalty. They are "the flesh and blood mistakes of the death penalty," says Richard Dieter of the Death Penalty Information Center.

Timeout Sought

Executions have been rare since the death penalty was reinstated in 1976. But the pace is picking up. There are now 3,517 prisoners on death row in the 38 capital-punishment states—an all-time high and a tripling since 1982. The 74 executions in 1997—the most since 1955—represented a 60 percent spike from the year before. Citing bad lawyering and mistaken convictions, the American Bar Association last year called for a death-penalty moratorium. This month, Illinois legislators will vote on such a ban. That state, more than any other, is grappling with the problem: It has exonerated almost as many men (nine) on death row as it has executed (11).

It's tempting to view the reprieved as proof that the legal system eventually corrects its mistakes. But only one of the nine men released in Illinois got out through normal appeals. Most have outsiders to thank. Northwestern University journalism professor David Protess and four of his students followed leads missed by police and defense attorneys to tie four other men to the rape and murders that put four innocent men in prison. "Without them, I'd be in the graveyard," says Dennis Williams, who spent 16 years on death row. "The system didn't do anything."

Most damning of the current system would be proof that a guiltless person has been executed. Credible, but not clear-cut, claims of innocence have been raised in a handful of executions since 1976. Leonel Herrera died by lethal injection in Texas in 1993 even though another man confessed to the murder. The U.S. Supreme Court ruled that, with his court appeals exhausted, an extraordinary amount of proof was required to stop his execution. Governors, the court noted, can still grant clemency in such cases. But what was once common is now so politically risky that only about one death row inmate a year wins such freedom.

How Wrongful Convictions Happen

Gary Gauger's calm gave a cop a hunch. But it was Gauger's trusting nature that gave police a murder tale that day in 1993. Gauger says that during 18 hours of nonstop interrogation, detectives insisted they had a "stack of evidence" against him. They didn't—but it never occurred to the laid-back farmer that his accusers might be lying. Instead, he worried he might have blacked out the way he sometimes did in the days when he drank heavily. So Gauger went along with police suggestions that, to jog his memory, he hypothetically describe the murders. After viewing photos of his mother's slit throat, Gauger explained how he could have walked into her rug shop next to the house ("she knows and trusts me"), pulled her hair, slashed her throat and then done the same to his dad as he worked in his nearby antique-motorcycle shop. To police, this was a chilling confession. Even Gauger, by this point suicidal, believed he must have committed the crimes.

False Confessions

Though police failed to turn up any physical evidence during a 10-day search of the farm, prosecutors depicted Gauger as an oddball who could have turned on his mother and father. He was a pot-smoking ex-alcoholic who once lived on a commune and brought his organic farming ways back to Richmond, Ill. The judge rolled his eyes during Gauger's testimony and, when defense attorneys objected, simply turned his back on Gauger. The jury took just three hours to reach a guilty verdict. "Nutty as a fruitcake," the jury foreman declared afterward.

A study by Profs. Hugo Bedau of Tufts University and Michael Radelet of the University of Florida found three factors common among wrongful capital convictions. One third involve perjured testimony, often from jailhouse snitches claiming to have heard a defendant's prison confession. (At Gauger's trial, a fellow inmate made a dubious claim to hearing Gauger confess. The man, contacted in jail by *U.S. News*, offered to tell a very different story if the magazine would pay for an interview.) One of every 7 cases, Bedau and Radelet found, involves faulty eyewitness identifications, and a seventh involve false confessions, like Gauger's.

False confessions occur with greater frequency than recognized even by law-enforcement professionals, argues Richard Leo of the University of California–Irvine. About a quarter, he estimates, involve people with mild mental retardation, who often try to hide limitations by guessing "right" answers to police questions. Children are vulnerable, too. Chicago police in September dropped murder charges against two boys, 7 and 8 years old, who confessed to killing 11-year-old Ryan Harris with a rock to steal her bicycle. After a crime laboratory found semen on the dead girl's clothes, police began looking for an older suspect. An educated innocent person, likely to trust police, may be especially prone to police trickery—which courts allow as often necessary to crack savvy criminals. "My parents had just been murdered and these were the good guys," Gauger says. "I know it sounds naive now, but when they told me they wouldn't lie to me, I believed them."

The falsely convicted is almost always an outsider—often from a minority group. In Illinois, six of the nine dismissed from death row were black or Hispanic men accused of murder, rape, or both of white victims. But the No. 1 reason people are falsely convicted is poor legal representation. Many states cap fees for court-appointed attorneys, which makes it tough for indigents to get competent lawyers. And it's been harder for inmates to find lawyers to handle appeals since Congress in 1996 stopped funding legal-aid centers in 20 states.

How Wrongful Convictions Get Discovered

Gary Gauger has a simple answer to how he won his freedom: "I got lucky." Of all the 74 released from death row, Gauger's stay was one of the briefest—just eight months. Shortly after his conviction, FBI agents listening in on a wiretap overheard members of a motorcycle gang discussing the murder of Ruth and Morrie Gauger. Last year, two members of the Outlaws Motorcycle Club, Randall "Madman" Miller and James

"Preacher" Schneider, were indicted for the Gauger killings. But a federal judge last month ruled the wiretaps were unauthorized and dismissed all the charges. The U.S. Attorney says he is seeking to reinstate them.

Even when another person confesses, the legal system can be slow to respond. Rolando Cruz and Alejandro Hernandez spent 10 years each on death row in Illinois for the rape and murder of 10-year-old Jeanine Nicarico. Shortly after their convictions, police arrested a repeat sex offender and murderer named Brian Dugan who confessed to the crime, providing minute details unknown to the public. Prosecutors still insisted Cruz and Hernandez were the killers—even after DNA testing linked Dugan to the crime. At Cruz's third trial, a police officer admitted that he'd lied when he testified Cruz had confessed in a "vision" about the girl's murder. The judge then declared Cruz not guilty. In January, seven police officers and prosecutors go on trial charged with conspiracy to conceal and fabricate evidence against Cruz and Hernandez.

Discarded Evidence

DNA profiling, perhaps more than any other development, has exposed the fallibility of the legal system. In the last decade, 56 wrongfully convicted people have won release because of DNA testing, 10 of them from death row. Attorneys Barry Scheck and Peter Neufeld, with the help of their students at New York's Cardozo School of Law, have freed 35 of those. But their Innocence Project has been hobbled by the fact that, in 70 percent of the cases they pursued police had already discarded semen, hair, or other evidence needed for testing.

Gauger had one other thing going for him that is key to overturning bogus convictions: outside advocates. Most important was his twin sister, Ginger, who convinced Northwestern Law School Prof. Lawrence Marshall (who also defended Cruz and organized next week's conference) to help her brother a week before the deadline for the final state appeal. In September 1994, Gauger's death sentence was reduced to life in prison.

Two years later, he was freed. Marshall visited Gauger in prison with the surprise news. "That's good," he said with a smile and his customary calm.

How to Prevent Wrongful Convictions

It's a fall afternoon and starlings are fluttering through the colorful maples that frame the Gauger farmhouse. Gary Gauger loads a dusty pickup with pumpkins, squash, and other vegetables. Inside, Ginger has taken up her mother's business of selling Asian kilims and American Indian pottery. A friend runs the vintage-motorcycle business, still called Morrie's Place, in an adjoining garage. For Gary Gauger, life seems normal again. Customers at his vegetable stand sort through bushels of squash. A hand-lettered sign advises: "Self Service: please place money in black box . . . thanks."

But there is pain, too, for his lost parents and for his 3 1/2 lost years. And it's that part of his story Gauger will share at the upcoming conference in the hope of sparing others such pain. Other conferees at the Northwestern event are expected to endorse a moratorium on executions at least until safeguards are in place such as increased legal aid, certification of capital-trial attorneys, limits on use of jail-house snitches, access to post-conviction DNA testing, and the recording of all police interrogations. There will also be appeals for accreditation of forensic experts: The first Cruz trial turned on a bloody footprint identified by an expert who was later discredited when she claimed she could tell a person's class and race by shoe imprints.

Gauger says the worst part about being wrongfully convicted is knowing that the guilty person is free. The victim Gauger most thinks about is 7-year-old Melissa Ackerman. The little girl was grabbed from her bicycle, sodomized, and left in an irrigation ditch, her body so unrecognizable that she could be identified only by dental records. She was killed by Brian Dugan, while Rolando Cruz and Alejandro Hernandez sat behind bars—falsely convicted of another child's murder committed by Dugan.

 Article Review Form at end of book.

How do police chiefs regard the effectiveness of the death penalty?

Death at Midnight... Hope at Sunrise

Steven Hawkins

Steven Hawkins is the executive director of the National Coalition to Abolish the Death Penalty.

If Connie Ray Evans was some awful monster deemed worthy of extermination, why did I feel so bad about it, I wondered. It has been said that men on death row are inhuman, cold-blooded killers. But as I stood and watched a grieving mother leave her son for the last time, I questioned how the sordid business of executions was supposed to be the great equalizer. I watched Connie's family slowly make their way to the parking lot, attempting to console each other over their private grief. "Is there ever an end to the pain?" I asked aloud, to no one in particular.

—Donald Cabana,
Death at Midnight: The Confession of an Executioner

As warden, from 1984 to 1989, Donald Cabana gave the order to execute men at the Mississippi State Penitentiary in Parchman. Yet, with each execution, Cabana came to realize more and more the utter pain, the profound waste and the senseless dehumanization that the death penalty places upon our society. His recently released book, *Death at Midnight: The Confession of an Executioner*, is a powerful account of the failings and inconsistencies of the death penalty by someone in the best position to make such an observation—the person in charge of carrying it out. It has been more than 70 years since we have had the benefit of such a perspec-

tive—not since Lewis Lawes, the warden at Sing Sing, gave us *Man's Judgment of Death* in 1924. Through their first-hand experience with the death penalty, both Cabana and Lawes became firmly opposed to capital punishment.

The failure of the death penalty as a crime-fighting measure also has been noted by law enforcement officials. In January 1995, Peter D. Hart Research Associates conducted a survey of randomly-selected police chiefs from around the nation. The Hart survey found that police chiefs rank the death penalty as the least effective way of reducing violent crime, placing it behind such alternatives as curbing drug abuse, putting more police on the streets, lowering the legal barriers to prosecution and improving the economic condition. With respect to public safety, the police chiefs also ranked the death penalty last among cost-effective priorities, putting at the forefront community policing, police training and equipment, neighborhood watch patrols, drug and alcohol programs and anti-gang efforts.

Apart from the lack of any value in deterring crime, the death penalty continues to be tainted with all the problems of its troubled past. In 1972, the U.S. Supreme Court struck down capital punishment because it was arbitrary and completely unpredictable in its selected fury. The only discernable pattern suggested a punishment reserved for the poor and racial minorities. In 1976, the

Supreme Court allowed the death penalty to return, but on the promise of fairness and justice in its administration. Twenty years later, that promise has not been fulfilled. The overwhelming majority of persons on death row still come from poverty-stricken backgrounds—more than 90 percent of them could not have hired a private attorney. And, more than half of the condemned still are members of racial and ethnic minorities. To make matters worse, nearly 60 people have been released from death row on grounds of their innocence.

While we have spent the last twenty years tinkering with the machinery of death—hopelessly trying to find a way to administer capital punishment in a consistent fashion, devoid of fatal error—the rest of the world has been moving away from the death penalty altogether. In fact, the majority of nations in the global community have abolished the death penalty either in law or in practice. Additionally, the execution of children (those under 18 years old at the time of the crime) has been eliminated in all but five countries—Iran, Pakistan, Yemen, Saudi Arabia . . . and the United States.

We may be at the midnight hour in our use of the death penalty, but there lies a dawn of hope as more people begin to question its legitimacy. The Academy Award-winning film, *Dead Man Walking*, shows us that sympathy for the pain and the plight of victims does not have to be synonymous with support for capital

"Death at Midnight . . . Hope at Sunrise," Steven Hawkins. *Corrections Today*, Vol. 58, No. 5, August 1996. Reprinted with permission from the American Correctional Association, Lanham, MC.

punishment. It takes courage to stand up and recognize this basic fact, but stand we must. As Cabana writes at the end of his book: "This is not a particularly good time in which to find myself an opponent of capital punishment. Paradoxically, however, if this is the worst of times to be against the death penalty, it may also be the best of times. Never has there been a greater need for rationality and clear thinking. Absent the emotionalism and histrionics that always have been characteristic of the debate, the present offers greater opportunity than ever for pragmatism and calm deliberation. There is much need, and room, for both.

 Article Review Form at end of book.

Identify two relatively recent events that have marked the differences that exist in the way European and African Americans react to policing strategies.

The Coca Cola Bottle Theory:

A Look at the Twentieth Century Effect of Exigency on Policing Strategies in the African American Community

Ramona Brockett, Ph.D., J.D.

Assistant Professor, Kent State University

Although America is often described as a melting pot, and those who live within its boundaries are supposed to be homogeneous, this description is a fallacy.[1] America is a place where Africans and Europeans live very differently. The difference in the way African Americans and European Americans are treated is often seen through the extreme use of social control exercised by the police. That difference is reflected not only in the way each group perceives the fairness of its treatment by those who exercise social control; in addition, those who exercise social control are often viewed as treating different groups differently. Further, police are often the ones blamed for excessive use of force. However, is it really the fault of police; or are the actions of police being sanctioned by the U.S. Supreme Court? The discussion in this paper focuses on the sweeping changes in Supreme Court decision making during the twentieth century, the effect on policing strategies and police aggressiveness, and the impact on African American citizens.

The 1990s in America have shown that police aggression affects European Americans and African Americans very differently. Two events during this decade that indicate a difference in the way European Americans and African Americans react to policing strategies are the Rodney King incident and the O. J. Simpson case. In both instances, African Americans overwhelmingly interpreted police aggression as violent and intrusive.[2] Further, in the case of O. J. Simpson, African Americans viewed the system of policing as unfair and prejudiced. African Americans overwhelmingly thought that O. J. Simpson was innocent and had been set up by the police because of his status as a wealthy African who did not know his "place" as a secondary citizen in America.[3] Interestingly, many African Americans presumed that O. J. Simpson was innocent because of their negative perception of police aggression, along with their distrust of police as an institution. On the other hand, European Americans, to a great extent, viewed the actions of the police and the justice system as justified in both the King and Simpson cases.[4] However, in both cases, the question left unanswered is: What is the true influence of police aggression? Has this country produced unruly groups of gun-wielding, anti-African American social control extremists? Or have the actions of the police been sanctioned by a more powerful legal authority?

The Influence of the Supreme Court on Race, Civil Liberties and the Approval of Police Aggression

Supreme Court decisions have affected police acts of aggression toward African Americans. Over time, U.S. Supreme Court rulings have defined acceptable and unacceptable police actions toward the public. Perhaps the explanation for why African Americans and European Americans are perceived as being treated very differently with regard to police aggression involves trends in the history of brutality that have been sanctioned by the Supreme Court's interpretation of the Constitution through criminal procedure and history. Social control theories focus on the strategies and techniques used to regulate human behavior, the purpose of which is to lead to obedience and conformity to society's rules (Adler et al. 1995). Thus, the Supreme Court is empowered to exercise its legal muscles to enforce such controls through various forms of punishment. This paper will further identify and analyze the legal controls of punishment that the Supreme Court uses to exercise social control and to sanction police aggressiveness.

The historic power of the U.S. Supreme Court over African American's rights includes the Court's dictating the African American's right to vote, own property, enjoy the privilege of citizenship, and ultimately, be considered equal. These rights, which were granted by the U.S. Supreme Court, often represented efforts by Africans not only to achieve equality but also to be treated fairly. Not having such rights placed African Americans in jeopardy. Interestingly, this same Supreme Court has, through legal decision making, placed the African citizen status in jeopardy once again through the denial of the protections under the Bill of Rights against unreasonable searches and seizures.

Historical Perspectives on Social Control, African Americans, European Americans, and the Supreme Court

Three controls promote the existence of social control in the court system: constitutional interpretation, the police, and "get tough on crime" legislation. Each of these mechanisms supports the punishment of incarceration, which directly affects the status of African Americans through various forms of social control (Petersilia 1997). For instance, the Thirteenth, Fourteenth, and Fifteenth Amendments, while used to secure the freedoms of formerly enslaved Africans, have been subjected to the interpretation of the meaning of the framers' original intent regarding freedom, equality, and fair treatment. The U.S. Supreme Court uses its decision-making authority to interpret the original framers' constitutional intent and apply its meaning to current social norms. Current trends in U.S. Supreme Court decision making as applied to constitutional interpretation further the notion of social control by usurping civil liberties in support of governmental intrusion. First, let us examine notions of social control in terms of privileges, immunities, and equal protection for African Americans as guaranteed by the Thirteenth, Fourteenth, and Fifteenth Amendments.

After the Civil War, the Thirteenth Amendment, ratified in 1865, abolished slavery and involuntary servitude.[5] The Fourteenth Amendment, ratified in 1868, provided citizenship and guaranteed equal protection for former slaves.[6] In addition to these two amendments, Congress enacted the Civil Rights Acts of 1866 after the ratification of the Thirteenth Amendment (Mann 1993). This was the first Civil Rights Act. It was passed in response to the Black Codes, which sought to reduce the status of African Americans to that of semi-slavery (Allport 1979). The Black Codes limited the rights of African Americans to own property, denied African Americans the right to testify against European Americans, prevented African Americans from being in the streets after dark, provided imprisonment for any breach of employment contract, and provided an employment provision that mandated the allocation of menial jobs to African Americans (Allport 1979 Miller 1966; Todd 1979; Marable 1983). Protection in terms of equality came with the ratification of the Fifteenth Amendment in 1870, which gave African Americans the right to vote.[7] Following the ratification of the Fifteenth Amendment, the Civil Rights Act of 1875, which was enacted during the Reconstruction Era, provided federal power to limit racial discrimination by redefining the titles of Americans as "citizens" instead of "blacks" or "whites."[8] Therefore, the promise of equality was delivered to African Americans upon the ratification and enactment of these provisions; however, the U.S. Supreme Court in the 1890s interpreted the framers' intent, redefining equality for African Americans and ultimately denying their rights. The analysis of Supreme Court intervention that follows will allow you to further understand the impact of the amendments and civil rights acts, in light of African Americans' rights to citizenship, equality, and fairness. An understanding of the impact of this portion of the paper will provide a possible explanation for the historic differences in the treatment of African Americans as a result of Supreme Court decision making.

First, prior to the Thirteenth Amendment and the Civil Rights Act of 1866, in the case of *Dred Scott v. Sanford,* 60 U.S. 393 (1857), the question being determined by the Court was whether a Negro whose ancestors were imported to this country as slaves could become a member of the political economy and community through the privileges and immunities clause guaranteed by the Constitution; and, further, whether that Negro could be considered a citizen of the United States. The U.S. Supreme Court unequivocally concluded no.[9] Further, the Court concluded that only those who presently held the right to be citizens could grant that same right to Negroes, upon the grantor's discretion.

The Supreme Court continued its rampage of racist decision making in the late 1800s, which mirrors the current rash of racist decision making. The first decision came in 1873 with the *Slaughter-House Cases.*[10] In these cases, the justices on the Court determined the need to restore the Dred Scott Doctrine after the Civil Rights Act of 1866 and the establishment of the Thirteenth, Fourteenth, and Fifteenth Amendments. This decision threatened the privileges and immunities clause of the Fourteenth Amendment by reinstating the idea of two classes of citizenship, chiefly national and state. Further, voting rights and the restoration of civil rights were given to the control of the states with the cases of *United States v. Cruishank* (1875)[11] and *United States v. Reese* (1875).[12] These decisions radically usurped the power of the Fourteenth and Fifteenth Amendments by granting states the right to enforce these amendments as they pleased. The decision that ultimately abolished the power of the Thirteenth Amendment and reinstated the philosophy of *Dred Scott* came from the language of the decision in the case of *Plessy v. Ferguson* (1896).[13] Supreme Court Justice Brown not only distinguished the differences in citizenship between African and European Americans, but he also described the Negro as abject, ignorant, childlike, and unfit. These particular words for describing the Negro in America have never been overturned. Further, these words justified the Court's decision to continue the dual classes of citizenship by constitutionally mandating separate but equal facilities for blacks and whites. This decision killed whatever remnants were left of the Act of 1875, which permitted people within the United States to be considered "citizens" instead of "black" or "white." Thus, the Supreme Court distinguished between African and European citizens, making African citizens less than European citizens. This was done through the legitimacy of legal decision making.

Presently, this debate of dual citizenship still exists and impacts African American and European Americans differently. First, in the late 1960s and mid 1970s, the Court wrestled once again with the Thirteenth Amendment, the Black Codes, and the rights associated with citizenship in terms of property ownership, the right to contract, and the right to attend private school. In two separate cases, *Jones v. Alfred H. Mayer Co.* (1968)[14] and *Runyon v. McCray* (1976),[15] the court considered the Act of 1866 and 42 U.S.C. sect. 1981, which prohibits racial discrimination in the making and enforcement of private contracts.[16] In both cases, the court dealt with the right to contract privately. In both cases, it determined that a Negro should be allowed to contract to buy a home or alternatively to go to private school, and that the contract should not be prohibited by the badge of indicia lodged in the color of skin. What becomes more important, however, in both of these cases are the dissenting opinions.

Justice Rehnquist, who presently is the Chief Justice of the current Supreme Court, along with Justices Harlan and White, stated in the dissents of both *Runyon* and *Jones*

that the basic law of contracts promotes the notion of mutual assent. Mutual assent in the law is the agreeing of two parties to a contract. This agreement is the basic constitutional right of each party to enter unencumbered into a contract. These justices sharing the same sentiment conclude that, in a contract, regardless of whether there is racial animus on the part of the white party, if the white person who is party to the contract does not want to contract with a black person, then no mutual assent exists. Without mutual assent, Rehnquist concludes, this supersedes the provision of 42 U.S.C. sect. 1981, which prohibits racial discrimination in the making of private contracts. Although this is part of the dissenting opinion, legal analysis has consistently revealed that dissenting opinions often have influence when the Supreme Court re-examines similar issues, becoming incorporated into the majority opinion in similar cases. The importance of the dissenting opinion is important in this study because Justice Rehnquist is now the Chief Justice of the Supreme Court. Further, as will be discussed *infra*, the decisions presently coming from the Supreme Court are vastly affecting African Americans more than European Americans. These decisions are affecting African Americans' civil liberties and property rights. The decisions are allowing police to actively seize property without the protections of the Bill of Rights and civil rights. Invariably, the owners of seized property are African Americans. Thus, the previous discussion on contracts merely states the influence that Justice Rehnquist has on the rights of the African citizen, which in turn affects approval rates of police aggression.

Our final consideration of constitutional interpretation involves how it relates to civil liberties and the Supreme Court's interpretation of the Fourth Amendment.[17] The Coca Cola Bottle Theory (Brockett, Jones 1995) examines the liberal and conservative interpretations by the U.S. Supreme Court of the Fourth Amendment bar against unreasonable search and seizure. Throughout the twentieth century, the Supreme Court has broadly and narrowly construed the breadth of Fourth Amendment guarantees in light of civil liberties. For

instance, the Warren Court of the 1960s recognized through the case of *Miranda vs. Arizona*[18] the importance of silence and being protected by the Constitution from unreasonable searches and seizures. The Coca Cola Bottle Theory notes the liberal and conservative legal decision-making discretion that the Court has had during the twentieth century with regard to citizens' rights to be protected. However, as the twentieth century ends and the twenty-first century begins, it is apparent that the Rehnquist Court is determined to abandon the protections guaranteed by the Fourth Amendment against unreasonable searches and seizures. In fact, the Rehnquist Court has narrowed the scope of protections guaranteed by the Constitution. Thus, in the Coca Cola Bottle analogy, the wide discretion the Warren Court sought for protecting the rights of citizens has now been replaced by the narrow neck of the bottle, in that the Rehnquist Court seems to no longer uphold citizens' rights against unreasonable searches and seizures.

The Rehnquist Court, Civil Liberties, Police Aggression, and Their Effect on African and European American Approval Rates

The Rehnquist Court has broadened the scope of exigency or emergency circumstances as a bar against providing a search warrant (*California v. Hodari D.*, 499 U.S. 621 [1991]; *Maryland v. Buie*, 494 U.S. 325 [1990]). Essentially, the Court condones the taking of a person's property at will if a government official, or police person, considers the property owner or the situation dangerous. The danger then is termed an emergency, which allows the government to take or seize property without a warrant. Chief Justice Rehnquist, in the case of *U.S. v. Ursery*, 116 S.Ct. 2135 (1995), ruled that double jeopardy does not exist when a defendant convicted of a federal criminal offense has his or her property forfeited simultaneously under a civil forfeiture proceeding. Thus, the Supreme Court condones the aggressive actions of police, invariably promulgated against African American suspects, by allowing police to seize evidence that would otherwise be protected by the fruits of the poisonous tree doctrine.

By the second half of Burger's Court, there was a vast difference between his earlier decisions and his decisions once Rehnquist joined the Court. However, what is more disturbing is the dissolution of the due process revolution. Chief Justice Warren, when delivering his opinion to the Court in the case of *Miranda vs. Arizona*, 384 U.S. 436 (1966), spoke of the insidious nature of custodial arrest and said that "officers are instructed to minimize the moral seriousness of the offense to cast blame on the victim or on society . . . so that the suspect can be put in a psychological state where his story is but an elaboration of what the police purport to know already . . . furthering notions that explanations to the contrary are dismissed or discouraged."[19] In other words, Chief Justice Warren recognized the importance of protecting certain defendants from police intrusion. Rehnquist, however, simply does not. In fact, those searches that could render "poisonous fruits" include: border searches, auto searches, consent searches, hot pursuit searches, plain view searches, searches incident to a lawful arrest, exigent searches, and stop and frisk searches (LaFave and Israel 1997). Exigent circumstances searches have become most important to the Burger and Rehnquist Courts. Further, these types of searches have opened the floodgates to usurping civil liberties for governmental intrusion.

The Burger and Rehnquist Courts have established in a series of cases where the issues of exigency supersede any warrant exception. For instance, in the case of *Katz v. U.S.*, 389 U.S. 347 (1967), while the Warren Court determined that an expectation of privacy existed and that the government cannot bug telephone lines, the Burger Court in *Oliver vs. U.S.*, 466 U.S. 170 (1984), determined that no expectation of privacy exists. Further, the nonexistence of the expectation allows government officials to seize a person's property and arrest at will.

Another example of the Supreme Court's use of constitutional guarantees to limit civil liberties is demonstrated by the Rehnquist Court in the case of *Arizona v. Hicks*, 480 U.S. 321 (1987), in which Justice Scalia, in a very liberal decision, determined that police cannot search from one room to another in a person's home, expecting to find incriminating evidence that ultimately is used against them in court. Scalia determined this was a violation of the Fourth Amendment guarantee against unreasonable searches and seizures. However, in the 1990 case of *Maryland vs. Buie*, 494 U.S. 325 (1990), Justice White, delivering the opinion of the Court, stated that police can go into someone's home, arrest them, and conduct a protective sweep. A protective sweep allows police to roam the home of the suspect at will, looking for anything that may be "dangerous," thus protecting others from danger or harm. The underlying reasoning for this falls under exigent circumstances, which means that if there is any emergency that could cause harm to others, then a warrantless search should ensue. This same type of reasoning was determined in the case of *Mapp v. Ohio*, 367 U.S. 643 (1961), twenty-nine years earlier, by the Warren Court to be an infringement of a person's civil liberties through the denial of Fourth Amendment protections.

Further, in the case of *Wilson v. Arkansas*, 514 U.S. 927 (1995), Justice Thomas wrote the opinion of the court and used the Seymanes[20] case. Justice Thomas determined in this opinion, using the precedent from the Kings Court of England in 1603, that police do not have to knock and announce if they think criminal activity is actively going on behind closed doors. Using the reasoning of the Kings Court in 1603, Thomas stated, "The king's purpose is to protect his kingdom and subjects," thus drawing the analogy between present-day policing strategies.[21]

Two more cases decided during the Burger and Rehnquist court era address civil liberties issues that affect the First and Eighth Amendments. For instance, in the case of *Wayte v. U.S.* 470 U.S. 598 (1985), Justice Powell, delivering the opinion of the court, determined that First Amendment privileges do not serve as a bar to a criminal conviction for anyone who does not register for selective service. Further, in the case of *United States v. Salerno*, 481 U.S. 739 (1987), the Court determined that holding a suspect without bail to prevent him or her from doing any further criminal acts is not in violation of the Eighth Amendment. Essentially, both of these cases criminalized the constitutional rights of defendants by limiting their actions through criminal sanctions. In the first case, a young man's right not to sign up for the draft was determined to be criminal because it went against the interest of the government. In the second case, the suspect was held in jail without bail because the government "thought" that he might commit more criminal acts. However, the suspect had not done the criminal acts and was being held for what he had not done.

Some criminologists have determined that this type of punishment is purposefully granted by the legal system of the United States through its laws and even its Constitution, and that further, it is not arbitrary (Russell 1984). Invariably, the Supreme Court's legal decision making condones the actions of police. Further, those who are affected by these actions generally are African Americans (Petersilia 1997). These liberties allow governmental takings at will, which is a denial of the right to property, speech, protection from unreasonable searches and seizures, *habeas corpus*, and self-incrimination. These same denials of rights were originally contained in the Black Codes. There is a correlation here between the Black Codes and current Supreme Court decisions that have directly affected African Americans by condoning proactive policing policies.

Conclusion

The scope of legal decision making by the Supreme Court has greatly affected the freedom of African Americans. Further, the Court's lessening of civil liberties has broadened governmental powers that directly prohibit the privacy and liberties of those over whom social control is exercised. Unfortunately, as seen by the studies and the literature, African

Americans are affected by police control and arrests at a greater rate than European Americans (Petersilia 1997, Mann 1993). Police control, however, does not simply lie in the hands of police personnel. The legislatures of each state and jurisdiction in which police have control are not at fault either. It appears that the issue of "control" has been promulgated by the U.S. Supreme Court. Decisions that narrow the scope of a person's civil liberties, replacing them with sanctioning of the government's exercise of social control are what lie at the heart of police brutality.

Exigency allows the police to act aggressively. Further, exigency allows police to not only forsake search warrants but also common courtesy in order to "protect" anyone or anything that might be harmed due to criminal misconduct. Thus, police aggression, or in many cases, brutality, is sanctioned by decisions coming from the "supreme" court of the land. Ultimately, police actions that cause death, severe injury, or loss of property are not the direct result of out-of-control, racist police personnel. Instead, they are a result of well-established legal thought and reasoning, for which cause and effect are deliberately felt in the African American community through aggression and brutality.

Notes

1. Dyson, Michael Eric. *Race Rules: Navigating the Color Line*. Vintage Books, 1997.
2. Fukurai, Hiroshi, Richard Kooth, and Edgar W. Butler. "The Rodney King Beating Verdicts." ed. Mark Baldassare, *The Los Angeles Riots: Lessons for the Urban Future*. Westview Press, 1997.
3. Barak, Gregg. *Representing O. J.: Murder, Criminal Justice and Mass Culture*. Harrow and Heston, 1996.
4. Newport, Frank, and Lyia Saad. "Civil Trial Didn't Alter Public's View of Simpson Case." *The Gallup Poll Monthly*, No. 377 (1997), pp. 21–23.
5. The Thirteenth Amendment was proposed by Congress on January 31, 1865; it was ratified on December 18, 1865. The amendment, when first proposed by a resolution in Congress, was passed by the Senate, 38 to 6, on April 8, 1864. On reconsideration by the House, on January 31, 1865, the resolution passed, 119 to 56. It was approved by President Lincoln on February 1, 1865. It reads in part: "1. Neither slavery nor involuntary servitude, except as a punishment for crime whereof the party shall have been duly convicted, shall exist within the United States or any place subject to their jurisdiction."
6. The Fourteenth Amendment was proposed to the legislatures by the Thirty-Ninth Congress on June 13, 1866, and declared to have been ratified in a proclamation by the Secretary of State on July 28, 1868.
7. The Fifteenth Amendment was proposed to the legislatures by the Fortieth Congress on February 26, 1869, and ratified in a proclamation by the Secretary of State on March 30, 1870.
8. Congress passed the Civil Rights Act on March 1, 1875, giving equal rights to blacks in public accommodation and jury duty. The act was invalidated in 1883 by the Supreme Court.
9. 60 U.S. 393 (1857).
10. 83 U.S.(16 Wall.) 36 (1873).
11. 92 U.S. 542 (1875).
12. 92 U.S. 214 (1875).
13. 163 U.S. 537 (1896).
14. 392 U.S. 409 (1968).
15. 427 U.S. 160 (1976).
16. 42 U.S.C. sect. 1981. Equal rights under the law: "All persons within the jurisdiction of the United States shall have the same right in every State and Territory to make and enforce contracts to sue, be parties, give evidence, and to the full and equal benefit of all laws and proceedings for the security of persons and property as is enjoyed by white citizens, and shall be subject to like punishment, pains, penalties, taxes, licenses, and exactions of every kind and to no other."
17. Fourth Amendment: No person shall be held to answer for a capital, or other infamous crime, unless on a presentment or indictment of a Grand Jury, except in cases arising in the land or naval forces, or in the militia, when the actual service is in time of war or public danger; nor shall any person be subject for the same offense to be twice put in jeopardy of life or limb; nor shall

be compelled in any criminal case to be a witness against himself, nor be deprived of life, liberty, or property, without due process of law; nor shall private property be taken for public use without just compensation.
18. 384 U.S. 436 (1966).
19. 384 U.S. 436, at 440.
20. K.B. 1603. This case is found in the original volume 5 of *Coke's Reports* and in the *English Reports*. It is an opinion handed down from the Kings Court of England in 1603.
21. 514 U.S. 927 at 940.

References

Adler, Freda, Gerhard O. W. Muller, and William S. Laufer. 1995. *Criminology*. New York: McGraw-Hill.

Allport, Gordon W. 1979. *The Nature of Prejudice*. Reading, Mass.: Addison-Wesley.

Brockett, Ramona, and Delores Jones. 1995. "The Role of the J.D. in Criminal Justice Education." In Nikki Ali Jackson, ed., *Contemporary Criminal Justice: Shaping Tomorrow's System*. New York: McGraw-Hill.

LaFave, Wayne R., and Jerold H. Israel. 1997. *Criminal Procedure*. St. Paul, Minn.: West Publishing Company.

Mann, Coramae. 1993. *Unequal Justice: A Question of Color*. Bloomington, Ind.: Indiana University Press.

Marable, Manning. 1983. "Racial Inequality: A Political-Economic Analysis." *Science and Society*, Vol. 47, No. 1, pp. 92–95.

Miller, Kent S. 1966. "Race Poverty and the Law." In *The Law of the Poor*. San Francisco, Calif.: Chandler Publishing.

Petersilia , Joan. 1997. "Racial Disparities in the Criminal Justice System: A Summary." In *Public Policy: Crime and Criminal Justice*, pp. 79–94, by Barry W. Hancock and Paul M. Sharp. Englewood Cliffs, N.J.: Prentice Hall.

Russell, Katheryn K. 1984. *The Color of Crime: Racial Hoaxes, White Fear, Black Protectionism, Police Harassment, and Other Macroaggressions*. New York: New York University Press.

Todd, Thomas N. 1979. "From Dred Scott to Bakke and Beyond: The Evolution of a Circle." *Dollars and Sense*, June–July, pp. 64–74.

Article Review Form at end of book.

Describe the differential punishments given to blacks in the United States during the period of slavery.

Differential Punishing of African Americans and Whites Who Possess Drugs:

A Just Policy or a Continuation of the Past?

Rudolph Alexander, Jr.

Rudolph Alexander, Jr. is an associate professor in the College of Social Work at Ohio State University. He has published more than 40 articles in refereed journals on issues related to justice, rights of offenders, mental health, and the law. Currently, he is writing a textbook on counseling offenders.

Jacquelyn Gyamerah

Jacquelyn Gyamerah is an assistant professor in the School of Social Work at the University of New York–Buffalo. Her interest areas are drugs, the African American family, and intervention with families of prisoners.

Five African Americans in Minnesota were arrested and charged with possession of a cocaine base, known on the street as crack. The statute that they were charged under provided that possession of 3 or more grams of crack cocaine was a third-degree

felony, punishable by up to 20 years of incarceration. In addition, the same statute provided that possession of 10 grams or more of a cocaine powder was a third-degree felony. Less than 10 grams of cocaine powder was a fifth-degree felony, punishable by up to 5 years. In Hennepin County in 1988, 97% of the persons arrested for cocaine base or crack were African Americans, and 80% of the persons arrested for cocaine powder were White. Because of these statistics and differential punishments, the five African Americans contested the constitutionality of the statute. After hearing the presentation of the issues, the Minnesota Supreme Court upheld the challenge and ruled the statute unconstitutional (*State v. Russell*, 1991).

The issue of whether African Americans are punished more severely than are White Americans by the criminal justice system and

whether the system is racist has been debated in the literature (Blumstein, 1982; Johnson, 1992, Peterson & Hagan, 1984). On one hand, some criminal justice professionals have called the charge of a racist criminal justice system a myth (Langan, 1985; Wilbanks, 1987) or have stated that the evidence is mixed (Petersilia, 1983; Peterson & Hagan, 1984). However, other professionals have stated the U.S. criminal justice system indeed is racist (Christianson, 1981/1991; Miller, 1991), and this racism traces itself back to slavery and the reconstruction period and continues today (Johnson & Secret, 1990). The purpose of this article is to recount this history, to discuss within this historical context the Minnesota case and the major federal cases involving charges of racial discrimination in the criminal justice system, and to propose a change in policy regarding possession of crack.

Rudolph Alexander, Jr. and Jacquelyn Gyamerah, *Journal of Black Studies*, Vol. 28, No. 1, September 1997, pp. 979–111. Copyright © 1997 by Sage Publications, Inc. Reprinted by permission of Sage Publications, Inc.

The Origins and Course of Differential Punishing of African Americans

The genesis of differential criminal treatment of African Americans is the slavery period in the United States. Controlling slaves required slave owners to subject slaves to sanctions for behaviors that were not offenses if committed by Whites. Punishable offenses for slaves included leaving the plantation without a pass, being out of their quarters after curfew, and being in a group of more than five slaves without a White man present. Slaves could not own firearms or animals, buy alcohol, give medicine to Whites, work in a drugstore, or work in a printing shop (Sellin, 1976). Moreover, slaves could not address a White person rudely or strike a White person even in self-defense, and these offenses were punishable crimes (Meier & Rudwick, 1976).

Slave-holding legislators did not view their traditional courts for free Whites as adequate for controlling slaves. Punishment for slaves had to be harsher than punishment for Whites because of a need to instill fear and obedience in slaves. As a result, state legislators created special courts to try slaves. These courts were called "Negro courts" and the judges were a combination of county justices and slave owners. For instance, Louisiana tried slaves for noncapital offenses before a court consisting of one justice and four slave holders. Mississippi tried slaves before a court consisting of two justices and five slave holders. Georgia tried slaves before three justices. Punishment decreed in these courts was swift and consisted primarily of whippings (Haunton, 1972/1992). In 1850, Georgia abolished its Negro courts and allowed its regular legal system to handle offenses by slaves, but in the other slave states the Negro courts existed to the end of slavery (Sellin, 1976).

Following slavery and the Civil War, both Presidents Lincoln and Johnson provided considerable latitude to Southern states to address the South's depressed economies, which were no longer going to be based on slave labor. Southern legislators responded with a series of laws, called the Black Codes, designed to reenslave African Americans and reestablish White supremacy (Levesque, 1989/1992; Wilson, 1980). As an example, the vagrancy law was vigorously enforced. Any African American without a permanent address or unemployed could be arrested and fined. If unable to pay the fine, he or she would be bound out to a plantation or leased (Adamson, 1983; Sisk, 1958/1992; Wilson, 1980). As W.E.B. Dubois wrote in 1901, many African Americans in the rural South were peons, "bound by law and custom to economic slavery, from which the only escape is death or the penitentiary" (Dubois, 1970, p. 124).

Wanting to increase the numbers of Africans in prisons in order to control them more effectively, Southern states enacted a series of laws targeting African Americans for differential punishments. As an example, several states increased the penalties for stealing livestock, making such acts grand larceny. Thus, stealing pigs or chickens could be punished by up to 10 years of incarceration (Adamson, 1983). To counter some of these unfair laws, Congress passed the first of a series of civil rights acts and the Fourteenth Amendment. Although the Fourteenth Amendment exists for all Americans, its origin was to address the legal problems of African Americans. As Jacob M. Howard, a member of the Senate Joint Committee on Reconstruction, reportedly wrote, the Fourteenth Amendment "prohibits the hanging of a black man for a crime for which the white man is not to be hanged" (Meltsner, 1973, p. 74).

However, the Fourteenth Amendment failed to provide this protection to African Americans because states continue to punish African Americans more seriously than Whites. The effect of targeting African Americans is seen in their increase in the penal systems. For example, in 1875, North Carolina had 569 African Americans in its penal institutions but only 78 Whites (Sellin, 1976). Similarly, Louisiana had 1,143 persons in its penal institutions in 1901 and 984 were African Americans (Sellin, 1976). In addition, Alabama created its "chain gang" in the 1920s, discarding its lease system. By the end of 1941, Alabama had 25 camps and all 1,717 prisoners in these camps were African Americans (Sellin, 1976). The South Carolina's chain gangs in 1926 contained 1,017 African Americans and 298 Whites (Sellin, 1976). These disparate numbers suggest either that African Americans were committing more crimes or states were imposing punishments on African Americans that were not generally imposed on Whites. This latter explanation seems more correct.

For instance, all the persons executed by South Carolina and Virginia for *attempted rape* were African Americans (Bowers, 1984). In one case upholding a death sentence for an African American for attempted rape, the Virginia Supreme Court stressed that prompt convictions and severe penalties were needed in rape or attempted rape cases to decrease the likelihood of lynch law (*Hart v. Commonwealth*, 1921). The Court's observation reveals the racial overtones in sexual assault cases, but it does not explain other instances where African Americans were punished more severely than Whites. For example, a few individuals have been executed for armed robbery in this country, and all but one were African Americans (Bowers, 1984).

A few laws were written during slavery that targeted African Americans and survived into the 20th century. For example, Georgia passed an antislave insurrection law involving printed materials in 1861, and the penalty was death. The law was broadened in 1871 to include speech and a lesser penalty was included ranging from 5 to 20 years. The law was used in the 1930s in Atlanta, Georgia to try an African American named Angelo Herndon who advocated social equality and self-determination for all African Americans. The prosecutor sought the death penalty for the defendant, but the jury recommended mercy and a sentence of 18 to 20 years at hard labor (Herndon, 1937).

Placed in an overall context of discriminatory responses by the criminal justice system, the issue of differential punishing of African Americans for possessing crack cocaine seems to be a continuation of historical policy. As one article revealed, White individuals use illicit drugs in substantial numbers, but their arrest numbers are substantially lower than for African Americans ("More Whites Use Drugs," 1992). Furthermore, when Whites are arrested and subsequently convicted, they, as the Minnesota case suggests, may face lesser punishment.

The following discussion explores the Minnesota case in more detail and the analytic framework used by courts to decide whether African Americans have been denied their Fourteenth Amendment right to equal protection of the law.

State v. Russell

In 1989 and 1990, the Minnesota legislature grappled with the issue of drug possession and prescribing appropriate penalties. Following legislative testimonies, it decided that possession of 3 or more grams of cocaine base [hereinafter referred to as crack cocaine] was a third-degree felony (Minnesota Statute § 152.023, 1989), and according to its criminal law, a third-degree felony is punishable by up to 20 years. The following year, the Minnesota legislature decreed that possession of 10 or more grams of cocaine powder was a third-degree felony and less than 10 grams of cocaine powder was a fifth-degree felony (Minnesota Statute § 152.025, 1990) and punishable by up to 5 years. Essentially, possession of 3 grams of crack could be punishable by up to 20 years, but an equal amount of cocaine powder was punishable only by up to 5 years.

Five African Americans, charged with possessing three or more grams of crack and facing up to 20 years in the state penitentiary, asked a trial judge to dismiss charges against them. Particularly, the Black defendants contended that there is no substantial difference between crack cocaine and cocaine powder, but the statutes punished them differently and more harshly for crack. Because 97% of the persons arrested for possession of crack in 1988 were African Americans and 80% of those arrested during that same year for cocaine powder were Whites, the statutes had a discriminatory impact and violated the equal protection clauses of both the U.S. and Minnesota Constitutions.

The trial judge, an African American woman, dismissed the charges and certified the following question to the Minnesota Supreme Court for a ruling: Does Minnesota Statute § 152.023, Subdivision 2(1) (1989), as it is applied, violate the equal protection clauses of the Fourteenth Amendment of the United States Constitution and the Minnesota Constitution, Article 1, Section 2? After considering its precedents, a majority of the justices held that the statute in question violated the Minnesota Constitution.

The majority justices arrived at its decision by noting differences in Minnesota's rational basis test and the federal test when challenges are made that a statute violates equal protection of the law. The federal rational basis test requires that (a) the statute serves a legitimate purpose and that (b) it was reasonable for legislators to believe that the statute would serve that purpose. However, Minnesota's rational basis test is substantially higher and requires that

(1) the distinctions which separate those included within the classification from those excluded must not be manifestly arbitrary or fanciful but must be genuine and substantial, thereby providing a natural and reasonable basis to justify legislation adapted to peculiar conditions and needs; (2) the classification must be genuine and relevant to the purpose of the law; that is there must be an evident connection between the distinctive needs peculiar to the class and the prescribed remedy; and (3) the purpose of the statute must be one that the state can legitimately attempt to achieve. (*State v. Russell*, 1991, p. 888).

Hence, the Minnesota's rational basis test is less deferential to the state than the federal test and requires a reasonable connection between the *actual* effects and the statutory aims.

Accordingly, the challenged statute was unconstitutional under Minnesota's rational basis test for three reasons. First, the statute failed to distinguish genuinely and substantially those individuals inside and outside the class. The state's primary justification for prescribing differences in punishment between those persons who possess 3 grams of crack and less than 10 grams of cocaine came from the legislative testimony of one lone prosecutor. According to this prosecutor, these

levels indicate whether one is using drugs or selling drugs. That is, a person who possesses 3 or more grams of drugs is a dealer, and a person who possesses 10 or more grams of cocaine powder is also a dealer. However, a report by the Minnesota Department of Public Safety Office of Drug Policy revealed that most prosecutors in Minnesota and other law enforcement officers did not accept the 3 and 10 distinction levels.

The second defect of the statute is that the defenders of it contended that the Minnesota legislature considered crack to be more addictive and dangerous than cocaine powder, and thus the legislature was justified in prescribing harsher penalties for crack possession. However, the majority, viewing this justification similar to the first, stated that the state had failed to establish a genuine and substantial difference between those inside and outside the class. The legislative view that crack is more addictive and dangerous than cocaine powder came from the testimony of a Minneapolis narcotic officer, who was not a trained chemist or scientist. But at the pretrial hearing, a certified chemist testified that crack and cocaine powder react differentially on the central nervous and respiratory systems when crack is smoked and cocaine powder is inhaled. The primary difference is that a smaller amount of crack will produce the same effect as a slightly higher amount of cocaine powder. However, there is no difference in the two drugs' effect if cocaine powder is dissolved in water and injected. Thus, cocaine powder has the same effect as crack if it is injected rather than inhaled.

Third, the state contended that it was justified in prescribing higher penalties for crack because there is more violence associated with crack than with cocaine powder. The majority understood this justification to be the state's contention that crack had a pharmacological effect that leads to violence, but the majority rejected it. The majority, looking at sociological evidence, associated the violence surrounding crack to gang warfare and group dynamics, which do not justify distinguishing statutorily crack and cocaine powder.

The majority also considered the statute to be unconstitutional because the classification between the two drugs did not serve the statutory purpose. Indeed, the state has the right to try to eliminate drug problems by punishing individuals who possess drugs. However, without more substantial evidence, other than the anecdotal testimony, the statute failed to achieve its aims. A person who possesses 3 grams of crack may be a user rather than a dealer, and a person who possesses less than 10 grams of cocaine may be a dealer who intends to convert the drug into more than 3 grams of crack. Thus, the statute is arbitrary and unreasonable. Moreover, the majority considered the statute to be unconstitutional because it assumes that an individual intends to deal drugs, on the basis of the amount possessed, without proof and thus violates due process of law.

Federal Decisions Involving Differential Punishing

The U.S. Supreme Court has decided numerous cases that involve racial issues, such as deciding whether African American defendants were deprived of due process of law in the availability of persons for jury duty, and peripherally decided cases involving differential punishing of African Americans. For instance, in 1970, the Court reversed on procedural grounds a death sentence for an African American defendant who had been convicted of rape of a White female. However, in that same case in the court of appeals, the issue of discriminatory practices in rape cases was raised by the defendant's attorneys on the basis of a study by Marvin Wolfgang. Justice Blackmun wrote the majority decision by a three-judge panel and stated that statistical evidence resulting from a study of several states failed to provide convincing evidence of racial discrimination. Particularly, the study showed that the death penalty for rape was primarily given to African Americans who had been convicted of raping White females, but Justice Blackmun noted that the study did not involve the county in which the defendant was convicted (*Maxwell v. Bishop*, 1968).

Arguments continued to be presented to the Court about the racial effects in rape cases, and the Court decided eventually that the death penalty for rape was unconstitutional. In ruling as it did, the Court did not consider the equal protection argument or directly discuss the statistical evidence presented to them. Instead, it focused on the small number of states that retain the death penalty for rape and the seemingly consensus of society that the death penalty for rape was no longer a valid punishment. As a result, the death penalty for rape violated the Cruel and Unusual Punishment Clause of the Eighth Amendment (*Coker v. Georgia*, 1977). Observers speculated, however, that the Court was persuaded by the racial arguments but did not want to state that it had been influenced by the impact of the racial evidence and arguments (*McCleskey v. Kemp*, 1987).

However, the Court had considered several cases involving contentions that official actions were motivated by racial discrimination or had a discriminatory impact and thus violated the Equal Protection Clause of the Fourteenth Amendment. The effect of these decisions was the formulation of a legal framework for deciding cases involving violations of the Equal Protection Clause. In one case, the Court decided whether African American plaintiffs were denied the equal protection of the laws in a zoning case and as a result decided how courts should view officials' decisions that have been alleged to have had a discriminatory effect on African Americans.

The case involved a collaboration between a nonprofit corporation in partnership and a religious order to build low-income housing in Arlington Heights, Illinois, a suburb of Chicago. The area was zoned for detached family homes, and the proposed project required a zoning change to attached multifamily homes. The zoning commission, following heated input by residents, denied the request for a zoning change. The builder, along with several African Americans, filed a lawsuit, contending that the denial of the zoning change had a discriminatory effect on the plaintiffs in that they were more likely to need low-income

housing. The U.S. district court ruled for the zoning commission, but the court of appeals reversed the lower court decision. By a 5 to 3 decision, the U.S. Supreme Court reversed the court of appeals and upheld the district court (*Arlington Heights v. Metropolitan Housing Corp.*, 1977).

Central to *Arlington Heights* was how courts should decide cases involving alleged discriminatory effects that result in a racially disproportionate impact. The Court stated that official action will not be held unconstitutional just because it results in a racially disproportionate impact. It is an issue to consider, but alone it does not rise to racial discrimination in violation of the Equal Protection Clause. Although the impact of official action and whether it bears more heavily on one race than another is an important starting point, a racially disparate outcome is not conclusive proof of official discrimination. A plaintiff, to establish a violation of the Equal Protection Clause, must establish proof of racially discriminatory intent or purpose. One evidentiary factor is the historical background of the decision. Another is the sequence of events leading to the challenged decision, such as when the officials did have one policy and suddenly change when learning that an integrated event had been proposed and is about to be presented. Further, minutes, reports, and the testimony of officials may provide evidence of purpose. Although these sources are not conclusive, they are some of the sources that plaintiffs must present to the courts for the determination of discrimination (*Arlington Heights v. Metropolitan Housing Corp.*, 1977).

A second prong in analyzing equal protection lawsuits was gleaned by the Eleventh Circuit Court of Appeals (*Underwood v. Hunter*, 1984) and seconded by the Court in *Hunter v. Underwood* (1985). The case involved an African American and a White plaintiff. Both were convicted of passing worthless checks, a misdemeanor in Alabama, and denied the right to vote because such conviction indicated, according to the Alabama Constitution, flaws in their moral turpitude. Both filed lawsuits against the Alabama registrars, contending that this law had a racist origin and violated the Equal Protection Clause. All parties agreed that the Alabama Constitutional Convention that was called in 1901 had as its primary aim the disenfranchisement of African Americans and poor Whites so as to promote White supremacy. The U.S. district court acknowledged that the 1901 convention had a racist agenda, but the plaintiffs had failed to prove that the Alabama registrars exemplified this same racism in disenfranchising them.

However, the Eleventh Circuit Court of Appeals reversed the U.S. district court. The court of appeals wrote that

to establish a violation of the Fourteenth Amendment in the face of mixed motives, plaintiffs must prove by a preponderance of the evidence that racial discrimination was a substantial or motivating factor in the adoption of section 182 [Alabama Disenfranchisement Law]. They shall then prevail unless the registrars prove by a preponderance of the evidence that the same decision would have resulted had the impermissible purpose not been considered. (Underwood v. Hunter, 1984, p. 617)

Using this test, the court of appeals ruled that the plaintiffs had met this burden and the registrars had not.

The court of appeals observed that before 1901, the Alabama Constitution denied persons who had been convicted of felonious crimes from voting. The conveners of the convention in 1901 were looking for legal reasons to disenfranchise African Americans and poor Whites. They consulted the Alabama justices of the peace, who had responsibility for trying African Americans during and after slavery and learned what crimes African Americans were more likely to be accused of committing and brought to courts. As a result, the 1901 delegates added to the list of disenfranchising offenses those crimes that African Americans were more likely to commit. In addition, they added a catchall phrase, moral turpitude, to embrace behaviors such as living in adultery. Enactment of this statute disenfranchised 10 times as many African Americans as Whites, and the effects of this law were still felt in the 1980s. The Alabama officials tried to defend this law by saying that it disenfranchised Whites and Blacks and, therefore, equal protection of the law was not

violated. However, the court of appeals recognized the registrars' impartiality in administering the statute, but their impartiality could not cleanse a purposefully discriminatory law that had current effects.

Later, the Supreme Court examined an equal protection claim by a criminal defendant. The case involved Warren McCleskey, an African American, who was convicted in Atlanta, Georgia, of killing a White police officer and given the death penalty. On the basis of a study by Baldus, he argued that he was denied the equal protection of the law because African American defendants who have killed Whites were more likely to receive death sentences than were White defendants. The Court began its analysis of this equal protection claim by stating that a defendant alleging violation of equal protection shoulders the burden of proving the existence of purposeful discrimination. A corollary of this principle is that a criminal defendant also must prove that the purposeful discrimination had a discriminatory effect on him or her. Thus, McCleskey, to prevail in his equal protection argument, must show that the judicial officials in his case acted with discriminatory purpose. According to the majority, McCleskey did not and the Baldus study is insufficient. Also, McCleskey contended that the state of Georgia's capital punishment statute violated the Equal Protection Clause and allowed it to remain in force despite its discriminatory application. The Court stated that for McCleskey to prove this aspect, he must prove that the Georgia legislature enacted and maintained the death penalty statute *because* of an anticipatory racially discriminatory effect. However, the Court stated that he had failed to prove this claim, and as a result, his claim of a denial of equal protection must fail (*McCleskey v. Kemp*, 1987).

In sum, federal jurisprudence involving an equal protection claim in the criminal context requires a criminal defendant to prove that state officials acted specifically against him or her. This is a higher burden to overcome than the burden a person involved in a civil action must overcome. Moreover, although studies that show discriminatory racial effects are a starting point in determin-

ing a violation of equal protection in a civil matter, they have little effect in a criminal case, and a criminal defendant must show that state officials specifically behaved in a racially discriminatory manner toward him or her.

The federal legal test, applied to *Russell* and considered in federal courts, would result in upholding the constitutionality of Minnesota's statute and its penalties. Simply, African Americans would not be able to prove that the Minnesota's legislators enacted the statute specifically for racial reasons. In addition, the federal legal test has been used to uphold differential punishing of persons convicted of the federal Anti-Drug Abuse Act of 1986. This act provides a 100-to-1 ratio, which means that for punishment purposes 100 grams of cocaine powder equal 1 gram of crack (*State v. Russell*, 1991).

Conclusion

Russell and *McCleskey* represent two divergent views on differential punishing of African Americans. The rationale adopted by the Minnesota Supreme Court clearly is the more enlightened approach and promotes social justice. Directly and indirectly targeting African Americans for differential punishing, as this article has discussed, has a long history in the United States and continues today. In the past, state legislatures were blatant in their racial intentions, knowing that African Americans did not have recourse in the courts. Now that African Americans' rights are more recognized, the discrimination is not as blatant and direct and has become more subtle and indirect. Whether blatant or subtle, the effect is the same. All courts, as a result, should look closely at the outcomes and adopt the standard used in Minnesota.

The effect of ensnaring more African Americans in the criminal justice system through drug laws is devastating and represents a major factor in their sharp increase in prisons across the country (Mauer, 1990; Miller, 1992). When vast numbers of middle-class Whites in the 1960s were being threatened with felony convictions for possessing marijuana, the response of policy makers and legislators was to make possession of small amounts a misdemeanor (Peterson & Hagan, 1984). Now, a similar response should be initiated for crack. Mere possession of crack should not be a crime, or if it is a crime, it should not be more than a misdemeanor. In this manner, African Americans will be treated with the same concern as Whites were in shaping social policy regarding marijuana.

References

Adamson, C. R. (1983). Punishment after slavery: Southern state penal system, 1965–1980. *Social Problems*, 30, 555–569.

Anti-Drug Abuse Act of 1986, Pub. L. No. 104–316, 19 U.S.C. § 2081 (1986).

Arlington Heights v. Metropolitan Housing Corp., 429 U.S. 252 (1977).

Blumstein, A. (1982). On the racial disproportionality of United States prison populations. *Journal of Criminal Law and Criminology*, 73, 1259–1281.

Bowers, W. J. (1984). *Legal homicide: Death as punishment in America, 1964–1982*. Boston: Northeastern University Press.

Christianson, S. (1991). Our Black prisons. In K. C. Haas & G. P. Albert (Eds.), *The dilemmas of corrections* (2nd ed., pp. 62–74). Prospect Heights, IL: Waveland. (Reprinted from *Crime and Delinquency*, 1981, 27, 364–375).

Coker v. Georgia, 433 U. S. 584 (1977).

Dubois, W.E.B. (1970). The freedman's bureau. In L. J. Austin, L. H. Fenderson, & S. P. Nelson (Eds.), *The Black man and the promise of America* (pp. 112–124). Glenview, IL: Scott, Foresman.

Hart v. Commonweath, 131 Va 726 (1921).

Haunton, R. H. (1992). Law and order in Savannah, 1850–1860. In P. Finkelman (Ed.), *Race, law, and American history 1700–1990* (pp. 189–212). New York: Garland. (Reprinted from *Georgia Historical Society*, 1972, 56, 1–24).

Herndon, A. (1937). *Let me live*. New York: Random House.

Hunter v. Underwood, 471 U. S. 222 (1985).

Johnson, J. B., & Secret, P. E. (1990). Race and juvenile court decision making revisited. *Criminal Justice Policy Review*, 4, 159–187.

Johnson, W. W. (1992, November). *Racial distribution and punishment: An analysis of state level data in the 1980s*. Paper presented at the annual meeting of the American Society of Criminology, New Orleans, LA.

Langan, P. A. (1985). Racism on trial: New evidence to explain the racial composition of prisons in the United States. *Journal of Criminal Law and Criminology*, 76, 666–683.

Levesque, G. A. (1992). Black political power and criminal justice: Washington county, Texas 1868–1884. In P. Finkelman (Ed.), *Race, law and American history 1700–1990* (pp. 268–279). New York: Garland. (Reprinted from *American Journal of Southern History*, 1989, 55, 391–420).

Mauer, M. (1990). *Young Black men and the criminal justice system: A growing national problem*. Washington, DC: The Sentencing Project.

Maxwell v. Bishop, 398 F. 2d 138 (1968).

McCleskey v. Kemp, 481 U. S. 279 (1987).

Meier, A., & Rudwick, E. (1976). *From plantation to ghetto* (3rd ed.) New York: Hill & Wang.

Meltsner, M. (1973). *Cruel and unusual: The supreme court and capital punishment*. New York: Random House.

Miller, J. G. (1991). *Last one over the wall*. Columbus: Ohio State University.

Miller, J. G. (1992). *Hobbling a generation: Young African-American males in D. C.'s criminal justice system*. Alexandria, VA: National Center on Institutions and Alternatives.

Minnesota Statute § 152.023 (1989).

Minnesota Statute § 152.025 (1990).

More Whites use drugs, more Blacks arrested. (1992, November). *Columbus Dispatch*, p. 14A.

Petersilia, J. (1983). *Racial disparities in the criminal justice system*. Washington, DC: National Institute of Corrections.

Peterson, R. D., & Hagan, J. (1984). Changing conceptions of race: Towards an account of anomalous findings of sentencing research. *American Sociological Review*, 49, 56–70.

Sellin, J. T. (1976). *Slavery and the penal system*. New York: Elsevier.

Sisk, G. S. (1992). Crime and justice in the Alabama Black belt, 1875–1917. In Finkelman (Ed.), *Race, law, and American history 1700–1990* (pp. 432–439). New York: Garland. (Reprinted from *Mid-America*, 1958, 40, 106–113).

State v. Russell, 477 N. W. 2d 886 (Minn. 1991).

Underwood v. Hunter, 730 F. 2d 614 (1984).

Wilbanks, W. (1987). *The myth of a racist criminal justice system*. Monterey, CA: Brooks/Cole.

Wilson, W. J. (1980). *The declining significance of race: Black and changing American institutions* (2nd ed). Chicago: University of Chicago Press.

 Article Review Form at end of book.

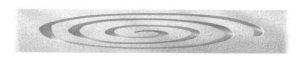

- Most individuals wrongfully convicted to death are members of minority groups.

- The death penalty is not viewed as an effective way of reducing violent crime.

- The rationale adopted by the Minnesota Supreme Court promotes social justice.

R.E.A.L. Sites

This list provides a print preview of typical **Coursewise** R.E.A.L. sites. (There are over 100 such sites at the **Courselinks**™ site.) The danger in printing URLs is that web sites can change overnight. As we went to press, these sites were functional using the URLs provided. If you come across one that isn't, please let us know via email to: webmaster@coursewise.com. Use your Passport to access the most current list of R.E.A.L. sites at the **Courselinks** site.

Site name: The Black World Today

URL: http://www.tbwt.com/

Why is it R.E.A.L.? This site contains a chronicle of the daily social, political, cultural, and economic realities of black communities in the United States and abroad. It is an excellent source of current information on issues pertaining to race and crime.

Key topics: race, crime, news, South Africa, police, prisons

Try this: Refer to a current event that shows that racism is still taking place in the United States.

....

Site name: Race and Racism

URL: http://www.users.interport.net/~heugene/race_racism.html

Why is it R.E.A.L.? This site contains articles, reviews, and essays on race and racism. It also contains poems and pictures that emphasize the racism that still takes place in the United States. Also, this site contains links and information on critical theory in an attempt to explain why racism occurs.

Key topics: media, postmodernism, race, racism, affirmative action, critical theory

Try this: Describe the main premises of critical theory.

....

Site name: Racetalks Initiatives

URL: http://www.law.upenn.edu/racetalk/

Why is it R.E.A.L.? This site seeks to develop new paradigms for linking racial and gender justice to the project of building more inclusive institutions. It contains online race-related articles and offers links to similar sites. While the articles at this site cover an array of issues pertaining to race, some specifically address race and crime-related issues.

Key topics: affirmative action, race, college admission, bias

Try this: What is the future of affirmative action?

....

section 4

Justice's Blindfold: A Myth or a Reality?

Learning Objectives

After studying this section, you will know

- that there is still a racially demarcated jury system that discriminates against blacks and their participation as jurors.

- that the *Whren* decision may allow law enforcement agents to use traffic codes to abuse Fourth Amendment rights.

- that the U.S. sentencing guidelines and the mandatory minimum statutes have not been successful in reducing racial disparity in sentencing in federal court.

- that individuals are seriously considering the consequences of using the race card.

 **WiseGuide Intro**

The criminal justice system prides itself on the principle of equality. The argument is put forth that the criminal justice system is objective and that decisions are predicated on the law. We are led to believe that the law is an objective construct. Judges, we are told, are instrumental in interpreting the law. There is also the notion of advocacy in the courtroom and the belief that those accused of crimes have rights that will not be compromised. Those who romanticize about the criminal courts are fond of saying, "Where justice ends, tyranny begins" or "equal justice for all." The point of this section is that these romanticized notions do not square with reality. There are, for example, studies purporting to show that nonlegal variables (race, social economic status, etc.) may weigh as heavily as legal variables (offense, prior history, etc.).

It is widely known that African Americans use crack cocaine and that cocaine use is high among whites, yet the penalties are disparate. This is true despite knowledge that cocaine is a purer and stronger substance. In fact, possession of only 5 grams of crack cocaine, compared with possession of 500 grams of powder cocaine (used largely by whites), results in a mandatory minimum five-year sentence. The net effect is that African Americans receive stiffer penalties when compared with their white counterparts.

With regard to politics and the courtroom, it has become vogue to put forth the belief that judicial restraint is important. Judges who run for office may make this the cornerstone of their political campaigns. The assumption is that these individuals will not make law, but interpret it. The reality is that those who favor judicial restraint are as political as so-called judicial activists. Those who advocate restraint are also "activists," with a passion for maintaining the status quo. From this perspective, there are judges on the bench with various agendas, bringing their biases into the courtroom. This contributes to inequalities in the sentencing of majority versus minority offenders. On the issue of the jury pool, the selection process may not result in large numbers of minorities serving on jury panels. The absence of minority members on juries surely affects the deliberations.

Another issue pertains to an increasing number of African American citizens who have come forward to suggest that they are vulnerable on the highway and subject to more stops by law enforcement than their white counterparts. An emerging body of evidence is beginning to support the widespread belief by black motorists that traffic stops and citations may stem from race. It may be that blacks are vulnerable for many reasons—they may be politically disenfranchised or easier targets for black and white police officers. Other traffic stops may be determined by perceptions of African Americans as drug users and drug couriers.

While some of the questions raised here are rhetorical, many are real. The evidence suggests that justice is not blind. The system responds to wealth, as evidenced by major criminal and civil trials of wealthy defendants, resulting in various outcomes based on the defendant's ability to marshal a strong defense with competent counsel.

To capsulize, the system is very political; the members of the courtroom workgroup have strong allegiances to the criminal justice organization, impacting advocacy and pointing toward cooptation of its members. Concerned citizens must explore and act on judicial selection. The number of minority judges in American society is low. More minority judges may bring a sensitivity and identification with black and Hispanic offenders, thereby reversing the disproportionality of minorities in our nation's prisons.

It is hoped that, in reading the articles in this section, you will be receptive to the research findings and will ponder their implications. What do they mean? What can be done differently? Lady justice does frequently wink her eyes; she is not at all blind!

Questions

Reading 17. Is there a racially demarcated jury system that discriminates against blacks and their full jury participation? Explain.

Reading 18. Describe the possible negative effects the U.S. Supreme Court's 1996 *Whren* decision may have on minorities.

Reading 19. What effect did the U.S. sentencing guidelines and mandatory minimum statutes have on African Americans?

Reading 20. Is it ethical for blacks to play the race card?

Is there a racially demarcated jury system that discriminates against blacks and their full jury participation? Explain.

Where Did Black Jurors Go?

A Theoretical Synthesis of Racial Disenfranchisement in the Jury System and Jury Selection

Hiroshi Fukurai

Hiroshi Fukurai is Assistant Professor in the Board of Studies at the University of California, Santa Cruz. His research interests include jury analyses, racial inequality in jury selection, and advanced quantitative statistics. His publications include Race and the Jury *(Plenum, 1992),* Anatomy of the McMartin Case *(Rutgers University Press, 1992), and "A Cross Sectional Jury Representation or Systematic Representation?" in* Journal of Criminal Justice.

Edgar W. Butler

Edgar W. Butler is Professor in the Department of Sociology at the University of California, Riverside. Current publications include Atlas of Mexico *(Westview, 1989),* Race and the Jury *(Plenum, 1992),* Anatomy of the McMartin Case *(Rutgers University Press, 1992), and numerous articles on fertility and historical migration patterns in Mexico, jury selection, environmental hazards, and the social networks and social support patterns of the elderly.*

Richard Krooth

Richard Krooth, a practicing attorney, is Visiting Scholar at the University of California, Berkeley. His publications include Common Destiny: Japan and the U.S. in the Global Age *(McFarland, 1990) and* Great Homestead Strike of 1892 *(Ramparts, 1991). His research interests include sociology of law, industrial sociology, jury selection, and the U.S-Japan sociopolitical relations.*

The jury system evolved as an essential ingredient of America's judicial framework. In recent years, however, frailties of the jury system in respect to its lack of fairness for women, Blacks, Latinos, and the poor have increasingly become the center of controversy. Federal law is clear that these groups have the right to participate in court as jurors, according to two key concepts: There must be a random selection of jurors, and it must be representative within specified geographic districts wherein a particular court convenes (U.S. 90th Congress House Report, 1968: Section 1961). The logic is that qualified residents of a given geographic domain should be part of the pool from which a jury is selected—on the basis of a chance-opportunity for each to serve on a jury panel. Recent U.S. Supreme Court decisions have held that any substantial violation of these basic requirements of representativeness in jury selection is a prima facie case of discrimination (Alker & Barnard, 1978; Fukurai & Butler, 1987; Fukarai, Butler, & Krooth, in press; Horowitz, 1980).[1]

Challenges concerned with the underrepresentation of minorities have been brought claiming violation of the Sixth Amendment, which requires a representative jury selection from a fair cross-section of the community (Burns, 1987; Jalee, 1968).[2] Yet, the lack of a fair cross-section has been shown in a variety of cases. Careful research indicates that discrimination in jury selection procedures occurs by gender, age, race, and socioeconomic status (Carp, 1982, pp. 257–277; Chevigny, 1975, pp. 157–172; Diamond, 1980, pp. 85–117; Fukurai, Butler, & Huebner-Dimitrius, 1987; Fukurai, Butler, & Krooth, 1991).[3]

In terms of the race of empanelled juries, however, the literature deals almost exclusively with the *surface* phenomenon of the lack of adequate Black representation. Clearly more elaborate research on judicial disenfranchisement is needed to examine the social mechanisms that produce and maintain the subservient condition of Black people, women, and other U.S. citizens with Third World backgrounds. This is particularly important because there

Hiroshi Fukurai, Edgar W. Butler, and Richard Krooth, *Journal of Black Studies*, Vol. 22, No. 2, December 1991, pp. 196–215. Copyright ©1991 Sage Publications, Inc. Reprinted by permission of Sage Publications, Inc.

has been a paucity of research examining the impact of the social and structural mechanisms that historically have perpetuated the subordination of Blacks in the jury system and jury selection.

The next section provides the theoretical synthesis to the problematique of judicial inequities in the jury system and jury selection by examining four specific determinants of disproportionate racial representation on juries: (a) racial discrimination in jury selection procedures, (b) socioeconomic barriers preventing full-community participation by Blacks and other racial minorities, (c) judicial discrimination that allows racially demarcated jury representation, and (d) institutional racism and bureaucratic discrimination in perpetuating judicial inequality. The remainder of this article, then, demonstrates that there still exists a racially demarcated jury system that systematically discriminates against Blacks and their full jury participation.

Racial Discrimination in Jury Selection Procedures

Jury selection procedures have long established effective mechanisms for racially demarcating jury participation. Here, then, are several of the legal mechanisms used to subjugate Blacks. An example is ensuring underrepresentation of racial minorities is the use of registered voters' rolls (ROV) as source lists from which potential jurors are to be selected. ROV lists provide a legal mechanism effectively enforcing the "rule of exclusion," because minorities are less likely to register to vote, and, thereby, jury pools consist primarily of Anglos (Butler, 1980; Fukurai & Butler, 1987; Fukurai, Butler, & Krooth, 1991).

Administration of qualification questionnaires also helps eliminate racial minorities from serving on juries. Psychological qualification examinations to select jurors in some counties in California have eliminated a large number of potential Black jurors (Boags & Boags, 1971, pp. 48–64).[4] Other subjective criteria and language requirements are also used to limit full community participation by eligible Black jurors. There

also are various different statutory qualifications at the state level to serve on juries. Those are:

1. mentally sound, 38 states
2. no conviction, 35 states
3. physically sound, 33 states
4. age, 30 states
5. ability to read, write, and speak English, 27 states
6. prior jury service, 27 states
7. key-man characteristics, 26 states
8. resident or citizen of the state, 24 states
9. resident or qualified elector, 23 states
10. resident or citizen of the country, 22 states
11. U.S. citizen, 17 states
12. jury solicitation, 8 states. (Benokraitis, 1975)

The important notion here is that some of these mandatory qualifications (1, 3, and 7) are subjective criteria. Past jury research has pointed out that, of the 11 southern states, 10 require that a prospective juror be mentally sound; eight require physical soundness; and eight states stipulate that prospective jurors have "key man" qualifications of "good character," "sound judgment," and "intelligence" (Benokraitis, 1975, p. 38). California law similarly reiterates the subjective discretion by stating "the qualified jury list . . . shall include persons suitable and competent to serve on juries. In making such selections there shall be taken only the names of persons . . . who are in the possession of their natural faculties, who are of fair character and approved integrity, and who are of sound judgment" (CA. 1981, Section 17.205(a)). Those subjective criteria are used to impose a limit on Black participation on juries. Because of a variety of selection criteria involving subjective qualifications, it is expected that greater disproportionate racial representation is found where jury commissioners and district clerks have substantial discretion regarding both the sources and methods of selection.

Personnel involved in the jury selection process, thus, play an important role in generating Black underrepresentation on juries. For instance, the systematic selection by jury clerks has been found to be an important factor in maintaining disproportionate jury representation. In *Avery v. Georgia* (1953), the U.S. Supreme Court found that jury panels in Georgia were drawn from a jury box that contained county tax returns with names of prospective Anglo jurors printed on White tickets and names of potential Black jurors printed on yellow tickets. Jury clerks consciously sought White jurors for trials, excluding potential Black jurors from serving on juries.

Jury commissioners also played a crucial role in limiting the full-community participation of Black jurors. Review of litigated cases by the Supreme Court has overwhelmingly revealed an implicit view of Blacks as inferior, reaffirmed by the limitations imposed to manipulate the jury selection process. In *Akins v. Texas* (1954), testimony revealed that all three jury commissioners in Dallas County consciously sought only one Black grand juror. Consequently, Black participation on grand juries was severely limited. Further, in *Cassell v. Texas* (1950), the Court discovered evidence of systematic selection exercised by jury commissioners. The statements of jury commissioners revealed that they chose those they knew for grand jury service, and that they knew no eligible Blacks in a county where Blacks made up approximately one seventh of potentially eligible jurors. The systematic selection by jury commissioners was further compounded by the manipulation of selected Black jurors to set a proportional limit on Black jury participation. For instance, in *Smith v. Texas* (1940), the Court found that between 1931 and 1938, a list for grand jurors had 512 Anglos and only 18 Blacks. Of them, 13 Blacks were at the bottom of the list; only one was put among the first 12. Further, only five Blacks took places in the grand jury room, and the same individual served in three separated instances. In the same period, 379 Anglos were allowed to serve as grand jurors.

The racial composition of the jury is also affected by lawyers using peremptory challenges in voir dire (Blauner, 1972). Because so many different persons are allowed to use individual discretion in deciding who would be excused and who would serve, the possibility of individual prejudice influencing excuses and exemptions is great (Van Dyke, 1977, p. 391). Some of the uncharted consequences may be corrected by recent U.S. Supreme Court rulings (see *Batson v. Kentucky*, 1986), but eliminating peremptory challenges and replacing them with reasons for all challenges will still not guarantee that the parties challenging minorities will give the real reasons: racism, sexism, xenophobia, and ageism.

Minorities have to operate within the framework of a racially oppressive institutional system. As a result, Blacks and other racial minorities have learned to mistrust the fairness inherent in most Anglo-dominated institutions of power, such as law enforcement agencies and courts that make decisions via racially disproportionate juries (see *Batson v. Kentucky*, 1986; Van Dyke, 1977, p. 32). One dominant ideological underpinning suggests that criminality is inherent in minority groups, and they need to be controlled by the legal system (Cullen & Link, 1980; Hepburn, 1978; Kramer, 1982). In modern phraseology, the "black community takes a permissive view of crime within its border. As a result, the black community is vulnerable to its own criminal element as well as to the criminal element of the white community" (*Yale Law Journal*, 1970, p. 534).

Crimes, criminals, and trials of those accused are also obviously linked. Those accused of crimes may defend themselves, but courts, judges, and juries seem locked into legal structures handed down from a past of discrimination and racism. The past has in fact contoured the underrepresentation of minorities on jury panels in our time. And such racial prejudgment generates different outcomes in various trials. In at least one Black Panther murder trial, the contention was made that the race of the defendant itself predisposed certain jurors to a negative verdict (Rokeach & McLellan, 1970). Studies covering the psychology of juries provide numerous examples

of racial prejudice impacting verdicts (*American Criminal Law Review*, 1980; Hans & Vidmar, 1986; Lipton, 1979; Starr & McCormick, 1985; Wishman, 1986).

A wall of hatred and noncommunication is put up between Black and Anglo populations, despite—and because of—such ideological justifications and structured practices like underrepresentation of minority jurors (Kairys, Kadane, & Lehoczky, 1977). Through their nonparticipation, however, racial minorities are forced to participate in strengthening the legitimation of Anglo-dominated judicial systems. And without such participation, racial supremacy is structurally reinforced by the dominant population, perpetuated by individual racism and the withdrawal of support by minorities. In fact, the large proportion of Blacks who do not respond to jury qualification questionnaires or summonses have been classified as "recalcitrants" and eliminated from subsequent jury selection procedures (Fukurai, 1985; Fukuria et al., in press; Van Dyke, 1977).

Socioeconomic Barriers and Handicaps

The economic life of a disenfranchised people makes that of the colonizing people possible. If the disenfranchised must be moved physically to make the colonizers' labor system efficient, the stability of residence and life of the colonized can be disregarded. In the oppressive legal system set up in the United States, indentured servants and slaves were replaced by new sources of cheap labor, with unsteady migratory labor uprooting large segments of the Black and other minority populations.

Obviously such labor market positions are closely related to residential mobility and affect jury representation by racial minorities. Since jury summonses and qualification questionnaires are generally sent by mail, one's labor market position as a migrant enhances the probability of being excluded from a jury pool, as those who move and fail to receive jury summonses (called "undeliverables") or to return jury qualification

questionnaires ("recalcitrants") cannot qualify for selection. In fact, such persons are systematically eliminated. Thereby a potential juror who has just entered the job market and/or is placed in a secondary labor market tends to be eliminated long before being called into the courthouse for jury service. Even those who make it into the courthouse are likely to be granted an excuse for reasons of economic hardship.

Two principal factors explain the high residential mobility among unskilled minority laborers. First, their position in the labor market involves low wages, seasonal work, and thus a high degree of occupational instability (Featherman & Hauser, 1978; Lipset & Bendix, 1959). Unstable job markets and economic shifts in production location and volume are conducive to a high level of geographic mobility in search of steady employment (Edward, Reich, & Gordon, 1975; Gordon, 1972).

An internal labor market that calls up temporary or seasonal workers also makes sedentary life impossible for colonized labor. The migratory search for jobs is the lifebread of the nation's poorest, hence its Blacks, other minorities with a Third World background, and women. The high geographic mobility of racial minorities creates the largest segment of those who do not receive jury qualification questionnaires and who are thereby classified as undeliverables (Fukurai, 1985). Forcing jury commissioners to track down those undeliverables is rare, even though such follow-up is required by law (CA. 1981, Sec 13. 204.3(b)).

Those who must move often to find work are more likely to be renters than owners of a residence (see Butler & Kaiser, 1971; Butler et al., 1969; Sabagh, Van Arsdol, & Butler, 1969). Low residential ownership plays an important role in generating high incidences of residential mobility among Blacks and other members of racial minorities.

The results are that youths, laborers with low income and education, and particularly Blacks are mobile workers subject to systematic jury exclusion and thus are underrepresented on jury pools (Fukurai et al., 1991; Zeigler, 1978). For example, for a three-year interval, using national data, a study found that 48.0% of Blacks moved, while 25.2% of Anglos moved (McAllister, Kaiser, & Butler, 1971). During a one-year time period in Los Angeles County, 49.8% of the age group between 15 and 29 moved, while only 12.8% of those 60 and over moved. The mobile groups were predominantly members of racial minorities (Feagin, 1984; Fukurai et al., in press; Van Arsdol, Maurice, Sabagh, & Butler, 1968).

This is in contrast to prospective jurors who work in large companies and are more likely to be reimbursed for jury service. They usually have a greater chance of surviving the jury selection process; and, in the world of job-structured benefits, they are predominantly Anglos (Fukurai et al., in press).

Judicial Discrimination Against Black and Minority Jurors

In a racially demarcated society, oppressive institutions use restrained power and regimented administrations to benefit one group at the expense of others. The racially demarcated society can be based on overt violence, such as slavery, or on covert structures that brandish the symbols of freedom but establish conditions for subjugation. The institutions of the greatest legitimation of authority and discrimination are the systems of laws and courts.

Echoes of such institutionalized inequality in the United States today appear as four judicial dimensions that set limits on racial participation on juries. First, there is the "blue ribbon jury," which systematically and disproportionately excludes minorities. Second, juries of unusually small size undercut minority participation. Third, jurors may be empowered to enforce less than unanimous decisions, so that minority opinions can be disregarded, and fourth, in selecting jurors, the process of constructing gerrymandered judicial districts may systematically exclude minority-dominant neighborhoods but include majority-dominant areas.[5]

Under a blue ribbon system, special jurors are selected from the general panel based on perceived special qualifications to hear important and intricate cases. Narrowly qualified jurors present an insurmountable fairness problem. Jury studies indicate that homogeneous panels selected with certain criteria may be less adept at reaching reasonable verdicts than are the heterogeneous ones. The latter bring to the decision-making process a rich mix of points of view and life experiences, and they are more likely than the homogeneous jury to recognize and offset one another's biases (Van Dyke, 1977).

Although the blue ribbon jury has not met the "fair cross-section of community" criterion demanded by the Sixth Amendment (*Fay v. New York*, 1947), the Supreme Court has nevertheless given constitutional sanction to the practice. Blue ribbon juries are thereby still empowered to parade their constitutionality and give judicial justification to the systematic exclusion of racial minorities from juries (Mills, 1969, pp. 338–339; *Yale Law Journal*, 1970).

Nor does the Constitution require a jury of 12; a state may use a jury of 6 in criminal trials, even when the sentence is as severe as life imprisonment, the U.S. Supreme Court declared in *Williams v. Florida* (1972). Numerous studies show that without an adequate theory of group dynamics, the Supreme Court was in error in assuming that there are no differences in the behavior of 12- and 6-member juries (Kaye, 1980; Roper, 1980). The fact is that smaller juries have a greater propensity to be controlled by a dominant group or person. A change of verdict may sometimes be attributed to an authoritarian personality who can control and influence small groups easier than large groups (Goffman, 1959; Hastie et al., 1983). Distinct or authoritarian personality traits are often characterized by the dominant ideology that shapes perceptions and affects everyday interactions (Hans & Vidmar, 1986). Because the prevailing ideology is likely to reflect the dominant group in society, the minority's alternate view—once formulated— may be side-stepped by controlling participation in judicial decision-making processes or disregarding their opinions.

A clear pattern of racial discrimination is found in death penalty cases. Blacks are more likely to receive the death sentence than Whites, particularly if the victim was White. In Florida, for example, if a Black person killed a White person, the chances of receiving a death sentence were about 1 in 5; if a White killed a White, the chances were about 1 in 20; if a Black killed a Black, the chances were about 1 in 167; and if a White killed a Black, the probability of a death sentence was zero (Bowers & Pierce, 1980). When a large number of extraneous factors was controlled (e.g., crime severity, past criminal records, and the number of charges), the basic pattern of racial discrimination remained. One explanation is simple racism; a White life is more valued than a Black life. Another explanation is that Whites are much more supportive of the death penalty than Blacks, and the White community therefore may pressure the prosecutor to ask for the death penalty when a White victim is killed (Baldus, Pulaske, & Woodsworth, 1983). Given the prevalence of White overrepresentation on juries and the impact on the jury decision-making process, a smaller size jury exhibits a greater propensity to be controlled by the dominant ideology reflected by White jurors.

Less than unanimous decisions also pose problems for racial minorities. In *Apodaca v. Oregon* (1972) and *Johnson v. Louisiana* (1972), the Court voted by a narrow margin not to apply the unanimity rule to state jury cases, concluding that the rule lacked constitutional authority.[6] Rejecting the previous pronouncements on unanimity requirements as inconclusive, the Supreme Court majority upheld verdicts in which the juries had voted 11–1, 10–2, and 9–3 for conviction. One study shows that the elimination of the unanimity rule favors the prosecution and increases the conviction rate (Kalven & Zeisel, 1966, p. 466). It is clear that relaxing the unanimity rule allows the opinions of racial minorities to be ignored and undermines the nature of justice and fairness in the judicial system. The new rule becomes especially problematic in cases of possible hung juries. In some capital punishment cases, for instance, the discrepant initial vote on the verdict, which eventually led to a final unanimous decision, was racially demarcated (*Harris v. People of California*, 1984).[7] Thus, frequent incidents of racially disproportionate votes in deliberation can be used to empower the racial majority ideologically (Fukurai et al., in press).

Racially demarcated points of view are found in cases involving interracial sex. A study found that White jurors were more likely to find a defendant culpable of rape when he was Black and the victim was White than in other racial combinations. Blacks, on the other hand, were more likely to judge that a White defendant was culpable when the victim was Black (Ugwuegbu, 1979). In a rape simulation study, Black defendants were treated more harshly than White defendants (Feild, 1979). Further, race was a significant factor when the evidence was more clear-cut in favor of guilt or innocence. Less than unanimous votes, thus, become particularly problematic because relaxing the unanimity rule is likely to disregard votes by racial minorities. Racially demarcated votes in deliberation can be used to delete the power of racial minorities.

Another effective mechanism in maintaining the racially dominant judicial institution is the construction of gerrymandered judicial districts. How this has been done is an adventure in mental and legal gymnastics. To begin, it is known that vicinity requirements are an essential ingredient of the Sixth Amendment. As a prime example, the legislature in California long ago defined a judicial district in Los Angeles County as the area within a 20-mile radius of each courthouse. Early in the 1970s, the Los Angeles County Board of Supervisors adopted this rule because Los Angeles County had wide geographic boundaries. The Senate approved the bill, A.B. 1454, which added the 20-mile rule to the *California Code of Civil Procedure*. Research has demonstrated that in fact the 20-mile rule for judicial districts has not been followed. Rather, systematic inclusion and exclusion of certain neighborhoods has led to a significant underrepresentation of minority populations (Fukurai, et al., 1991, in press). By regulating the degree of minority participation on jury

panels, and thus ultimate judicial decision-making, the dominant population's control over the political and judicial apparatus creates an effective mechanism for gerrymandering geographic definitions of judicial districts. Particular neighborhoods with a high concentration of Blacks and other racial minorities have simply been excluded from the defined boundary of judicial districts (Fukurai & Butler, 1987).

Institutional Discrimination: Subordinating Blacks

Numerous Supreme Court decisions have also perpetuated and legitimized the domination and racial supremacy of the majority in both judicial and political spheres. The very apparatus of law regulates racial participation, and Court decisions reify the dominant bureaucratic system, elevating the "rule of law" while degrading rights of Blacks.

In *Carter v. Jury Commission of Greene County* (1970), for example, the petitioner claimed that the entire state apparatus—which included the county jury commissioners, their clerks, the local circuit judge, and even the governor of Alabama—was in conspiracy in perpetuating racial inequality in jury selection. The appellant (*Carter v. Jury Commission of Green County*, 1970) sought to establish three principles in the case:

1. A *declaration* that qualified Blacks were systematically excluded from grand and petit juries in Greene County, making the Alabama statutes unconstitutional, and that the jury commissioner operated illegally through his deliberate segregation of a governmental agency.

2. A *permanent injunction* forbidding the systematic exclusion of Blacks in juries, thereby requiring all eligible Blacks to be placed on the jury roll.

3. An *order to vacate the appointment* of jury commissioners and to compel the Alabama governor to select new members without racial discrimination.

Further, *Turner v. Fouche* (1970), announced the same day as *Carter*, also argued the notion of institutional discrimination against potential Black jurors. The petitioner alleged that the county board of education, which consisted of five freeholders, was selected by the grand jury, which in turn was drawn from a jury list selected by the six-member county jury commission. The commissioners were appointed by the judge of the state superior court for the circuit in the county. The problem here is that all board of education members were White, selected by all-White grand juries, which in turn, had been selected by all-White jury commissioners. Because of racial oppression against Blacks, the petitioner alleged that "the board of education had deprived the Negro school children of text books, facilities, and other advantages" (*Turner v. Fouche*, 1970).

The notion of a racially discriminatory judicial system is also reported elsewhere. In the Huey Newton trial, for instance, ethnographic research confirmed the notion of White supremacy in the criminal court system. The study notes that:

a black man like Huey Newton is tried under a system of law developed by white Western European jurists. He is confronted in the black ghetto by white police officers, then indicted by an all-white, or predominantly white, grand jury, prosecuted by a team of all-white district attorneys, tried by a white judge, convicted by a predominantly white jury, and denied bail on appeal by white state appellate courts and a white federal judge. It is not simply the color of the principals that is at issue, but the more profound point that the various officials and processes in the system represent institutions that reflect and are responsive to values and interests of the white majority—a power structure and a community that benefit from keeping black people in "their place," namely, in the ghetto and without power. (Blauner, 1972, p. 253)

Elsewhere we have documented the precise way in which this was done (Fukurai & Butler, 1987; Fukurai et al., in press). Yet, this is only a single case, and further evidence of institutional racism is required of future investigators.

In the view of those who feel they are oppressed, the judicial and legal structures are grounded upon

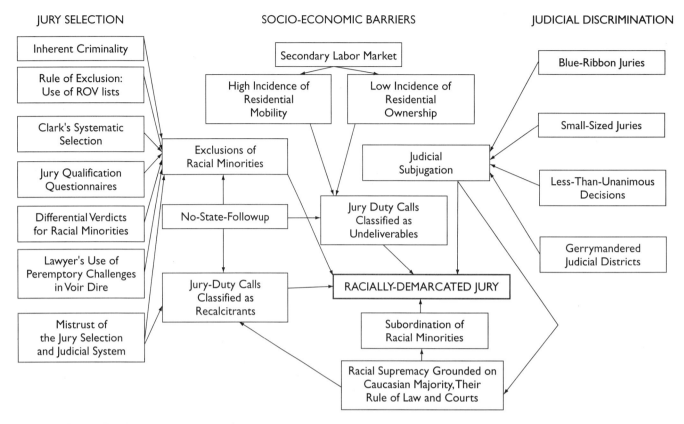

JURY SELECTION   SOCIO-ECONOMIC BARRIERS   JUDICIAL DISCRIMINATION

Figure 1. Racial disenfranchisement in the jury system and jury selection.

Anglo supremacy and create the opportunity to maintain oppressive social conditions that—while gradually undergoing change awarding minorities some rights—continuously reproduce the subordination of Blacks. The theoretical tenet of discrimination against Blacks in the jury system and jury selection is summarized in Figure 1.

Conclusions

This article argued that the racially demarcated social system in the United States still exists in the form of oppressive legal and judicial structures that continuously reproduce, maintain, and perpetuate the subordination of Blacks. Historically they are discouraged, if not prevented, from full-community participation in labor markets, political structures, courts, and the judicial decision-making processes. Up until the last few decades, the jury-participation privilege was largely reserved to the Anglo majority.

Specific mechanisms still exist today and are used to sculpt system-

atically a racially demarcated jury. Potential sources of institutional biases in jury selection include various forms of structural and individual racism that prevent full-community jury participation, thereby perpetuating and maintaining racially demarcated juries. Labor market characteristics also set limits on racial minorities, who are likely to be in secondary markets with a high degree of residential mobility, so that the call to jury service legally become "undeliverable" and they become "recalcitrants" who do not respond. As well, judicial discrimination points to various strategies that regulate the degree of minority participation on juries: the use of blue ribbon juries, a smaller-size jury, less than unanimous decisions, and gerrymandered judicial districts.

Perhaps more important is the notion that the entire jury system and jury selection are grounded on Anglo-controlled institutions and structural ideas of supremacy. Only time will reveal if the United States can free itself of such powerful forces, which set limits on the rights

of Black people and curtail their freedom to participate equally in the judicial decision-making process. What can be said, though, is that until it overturns the past, such a society will be the target of those still unfree who view its courts and other institutions as chains to be broken not to be shackled by.

Notes

1. For additional information, see Benokraitis, 1975; Butler et al., in press; Erlanger, 1970, pp. 345–370; Fukurai et al., 1987; *Iowa Law Review*, 1973, pp. 401–419; *The Yale Law Journal*, 1970, pp. 531–550.
2. Also see Cromer, 1910; Krooth, 1975, 1980; Lewis, 1984.
3. For additional information, see Alker, Hosticka, & Mitchell, 1976, pp. 9–41; Brady, 1983, pp. 241–263; De Cani, 1974, pp. 234–238; Finkelstein, 1976, pp. 338–376; Heyns, 1979; Kairys, 1972, pp. 771–806; Kairys et al., 1977, pp. 776–827; Mills, 1969, pp. 329–339; Morris, 1965; Roberts, 1939; Robinson, 1950, pp. 73–78; Staples, 1975, pp. 14–22; Summers, 1961, pp. 35–42; *U.S. 90th Congress Senate Report No. 891*, 1967; *U.S. 90th Congress House Report No. 1076*, 1968; Whyte, 1956.

4. Research in Oakland found that 81.5% of Blacks and 14.5% of Anglos failed to qualify as jurors; in central Los Angeles, 38% of Blacks and 8.5% of Anglos failed the examination; and in Long Beach failure rates were 40% for Blacks and 13% for Anglos.

5. The cumulative effect of institutional racism is crucial in eliminating racial groups during the jury selection process. For example, research in Maryland found substantial bias against those with less than 12 years of formal education. Because inequality in the quality and accessibility of education leads to fewer Blacks finishing high school, and because most jurors are expected to have a high school education, many Blacks are disqualified from jury lists.

6. Rulings in both *Johnson v. Louisiana* (1972) and *Apodaca v. Oregon*, (1972) were by 5–4 votes.

7. Postverdict interviews revealed that the first vote on the penalty was 9–3 in favor of death. The three jurors who voted against the death penalty were Black. The second vote resulted in a unanimous decision in favor of life without possibility of parole. Postverdict interviews also indicated that one Black male juror walked into the deliberation room after hearing all the penalty phase evidence and said: "I'm not going to vote for the death penalty and no one is going to change my mind." Ultimately, the assertiveness of that one Black juror, working his chemistry with the others, significantly affected their final verdict, changing the first vote of death to life without possibility of parole (for more detailed descriptions of the case, see Fukurai et al., in press).

References

Akins v. Texas. 325 U.S. 398 (1954).

Alker, H. R., Jr., & Barnard, J. J. (1978). Procedural and social biases in the jury selection process. *The Justice System Journal*, 3, 220–241.

Alker, H. R., Jr., Hosticka, C., & Mitchell, M. (1976). Jury selection as a biased social process. *The Law and Society Review*, 9, 9–41.

American Criminal Law Review (1980). "Grigsby vs. Mabry" a new look at death qualified juries. Vol. 18, pp. 145–163.

Apodaca v. Oregon, 406 U.S. 404 (1972).

Avery v. Georgia, 345 U.S. 559 (1953).

Baldus, D. Pulaske, C., & Woodsworth, G. (1983). Judicial review of death sentences. *Journal of Criminal Law and Criminology*, 74, 661–753.

Batson v. Kentucky, 106 S. Ct. 1712 (1986).

Benokraitis, N. (1975). *Institutional racism: An empirical study of Blacks and jury selection process in ten Southern states*. Unpublished doctoral dissertation, University of Texas, Austin.

Berle, A. (1959). *Power without property: A new development in American political economy*. New York: Harcourt, Brace.

Blauner, R. (1973). *Racial oppression in America*. New York: Harper & Row.

Boags, C. D., & Boags, R. M. (1971). The misuse of a so-called psychological examination for the selection of jurors. In C. Thomas (Ed.), *Boys no more: A Black psychologist's view of community* (pp. 48–64). Beverly Hills, California: Glencoe.

Bowers, W., & Pierce, G. (1980). Arbitrariness and discrimination under post-Furman capital statutes. *Crime & Delinquency*, 26, 563–635.

Brady, J. (1983). Fair and impartial railroad: The jury, the media, and political trials. *Journal of Criminal Justice*, 11, 241–263.

Burns, J. F. (1987, October 17). After echoes of empire, countries are on edge. *New York Times*.

Butler, E. W. (1980). Torrance Superior Court panels and population analysis. University of California, Riverside.

Butler, E. W., Chapin, S., Jr., Hemmens, G. C. Kaiser, E. J., Stegman, M. A., & Weiss, F. S. (1969). *Moving behavior and residential choice: A national survey*. Washington, DC: National Academy of Science.

Butler, E. W., Fukurai, H., & Huebner-Dimitrius, J. (in press). *Anatomy of the McMartin case*. New Brunswick, NJ: Rutgers University Press.

Butler, E. W., & Kaiser, E. J. (1971). Prediction of residential movement and spatial allocation. *Urban Affairs Quarterly*, 6, 477–494.

Carp, R. A. (1982). Federal grand juries: How true a "cross section" of the community. *The Justice System Journal*, 7, 257–277.

Carter v. Jury Commission of Greene County, 396 U.S. 332 (1970).

Cassell v. Texas, 339 U.S. 282 (1950).

Chevigny, P. G. (1975). The Attica case: A successful jury challenge in northern city. *Criminal Law Bulletin*, 11, 157–172.

Cromer, E. (1910). *Ancient and modern imperialism*. New York: Longmans, Green.

Cullen F. T., & Link, B. G. (1980). Crime as an occupation. *Criminology*, 18, 399–410.

De Cani, J. S. (1974). Statistical evidence in jury discrimination cases. *The Journal of Criminal Law and Criminology*, 65, 234–238.

Diamond, W. H. (1980). Federal remedies for racial discrimination in grand jury selection. *Columbia Journal of Law and Social Problems*, 16, 85–117.

Edward, R., Reich, M., & Gordon, D. (1975). *Labor market segmentation*. Lexington, MA: D. C. Heath.

Erlanger, H. S. (1970). Jury research in America. *Law and Society Review*, 5, 345–370.

Fay v. New York, 332 U.S. 261 (1947).

Feagin, J. R. (1984). *Racial and ethnic relations*. Englewood Cliffs, NJ: Prentice-Hall.

Featherman, D. & Hauser, R. (1978). *Opportunity and change*. New York: Academic Press.

Feild, H. (1979). Rape trials and jurors' decisions: A psychological analysis of the effects of victim, defendant, and case characteristics. *Law and Human Behavior*, 3, 261–284.

Finkelstein, M. O. (1976). The application of statistical decision theory to the jury discrimination cases. *Harvard Law Review*, 80, 338–376.

Fukurai, H. (1985). *Institutional racial inequality: A theoretical and empirical examination of the jury selection process*. Unpublished doctoral dissertation, University of California, Riverside.

Fukurai, H., & Butler, E. W. (1987). *Jury selection: Institutionalized racial inequality*. Unpublished manuscript.

Fukurai, H., Butler, E. W., & Huebner-Dimitrius, J. (1987). Spatial and racism imbalances in voter registration and jury selection. *Sociology and Social Research*, 77, 33–38.

Fukurai, H., Butler, E. W. & Krooth, R. (1991). A cross sectional jury representation or systematic jury representation? Simple random and cluster sampling strategies in jury selection. *Journal of Criminal Justice*, 19, 31–48.

Fukurai, H., Butler, E. W. & Krooth, R. (in press). *Race and the jury: Racial disenfranchisement and the search for justice*. New York: Plenum.

Goffman, E. (1959). *The presentation of self in everyday life*. New York: Doubleday Anchor.

Hans, V., & Vidmar, N. (1986). Judging the jury. New York: Plenum.

Hastie, R., Penrod, S. D., & Pennington, N. (1980). *Inside the jury*. Cambridge, MA: Harvard University Press

Harris v. People of California, 36 Cal 3d. 36 (1984).

Hepburn, J. R. (1978). Race and the decision to arrest: An analysis of warrants issued. *Journal of Research in Crime and Delinquency*, 15, 54–73.

Heyns, B. (1979). *1979 jury analysis*. No. A–344097. Los Angeles, CA: Superior Court, County of Los Angeles.

Horowitz, I. A. (1980). Jury selection: A comparison of two methods in several criminal cases. *Journal of Applied Social Psychology*, 10, 86–99.

Iowa Law Review. (1973). "Jury-mandering": Federal jury selection and the generation gap. Vol. 59, pp. 401–419.

Jalee, P. (1968). *The pillage of the Third World*. New York: Monthly Review Press.

Johns, M. A. (1960). *American immigration*. Chicago: University of Chicago Press.

Johnson v. Louisiana, 406 U.S. 356 (1972).

Kairys, D. (1972). Juror selection: The law, a mathematical method of analysis, and a case study. *American Criminal Law Review*, 12, 771–806.

Kairys, D., Kadane, J. B., & Lehoczky, J. P. (1977). Jury representativeness: A mandate for multiple source lists. *California Law Review*, 65, 776–827.

Kalven, H., Jr., & Zeisel, H. (1966). *The American jury*. Boston: Little, Brown.

Kaye, D. (1980). And then there were twelve: Statistical reasoning, the supreme court, and the size of the jury. *California Law Review*, 46, 461–474.

Kramer, R. C. (1982). From "habitual offenders" to career criminals. *Law and Human Behavior*, 6, 273–293.

Krooth, R. (1975). *Empire: A bicentennial appraisal*. Santa Barbara, CA: Harvest.

Krooth, R. (1980). *Arms and empire: Imperial patterns before World War II*. Santa Barbara, CA: Harvest.

Lewis, G. C. (1984). *On the government of dependencies* (C.P. Lucas, Ed.). Oxford.

Lipset, J. M., & Bendix, R. (1959). *Social mobility in industrial society*. Berkeley: University of California Press.

Lipton, J. P. (1979). *Sociocultural and personality perspectives on jury behavior and decision making*. Unpublished dissertation, University of California.

McAllister, R. J., Kaiser, E. J., & Butler, E. W. (1971). Residential mobility of blacks and whites: A national longitudinal survey. *American Journal of Sociology*, 77, 445–456.

Mills, E. S. (1969). A statistical profile of jurors in a United States district court. *Law and the Social Order*, 1, 329–339.

Morris, R. (1965). *Government and labor in early America*. New York: Harper & Row.

Roberts, G. (1939). *The Nazi: Claims to colonies*. London: John Murray.

Robinson, W. S. (1950). Bias, probability and trial by jury. *American Sociological Review*, 15, 73–78.

Rokeach, M., & McLellan, D. D. (1970). Dogmatism and the death penalty: A reinterpretation of the Duquesne poll data. *Duquesne Law Review*, 81, 125–129.

Roper, R. T. (1980). *The American profile poster: Who own what, who makes how much, who works where, and who lives with whom*. New York: Pantheon.

Sabagh, G., Van Arsdol, M. P., & Butler, E. W. (1969). Some determinants of intra-metropolitan residential mobility: Conceptual considerations. *Social Forces*, 48, 88–98.

Smith v. Texas, 211 U.S. 128 (1940).

Staples, R. (1975). White racism, black crime, and American justice. *Phylon*, 36, 14–22.

Starr, V. H., & McCormick, M. (1985). *Jury selection*. Boston, Little, Brown.

Summers, M. R. (1961). A comparative study of the qualifications of state and federal jurors. *Wisconsin Bar Bulletin*, 34, 35–42.

Turner v. Fouche, 396, U.S. 346 (1970).

Ugwuegbu, D. (1979). Racial and evidential factors in juror attributions of legal responsibility. *Journal of Experimental Social Psychology*, 15, 133–146.

U.S. 90th Congress Senate Report. 1967. No. 891. Washington, DC: U.S. Government Printing Office.

U.S. 90th Congress House Report. 1968. No. 1076. Washington, DC: U.S. Government Printing Office.

Van Arsdol, J., Maurice, D., Sabagh, G., & Butler, E. W. (1968). Retrospective and subsequent metropolitan residential mobility. *Demography*, 5, 249–267.

Van den Berghe, P. L. (1974). Bringing beast back in. *American Sociological Review*, 39, 777–788.

Van Dyke, J. M. (1977). *Jury selection procedure*. Cambridge, MA: Ballinger.

Whyte, W. (1956). *Organization man*. Garden City, NY: Doubleday.

Williams v. Florida, 406 U.S. 356 (1972).

Wishman, S. (1986). *Anatomy of a jury*. New York: Times.

Yale Law Journal. (1970). The case for Black juries. Vol. 79, pp. 531–550.

Zeigler, D. H. (1978). Young adults as a cognizable group in jury selection. *Michigan Law Review*, 76, 1045–1110.

Article Review Form at end of book.

Describe the possible negative effects the U.S. Supreme Court's 1996 *Whren* decision may have on minorities.

"Driving While Black" and All Other Traffic Offenses:

The Supreme Court and Pretextual Traffic Stops

David A. Harris

Eugene N. Balk Professor of Law and Values, University of Toledo College of Law

I. Introduction

The Supreme Court's decision in *Whren v. United States*[1] could not have surprised many observers of the Court's Fourth Amendment jurisprudence. In *Whren*, police officers used traffic violations as a pretext to stop a car and investigate possible drug offenses; the officers had neither probable cause nor reasonable suspicion to stop the driver for narcotics crimes.[2] In the Supreme Court, the government advocated the "could have" standard: any time the police *could have* stopped the defendant for a traffic infraction, it does not matter that police *actually* stopped him to investigate a crime for which the police had little or no

My thanks to Jeffrey Gamso, Deborah Jeon, Mark Kappelhoff, Tom Perez, Daniel Steinbock and Lisa Burget Wright for helpful comments on an earlier draft of this piece. Thanks also to Eric Crytzer and Mary L. Sawyers for research and editorial assistance.

evidence.[3] The defense asked the Court to adopt a "would have" rule: a seizure based on a traffic stop would only stand if a reasonable officer *would have* made this particular stop.[4] The Court sided with the government. If police witness a traffic violation, the Court said, they have the simplest and clearest type of probable cause imaginable for a stop.[5] Requiring more would force lower courts to make post hoc Fourth Amendment judgments based on either the mindset of a reasonable officer or the actual (perhaps ulterior) motives of the arresting officer, neither one of which the Court saw as necessary, useful, or relevant to the task of judging the constitutionality of a seizure.[6] After *Whren*, courts will not ask whether police conducted a traffic stop because officers felt the occupants of the car were involved in some other crime about which they had only a hunch; rather, once a driver commits a traffic infraction, the officer's "real" purpose will make no difference at all.[7]

For the sake of of argument, I will concede that the decision in *Whren* makes some sense, at least from the point of view of judicial ad-

ministration. But examined more carefully, *Whren* does more than opt for a more workable rule: it approves two alarming law enforcement practices. Neither are secret; on the contrary, the law of search and seizure has reflected both for a long time.[8] But both represent profoundly dangerous developments for a free society, especially one dedicated to the equal treatment of all citizens.

First, the comprehensive scope of state traffic codes makes them extremely powerful tools under *Whren*. These codes regulate the details of driving in ways both big and small, obvious and arcane. In the most literal sense, no driver can avoid violating *some* traffic law during a short drive, even with the most careful attention. Fairly read, *Whren* says that any traffic violation can support a stop, no matter what the real reason for it is; this makes any citizen fair game for a stop, almost any time, anywhere, virtually at the whim of police. Given how important an activity driving has become in American society, *Whren* changes the Fourth Amendment's rule that police must have a reason to forcibly interfere in our business—some basis to

Reprinted by special permission of Northwestern University School of Law. *Journal of Criminal Law and Criminology*, Vol. 87, Issue 2, 1997.

suspect wrongdoing that is more than a hunch.[9] Simply put, that rule no longer applies when a person drives a car.

This alone should worry us, but the second police practice *Whren* approves is in fact far worse. It is this: Police will *not* subject *all* drivers to traffic stops in the way *Whren* allows. Rather, if past practice is any indication, they will use the traffic code to stop a hugely disproportionate number of African-Americans and Hispanics. We know this because *it is exactly what has been happening already*, even before receiving the Supreme Court's imprimatur in *Whren*. In fact, the stopping of black drivers, just to see what officers can find, has become so common in some places that this practice has its own name: African-Americans sometimes say they have been stopped for the offense of "driving while black."[10] With *Whren*, we should expect African-Americans and Hispanics to experience an even greater number of pretextual traffic stops. And once police stop a car, they often search it, either by obtaining consent, using a drug sniffing dog, or by some other means.[11] In fact, searching cars for narcotics is perhaps *the* major motivation for making these stops.

Under a Constitution that restrains the government vis-a-vis the individual[12] and that puts some limits on what the authorities may do in the pursuit of the guilty, the power of the police to stop any particular driver, at almost any time,[13] seems oddly out of place. And with the words "equal justice under law" carved into the stone of the Supreme Court itself, one might think that the use of police power in one of its rawest forms against members of particular racial or ethnic groups might prompt the Court to show some interest in curbing such abuses.[14] The defendant-petitioners presented both of these arguments— the almost arbitrary power over any driver inherent in the "could have" approach, and the racially biased use of traffic stops—to the Court. Yet the Court paid little attention to these obvious implications of its decision.*Whren* is more than a missed opportunity for the Court to rein in some police practices that strike at the heart of the ideas of freedom and equal treatment; *Whren* represents a clear step in the other direction— toward authoritarianism, toward racist policing, and toward a view of minorities as criminals, rather than citizens.

II. The Case

Whren presented the Court with relatively simple facts. Plain clothes vice officers in an unmarked police car saw two young men driving a vehicle with temporary tags in an area known for drug activity.[15] The police observed the vehicle pause at a stop sign for longer than usual.[16] While the officers did not see the men do anything to indicate involvement in criminal activity, they still became suspicious.[17] The driver turned without signalling and sped off.[18] The police stopped the vehicle, and observed the passenger holding a bag of cocaine in each hand.[19]

The government argued that the traffic violations the driver committed—not giving "full time and attention to the operation of the vehicle,"[20] failing to signal,[21] and travelling at a speed "greater than is reasonable and prudent under the conditions"[22]—gave the police probable cause to stop the car. The government contended that with probable cause arising from the traffic violations, the stop of the car passed constitutional standards, regardless of the fact that the officers may actually have intended to investigate drug offenses and not traffic infractions.[23] The defense asserted that the officers had no actual interest in traffic enforcement, and had used the traffic infraction only as a pretext. For the real objection of the police—searching for evidence of possible drug offenses—no probable cause or reasonable suspicion existed.[24] The defense contended that this made the stop (and the resulting seizure of the cocaine) unconstitutional.[25] The District Court admitted the evidence, and at trial both defendants were found guilty.[26] The U.S. Court of Appeals for the District of Columbia Circuit affirmed, stating that "a traffic stop is permissible as long as a reasonable officer in the same circumstances *could have* stopped the car for the suspected traffic violation," despite the fact that the officer may subjectively believe that those in the car may be engaging in some other illegal behavior.[27]

The Supreme Court adopted the "could have" theory. The Court said that any time a police officer observes a traffic violation, she has probable cause to stop the vehicle, regardless of the fact that the detailed nature of traffic codes enables any officer that wishes to do so to stop virtually any motorist at almost any time by using the traffic infraction as a pretext.[28] The Court discounted statements in prior cases that seemed to cast pretextual stops in an unfavorable light,[29] and stated that the law actually supported the opposite proposition: An officer's motive does not "invalidate[ ] objectively reasonable behavior under the Fourth Amendment."[30] Relying heavily on *United States v. Robinson*[31] and *Scott v. United States*,[32] the Court said that the officer's state of mind in a Fourth Amendment situation is irrelevant, "as long as the circumstances viewed objectively, justify that action."[33] "We think," the Court went on, that *Robinson* and other cases "foreclose any argument that the constitutional reasonableness of traffic stops depends on the actual motivation of the individual officers involved."[34]

Addressing the "would have" standard that the defendant proposed, the Court rejected the notion that the results of a suppression motion should turn on whether a reasonable officer, under the police practices and regulations in the jurisdiction in which the case arose, would have made the stop for the purposes of traffic enforcement.[35] Trial courts would find such a test much too difficult to administer, the Court said, and would end up "speculating about the hypothetical reaction of a hypothetical constable—an exercise that might be called virtual subjectivity."[36] The result would be that the application of Fourth Amendment law would vary from place to place, depending on police regulations and practices, a result the Court found unacceptable.[37] But the Court failed to acknowledge that the district court in *Whren* would not have needed to speculate to apply the "would have" standard. District of Columbia Police regulations prohibited officers in plain clothes and officers in unmarked vehicles from making traffic stops unless the violations posed an immediate threat to others.[38] The officers clearly violated this rule in *Whren*; thus, there is little doubt that their conduct was not what a reasonable officer in their department would do, at least assuming that a reasonable officer follows regulations. Additionally, there was no doubt that their traffic enforcement actions were a pretext for drug investigation without probable cause or reasonable suspicion.[39]

The Court gave short shrift to the argument that police would use the power to make traffic stops disproportionately against minorities. Of course, the Constitution forbids racially biased law enforcement, the Court said, but the proper source for a remedy is the Equal Protection Clause, not the Fourth Amendment.[40] Dismissing this point in a few tepid lines buried in the middle of the opinion, the Court read the racial question out of the case without any substantive discussion. The real reasons police act, as opposed to the legal justification proffered for their actions, "play no role in ordinary, probable-cause Fourth Amendment analysis."[41] It is difficult to say what is more striking: the blandness of these words, or the blindness of what they assert.

The Court's brief treatment of a position so central to the petitioners' case suggests that the Justices may not have taken the argument seriously. But it is the substance of the Court's answer, not its brevity, that confirms this feeling. On the practical level, equal protection will provide few of those subjected to this treatment with any solace; indeed, for each of the few successful suits brought to protest racially biased law enforcement practices,[42] police may stop and search thousands of people who have no hope of redress. They do not have the resources, knowledge, or wherewithal to complain; they have learned that complaining about this treatment brings nothing (except maybe trouble), or that they may make unattractive plaintiffs unlikely to engender any jury's sympathy, regardless of the injuries to their rights.[43]

Aside from these practical considerations, the Court's reference to the Equal Protection Clause seems to mean that persons aggrieved by racially biased stops and searches

should attempt a statistical demonstration that pretextual traffic stops have a racially disproportionate impact. But plaintiffs in such suits would have to confront the Court's long-standing precedents barring proof of equal protection claims by a showing of disparate impact.[44] Moreover, the Court has shown hostility toward the demonstration of constitutional violations through statistics. In *McCleskey v. Kemp*,[45] a statistical study showed undeniable racial patterns in the administration of the death penalty in Georgia. If the victim was white and the perpetrator was black, the state sought the death penalty 70 percent of the time;[46] if the victim was black and the defendant was white, the state sought the death penalty in only 19 percent of the cases.[47] If the victim and defendant were either both white or both black, the figures were 32 percent and 15 percent, respectively.[48] McCleskey claimed that the statistics demonstrated that he was discriminated against because of his race and the race of his victim.[49] As striking as these statistics may have been, the Court found them meaningless. "At most," the Court said, "the . . . [statistical] study indicates a discrepancy that appears to correlate with race," but it "does not demonstrate a constitutionally significant risk of racial bias affecting the Georgia capital-sentencing process."[50] McCleskey, the Court said, "must prove that the decision-makers in *his* case acted with discriminatory purpose."[51] In other words, only evidence of racial animus of the most direct nature in the defendant's own case could prove an equal protection violation; statistical proof showing patterns of racial bias, the more logical way to demonstrate discriminatory application of the law, would be unacceptable.[52]

Another example is *United States v. Armstrong*,[53] a selective prosecution case decided during the same Supreme Court term as *Whren*. In *Armstrong*, the defendants presented a study that showed that all 24 crack cocaine cases the district federal public defender had closed over the prior year involved only black defendants.[54] Finding this evidence insufficient, the Court sided with the government and made the already daunting challenge of proving a se-

lective prosecution claim even more difficult: the defendant will have no right of access to the prosecutor's files unless he first introduces evidence that the prosecutor did not prosecute others similarly situated and acted out of racial hostility in the defendant's case.[55] Thus, the defendant must furnish evidence of the correctness of his claim, without access to the very evidence needed to prove his claim—a Catch 22 if ever there was one.[56]

McClesky and *Armstrong* make a jarring backdrop for the Court's blithe assertion in *Whren* that the Equal Protection Clause represents the proper way to address claims of discrimination in law enforcement. It is hard to avoid the conclusion that, given *McClesky* and *Armstrong*, the Justices do not mean for many equal protection cases to succeed.

Even though I disagree strongly with some parts of *Whren*, I will concede for the sake of argument that the Court's reasoning is not entirely wrong. There is no question that it will be easier for lower courts to work with the "could have" rule than the "would have" rule. The "could have" rule requires very little evidence; the officer need only testify that she observed a traffic violation and stopped the car. The court will either believe the testimony or reject it.[57] By contrast, the "would have" test might require testimony about regular police practices, departmental regulations, and in the end a judgment from the court about whether the actions of the officer in a particular case were those a reasonable officer would have taken. These difficulties do not persuade me that courts *could not* cope with a "would have" rule; in fact, they make such judgments all the time in *Terry* stop cases, which require a decision about the reasonableness of the officer's actions in a given situation.[58] Nevertheless, the "could have" test would no doubt prove easier to administer.

To be sure, there are negative points to the opinion beyond those I have already mentioned. For example, one can make a good argument that the Court used a strained reading of its cases to reject the "would have" test. This seems especially true of the Court's treatment of *Robinson*. The Court was correct in

Whren: *Robinson* said that the actual motivation of the officer does not determine the search's objective reasonableness.[59] But this is hardly a fair description of the actual thrust of the case. *Robinson* posed the question whether the search of the defendant incident to arrest met constitutional standards. The facts did not point to any danger to police or to the destruction of any evidence—the twin justifications for a search incident to an arrest until the *Robinson* decision.[60] Nevertheless, the Court in *Robinson* found that the arrest alone justified the search. In other words, a full search can always follow a legitimate arrest; that is, an arrest which police make for the purpose of apprehending an offender, not for the purpose of making the search. Thus, while the irrelevancy of the actual beliefs of the officer is consistent with the rest of *Robinson*, it hardly seems substantial enough to be the basis of the decision in *Whren*. Indeed, from the point of view of the proper use of cases and doctrine, the Court should simply have conceded in *Whren* that precedent did not supply a ready answer to the question of how to handle pretextual stops. The opinion could have said (1) our cases do not dictate which way to decide this issue, so (2) we think the "could have" rule clearly preferable for reasons of judicial administration, police understanding of the rule, and crime control.

But these arguments are not the primary reasons that *Whren* should disturb us. The real danger of *Whren* is not its use of precedent, its facile logic, or its rejection of one proposed test for another. Rather, *Whren's* most troubling aspects lie in its implications—the incredible amount of discretionary power it hands law enforcement without any check—and what this means for our everyday lives and our freedom as citizens.

III. The Fourth Amendment and Traffic Offenses

Commentators have criticized the Supreme Court's Fourth Amendment jurisprudence, with considerable justification. As the Court lurches between protecting what it considers bedrock Fourth Amendment values—the sanctity of the home, for example[61]—and the undesirable and distasteful result of suppressing probative evidence of guilt, it has generated a hodgepodge of conflicting rules so technical that law professors—let alone law *enforcers*—find them difficult to understand.[62] Even so, some basic search and seizure rules seem firmly ensconced in the law. Perhaps this is because they are so fundamental that disturbing them would create an even larger doctrinal mess than the one that already exists; perhaps it is because there is present-day consensus accompanied by historical evidence on these points. Whatever the reason, we can discuss two key rules, secure in the knowledge that they are accepted by the Court.

First, the police must usually have a reason to forcibly stop a person.[63] When I say "forcibly stop," I do not mean the application of force to a suspect, though that may be part of a seizure. And I am not referring to casual encounters with police, in which a citizen is asked whether he or she would mind talking to police. Even though it seems more than just plausible to argue that such encounters always carry with them some element of coercion,[64] I am willing to accept, for the purposes of argument, the idea that such encounters remain consensual. In contrast, a forcible stop *is* by its nature coercive. When a police officer *orders* a citizen to halt, questioning, a search of some kind, or even arrest may follow. Police cannot force a citizen to stop and submit in this way without probable cause or at least reasonable suspicion to believe that a crime has been or is about to be committed by the suspect.[65] The Supreme Court reaffirmed this standard just a few years ago in *Minnesota v. Dickerson*,[66] in which Justice White stated clearly that this rule had not changed. The police must still have a reason to force a citizen to stop and submit to their authority, something more than just a hunch.[67]

The other basic rule important to our discussion is this: if police do not have the probable cause or reasonable suspicion necessary for a forcible stop, a citizen may ignore police requests to stop, respond to questions, produce identification, or submit to any further intrusion. The Supreme Court has reiterated this rule in a number of cases stretching over many years. For example, in *Brown v. Texas*,[68] police stopped a man in an area with a "high incidence of drug traffic"[69] because "the situation 'looked suspicious and we had never seen [the] subject in that area before.'"[70] The officers arrested the man under a Texas statute that criminalized any refusal to give police a name and address upon a legitimate stop.[71] The Supreme Court invalidated the statute, and declared that nothing in the facts of the case allowed the officers to make a legitimate stop, even the defendant's presence in an area known for narcotics trafficking. The defendant had every right to walk away and to refuse to produce identification in such a situation, and any law to the contrary did not meet constitutional standards.[72] The Court carried this doctrine forward in *Florida v. Royer*,[73] in which it stated that "[a citizen] may not be detained even momentarily without reasonable, objective grounds for doing so; and his refusal to listen or answer does not, without more, furnish those grounds."[74] And in *Florida v. Bostick*,[75] the Court reaffirmed this principle, declaring that while the police may question a person about whom they have no suspicion, "an individual may decline an officer's request without fearing prosecution."[76]

To be sure, I have not made the mistake of assuming that these legal rules necessarily reflect reality. I know that even though the cases discussed here may guarantee citizens the right to walk away from curious police without interference, the right may exist more in theory than in practice.[77] It may be that the mere appearance of authority—nothing more than the officer's uniform, badge and squad car, to say nothing of her weapon—will cause most people to do what she says or answer her questions. But the point is that even if the law remains more an ideal than anything else, the Court's pronouncements on the subject all point in one direction: the police need at least reasonable suspicion to forcibly interfere with one's movement, and if they do not have it the citizen may walk away.

Whren alters all of this for anyone driving a car. Simply put, it is difficult to imagine a more American activity than driving a car. We use our cars for everything: work (both as transportation to get to and from work and as mobile offices and sales platforms), play, and myriad other activities that make up everyday life. Of course, many Americans do not own cars, and some have even found it unnecessary to learn to drive. But this is not the norm. Most American kids date their emergence from adolescence not from high school graduation or a religious or cultural ceremony, but from something far more central to what they really value: the day they receive their driver's licenses. Americans visiting Europe for the first time often return with the observation that one can get to and from almost any little town entirely on public transportation. Europeans visiting America are often surprised at the lack of public transportation facilities and options outside of major urban centers, and at the sizeable cities that rely entirely on automobile transportation. Despite energy crises, traffic congestion, and the expense of owning a car, most Americans prefer to drive wherever they go.[78] In short, there are few activities more important to American life than driving.[79]

With that in mind, consider traffic codes. There is no detail of driving too small, no piece of equipment too insignificant, no item of automobile regulation too arcane to be made the subject of a traffic offense. Police officers in some jurisdictions have a rule of thumb: the average driver cannot go three blocks without violating some traffic regulation. Reading the codes, it is hard to disagree; the question is how anyone could get *as far as three blocks* without violating the law.

When we think of traffic offenses, we think of "moving violations"—exceeding the speed limit, crossing dividing lines, and the like. But in fact traffic codes regulate many other aspects of driving-related activity, including some that seem almost wildly hypertechnical. And some of these offenses have nothing to do with driving at all. Rather, they are "equipment violations"—offenses in which driving with incorrect, outdated, or broken equipment consti-

tutes the violation. And then there are catch-all provisions: rules that allow police to stop drivers for conduct that complies with all rules on the books, but that officers consider "imprudent" or "unreasonable" under the circumstances, or that describe the offense in language so broad as to make a violation virtually coextensive with the officer's unreviewable personal judgment.

For example, in any number of jurisdictions, police can stop drivers not only for driving too fast, but for driving too slow.[80] In Utah, drivers must signal for at least three seconds before changing lanes; a two second signal would violate the law.[81] In many states, a driver must signal for at least one hundred feet before turning right; ninety-five feet would make the driver an offender.[82] And the driver making that right turn may not slow down "suddenly" (undefined) without signalling.[83] Many states have made it a crime to drive with a malfunctioning taillight,[84] a rear-tag illumination bulb that does not work,[85] or tires without sufficient tread.[86] They also require drivers to display not only license tags, but yearly validation stickers, pollution control stickers, and safety inspection stickers; driving without these items displayed on the vehicle in the proper place violates the law.[87]

If few drivers are aware of the true scope of traffic codes and the limitless opportunities they give police to make pretextual stops, police officers have always understood this point. For example, the statements by police officers that follow come from a book written in 1967:

You can always get a guy legitimately on a traffic violation if you tail him for a while, and then a search can be made.

You don't have to follow a driver very long before he will move to the other side of the yellow line and then you can arrest and search him for driving on the wrong side of the highway.

In the event that we see a suspicious automobile or occupant and wish to search the person or the car, or both, we will usually follow the vehicle until the driver makes a technical violation of a traffic law. Then we have a means of making a legitimate search.[88]

These officers may not fully understand search and seizure law; for example, even in 1967, it was far from clear that a search could follow

any traffic stop that police "legitimately" made. But they are absolutely correct on the larger point: with the traffic code in hand, any officer can stop any driver any time. The most the officer will have to do is "tail [a driver] for a while," and probable cause will materialize like magic. *Whren* is the Supreme Court's official blessing of this practice, despite the fact that police concede that they use this technique to circumvent constitutional requirements.

But the existence of powerful and unreviewable police discretion to stop drivers is not the most disturbing aspect of *Whren*. That dubious honor is reserved for the way in which the police will *use* this discretion.

IV. Who Will Be Stopped?

Once we understand that *Whren* will permit police to stop anyone driving a car whenever they observe the ever-present violations of the traffic code, the question becomes *who* the police will stop. At first blush, the question might seem unnecessary. After all, if *Whren* allows the police to stop any driver at virtually any time, everyone faces the risk of a pretextual stop. But while *Whren* certainly makes it *possible* for the police to stop anyone, the fact is that police *will not* stop *just anyone*. In fact, police will use the immense discretionary power *Whren* gives them mostly to stop African-Americans and Hispanics. I say this not to imply that individual officers will act out of racist motivations. Though some will, I believe most will not. Rather, my point is that whatever their motivation, viewed as a whole, pretextual stops will be used against African-Americans and Hispanics in percentages wildly out of proportion to their numbers in the driving population.

It may seem bold that I make this assertion as a fact. In fact, I lack the kind of systematically gathered and analyzed data anyone making such a statement would prefer to have. This is because virtually no one—no individual, no police department, and no other government agency—has ever kept comprehensive statistics on who police stop: basis for the stop, race of suspect, type of police activity after stop (e.g., questioning, search of suspect, search of car, use of drug-sniffing dog, whether consent was given), and the like. Of course, one type of record does follow some percentage of stops: traffic tickets and warnings, and arrest, charging and prosecution records of those suspects police find with contraband. But looking only at the records of those charged and prosecuted can mislead, and says nothing about the many other stops that result in no ticket and yield no contraband.

Even so, information uncovered in the last few years has begun to shed light on the use of pretextual traffic stops. This data reveals several patterns, which African-Americans and Hispanics understand quite well already: police use traffic regulations to investigate many innocent citizens; these investigations, which are often quite intrusive, concern drugs, not traffic; and African-Americans and Hispanics are the targets of choice for law enforcement. So even if we lack systemic data, we now have something that gives us a strong indication of current law enforcement realities and the direction of future trends. We can comfortably predict the effect of *Whren*: police will use the case to justify and expand drug interdiction efforts against people of color.

Here are four different stories of pretextual stops. They originate from different areas of the country: Florida in the South, Maryland in the Northeast, Illinois in the Midwest, and Colorado in the West. All involve independent police agencies. Other stories of this type of police activity exist,[89] but those presented here are among the best documented. Each of them teaches the same lesson. And with *Whren* on the books, we should expect more of what these stories tell, not less.

A. Volusia County, Florida

Located in central Florida, Volusia County surrounds a busy stretch of Interstate 95. In the late 1980's, this portion of highway became the focus of Sheriff Bob Vogel and his deputies. Using a group of officers called the Selective Enforcement Team, Vogel operated a major drug interdiction effort against drivers moving narcotics by car through his jurisdiction.[90] The deputies aimed not only to make arrests, but to make seizures

of cash and vehicles, which their agency would keep.[91]

As with most police agencies, the Volusia County Sheriff's Department did not keep records of stops and searches in which no arrests or seizures occurred in the three years that the Selective Enforcement Team operated.[92] Thus no one might ever have learned about the Selective Enforcement Team's practices, except for one thing: Volusia County deputies' cars were fitted with video cameras.[93] Deputies taped some of the I-95 stops; using Florida's public records law, *The Orlando Sentinel* obtained 148 hours of the videotapes.[94] Deputies made no tapes for much of the duration of the interdiction effort, and they sometimes taped over previously recorded stops.[95] But the tapes the newspaper obtained documented almost 1,100 stops, and they showed a number of undeniable patterns.

First, even though African-Americans and Hispanics make up only about five percent of the drivers on the county's stretch of I-95,[96] more than *seventy percent* of all drivers stopped were either African-American or Hispanic.[97] The tapes put this in stark terms. One African-American man said he was stopped seven times by police; another said that he was stopped twice *within minutes*. Looking at figures for all of Florida, seventy percent is vastly out of proportion to the percentage of Blacks among Floridians of driving age (11.7 percent), the percentage of Blacks among all Florida drivers convicted of traffic offenses in 1991 (15.1 percent), or to the percentage of Blacks in the nation's population as a whole (12 percent).[98] (Hispanics make up about nine percent of the population).[99] Second, the deputies not only stopped black and Hispanic drivers more often than whites; they also stopped them *for longer periods of time*. According to the videotapes, deputies detained Blacks and Hispanics for twice as long as they detained whites.[100] Third, the tapes showed that police followed a stop with a search roughly half the time; *eighty percent* of the cars searched belonged to Black or Hispanic drivers.[101]

It should not surprise anyone to know that deputies said they made these 1,100 stops based on "legitimate traffic violations."[102] Violations

ranged from "swerving" (243), to exceeding the speed limit by up to 10 miles per hour (128), burned-out license tag lights (71), improper license tags (46), failure to signal before a lane change (45), to a smattering of others.[103] Even so, only nine of the nearly eleven hundred drivers stopped—considerably less than one percent—received tickets,[104] and deputies even released several drivers who admitted to crimes, including drunk driving, without any charges.[105] The tapes also showed that the seizure of cash remained an important goal of the stops, with deputies seizing money almost three times as often as they arrested anyone for drugs.[106] With regard to the seizures of cash, race also played a role: Ninety percent of the drivers from whom cash was taken, but who were not arrested, were Black or Hispanic.[107]

Notwithstanding these numbers, Sheriff Vogel said there was no racial bias in his department's work. Prior to the release of the tapes, he stated that the stops were not based on skin color and that deputies stopped "a broad spectrum of people."[108] The tapes eventually led to two lawsuits in federal court in which plaintiffs alleged violations of their civil rights because they were targeted for stops on the basis of their race.[109] In both cases, a judge refused to certify a class of all minority citizens illegally stopped; this resulted in the dismissal of the cases when they went to trial.[110] On appeal, the United States Court of Appeals for the Eleventh Circuit affirmed the dismissals.[111]

The experience of drivers in Volusia County shows what we can expect under *Whren*. Police will use traffic regulations as an excuse to stop drivers they suspect of narcotics trafficking, and most of those stopped will be people of color. Of course, this is exactly the type of police activity that African-Americans and Hispanics have complained of for years, but few have listened.

B. Robert Wilkins and the Maryland State Police[112]

In the early morning hours of May 8, 1992, a Maryland State Police officer stopped a new rental car carrying four African-Americans on Interstate 68. The four, all relatives, were returning to the Washington, D.C. area from a family member's funeral in Chicago.[113] After obtaining the driver's license, the officer asked the driver to step out of the car and sign a form giving consent to a search.[114] At that point, Robert Wilkins, one of the passengers in the car, identified himself as an attorney with a 9:30 a.m. court appearance in the District of Columbia Superior Court. Wilkins told the officer that he had no right to search the car without arresting the driver; the officer replied that such searches were "routine." After all, the officer said, if Wilkins and his relatives had "nothing to hide, then what [was] the problem?"[115] Another officer joined the first, and they detained the group for an additional half hour while other officers brought a drug-sniffing dog to the scene.[116] The driver asked whether he would receive a ticket; the officer said he would only give the driver a warning. The driver asked that the warning be written so that the group could leave, and Wilkins asserted that continued detention in order to bring the dog violated the Constitution; the officer ignored both of them.[117] When the dog arrived, the officers ordered Wilkins and his relatives out of the car, despite their expressed fears of the dog and the fact that it was raining.[118] They were forced to stand in the rain as the dog sniffed in and around the car.[119] When the dog failed to react in any way, Wilkins and the others were then allowed back in the car—while the officer who had stopped them wrote the driver a $105 speeding ticket.[120]

Civil rights lawyers sometimes say that despite the volume of complaints they receive about racially biased traffic stops, victims of this treatment feel reluctant to become plaintiffs in legal actions for redress.[121] Perhaps they fear retaliation; others may want to avoid the hassle of becoming involved in a very public way in complex and often politically charged litigation. Still others may fear that opposing lawyers may discover dirt in their pasts and use it against them. Not so with Robert Wilkins. A Harvard Law school graduate, Wilkins worked as a public defender for the highly-regarded Public Defender Service in Washington,

D.C.[122] As an attorney with an active practice in criminal law, he was no doubt thoroughly familiar with the law that governed the situation in which he and his family members found themselves.[123] The prospect of public litigation against a police agency obviously did not scare him. Individually and on behalf of a class of all others treated similarly, he and his family members sued the Maryland State Police, supervisory and command personnel at the agency, and the individual officers involved. They alleged civil rights violations and other wrongs, stating that the officers had illegally stopped and detained them on the basis of a "profile" that targeted people based on their race.[124] State Police officials denied Wilkins' allegations; a spokesman said the practice of stopping a disproportionate number of blacks simply represented "an unfortunate byproduct of sound police policies."[125] The implication was clear: African-Americans commit the most crime; to stop crime, we must stop African-Americans. Officials maintained this supposedly race-neutral explanation even in the face of an official document that surfaced during litigation. Dated just days before the State Police officers stopped Wilkins and his family members, it warned officers operating in Allegheny County—the very county in which police stopped the Wilkins group—to watch for "dealers and couriers (traffickers) [who] are predominantly black males and black females. . . . utilizing Interstate 68. . . ."[126]

The case eventually produced a settlement, in which the Maryland State Police agreed not to use any race-based drug courier profiles and to cease using "race as a factor for the development of policies for stopping, detaining, and searching motorists."[127] The State Police also agreed to conduct training that would reflect the prohibition on the use of race as both departmental policy and state law,[128] and to pay monetary damages and attorney's fees.[129] Perhaps more significantly, the State Police agreed that for a period of three years, they would:

maintain computer records of all stops in which a consent to search was given by a motorist stopped on any Maryland roadway by the Maryland State Police and all stops on any Maryland roadway by

Maryland State Police in which a search by a drug-detecting dog is made, "minimally including in such records: date, time, and location of consent or search; name of officer(s) requesting consent to search or directing search by drug dog; race of persons(s) stopped, detained, or searched; year make and model of vehicle; and grounds for requesting that consent to search be given or search by drug dog made, if any."[130]

The State Police have, in fact, maintained these records, and submitted them to the court. The latest figures available track stops followed by consent searches and dog sniffs from January 1995 through June 1996, and they bear a striking similarity to the information revealed by the Volusia County videotapes. Of the 732 citizens detained and searched by the Maryland State Police, 75% were African-Americans, and 5% were Hispanics.[131] The Maryland numbers are also broken down by officer; of the twelve officers involved, six stopped over 80% African-Americans, one stopped over 95% African-Americans, and two stopped only African-Americans.[132] Based on this information, provided to the court by the State Police, the plaintiffs and their attorneys are preparing to reopen the litigation, as the Settlement Agreement allows.[133] Sad to say, the numbers show that very little has changed, despite the Wilkins suit and the Settlement Agreement.[134]

C. Peso Chavez and the Illinois State Police

During recent years, African-Americans and Hispanics have made hundreds of complaints to the Illinois affiliate of the American Civil Liberties Union, alleging that the Illinois State Police targeted them for pretextual traffic stops.[135] The A.C.L.U. eventually filed suit; a man named Peso Chavez became the lead plaintiff. However, Mr. Chavez's 1994 encounter with the Illinois State Police did not happen by chance.

Chavez was a private investigator with twenty years of experience and a former elected official in Santa Fe, New Mexico. In 1994, a lawyer for an Hispanic man who alleged that Illinois State Police had stopped him illegally hired Chavez to drive a late model sedan across areas of Illinois that had been the source of complaints of illegal stops and searches of minority motorists.[136] The plan called for Chavez, a man with an Hispanic appearance, to drive cautiously, taking care not to break the traffic laws; a paralegal in another car would follow at a distance to observe his driving. The idea was a "reverse sting."[137]—an attempt to catch police in the act of making illegal stops and searches.

On February 18, 1993, in Bureau County, Illinois, Officer Thomas of the Illinois State Police began to follow Chavez. He followed Chavez for twenty miles, through Bureau and LaSalle Counties.[138] Eventually, Thomas activated his emergency lights and pulled Chavez over.[139] Thomas was soon joined at the scene by another officer. Officer Thomas told Chavez that he had stopped him for a traffic violation, and asked Chavez for his license and rental agreement. Chavez supplied both.[140] After questioning Chavez, Thomas gave Chavez a warning for failing to signal when changing lanes. This supposed infraction was an obvious and unfounded pretext for the stop; the paralegal following Chavez saw no such violation.[141] The other officer then asked Chavez if he could search his car. Chavez asked whether he had to allow the search; the officer said that he wanted a drug-sniffing dog to walk around Chavez' car. Chavez unequivocally refused and asked to be allowed to leave, but the officers detained him.[142] Another officer then led a dog around Chavez' car; the officers told Chavez that the dog had "alerted" to the presence of narcotics, and ordered him into the back seat of a patrol car.[143] For the next hour, Chavez watched as the interior, trunk, and engine compartment of his car were thoroughly searched. The police opened his luggage and searched through his personal possessions.[144] Meanwhile, an officer in the patrol car with Chavez questioned him about his personal life.[145] The police found nothing, and eventually allowed Chavez to leave.[146]

Despite his background as an investigator, his government experience, and the knowledge that he was part of a reverse sting, Chavez found the experience more than unnerving. Watching police search his car and

being told that the dog had detected drugs, Chavez said, "I became very frightened at what was happening. I never had my mouth as dry as it was—it was like cotton."[147]

Chavez is now the named plaintiff in a lawsuit in federal court that seeks injunctive relief against the State Police to stop racially based searches and seizures, as well as other relief and damages. The suit seeks certification of a class of persons subjected to the same treatment. Many other African-Americans and Hispanics who were subjected to illegal stops and searches have become named plaintiffs.[148] At this writing, discovery is ongoing.[149]

D. Eagle County, Colorado

In the late 1980's, the Eagle County, Colorado Sheriff's Department established a highway drug interdiction unit. The "High Country Drug Task Force" used a drug courier profile made up of twenty-two "indicators" to stop cars along Interstate 70; prominent among them was "race or ethnicity, based on 'intelligence information' from other law agencies. . . ."[150] Although the Task Force used traffic infractions as a pretext to stop many people, not one person received a ticket.[151]

The story of one of the people stopped speaks volumes about what happened in Eagle County. On May 3, 1989, Eagle County deputies stopped Jhenita Whitfield as she drove from San Diego to Denver to visit relatives. With her were her sister and their four children.[152] A disabled vehicle in the roadway forced them to change lanes; soon after, an officer pulled them over for failing to signal before changing lanes.[153] The deputies told her explicitly that she " 'fit the profile' of a possible drug runner," and asked if they could search her car.[154] Whitfield wanted to refuse, but felt concerned that if she did, she might be "set up."[155] She also felt she had no choice because the children were hungry and one needed to use a bathroom, so she consented.[156] The experience left Whitfield, an African-American, shaken, and it has changed her life in a significant way. Despite the fact that she has family out of town, she does not visit them. "I do not travel anymore," she said.[157]

Seven people who, like Jhenita Whitfield, had been stopped by Eagle County deputies filed a class action suit in 1990, asking the court to halt the Task Force's practice of race-based profile stops.[158] The court eventually certified a class consisting of 400 individuals who had been stopped.[159] Among them were African-Americans and a large number of Hispanics, who alleged that deputies stopped them because of their ethnicity.[160] In November of 1993, a federal court ruled that the Task Force had violated constitutional protections against unreasonable searches and seizures. With appeals pending, the parties reached a settlement requiring Eagle County to pay damages to each person searched, amounting to a total of $800,000. The County also agreed to abandon the Task Force program, and agreed not to stop, search, seize evidence or detain a person "unless there is some objective reasonable suspicion that the person has done something wrong."[161]

E. Living with Pretextual Stops

These cases from Florida, Maryland, Illinois and Colorado show in no uncertain terms the impact *Whren* will have: The drivers police will stop for pretextual traffic violations will come from minority groups in disproportionate numbers. Police have done it in the recent past; in the Maryland case, police continue to do so despite a settlement reflected in a court order specifically prohibiting these practices. *Whren* insulates this activity by pronouncing any stop for a traffic violation proper and reasonable, whatever its real purpose.

But seeing the big picture should not prevent us from asking what effect pretextual stops have on the individuals who experience them. The answer highlights the hidden cost of racially skewed law enforcement techniques in a profound way.

For those stopped, the situation may produce fear, anger, humiliation, and even rage. Jhenita Whitfield, the African-American woman stopped in Eagle County, has given up travelling because she once had to balance her desire not to submit to a search against her fear that not consenting would lead the police to plant evidence on her.[162] Peso Chavez, the experienced investigator stopped while driving through Illinois, knew he had no narcotics with him, knew he had a witness to prove that he had broken no laws, and knew and insisted upon his rights. Still, his mouth went dry with fear as officers reported that a dog had been alerted to drugs in his car and the officers proceeded to search through the car and his private effects.[163] Robert Wilkins and his family members, forced to stand in the rain while a dog sniffed through their car, felt degraded. "You can't imagine the anger and humiliation I felt during the entire episode," said Aquila Abdullah, a passenger in the car with Wilkins that night.[164] Wilkins himself expressed a sense of helplessness. "Part of me feels like there is nothing that I could have done to prevent what happened. You know, I was calm and respectful to the police. I tried to explain to the officer what my rights are."[165] Beyond the price paid by the person stopped, other African-Americans and Hispanics feel the effects, too. Because these pretextual police stops of blacks are so common—frequent enough to earn the name "driving while black"—many African-Americans regularly modify the most casual aspects of their driving behavior, travel itineraries, and even their personal appearance, to avoid police contact. Salim Muwakkil, an academic and journalist, makes trips in the Midwest in a nondescript rental car, strictly obeys the speed limit, and never wears his beret behind the wheel.[166] Before he adopted this strategy, police stopped Muwakkil so often that he would compute the time these stops took into his travel time.[167] When lawyer and lobbyist Wade Henderson drives from Washington, D.C., to Richmond, Virginia, to teach, he eschews flashy rental cars for conservative ones, even though he is graying and wears a suit.[168] Others restrict their movements; they avoid driving in areas where a black person attracts "stares."[169] And when police stop Christopher Darden, one of the prosecutors in the O.J. Simpson case, he doesn't move, keeps his hands on the wheel, and makes no sudden gestures; he calls these "African American survival techniques."[170]

But perhaps we should examine the issue from another perspective: that of law enforcement.[171] And that outlook would no doubt seem quite different from what I have said so far. In a nutshell, it is this: Stopping a disproportionate number of African-Americans is not racist; it is just plain good police work. After all, African-Americans make up a large share of those arrested, prosecuted and jailed in this country. Police know jails are full of criminals, a substantial portion of whom are black, and that a high percentage of black males are under the control of the criminal justice system in one way or another.[172] The police have no interest in harassing black or Hispanic people; rather, their motivation remains the apprehension of criminals. Race may play a part in law enforcement, but only as a proxy for a higher probability of criminal activity. In other words, racial disparities in stops and searches are nothing more than "an unfortunate byproduct of sound police policies."[173] Lt. Col. Ernest Leatherbury, commander of field operations for the Maryland State Police, puts it this way: "The facts speak for themselves. . . [W]hen you got a high number of these consent searches resulting in drug arrests do we in law enforcement or the public want to say the state police should discontinue these searches?"[174] In other words, police target blacks and Hispanics because they are the right ones, and this technique gets results. And if it works, we should not let the niceties of search and seizure law get in the way of catching the bad guys.

But this argument contains a flaw, and it is not a small one. Behind the race-neutral reasons police give lies a stark truth. When officers stop disproportionate members of African-Americans because this is "just good police work," they are using race as a proxy for the criminality or "general criminal propensity" of an entire racial group.[175] Simply put, police are targeting all African-Americans because some are criminals. In essence, this thinking predicts that all blacks, as a group, share a general propensity to commit crimes. Therefore, having black skin becomes enough—perhaps along with a minimal number of other fac-

tors, perhaps alone—for law enforcement to stop and detain someone. Under this view, all black citizens become probable criminals—suspects the minute they venture out of their homes.

The wrongheadedness and unfairness of treating all members of a group as criminals just because some are seems obvious. But even if not everyone feels this way, treating race as a proxy for criminality suffers from other serious problems. First, implicit in this view is the assumption that blacks are disproportionately more likely than whites and others to be involved with street crimes.[176] Even if this is true, African-Americans being more likely than whites to be involved in street crime is a far cry from any evidence that would strongly support the assertion that any particular black person is committing a crime. Yet that is the way police use this information. Second, even if we accept the assumption of the disproportionate involvement of blacks in street crime, police still greatly overestimate the value of race as a predictor of criminal behavior.[177] Using race as a proxy for criminality may result in "double counting."[178] If, for example, criminal involvement is strongly correlated with poverty, with presence in so-called "high crime areas," or with both, and if African-Americans are disproportionately poor and living in such neighborhoods,[179] race would add little to a police officer's ability to predict criminal involvement beyond what poverty and geography already reveal.[180] As Professor Sheri Lynn Johnson has said, "(a)lthough probabilistic constraints may not preclude general racial propensities to commit crime, they clearly militate against according them substantial weight."[181]

V. What Happens after the Stop?

Once police stop a person for a traffic offense, what happens? By posing this question, I do not mean to imply that the stop itself is insignificant. On the contrary, the stop is itself not only unnerving but potentially dangerous, especially if it is ordered by an officer in plain clothes or in an unmarked car.[182] Although pretextual traffic stops may be problematic in themselves, they are also disturbing because they may lead to searches. What rules govern what happens *after* a pretextual stop?

First, if police have probable cause to stop a vehicle, this alone does not entitle them to search it. There must be something more than the traffic offense to justify a search, some combination of facts that gives police probable cause to believe that an offense has been or is being committed or that the vehicle contains contraband. While we can argue *whether* any particular set of facts actually gives rise to probable cause or reasonable suspicion, the bottom line is that *something* is required to justify a search.[183]

There are several variations on this theme. If police arrest the driver, they may search not only the driver but the interior of the car, closed parts of the interior like the glove box, and any closed containers inside the interior.[184] And if the police see evidence of crime in plain view, of course, they may seize it and then arrest and search as appropriate. This, in fact, is what happened in *Whren*: Police stopped the vehicle, and upon looking inside—without any further searching—saw two bags of cocaine.[185]

But in the great bulk of cases, there is no offense other than the traffic violation, no arrest occurs for the traffic offense, and police find nothing incriminating in plain view. Instead, police accomplish their goal of searching those they stop in two other ways.

The first is simple: officers ask the people they stop to consent to a search. While those asked need not consent, many do. The reasons for this seem as varied as human beings are, but several causes predominate. People simply may not know that they can refuse, and the Constitution does not require the police to tell citizens that they can withhold their consent.[186] Consequently, some undoubtedly feel they have no choice. Others surely feel intimidated, as Jhenita Whitfield said she did in Eagle County. Intimidation was no doubt what the Maryland State Police officer intended when he told Robert Wilkins that searches were "routine" and that if he had nothing to hide, he should permit the search—leaving in the air the obvious implication that a refusal would show Wilkins' guilt.[187]

But the predominant reason drivers consent lies with police officers. Their goal, plain and simple, is to get people to agree to a search. They are accomplished at the verbal judo necessary to subjugate their "opponents," they have the authority of their office behind them, and they make it their business to get what they want. The officer starts with innocuous sounding questions: Where are you coming from? Where are you headed? Who's the person you're visiting? What's her address? Who's with you in the back seat? Then the questions often get more personal. They are designed to find contradictions that show the driver might have something to hide, and to put the driver in the frame of mind of responding to the officer's authority. Police call it "sweet talk," and it almost always leads to a consensual search. None of this is accidental; rather, it is a well-honed, calculated psychological technique that police departments teach their officers.[188] And it works. In the course of 150 stops over two years, one Indiana state trooper said, "I've never had anyone tell me I couldn't search."[189]

But what if the occupants of the car refuse? Must the police allow them to leave, ending the encounter? Not necessarily, as the Wilkins case and others show. If police encounter a person like Wilkins—one who knows he does not have to answer questions or consent to a search, one who will insist on his rights—they use another technique: they use a dog trained to detect drugs. If the dog gives the signal that it has smelled drugs, this provides the police with probable cause for a full-blown search of the vehicle and its contents. According to *United States v. Place*,[190] the use of such a dog does not constitute a search for purposes of the Fourth Amendment; therefore, use of the dog requires neither probable cause nor reasonable suspicion. *Place* gives the police just what they need if a driver refuses consent: a search for which consent is not necessary, which may yield the justification they need to do the very search the driver refused to allow.

There is one important wrinkle in this argument. Once the driver refuses consent, the police must not hold her any longer unless there is probable cause or reasonable suspicion to do so. Can the police hold someone long enough to have a drug detecting dog brought to the scene? The Supreme Court has not yet supplied a definitive answer, but analogous cases indicate that if the police have reasonable suspicion to suspect someone of involvement in a crime, they can detain the person for a "reasonable" period of time to allow the dog to be brought. In *Place*, a passenger's luggage was held for ninety minutes to allow for a dog to sniff it; the Court found this unreasonable, because the law enforcement officials had advance warning and could have gotten the dog there in much less time.[191] And in *United States v. Sharpe*,[192] the Court found a twenty minute detention reasonable, because the delay was caused by the suspect's flight.[193] How the Court will ultimately resolve this question is anyone's guess; the most likely possibility is case by case discussion of what length of detention is reasonable under the circumstances. But given the Court's unbounded analysis of the Fourth Amendment implications of the use of dogs, the argument over the reasonableness of the length of detention will be the only argument any driver has left.

VI. Recommendations

Whren represents the Supreme Court's official approval for the use of pretextual stops by police. Defendants may no longer argue successfully that particular traffic stops were purely excuses to allow investigation of other crimes about which there was neither probable cause nor reasonable suspicion.[194] If I am right, all motorists are now fair game for police, and African-Americans and other people of color will suffer the great bulk of this treatment. Where does all of this leave us? Can anything be done to address these practices and the disparate impact they seem almost certain to have?

If *Whren* does nothing else, it takes courts out of the business of supervising this type of police conduct. Now, police need not come up with any rationale for stopping motorists save the easy and obvious one: violation of the traffic code.[195] Given that the door of judicial redress has closed, and that the Supreme Court's suggested equal protection remedy seems unlikely to bear any fruit, what other avenues are open to help grapple with the police practices highlighted here? Two modest suggestions follow.

A. Administrative Regulations

In a time when we continue to focus on courts to control police discretion, another tool is often overlooked: Police department policy and regulation. If unchecked discretion and racially biased traffic enforcement tactics infect a police agency's operations, written policies and regulation could fill the vacuum created by the Supreme Court's abdication of supervisory responsibility. Any time official discretion exists, we must ask not only how to eliminate unnecessary discretion, but also how to regulate and constrain the discretion that must exist as part of the system.[196] Departmental regulations have the potential to do both.

In the recent past, courts, especially the Supreme Court, played the dominant rulemaking role for law enforcement at the level of constitutional enforcement. This has been especially true in the Fourth Amendment area. This resulted from the fact that other agencies—the legislative branch, executive agencies, and police departments themselves—failed to take any significant role in regulation of police.[197] Courts in the post-*Mapp* era rushed to fill this void; in the Fourth Amendment field, this has been done through adjudication of search and seizure cases.

But, as Professor LaFave has said, this has begun to change.[198] Many police departments now put their practices down in written form as official policies or guidelines.[199] And the fact that police agencies themselves construct these self-regulatory systems has some important advantages. First police rulemaking makes for better police decisions, if only because it focuses the department on policy making and on the implications to the community of the police practices being regulated.[200] Second, rules reduce the influence of bias because they make training more uniform, and be-

cause they guide and control discretion.[201] Third, police-made rules are most likely to be followed and enforced by police.[202] Last—but certainly not least—is the fact that, in cases such as *Whren*, the Supreme Court has simply taken the judiciary out of the equation. If there is no regulation at the agency level, there may simply be no regulation at all.

One line of the Supreme Court's own cases suggests that the practices highlighted in this essay might be successfully addressed through police regulation. Beginning with *South Dakota v. Opperman*,[203] the Court passed upon the reasonableness of searches done pursuant to departmental inventory procedures. In *Opperman*, the police discovered marijuana in the glove compartment of a vehicle they had towed to an impound lot before they inventoried the contents of the car. The Supreme Court found the inventory search reasonable, perhaps because police performed the inventory "pursuant to standard police procedures."[204] In the most recent inventory case, *Colorado v. Bertine*,[205] police discovered contraband in a backpack found in the defendant's vehicle during an inventory search. In *Bertine*, the Court was much clearer in delineating the place of police rules and rulemaking in search and seizure law: "reasonable police regulations relating to inventory procedures administered in good faith satisfy the Fourth Amendment, even though courts might as a matter of hindsight be able to devise equally reasonable rules requiring a different procedure."[206] As Professor LaFave points out, to the extent that *Opperman* and *Bertine* encourage or require departments to make rules for inventories, this is all to the good. Since, according to *Bertine*, an inventory search may be reasonable without either probable cause or a warrant,[207] standardized police procedures for inventories will limit and channel police discretion and prevent arbitrary police action.[208]

We should consider using the same approach to confine and regulate police discretion vis-a-vis the conduct of traffic stops. While *Whren* allows the police to stop motorists any time an officer could have done so, this need not be the rule within any given police department. In fact,

it was not the rule in the District of Columbia, where *Whren* arose; departmental regulations prohibited the making of traffic stops except within certain well-defined parameters.[209] Departments could make rules that set out criteria for situations in which officers can stop cars when there is no intention of giving a traffic citation or performing other enforcement activities related to operation of the vehicle. At the very least, departmental regulations could prohibit the targeting of racial or ethnic groups for traffic stops and searches. To encourage rulemaking (or review of existing rules) along these lines, federal and state governments might offer incentives in the form of increased funding to those departments that make changes in their existing regulations or implement new ones. Alternatively, of course, there might be financial penalties for departments that do not comply, or some combination of carrot and stick.

B. Collection of Data on Traffic Stops and Searches and the Rules Put in Place to Govern Them

A second step we might take to address the problem of pretextual stops involves the collection of data. Police departments could be required (or financially encouraged) to collect data on all traffic stops. This data should include the reason for the stop, the race, ethnicity, and other identifying information concerning the person stopped, whether the driver received a citation or warning and for what, whether a search followed the stop, the basis for the search (consent, observation of incriminating items, or the like), whether a dog was used as part of the procedure, whether contraband was found and if so what kind, and whether any property was seized under forfeiture laws.

The collection of this data would allow for large-scale study of traffic stops and the issues they raise, and would allow for a more rigorous analysis than I have presented here. While the numbers of persons stopped in my examples are large—in Volusia County alone, for example, the number of stops on the video tapes is almost eleven hundred—any social scientist would no doubt prefer a more systematic collection of data. And even in the Maryland case, in which stops must be recorded, the court did not order Maryland State Police to collect all the information that might prove useful to someone studying these practices. On the contrary, only stops followed by consent searches or searches with dogs are included, whereas a more complete picture would, at the very least, require that all stops be tallied, whether or not followed by a search. A widespread, standardized study of a number of police departments in a wide variety of geographic areas would give us the opportunity to arrive at a better understanding. If the data show that, in fact, African-Americans or other racial or ethnic groups are being targeted by police,[210] there would be no dismissing their experiences as isolated incidents or the work of just one or another particular police department. We might at last have the information necessary to understand fully what happens in these situations, and perhaps to finally persuade legislators and other leaders that we must take concrete steps toward solutions.[211]

Such data collection would also allow us to study the effectiveness of the police regulations proposed above. Departments with and without such regulations could collect data, and the side by side comparison this would allow would give us a better understanding of the effectiveness of this approach.

One can imagine at least two possible problems that might be suggested concerning the collection of data on police/motorist encounters. First, individual police officers might be reluctant to report information concerning their traffic stops. After all, would academics, policy makers, and others not use the data to attempt to prove police racism, either on the part of the individual or the institution? And would this concern not result in either incomplete and perhaps stilted reporting, or even reluctance to report at all, especially if the officer could be seen to be acting in contravention of departmental regulations? While these concerns are understandable, they would not be hard to address. Data collection could be anonymous, certainly as to

the activities of individual officers. And if part of what we wish to study is whether departmental regulations might help limit or curb objectionable elements of police discretion in this area, the identity of the police *department* the data have come from might be hidden, too. With anonymity safeguarding them from implicating themselves in any way, there is no reason to believe that police and their superiors would not fairly and fully report their traffic stop activities. As an example, recall that the Maryland State Police have been reporting all stops resulting in canine and consent searches for many months now. While they do this pursuant to a court order, there is still every reason to believe that the Maryland State Police officers might feel reluctant to report fully and accurately for just the reasons I have described. In fact, their feelings might even be somewhat more intense, since the data collected in Maryland is broken down officer by officer, with names attached. Thus if one could imagine a scenario in which police might fail to fully and fairly report their actions, the Maryland case would be it. But that does not seem to be happening. While no one but the individual officers involved knows for sure whether some stops are not being reported, it would seem that underreporting would skew the data away from any racial bias in stops, since all of the officers know that this was the problem from which the reporting obligation arose in the first place. Yet after eighteen months, the data show that roughly eighty percent of the stops counted still involve people of color. In other words, if the officers were trying to affect the numbers (and one could argue that if anyone had incentive to do so, they do), they are doing a poor job of it. The other explanation, of course, is that they are not doing this at all.

The other problem that might be raised concerns the practical side of reporting. What officer will want to fill out a form, even a simple one, for every traffic stop? Police are already busy trying to do the job we send them out to do. Why should they do extra paperwork to help study that job? The first answer to this objection is that many police departments already request a short re-

port on every stop, whether or not the officer issues a citation or a warning. The second answer lies with technology. Already, many police vehicles carry not just radios, but computer terminals that can be used to check a car's license plate number or a motorist's drivers license, or to see if a person is wanted on outstanding warrants. It would take little more to enter the basic information on traffic stops discussed above into such a computer. The process would involve little more than punching agreed-upon code numbers into the available machine. In fact, small hand-held units now exist that can handle quite a bit of simple data. Waiters and waitresses in restaurants sometimes carry these small devices, on which an order can be taken, transmitted to the kitchen, tallied for billing purposes, and then saved for marketing and other business purposes. Such a machine would be more than capable of receiving and storing the relatively small amount of data that would be generated by traffic stops, and transfer of the data into analyzable form would involve no extra work. Another possibility is to do what Volusia County did: have the police cars in departments under study fitted with video cameras which would be turned on and off each time a stop was made. This arrangement would also benefit the police by providing evidence in stops resulting in arrests. Police could simply turn the tapes in, without having to do extra paperwork. Researchers would then gather the statistics. While particulars would have to be worked out, using video cameras might be the easiest way to do this.

VII. Conclusion

Whren leaves us in an unsatisfactory situation. Any time we use our cars, we can be stopped by the police virtually at their whim because full compliance with traffic laws is impossible. And we can feel relatively certain that past will be prologue: African-Americans and Hispanics will suffer the bulk of this treatment. Whites will not have to endure it very often; if they did, it probably would not happen. And, once police stop drivers, the officers will be able to search almost everyone they want, some with consent and others with dogs. I, for one, feel considerably less than comfortable with this outcome.

We may not always agree on the full contours of the Fourth Amendment, but if nothing else it stands for—indeed, imposes—restraint on the government's power over the individual in the pursuit of crime. At the very least, the police must have a reason—probable cause, or at least reasonable suspicion—to pursue, stop and search citizens. The point is not that the police are powerless until criminals strike, but rather that police cannot treat everyone like a criminal in order that some secretive wrongdoers be caught. From every practical vantage point, *Whren* upends this venerable and sensible principle in the name of the war on drugs. Its implications are clear: everyone is fair game; members of minority groups will pay the largest price, but there are casualties in war, so African-Americans and Hispanics will just have to bear the cost. The Supreme Court could have used *Whren* as an occasion to repudiate the worst of what this tragic and ultimately unwinnable war has brought us. Instead, it increased police power and discretion. We are all the losers for it, but unfortunately some of us—those of us with dark skin—will lose a lot more than the rest. Perhaps police departmental regulation, and further study, can lead us in new directions.

Notes

1. 116 S. Ct. 1769 (1996).
2. See infra notes 15 through 19 and accompanying text. To legally stop a person, a police officer must have at least reasonable suspicion of criminal activity. Terry v. Ohio, 392 U.S. 1 (1968).
3. Brief for the United States at 5–6, United States v. Whren, 116 S. Ct. 1769 (1996) (No. 95–5841).
4. Whren, 116 S. Ct. at 1773 (defendant petitioners asked that the standard be "whether a police officer, acting reasonably, *would have* made the stop for the reason given" (emphasis added)).
5. Id. at 1772.
6. Id. at 1773–76.
7. Id.
8. See, e.g., infra note 27; Wayne R. LaFave & Jerold Israel, *Criminal Procedure* § 3.1, at 2 (1996 Supp.) Indeed, I would be remiss not to mention that the subject of pretextual Fourth Amendment activity has garnered a considerable amount of attention over the years. E.g., John M. Burkoff, The Court That Devoured the Fourth Amendment: The Triumph of an Inconsistent Exclusionary Doctrine, 58 *Ore. L. Rev.* 151 (1979); John M. Burkoff, Bad Faith Searches, 57 *N.Y.U. L. Rev.* 70 (1982); John M. Burkoff, The Pretext Search Doctrine: Now You See It, Now You Don't, 17 *U. Mich. J.L. Ref.* 523 (1984); James B. Haddad, Pretextual Fourth Amendment Activity: Another Viewpoint, 18 *U. Mich. J.L. Ref.* 639 (1985); Rejoinder: Truth, Justice, and the American Way—Or Professor Haddad's Hard Choices, 18 *U. Mich. J.L. Ref.* 695 (1985); 1 Wayne R. LaFave, *Search and Seizure: A Treatise On The Fourth Amendment* 1.4(e) (3d ed. 1996). This excellent commentary has framed the debate well. But my argument is different. *Whren* means that as long as a traffic infraction occurs—and one almost always will—no inquiry into pretext of any type is even necessary.
9. [E]xcept in those situations in which there is at least articulable and reasonable suspicion that a motorist is unlicensed or that an automobile is not registered, or that the vehicle or an occupant is otherwise subject to seizure for violation of law, stopping an automobile and detaining the driver in order to check his driver's license and the registration of the automobile are unreasonable under the Fourth Amendment. Delaware v. Prouse, 440 U.S. 648, 663 (1979); see Terry v. Ohio, 392 U.S. 1, 27 (1968).
10. I heard this phrase often from clients I represented in Washington, D.C. and its surrounding Maryland counties; among many of them, it was the standard way of describing the common experience of constant stops and harassment of blacks by police. Thus I was not surprised to see the phrase show up recently in the popular press. E.g., Michael Fletcher, Driven to Extremes: Black Men Take Steps to Avoid Police Stops, *Wash. Post*, March 29, 1996, at A1 (black men are stopped so often they say they are stopped for the offense one of them "calls DWB—driving while black."). See also Henry Louis Gates, Thirteen Ways of Looking at a Black Man, *New Yorker*, October 23, 1995, at 59 (constant stops by police is what "many African-Americans know as D.W.B.: Driving While Black.").
11. See infra notes 184–193 and accompanying text.
12. See, e.g., Wayne R. LaFave, *Search and Seizure, A Treatise On The Fourth Amendment*, § 1.1, at 3–5 (1996) (Fourth Amendment grew out of English and colonial experiences with abuses of general warrants and writs of assistance); Tracey Maclin, When the Cure for the Fourth Amendment Is Worse Than the Disease, 68 *S. Cal. L. Rev.* 1, 5–6 (1994) (noting that the history and purpose of Fourth Amendment is about limitation of executive and police power).
13. Indeed, described this way, the Court would no doubt disagree and say that police behavior like this surely *does* violate the Fourth Amendment. E.g., Delaware v. Prouse, 440 U.S. 648 (1979) (random stops of automobiles prohibited). This may be true, but my intent is to describe what the law *does*, not what it *says*.
14. Brief for Petitioners at 17–30. Whren (No. 95–5841).
15. Whren v. United States, 116 S. Ct. 1769, 1772 (1996). Both of the young men were African-Americans.
16. Id.
17. Id. While the Court's opinion notes that the occupants were "youthful," that the vehicle was "a dark Pathfinder," and that the driver seemed to be looking down into the lap of the passenger, id., there was no indication of criminal activity. As the Brief for the Petitioners notes, the main officer involved testified that the stop of the car was performed not to investigate specific acts of the occupants indicating criminality, but simply to speak to the driver about his poor driving. Brief for Petitioners, *Whren*, at 5–7 (No. 95–5841). This seems a transparently obvious lie; with *Whren* on the books, police will have no reason to tell such stories, since pretextual stops have been approved, and no "innocent" motivation need be voiced for the court reviewing a motion to suppress.
18. Whren, 116 S. Ct. at 1772.
19. Id.
20. 18 *D.C. Mun. Regs.* § 2213.4 (1995).
21. Id. at § 2204.3
22. Id. at § 2200.3.
23. When a police officer has observed a motorist commit a traffic offense, the officer has probable cause to justify a stop. . . . [A]ny argument [to the contrary] . . . conflicts with this Court's teaching that the validity of a search or a seizure under the Fourth Amendment turns on an objective assessment of the officer's actions in light of the facts and circumstances confronting him at the time. . . . Brief for the United States, Whren, at 7–8 (No. 95–5841).
24. Transcript, U.S. v. Whren, U.S. D. Ct., D.D.C., Nos. 93–cr00274–01 and 93–cr00274–02, at 122–24, 126–30; see also Brief for Petitioners, Whren, at 13–14 (no. 95–5841).
25. Transcript, supra note 24, at 124, 130; Brief for Petitioners, Whren, at 14 (no. 95–5841).
26. Id. at 10–11.
27. Whren v. United States, 53 F.3d 371, 374–75 (D.C. Cir. 1995). The D.C. Circuit's decision put it in line with eight other circuits that had adopted some form of the "could have" rule. U.S. v. Botero-Ospina, 71 F.3d 783, 787 (10th Cir. 1995) (en banc); U.S. v. Johnson, 63 F.3d 242, 247 (3d Cir. 1995), petition for cert. filed, No. 95–6724

(Nov. 13, 1995); U.S. v. Scopo, 19 F.3d 777, 782–84 (2d Cir 1994), cert. denied, 115 S. Ct. 207 (1994); U.S. v. Ferguson, 8 F.3d 385, 389–91 (6th Cir. 1993) (en banc), cert. denied, 115 S. Ct. 97 (1994); U.S. v. Hassan El, 5 F.3d 726, 729–30 (4th Cir. 1993) cert. denied, 114 S. Ct. 1374 (1994); U.S. v. Cummins, 920 F.2d 498, 500–01 (8th Cir. 1990); U.S. v. Trigg, 878 F.2d 1037, 1039 (7th Cir. 1989); U.S. v. Causey, 834 F.2d 1179, 1184 (5th Cir. 1987) (en banc). Two other circuits had adopted the "would have" rule. U.S. v. Cannon, 29 F.3d 472, 475–76 (9th Cir. 1994); U.S. v. Smith, 799 F.2d 704, 709 (11th Cir. 1986).

28. Whren v. United States, 116 S. Ct. 1769, 1772–1773 (1996).

29. Id. at 1773–74 (citing Florida v. Wells, 495 U.S. 1 (1990) (impoundment of vehicles); Colorado v. Bertine, 479 U.S. 367 (1987) (same); New York v. Burger, 482 U.S. 691 (1987) (administrative inspections of businesses)).

30. Whren, 116 S. Ct. at 1774.

31. 414 U.S. 218 (1973).

32. 436 U.S. 128 (1978).

33. Whren, 116 S. Ct. at 1774 (quoting Scott, 436 U.S. at 138).

34. Id. at 1774.

35. Id. at 1775.

36. Id.

37. Id. at 1775.

38. D.C. Metropolitan Police Department General Order 303.1 (Traffic Enforcement) (eff. April 30, 1992) ("Traffic enforcement may be undertaken as follows: . . . Members who are not in uniform or are in unmarked vehicles may take enforcement action only in the case of a violation that is so grave as to pose an immediate threat to the safety of others.").

39. The main officer involved in the case testified that he was "out there almost strictly to do drug investigations" and that he stops drivers for traffic offenses "[n]ot very often at all." Transcript, supra note 24, at 78. Despite these statements, and the fact that the district judge was troubled by a "lengthy pause" before the officer's answer to the question whether he in fact stopped the vehicle because he was suspicious of a new car with two young black men inside, id. at 66–67, 76–77, 138, the court found the traffic stop proper under the "could have" test.

The court also declared that the case need not be resolved by a balancing of interests. Past cases, the court said, made a balancing of the government's interest in such stops against the individual's interests in freedom from such interference necessary only in situations without probable cause or in cases featuring an extraordinary search or seizure—for example, seizing a fleeing suspect by using deadly force. Whren, 116 S. Ct. at 1776 (citing Tennessee v. Garner, 471 U.S. 1 (1985) (balancing interests to

determine that using deadly force to seize a fleeing felon is an unreasonable seizure)). Since, by hypothesis, probable cause exists in a pretextual traffic stop case, courts need not do any balancing because "[t]he making of a traffic stop out-of-uniform does not remotely qualify as such an extreme practice." Id. at 1777. While a stop by an individual in plain clothes in a nondescript car may not be as "extreme" as shooting someone, the experience could still be quite frightening or even dangerous. See, e.g., State v. Auxter, No. OT–96–004, 1996 WL 475926, at *2 (Ohio Ct. App. August 23, 1996) (drunk driving case dismissed because officer made stop and arrest in unmarked car, and Ohio law prohibits officer who does so from testifying in case in order to curb abusive use of speed traps and *to provide for the safety of persons being stopped*" (emphasis added)); Rose Kim, Family Wants Answers, *Newsday*, March 20, 1996, at 4 (family members allege that physician killed by police officers because police officers were in unmarked cars and not in uniform, precipitating violent incident); Pennsylvania Bill Would Bar Use of Unmarked Police Cars, *N.Y. Times*, Oct. 13, 1996, at A12 (proposed bill targeted at crimes by police impostors using unmarked cars).

40. Whren, 116 U.S. at 1774.

41. Id.

42. See infra notes 89–161 and accompanying text.

43. See infra note 120.

44. In making this suggestion, the Court seemed to ignore its cases, which say disparate racial impact of a practice or policy is not enough to prove a violation of the Equal Protection Clause. Rather, to prove such a violation, "the invidious quality of a law claimed to be racially discriminatory must ultimately be traced to a racially discriminatory purpose." Washington v. Davis, 426 U.S. 229, 240 (1976); see also Village of Arlington Heights v. Metropolitan Housing Development Corp., 429 U.S. 252, 264–65, 271 (1977) (proof of racially discriminatory aim is required to show a violation of the equal protection clause, and inference of discriminatory "ultimate effect" did not make out a constitutional claim). While the exact contours of *what* the Court would require in order to make out a claim remain unclear, *Davis* and the cases that follow seem to say that lawsuits over the racially discriminatory effect of facially race-neutral rules are to be "conducted as a search for a bigoted decision-maker," Lawrence Tribe, *American Constitutional Law* 1509 (2d ed. 1988), a difficult standard to meet in contemporary America. Thus a case like that of Robert Wilkins, see infra notes 112–134 and accompanying text, may succeed, since the evidence uncovered

in the case includes an actual memorandum explicitly targeting black men for pretextual stops. But the Wilkins case will prove to be the rare exception, because in most cases decision–makers will not commit such ideas to paper. The only equal protection cases that might provide some underpinning for the Court's equal protection suggestion in *Whren* are the peremptory challenge cases, in which discriminatory use of peremptory challenges may make out a prima facie case of discrimination that an adversary must then explain as stemming from nonracial reasons. E.g., Batson v. Kentucky, 476 U.S. 79 (1986) (applying rule to prosecutor's use of peremptories in criminal case); Edmonson v. Leesville Concrete Co., 500 U.S. 614 (1991) (applying rule to civil cases); Powers v. Ohio, 499 U.S. 400 (1991) (exclusion of white jurors in trial of black defendant prohibited). But the underlying rationale of these cases has to do not just with discriminatory racial impact and equal protection, but with barring particular groups from an important civic function—jury service—and in the undermining of public confidence in the jury system that might then result. Batson, 476 U.S. at 87; Georgia v. McCollum, 505 U.S. 42, 48–50 (1992) (same). Thus it is not at all clear that the Court would find the peremptory challenge cases applicable.

45. 481 U.S. 279 (1987).

46. Id. at 287.

47. Id.

48. Id.

49. Id. at 292.

50. Id. at 312–13.

51. Id. at 292.

52. But cf. United States v. Gordon, 817 F.2d 1538 (11th Cir. 1987) (error to reject "racial impact or results evidence," given defendant's allegations of selective prosecution of vote fraud laws by targeting majority-Black counties).

53. 116 S. Ct. 1480 (1996).

54. Id. at 1483.

55. Id. at 1488–89.

56. See David Cole, See No Evil, Hear No Evil, *Legal Times*, July 29, 1996, at S29 ("In effect, one must provide evidence of one's claim without access to the very evidence necessary to establish the claim.").

57. Given that lower courts nearly always take the word of the officer in these matters, even when it is obvious that the officer is lying, it seems unlikely in the extreme that courts will disbelieve officers' proffered justifications based on the traffic stops which *Whren* permits. See, e.g., David A Harris, Frisking Every Suspect: The Withering of Terry, 28 *U.C. Davis L. Rev.* 1, 6 (1994) (testifying falsely on search and seizure issues is an accepted practice in lower courts); Alan M. Dershowitz, Accomplices to Perjury, *N.Y. Times*, May 2, 1994, at A15 (when judges

accept perjurious police testimony, they bear responsibility for it).

58. See Terry v. Ohio, 392 U.S. 1, 21–22 (1968) (the question is whether "the facts available to the officer at the moment of the seizure or the search 'warrant a man of reasonable caution in the belief' that the action taken was appropriate").

59. Whren, 116 S. Ct. at 1774, (citing United States v. Robinson, 414 U.S. 218, 221 n.1 and 236 (1973)).

60. See, e.g., Chimel v. California, 395 U.S. 752 (1969).

61. See, e.g., Payton v. New York, 445 U.S. 573, 589–90 (1980) (the Fourth Amendment prohibits the police from making a warrantless and nonconsensual entry into a suspect's home in order to make a routine felony arrest).

62. E.g., Akhil Reed Amar, Fourth Amendment First Principles, 107 *Harv. L. Rev.* 757 (1994) (describing Fourth Amendment jurisprudence as a mess); Craig M. Bradley, Two Models of the Fourth Amendment, 83 *Mich. L. Rev.* 1468 (1985) (chaotic state of Fourth Amendment law comes from the pulling of courts between the poles of following the law as decided in previous cases and suppressing evidence, and the desire to have the evidence of crime that will convict the guilty admitted).

63. Terry v. Ohio, 392 U.S. 1 (1968), is of course the source of the rule that at least reasonable suspicion is necessary for a stop. I say this is usually the rule, because there are exceptions, such as the cases in which there is a special governmental need, e.g., Michigan Dep't of State Police v. Sitz, 496 U.S. 444 (1990) (permitting suspicionless searches at roadblocks due to the special need to fight drunk driving), or administrative searches, e.g., New York v. Burger, 482 U.S. 691 (1987) (administrative inspection of junkyards).

64. Tracey Maclin, "Black and Blue Encounters"—Some Preliminary Thoughts about Fourth Amendment Seizures: Should Race matter?, 26 *Val. U. L. Rev.* 243, 249–50 (1991) (describing encounters between police and citizens as always carrying some element of coerciveness).

65. Terry, 392 U.S. at 30. Even in the context of a *Terry* stop, the same rules have always applied. Justice Harlan's concurring opinion in *Terry* makes this clear. Without a justifiable stop, Harlan said, officers could not frisk to assure their safety. It is the right to stop the suspect in the first place that justifies getting close enough to the suspect that the officer might be in danger; the police cannot generate that danger by putting themselves at risk in the first place. Id. at 32–33 (Harlan, J., concurring).

66. 508 U.S. 366 (1993).

67. Id. at 372–73.

68. 443 U.S. 47 (1979).

69. Id. at 49.

70. Id.

71. Id.

72. Id. at 52–53. See also Ybarra v. Illinois, 444 U.S. 85, 92–93 (1979) (holding that police had no reasonable suspicion to detain the customer of a tavern, even if the police had a warrant to search the tavern and a general suspicion that drug sales took place at the tavern, when there was no indication that the customer himself was involved or armed).

73. 460 U.S. 491 (1983).

74. Id. at 498 (citing United States v. Mendenhall, 446 U.S. 544 (1980) ("a citizen who does not wish to answer police questions may disregard the officers' questions and walk away")).

75. 501 U.S. 429 (1991).

76. Id. at 437.

77. Professor Tracey Maclin has made this point in a persuasive way: It is all very well to say that a citizen need not respond to police inquiries; it is another to ask how many would actually resist and why they should have to do so. "The point is not [only] that very few persons will have the moxie to assert their fourth amendment rights, although we know that most will not. It is whether citizens in a free society should be forced to challenge the police in order to enjoy [their rights]." Tracey Maclin, The Decline of the Right of Locomotion: The Fourth Amendment on the Streets, 75 *Cornell L. Rev.* 1258, 1306 (1990). Professor Maclin has also argued that the situation may be worse for some members of our society than for others, depending on the color of their skin. Maclin, supra note 63, at 251–53 (describing numerous less-than-legal encounters between police and black men).

78. Thus it was no accident when, several years ago, the company that provides "genuine" General Motors parts and service for that company's automotive products ran a series of commercials in which a chorus of hearty voices sang out the words: "It's not just your car, it's your freedom." This jingle represented a perfect blending of the American attitude toward the automobile—the essential part of life, without which one surrenders the "freedom" to come and go at will—with a huckster's willingness to appropriate patriotic feelings and symbolism.

79. Steven Stark, Weekend Edition Sunday: America's Long-Term Love Affair with the Automobile, (National Public Radio broadcast, Aug. 18, 1996) ("It's virtually impossible to overstate the importance of the car in American life.").

80. E.g., N.M. Stat. Ann. § 66–7–305 (Michie (1994) (prohibits driving "at such a slow speed as to impede the normal

and reasonable movement of traffic"); 18 D.C. Mun. Regs. § 2200. 10 (1995).

81. Utah Code Ann. § 41–6–69 (1993).

82. Md. Code Ann. Transp. II § 21–604(d) (signal must "be given continuously during at least the last 100 feet"); N.M. Stat. Ann. § 66–7–325B (Michie 1994) (same); Ohio Rev. Code Ann. § 4511.39 (Banks-Baldwin 1993) (same); S.C. Code Ann. § 56–5–2150(b) (Law Co-op. 1991) (same).

83. E.g., Md. Code Ann. Transp. II § 21–604(e) (1992) ("If there is an opportunity to signal, a person may not stop or suddenly decrease the speed of a vehicle until he gives an appropriate signal"); N.M. Code Ann. § 66–7–325C (1994) ("No person shall stop or suddenly decrease the speed of a vehicle without first giving an appropriate signal. . ."); S.C. Code Ann. § 56–5–2150(c) (Law Co-op. 1991) (same).

84. E.g., Md. Code Ann, Transp. II § 22–204(a) (1992) ("[e]very motor vehicle. . . shall be equipped with at least 2 tail lamps mounted on the rear, which. . . shall emit a red light plainly visible from a distance of 1000 feet to the rear"); N.D. Cent. Code § 39–21–04(1) (1987) (same); S.C. Code Ann. § 56–5–4510 (Law Co-op. 1991) (same, except that red light must be visible from a distance of 500 feet).

85. E.g., Md. Code Ann. Transp. II § 22–204(f) (1992) (requiring "a white light" that will illuminate the rear registration plate "and render it clearly visible from a distance of fifty feet"); N.D. Cent. Code § 39–21–04(3) (1987) (same); S.C. Code Ann. § 56–5–4530 (Law Co-op. 1991) (same)

86. E.g., Md. Code Ann. Transp. II § 22–405.5(b) (1992) (tire considered unsafe if tread wear indicators are "flush with the tread at any place on the tire" or, in absence of tread wear indicators, do not meet precise measurements at three locations on the tire); S.C. Code Ann. § 56–5–5040 (Law Co-op. 1991) (tires "shall be in a safe operating condition").

87. E.g., S.C. Code Ann. § 56–5–5350(a) (Law Co-op. 1991) ("No person shall drive. . . any vehicle. . . unless there shall be in effect and properly displayed thereon a current certification of inspection").

88. Lawrence F. Tiffany et al., *Detection of Crime* 131 (1967). In its most recent case on traffic stops, in which the Supreme Court gave police making these stops the power to order passengers out of vehicles without any suspicion of wrongdoing or danger, Justice Kennedy's dissent points out just how powerful a tool *Whren* is. Maryland v. Wilson, No. 95–1268, 1997 U.S. Lexis 1271 (Feb. 19, 1997) (Kennedy, J., dissenting) (when coupled with *Whren's* grant of power to "stop vehicles in almost countless circumstances," majority opinion in

Wilson "puts tens of millions of passengers at risk of arbitrary control by the police.").

89. E.g., Duke Helfand & Susan Steinberg, Charges of Police Racism Tear at Beverly Hills' Image, *L.A. Times*, December 27, 1995, at A1 (African-Americans "go out of their way to avoid Beverly Hills for fear of being stopped by police" and six have filed suit as a result of stops); Barbara White Stack, The Color of Justice: The Race Question, *Pittsburgh Post-Gazette*, May 5, 1996, at A1 (common experience of police harassment has led some African-Americans to file suit).

90. Henry Pierson Curtis, Statistics Show Pattern of Discrimination, *Orlando Sentinel*, August 23, 1992, at A11.

91. Id.; Jeff Brazil and Steve Berry, Color of Driver to Key to Stops in I-95 Videos, *Orlando Sentinel*, August 23, 1992, at A1.

92. Id.

93. Id.

94. Id.

95. Id.

96. Curtis, supra note 90, at A11 (during five days of sampling, "about 5 percent of the drivers of 1,120 vehicles counted were dark skinned").

97. Id.; Brazil and Berry, supra note 91, at A1 ("Almost 70 percent of the motorists stopped were black or Hispanic, an enormously disproportionate figure because the vast majority of interstate drivers are white.").

98. Curtis, supra note 90, at A11.

99. Id.

100. Brazil & Berry, supra note 91, at A1 (Average length of stop in minutes: minority drivers, 12.1, white drivers, 5.1).

101. Id. at A1 (in 507 searches shown by the tapes, four out of five were of cars with Black or Hispanic drivers; note, however, that these numbers do "not include 78 possible searches/incomplete video").

102. Id.

103. Id.

104. Id.

105. Id. Even in these stops, race sometimes played a role. When a stopped white driver told a deputy he was not doing well, the deputy replied, "could be worse, could be black." Id.

106. Id. (89 seizures of cash and 31 drug arrest, respectively). Note also that almost 87 percent of stops were in the southbound lanes, "where any drug traffickers would more likely be carrying cash to Miami," and "[o]nly 13 percent of stops were in the northbound lanes, where the catch would more likely be drugs." Id.

107. Id.

108. Id.

109. Steve Berry, Drug Squad's I-95 Tactics Going On Trial, *Orlando Sentinel*, Jan 6, 1995, at A1; I-95 Cash-Seizure Stops, *Orlando Sentinel*, June 10, 1995, at D3 (first case denied class action status).

110. Washington v. Vogel, 880 F. Supp. 1542 (M.D. Fla. 1995); Steve Berry, Judge Throws Out Suit Against Vogel, *Orlando Sentinel*, Jan. 14, 1995, at A1 (cases dismissed because "plaintiff had not produced enough evidence to show that Vogel had used illegal tactics," but did not address "whether Vogel had a policy of targeting minority motorists"); Steve Berry, Bob Vogel Breezes Through Minorities' Legal Challenge, *Orlando Sentinel*, January 15, 1995, at A1 (first case dismissed at trial because judge refused to certify a class).

111. Washington v. Vogel, Nos. 95–2190, 95–3123, slip op. at 7 (11th Cir. Jan. 7, 1997) ("[The plaintiff's] evidence of a race-based policy, while highly disturbing, fails to demonstrate that the policy, and not traffic violations, prompted the individual officers in this case to conduct [plaintiff's] traffic stops.").

112. The facts described here are taken from the Complaint in the lawsuit Mr. Wilkins and others filed after the incident. See Complaint, Wilkins v. Maryland State Police et al., Civil No. MJG–93–468, (D. Md. 1993) [hereinafter Complaint].

113. Id. ¶ 16.

114. Id. ¶ 19.

115. Id. ¶ 20.

116. Id. ¶ 22.

117. Id. ¶ 23.

118. Id. ¶ 24–25.

119. Id. ¶ 26.

120. Id. ¶ 26–27.

121. Mark Pazniokas, Discrimination by Police Often Hard to Prove, *Hartford Courant*, May 2, 1994, at A11 ("[V]ictims [of racially biased police practices] are reluctant to sue" and "shrug off the [racially biased] stops as an annoying fact of life.")

122. Complaint, Wilkins, at ¶ 20 (Civ. No. MJG–93–468).

123. As recited in the Complaint, Wilkins demonstrated his familiarity with the law. Id. ¶ 20.

124. Id. ¶ ¶ 21, 37–57.

125. Fletcher, supra note 10, at A1.

126. Maryland State Police, Criminal Intelligence Report (April 27, 1992) (on file with author).

127. Settlement Agreement, Wilkins v. Maryland State Police, Civ. No. MJG–93–468 (D. Md.), Jan. 5, 1995, at ¶ 6 [hereinafter Settlement Agreement].

128. Id. ¶ ¶ 7, 8. Both of these paragraphs reference *Derricott v. State*, 611 A.2d 592 (Md. 1992), which outlaws the use of racial profiles in Maryland.

129. Settlement Agreement, supra note 127, at ¶ ¶ 13, 14.

130. Id. ¶ 9. Note that such records might tend to underestimate the total number of racially biased stops on the highways, because they only include stops that are followed by searches, and only two kinds of searches at that: searches by consent and searches with dogs. As the Volusia County data

indicates, there are often significant numbers of citizens stopped who are not searched. See supra note 101 and accompanying text.

131. Summaries of records of Maryland State Police searches, January 1995 through June 1996 [on file with the author]. These data were provided to the court and plaintiff's counsel in raw form; the summaries on file with the author were produced by the plaintiff's legal team.

132. Id.

133. Settlement Agreement, supra note 127, at ¶ 10. See also Plaintiff's Motion for Enforcement of Settlement Agreement and Further Relief, Wilkins v. Maryland State Police, Civ. No. CCB–93–468 (D. Md. Nov. 4, 1996).

134. Thus it was not surprising to find that the continuation of these practices by the Maryland State Police has led to the filing of yet another, separate lawsuit. Michael Schneider, State Police I-95 Drug Unit Found to Search Black Motorists 4 Times More Often than White, *Baltimore Sun*, May 23, 1996 (detailing the "deeply humiliating" roadside search of the vehicle and possessions of Charles and Etta Carter who were travelling on the occasion of their 40th wedding anniversary).

135. Andrew Fegelman, Suit Charges State Police Improperly Stop Minorities, *Chi. Trib.*, August 31, 1994, at 4 (Chavez's suit "echo[ed] complaints the organization has received from motorists for six years"); Illegal Searches Used in Illinois, Suit Alleges, *N.Y. Times*, Sept. 4, 1994, at 24 (suit filed after "hundreds of complaints from motorists") (hereinafter Illegal Searches); Profiles in Prejudice, *St. Louis Post-Dispatch*, September 19, 1994, at 6B.

136. Illegal Searches, supra note 135, at 24.

137. Illinois Drug Searches Prompt Lawsuit By ACLU, *Orlando Sentinel*, September 1, 1994, at A12.

138. Fourth Amended Complaint, Chavez v. Illinois State Police, Civil No. 94 C 5307 (N.D. Ill. 1994), at ¶ ¶ 23, 24 (on file with author).

139. Id. ¶ 25.

140. Id. ¶ 26.

141. Id. ¶ 22; Sam Vincent Meddis, Suit Says Suspect 'Profiles' Are Racist, *USA Today* September 1, 1994, at 3A.

142. Fourth Amended Complaint, Chavez, at ¶ 29.

143. Id. ¶ ¶ 30, 31.

144. Id. ¶ ¶ 32.33.

145. Id. ¶ ¶ 33.

146. Id.

147. Meddis, supra note 141, at 3A.

148. Fourth Amended Complaint, Chavez, at ¶ ¶ 39–129. Many of these plaintiffs were stopped by the Illinois State Police more than once.

149. Telephone interview with Fred Tsao, Public Information Director of the American Civil Liberties Union, Chicago, Ill. (July 23, 1996).

150. Patrick O'Driscoll, 'Drug Profile' Lawsuit Settled, *Denver Post*, November 10, 1995, at A1.

151. Robert Jackson, Minorities Win Suit Over Unfair I-70 Stops, *Rocky Mountain News*, November 10, 1995, at 4A ("Of the 402 people stopped between August 1988 and August 1990 on I-70 between Eagle and Glenwood Springs, none was ticketed or arrested for drugs. . . . ").

152. O'Driscoll, supra note 150, at A1.

153. Id.

154. Id.

155. Id.

156. Jackson, supra note 151, at 4A.

157. O'Driscoll, supra note 150, at A1.

158. Id. For a criminal case in which a suppression motion grew out of the Eagle County deputies' use of pretextual stops, see United States v. Laymon, 730 F. Supp. 332 (D. Colo. 1990), finding that an Eagle County deputy had used a traffic stop as a pretext, and that the consent that followed the stop was not valid.

159. O'Driscoll, supra note 150, at A1.

160. Id.

161. Jackson, supra note 151, at 4A.

162. See O'Driscoll supra note 150, at A1.

163. See Meddis, supra note 141, at 3A.

164. ACLU Sues Maryland Police, *Louisville Courier-Journal*, February 14, 1993, at 20A.

165. Fletcher, supra note 10, at A1.

166. Id.

167. Id.

168. Id.

169. Id.

170. Id.

171. Indeed, I would be remiss if I did not look to the position of law enforcement, given the Supreme Court's pronouncements on the right way for lower courts to make judgments on whether or not officers had reasonable suspicion or probable cause. See United States v. Cortez, 449 U.S. 411, 418 (1981) ("[T]he evidence thus collected must be seen and weighed not in terms of library analysis by scholars, but as understood by those versed in the field of law enforcement.").

172. Marc Mauer & Tracy Huling, *Young Black Americans And The Criminal Justice System: Five Years Later* 3 (1995) ("Almost one in three (32.2% of black men in the age group 20–29) is under criminal justice supervision on any given day—in prison or jail, on probation or parole.").

173. Fletcher, supra note 10, at A1.

174. Id.

175. Sheri Lynn Johnson, Race and the Decision to Detain a Suspect, 93 *Yale L. J.* 214, 220, 236–237, 237–39 (1983) (police use minority race as a proxy for a greater probability of criminal involvement, even though, statistically and logically, this is problematic at best).

176. Professor Johnson makes this assumption, but is careful to say that if so-called "white collar crime" were counted, the numbers might look very different. Id. at 237.

177. Id. at 237–39.

178. Id. at 238–39.

179. See, e.g., David A. Harris, Factors for Reasonable Suspicion: When Black and Poor Means Stopped and Frisked, 69 *Ind. L.J.* 659, 677–678 (1994) (noting that segregation of urban areas usually means that minority group members often live and work in "high crime areas").

180. Johnson, supra note 175, at 238–39. Perhaps another way of looking at this, instead of "double counting," is that race becomes a proxy for poverty and presence in a high crime area, a view which makes little more sense than the one articulated in the text.

181. Id. In fact one commentator has gone even further, arguing that using race as a proxy for criminality "results from a self-fulfilling statistical prophecy: racial stereotypes influence police to arrest minorities more frequently than nonminorities, thereby generating statistically disparate arrest patterns that in turn form the basis for further selectivity." Developments in the Law—Race and the Criminal Process, 101 *Harv. L. Rev.* 1472, 1507–08 (1988). This argument involves some major assumptions, not the least of which is that because blacks are disproportionately arrested and incarcerated, we can assume that a disproportionate number are being stopped. I do not think it is necessary to my argument to go this far.

182. See supra note 39 and accompanying text.

183. Terry v. Ohio, 392 U.S. 1, 27 (1968) (reasonable suspicion requires more than officer's "inchoate and unparticularized suspicion or 'hunch,' [rather, it requires] the specific reasonable inferences which he is entitled to draw from the facts in light of his experience")

184. New York v. Belton, 453 U.S. 454 (1981). Note that *Belton* does not allow the police to search the trunk of the car, but once an arrest is made, the trunk might be opened and searched under proper inventory procedures, Colorado v. Bertine, 479 U.S. 367, 371–72 (1987), or if a drug sniffing dog alerts to the presence of narcotics in the trunk.

185. Whren v. United States, 116 S. Ct. 1769, 1772 (1996).

186. Ohio v. Robinette, 117 S. Ct. 417, 421 (1996) (Fourth Amendment does not require lawfully seized suspects to be told they are free to leave before suspect's consent to search is considered voluntary).

187. Kate Shatzkin & Joe Hallinan, Highway Dragnets Seek Drug Couriers—Police Stop Many Cars For Searches, *Seattle Times*, Sept. 3, 1992, at B6.

188. Id. ("'We definitely tell [our officers] to try to talk their way into a search,' said Lt. Mike Nagurny of the Pennsylvania State Police bureau of drug law enforcement.").

189. Id.

190. 462 U.S. 696 (1983).

191. Id. at 706. But see State v. Dickey, 684 A.2d 92 (N.J. Super Ct. App. Div. 1996) (hours-long detention of motorist before dog sniff held constitutional).

192. 470 U.S. 675 (1985).

193. In *Sharpe*, a DEA agent became suspicious of a Pontiac travelling in tandem with an overloaded truck and camper. The agent stopped the Pontiac, but the truck continued on, pursued by another officer. Once another officer arrived at the place where the Pontiac had been stopped, the DEA officer went in pursuit of the truck, which had been stopped and detained some miles up the road for about twenty minutes in anticipation of the agent's arrival. The Supreme Court said that in assessing whether an investigatory stop is too long, "we consider it appropriate to examine whether the police diligently pursued a means of investigation that was likely to confirm or dispel their suspicions quickly, during which time it was necessary to detain the defendant." Id. at 686. Sine the DEA agent acted "expeditiously" and the delay was attributable to the driver's own "evasive actions," the Court found the detention of twenty minutes entirely reasonable. Id. at 687–88.

194. Of course, given that there was a circuit split before *Whren* on the question of the correct standard to review pretextual traffic stops, see supra note 27, *Whren* did not change either the law or practice in some places.

195. Thus we can find at least one possible benefit of the decision, however else one feels about it: police will no longer have to perjure themselves in order to make these stops stand up in court. See supra note 17; Dershowitz, supra note 57.

196. Kenneth Culp Davis, *Discretionary Justice* 51 (1969).

197. Anthony G. Amsterdam, The Supreme Court and the Rights of Suspects in Criminal Cases, 45 *N.Y.U. L. Rev.* 785, 790 (1970).

198. Wayne R. LaFave, Controlling Discretion by Administrative Regulations: The Use, Misuse, and Non use of Police Rules and Policies in Fourth Amendment Adjudication, 89 *Mich. L. Rev.* 442, 446 (1990) (police use of written policies as instruments to control discretion grew "immeasurably but [to] a noticeable degree" between 1965 and 1990).

199. Id.

200. Id. at 451 (citing Anthony G. Amsterdam, Perspectives on the Fourth Amendment, 58 *Minn L. Rev.* 349, 421 (1974)).

201. Id.

202. Id.

203. 428 U.S. 364 (1976).

204. Id. at 372. I say "perhaps" because while there is no majority opinion, the plurality does say that "inventories pursuant to standard police procedures are reasonable," id., and Justice Powell, concurring, also takes care to say that the inventory "was conducted strictly in accord with the regulations of the Vermillion Police Department," under which all impounded vehicles are inventoried, including the glove compartment. Id. at 380 and n.6.

205. 479 U.S. 367 (1987). Note that *Illinois v. Lafayette*, 462 U.S. 640 (1983), which came between *Opperman* and *Bertine*, also dealt with an inventory search: a search of the contents of the backpack of a person who had been arrested. Since it was "standard procedure" to inventory all of an arrested person's possessions, id. at 642, the Court said that it was not unreasonable "for police, as part of the routine procedure incident to incarcerating an arrested person, to search any container or article in his possession, in accordance with established inventory procedures." Id. at 648.

206. Bertine, 479 U.S. at 374.

207. Id. at 371.

208. LaFave, supra note 198, at 454. It is worth noting that the majority opinion in *Bertine* treats the facts as if there were, in fact, regulations strictly governing inventory searches, *Bertine*, 479 U.S. at 374 n.6, and that three of the seven justices signing the majority opinion joined in a separate concurring opinion to say, explicitly, that inventory searches must follow "standardized police procedures" that ensure an "absence of [police] discretion" such that "it is permissible for police officers to open closed containers. . . only if they are following standard police procedures that mandate the opening of such containers in every impounded vehicle." Id. at 376–77 (Blackmun, J. concurring). But the dissenters vehemently disagreed with the majority's characterization of the regulations at issue. In fact, the regulations allowed the police a choice: upon the arrest of the driver, they could give custody of the vehicle to a third party; the vehicle could be parked and locked in the nearest public parking facility; or the vehicle could be impounded and its contents inventoried. Id. at 379–80. Thus the dissenters argued that "the record indicates that no standardized criteria limit [the] officer's discretion." Id. at 379 (Marshall, J., dissenting).

209. See supra notes 38–39 and accompanying text.

210. To make a valid comparison, we would also need to know the relative frequency of traffic violations by African-Americans vis-a-vis other groups. If this information is not already available, it should be easy to collect.

211. In fact, legislation has been introduced in the 105th Congress that would mandate just such a study. Traffic Stops Statistics Act of 1997, H.R. 118, 105th Cong. (1997). H.R. 118's sponsor is Representative John Conyers of Michigan. In its current form, the Act would mandate collection of a number of categories of statistical information on drivers stopped for traffic offenses, including race and ethnicity, the reason for the stop, and the rationale for any search that follows a stop. It also obligates the Attorney General to publish an annual summary of the data acquired, and attempts to encourage full and complete reporting by masking the identities of reporting officers and departments.

 Article Review Form at end of book.

What effect did the U.S. sentencing guidelines and mandatory minimum statutes have on African Americans?

The Impact of Federal Sentencing Reforms on African Americans

Marvin D. Free, Jr.

Marvin D. Free, Jr. is an assistant professor of sociology at the University of Wisconsin–Whitewater. He has recently published a book, African Americans and the Criminal Justice System, and has had articles appear in various sociological journals. His research interests focus on the issues of race and crime and the depiction of African Americans in criminology textbooks.

African Americans are disproportionately found in the inmate population of federal penal institutions. Although composing 12.1% of the total United States population (U.S. Bureau of the Census, 1992, p. 17), African Americans constituted 33.8% of all federal inmates in 1993 (Maguire & Pastore, 1994, p. 628). The overrepresentation of African Americans in federal prisons raises an interesting question: What effect have the U.S. sentencing guidelines, which emerged from the Sentencing Reform Act of 1984, and mandatory minimum statutes had on

Author's Note: A version of this article was presented at the 1996 Academy of Criminal Justice Sciences Annual Meeting in Las Vegas, Nevada.

African Americans?[1] Before reviewing the relevant empirical research, however, a succinct overview of recent sentencing reform is in order.

Sentencing Reform in the United States

Recent changes in federal sentencing are the result of two simultaneous and related forces. First, "mandatory minimums" (i.e., statutory requirements that a person convicted of a specific offense shall receive at least the minimum sentence prescribed by that statute), which, until lately, were used sparingly, have today been expanded to include entire classes of offenses (U.S. Sentencing Commission, 1991b). Second, the Sentencing Reform Act of 1984 has altered the processing of federal defendants. This act created the U.S. Sentencing Commission and charged it with the responsibility of developing sentencing guidelines for federal offenses. The guidelines, submitted to Congress in April 1987, became effective on November 1, 1987 (Heaney, 1991).

To place these changes in proper perspective, it is necessary to discuss separately mandatory minimum sentencing provisions and the sentencing guidelines. Because mandatory minimum statutes preceded the sentencing guidelines, mandatory minimums are examined first.

Mandatory Minimums

Federal mandatory minimum sentences were not widely used until 1956 when the Narcotic Control Act required mandatory minimum sentences for most offenses involving the distribution and importation of drugs. By 1970, however, virtually all mandatory penalties for drug violations were abolished when Congress passed the Comprehensive Drug Abuse Prevention and Control Act (U.S. Sentencing Commission, 1991b).

Federal mandatory minimum penalties returned in 1984.[2] The same comprehensive legislation that led to the development of the sentencing guidelines also established mandatory minimum penalty statutes. Within 10 years, more than 60 federal offenses carried mandatory minimum sentences (Vincent & Hofer, 1994, p. 2). Federal legislation emphasized crimes involving drugs and violence, with drug offenders being particularly affected by the mandatory minimum sentences.

Marvin D. Free, *Journal of Black Studies*, Vol. 28, No. 2, November 1997, pp. 268–286. Copyright © 1997 Sage Publications, Inc. Reprinted by permission of Sage Publications, Inc.

Between 1984 and 1990, 91% of the federal defendants sentenced to mandatory minimum sentences were convicted of drug-related crimes (Vincent & Hofer, 1994, p. 3). Moreover, the Bureau of Prisons estimates that 70% of the growth in the federal prison population can be attributed to longer sentences given to drug offenders (Vincent & Hofer, 1994, p. 9).

Changes in the processing of drug offenders occurred as a consequence of new legislation reflecting the "get tough" policy of the so-called War on Drugs. The Anti-Drug Abuse Act of 1986 established mandatory minimum penalties for offenses involving drug trafficking based on the quantity of drugs associated with the offense (U.S. Sentencing Commission, 1991b) and differentiated crack cocaine from powder cocaine for sentencing purposes (McDonald & Carlson, 1993). Given that African Americans were disproportionately likely to be charged with possession of crack cocaine, whereas Whites were substantially more likely to be charged with possession of powder cocaine (see *State v. Russell,* 1991), the establishment of stiffer sentences for crack cocaine possession had serious implications for Blacks.[3] Further contributing to racial disparity in sentencing was the *lack* of emphasis on treatment and prevention. Only 14% of the allocated funding was set aside for the treatment and prevention of drug abuse (Johnson, Golub, & Fagan, 1995, p. 288).

Two years later, Congress passed the Omnibus Anti-Drug Abuse Act, which provided for a mandatory minimum of 5 years in prison for possession of 5 grams of crack cocaine, the approximate weight of two pennies (Wallace, 1993, p. 10).[4] As with the earlier act, this legislation stressed law enforcement over treatment and prevention. The effect of this and similar federal legislation was that, by 1993, drug offenses composed the single most common offense in federal trials (Miller, 1995).[5]

Sentencing Guidelines

Although the sentencing guidelines are a form of mandatory sentencing in that they limit judicial discretion

and eliminate parole, they are somewhat more flexible than the statutory minimum penalties in that upward and downward departures from the guideline range are permitted under certain circumstances. Additionally, if the minimum of the guideline range does not exceed 6 months, nonimprisonment sentences (e.g., home confinement) can be imposed (Vincent & Hofer, 1994).

The sentencing commission, in developing the guidelines, was given the mandate that its guidelines and policy statements should be "entirely neutral as to race, sex, national origin, creed, and socioeconomic status of offenders" (cited in Heaney, 1991, p. 203). Under the guidelines, judges are prohibited from taking into consideration many personal attributes of the defendant, including (a) the defendant's mental health or alcohol or drug dependence, (b) the defendant's background, (c) prior victimization of the defendant, and (d) the potential impact of the sentence on the defendant or the defendant's family (Tonry, 1995). Depending on the offense, such information as victim injury, drug quantity, amount of dollar loss, and use of a weapon may be relevant to the sentencing process. Moreover, the guidelines stipulate that a judge *must* consider these facts, if present, even if they are not charged and even if the participants in the case have agreed that such facts will not be included (Nagel & Schulhofer, 1992).

A sentencing table is used for ascertaining the appropriate guidelines sentence. The table has two axes—one for the offense level (there are 43 offense levels), the other for the offender's criminal history (Karle & Sager, 1991). To locate the correct guidelines range, one must simply find the intersection of these two axes. A sentencing range between the maximum and minimum sentences of approximately 25% is typically specified by the guidelines (Nagel & Schulhofer, 1992).

Departures from the guidelines are tolerated under certain conditions. Downward departures (i.e., reductions in sentence length) under section 5K.1.1, the substantial-assistance provision, are permitted in cases where a defendant has provided assistance in the prosecution

of other offenders and the government has moved for a downward departure based on this assistance. Further, a two-level reduction for "acceptance of responsibility" may be awarded. If granted, this can have the effect of reducing the length of the sentence by about 25% (Nagel & Schulhofer, 1992).

Although parole was abolished for individuals engaging in federal crimes after the effective date of the guidelines, sentence reductions were still possible using good time credits earned in prison. Credit for up to 50 days annually can accrue to inmates exhibiting good behavior while incarcerated (Karle & Sager, 1991).

Sentencing Reform and Racial Discrimination

As indicated earlier, sentencing reform in the United States came packaged as either the U.S. Sentencing Commission's sentencing guidelines, which applied to *all* federal crimes committed on or after November 1, 1987, or legislatively mandated minimum sentences, which applied to only specified *classes* of crimes. Thus, to the extent possible, an evaluation of sentencing reform should analyze separately these two alterations in sentencing policy. Some caveats are necessary, however, prior to assessing the impact of sentencing reform on African Americans.

Obstacles to Demonstrating Discrimination in Sentencing

Whether a researcher finds evidence of differential treatment in sentencing is, in part, a function of the type of model the investigator employs. Commonly used in research are additive models that look at the effect of race on sentencing outcome. Alternatively, an interactive model allows the investigator to examine if race, in conjunction with other relevant variables, might result in differential processing. Terance Miethe and Charles Moore (1986) observed that the additive model conceals and suppresses racial differences in criminal processing, whereas the interactive model uncovers differential criminal processing between and within the two racial groups.

At least two additional problems related to statistical procedures can be identified. First, conventional regression techniques can distort one's findings so that the investigator incorrectly accepts the null hypothesis of no racial differences (Myers, 1985). Additionally, overreliance on statistical significance as a gauge of the importance of race in discrimination in the criminal justice system can result in overemphasizing minor relationships because statistical significance is, in part, a function of sample size.

Moreover, the way in which discrimination is operationalized will affect the conclusions of the investigator. Samuel Myers (1993) suggests that many researchers examining discrimination use measures of discrimination that are too narrow. Arguing for the employment of "residual differences" methodology, he posits that discrimination can exist even when systematic decisions are based on legitimate standards if their application differentially affects Blacks and Whites.

Difficulties further arise when investigators attempt to interpret their findings. Although harsher sanctions against African American defendants are typically construed as discriminatory in nature, do less severe penalties necessarily signify an *absence* of discrimination? As Wilbanks (1987) points out, greater leniency accorded African American offenders can, depending on the circumstances, be symptomatic of either nondiscriminatory or discriminatory behavior. For instance, a judge who devalues the lives of African Americans might sentence less severely the killers of Blacks than the killer of Whites. Because much murder is intraracial (i.e., offenders and victims are of the same race), this prejudicial attitude would typically translate into African American defendants receiving lighter sentences than their White counterparts. Racial discrimination might also be operative in cases where Black murderers are given shorter sentences because they are perceived as being prone to irrationality and impulsiveness and consequently less responsible for their actions.

The finding that Whites receive more severe sentences than African Americans may also mask racial discrimination if "selection bias" occurred during the presentencing stage (Blumstein, 1993). Illustrative of this would be a situation where a prosecutor is more likely to institute legal proceedings against African Americans than Whites. Hence, the White defendants coming to trial would, on average, have been involved in more serious crimes than their Black counterparts. Thus, even if a judge handles all cases the same, Whites would be subjected to more severe sentences due to their greater involvement in serious crime, thereby concealing the earlier discrimination.

Moreover, the use of aggregate data may result in a "canceling-out effect" that disguises the presence of racial bias (Wilbanks, 1987). If some judges are more likely to severely sanction African Americans, whereas others are more likely to severely sanction Whites, the overall impact would be a washing out of these differences if aggregate data were employed in the analysis. To effectively determine if individuals within the criminal justice system discriminate against African Americans, studies of individual decision makers are needed; yet, such research is almost nonexistent.

Further complicating the assessment of sentencing reform on African Americans are four problems associated with sentencing guidelines research. One such problem is a weak research design (Tonry, 1993). Evaluations typically compare sentencing patterns before and after the implementation of the guidelines, instead of the ideal (but legally impossible) situation where defendants are randomly assigned to the two sentencing systems.

Another problem stems from changes occurring in the federal criminal justice system since 1987, the year the guidelines took effect (Tonry, 1993). Since the mid-1980s, federal criminal justice policy has become increasingly politicized. The conservative political agenda of the Reagan and Bush presidencies culminated in the appointment of many conservative judges, such that by 1992, a majority of all federal judges were conservative. Given these changes, it is difficult to know if any detected changes are the result of the guidelines or some other factor(s).

Meaningful comparisons of pre- and postguidelines data are also problematic because preguideline data often do not contain information used in sentencing decisions under the guidelines (Tonry, 1993). Quantity of drugs, presence of an unused firearm, and other uncharged crimes are all relevant factors under the guidelines, yet preguideline cases do not regularly contain such information.

Additionally, the shifting of sentencing power from judges to prosecutors since the arrival of sentencing guidelines makes comparisons of pre- and postguidelines cases more onerous (Tonry, 1993). Under the new standards, such items as the specific offense with which one is charged and the quantity of drugs one is alleged to have sold or possessed take on even greater significance. With judges having limited discretion and prosecutors deciding what data will be included in the case, prosecutorial decisions become even more important under the new system. And with data on prosecutors' decisions being largely unavailable, racial bias can go undetected.

These limitations notwithstanding, a critical examination of the extant research is warranted given the racial disparity in federal incarceration rates. Although no single investigation is likely to lead to definitive statements about the impact of sentencing reform on African Americans, drawing on multiple studies makes it possible to derive some general conclusions.

Mandatory Minimums and Racial Bias

Using data for fiscal year 1990, the U.S. Sentencing Commission (1991b) observed that African Americans were more likely than Whites to be convicted under mandatory minimum provisions, even though they constituted a much smaller percentage of all federal defendants than their White counterparts. African Americans, who constituted 28.2% of all federal defendants, accounted for 38.5% of all federal defendants convicted under mandatory minimum provisions. Comparable figures for Whites were 46.9% and 34.8%, respectively.

The study also found that African Americans were more likely than either Whites or Hispanics to be sentenced at or above the indicated mandatory minimum. More than two thirds (67.7%) of all Black federal defendants convicted under the mandatory minimum provisions received sentences that were at or above the indicated mandatory minimum. In contrast, 54% of the White and 57.1% of the Hispanic federal defendants convicted under the mandatory minimum provisions received these sentences (U.S. Sentencing Commission, 1991b, p. 80).

Why are African Americans disproportionately convicted under the mandatory minimum provisions and why are they more likely than Whites and Hispanics to receive severe sentences under the mandatory minimum provisions? Much of the disparity can be attributed to the emphasis on drug offenses. This is readily seen by analyzing data from pre- and postguidelines periods, in that the guidelines reflected the increasingly severe penalties required under the mandatory minimum provisions. In 1986, the last full year prior to the implementation of the guidelines,[6] only 19% of all African Americans convicted in federal court were convicted of drug trafficking. By the first half of 1990, however, this figure had risen to 46%. The comparable White rates were 26% in 1986 and 35% for the first 6 months of 1990 (McDonald & Carlson, 1993, p. 10). Thus, prior to the implementation of mandatory minimum provisions for drug offenses, Whites were more likely than Blacks to be convicted of drug trafficking, whereas the reverse was true after these provisions went into effect.

The dramatic increase in drug convictions for African Americans mirrors the harsher sanctions attached to crack cocaine offenses. With the law equating 1 gram of crack cocaine with 100 grams of powder cocaine, even relatively modest quantities of crack cocaine can lead to rather severe penalties. A serious user of crack cocaine, for instance, could require 5 or more grams of the substance for the weekend. Yet, this amount presently carries a mandatory minimum prison term of 5 years (Vincent & Hofer, 1994, p. 23). Prior to this, federal judges typically placed first-time offenders on probation (Alschuler, 1991).

Not only are crack cocaine offenses more heavily sanctioned, they are also somewhat more likely than offenses involving powder cocaine to be sentenced at or above the indicated mandatory minimum. Data analyzed by the U.S. Sentencing Commission (1991b, p. 72) revealed that 67.5% of the offenses involving crack cocaine, compared to 64.9% of the offenses involving powder cocaine, were sentenced at or above the indicated mandatory minimum.

The significance of the harsher sanctions attached to crack cocaine offenses is disclosed in an investigation by Douglas McDonald and Kenneth Carlson (1993). They conclude that the single most important difference that contributed to the longer sentences for Black federal offenders was their overrepresentation in crack cocaine trafficking. Examining the potential impact of sentencing crack and powder cocaine traffickers the same for identical amounts of the drug, McDonald and Carlson (1993, p. 21) report that instead of African Americans receiving sentences that averaged 30% longer than that of Whites, the average sentence for African American cocaine traffickers would have been 10% *shorter* than that of their White counterparts. In addition, it would have reduced by half the Black/White difference in average prison sentence for all federal crimes.

Evidence of potential racial bias in the charging of Black defendants in federal court with the selling of crack cocaine has been detected by Richard Berk and Alec Campbell (1993).[7] Analyzing data sets from Los Angeles, they observed that although state charges for the sale of crack cocaine were similar to the sheriff's department arrest patterns, African Americans were overrepresented in federal cases when compared to their patterns of arrest by the sheriff's department. Also indicative of possible racial bias was the finding that over a 4-year period in federal court, *no* Whites were charged with the sale of crack cocaine.

Arguments in favor of maintaining a legal distinction between crack and powder cocaine frequently center on the assumption that crack is more dangerous because it is instantly addicting and is related to violence. Contradictory evidence, nonetheless, is beginning to surface. Data from the Careers in Crack Project tend to refute the notion that crack is any more instantly addicting than powder cocaine. Additionally, crack use did not appear to substantially alter the involvement of men in nondrug offending. Moreover, whereas the *use* of crack was unrelated to violent behavior, the *sale* of crack was strongly related to violence, thereby suggesting that the violence associated with inner-city crack culture is probably the result of systemic violence involved in the sale of illicit drugs, rather than the pharmacological properties of the drug itself (Johnson et al., 1995).

The continuation of a legal distinction between the two types of cocaine can also be challenged on other grounds. First, the mood-altering ingredient is the same in both. Second, powder cocaine, if dissolved in water and injected intravenously, has a similar effect to that of smoking crack cocaine. Finally, powder cocaine can be converted into crack cocaine by using baking soda and water to remove the hydrochloride from the powder cocaine (see *State v. Russell*, 1991).

Sentencing Guidelines and Racial Bias

Because the sentencing guidelines are anchored by mandatory minimum sentences, any discussion of the impact of the guidelines on African Americans is somewhat arbitrary. Though numerous studies have attempted to evaluate the effect of the new system on sentencing, few have specifically analyzed racial differences. Accordingly, care must be exercised when assessing the extant research.

Data analyzed by the U.S. Sentencing Commission (1991a) disclosed little sentencing disparity under the guidelines if offenders with similar criminal records are compared. When the commission limited the analysis to four major offenses (bank robbery, powder cocaine distribution, heroin distribution, and bank embezzlement), race was a factor ($p \le .05$) in sentencing outcome only for heroin distribution. Whereas 92.3% of all Whites convicted of heroin distribution were given sentences at the bottom of the guideline range, the comparable figures for African Americans and Hispanics were 82.6% and 56.7%, respectively (U.S. Sentencing Commission, 1991a, p. 310). Nonetheless, the small samples employed in the analyses of different offenses make any generalizations uncertain (for a critique of the study, see Tonry, 1993). The report further revealed that across all offense categories for the last half of fiscal year 1990, African Americans were *more* likely than either Whites or Hispanics to be sentenced at the bottom of the guidelines range.

An investigation by McDonald and Carlson (1993) found that substantial racial disparity in sentencing occurred after the guidelines were implemented. During the period 1986 to 1988, prior to full implementation of the new system,[8] White, African American, and Hispanic defendants received similar sentences in federal district courts. Average maximum prison sentences ranged from 51 months for Whites and Hispanics to 55 months for African Americans (p. 3). However, between January 20, 1989, and June 30, 1990, racial disparities in sentencing appeared. African Americans and Hispanics convicted of federal offenses and subject to the provisions of the Sentencing Reform Act of 1984 were more likely than Whites to be sentenced to prison. Further, African Americans received longer average prison sentences (71 months) than either Whites (50 months) or Hispanics (48 months) (p. 4). These disparities, the investigators note, were primarily the result of differences in the characteristics of the offenses and offenders that the law recognizes as legitimate for sentencing purposes. McDonald and Carlson (1993) conclude that the sentencing disparities they observed were generally not a consequence of the guidelines themselves with the exceptions of "the mandatory minimum sentencing laws passed for drugs, especially crack cocaine, and the particular way the Sentencing Commission arrayed guideline ranges above the statutory minima" (p. 21).

A study conducted by the U.S. General Accounting Office (1992) revealed that the effect of race on sentencing was not consistent under the guidelines. There were, nevertheless, some situations in which African Americans were at a disadvantage. Bank robbery and larceny, for instance, are offenses in which African Americans and Whites were less likely than Hispanics to have their counts reduced or dismissed and consequently received longer sentences for these crimes. Additionally, the data disclosed that African Americans were less likely than Whites and Hispanics to have their counts reduced or dismissed before going to trial for heroin distribution. And, though the reasons are unclear, African Americans were less likely than Whites to plead guilty, despite the fact that offenders convicted by plea generally received shorter sentences than those convicted at trial.

It additionally appears that the sentencing guidelines have increased the proportion of minority defendants processed in federal court. Methodological criticisms aside (see Schulhofer, 1992; Wilkins, 1992), Gerald Heaney's (1991, 1992) comparison of offenders sentenced under the guidelines to those sentenced under preguidelines law disclosed that African Americans accounted for 22.3% of the preguidelines defendants but composed 26.2% of the guidelines defendants. Hispanics fared even worse, going from 8.5% of the defendants under the preguidelines to 26.3% of the defendants under the guidelines (Heaney, 1991, p. 204; 1992, p. 781). In other words, Black representation increased by almost 4% and Hispanic representation grew by nearly 18% under the guidelines.

The investigator contends that two factors are primarily responsible for these changes (Heaney, 1991). First, he asserts, many law enforcement officials pursued their cases through federal court instead of state court believing that the defendants would be imprisoned longer under the new federal standards. The second factor attributed to the changes involves the filing of marginal cases. According to Heaney, some cases were filed in federal court that would otherwise not have been filed in either state or federal court because the guidelines now made the prosecution worth the effort.

Heaney (1991) also observed that under the guidelines, the average sentence increased most dramatically for African Americans. Although the average sentence for African Americans under preguidelines law in 1989 was 27.8 months, this figure swelled to 68.5 months for cases sentenced the same year under the guidelines. To be sure, the average sentence for Whites and Hispanics expanded as well under the guidelines, but the increases of 19 months for Whites and 13.7 months for Hispanics (p. 207) pale in comparison to that experienced by African Americans.

What accounts for the greater Black/White disparity under the new system? Heaney (1991) suggests that the emphasis on curtailing crack cocaine traffic, accompanied with the stiffer penalties attached to crack cocaine, contributed to the expansion of the average sentence for African Americans. Moreover, being more likely than Whites to possess a criminal record, African Americans are at a greater disadvantage in sentencing.

The negative impact of the guidelines on African Americans is apparently not confined to longer sentences: On average, African Americans are less likely than Whites to be given a probation-only disposition in federal court cases prosecuted under the new system (Heaney, 1991, 1992). The probability of receiving straight probation, of course, varies depending on the offense. For instance, Whites are over 3 times more likely than African Americans under the new standards to receive probation-only for offenses involving drugs and violence. On the other hand, African Americans are slightly more likely than Whites to receive a straight probation disposition for property crimes and have a 6% greater chance than Whites to receive this disposition in immigration cases (Heaney, 1991, p. 207; 1992, p. 780).

Most recently, *The Tennessean* newspaper in Nashville conducted a study of all 1992–1993 federal convictions using data furnished by the U.S. Sentencing Commission. The analysis of approximately 80,000 cases controlled for offense severity and prior record. Overall, the investigation revealed that African Americans received sentences that averaged 10% longer than those of comparable Whites (p. 1A). Although Hispanics received sentences similar to those of Whites, in 74 of the 90 federal court districts, African Americans received longer sentences than Whites charged with the same crimes (p. 6A). The amount of disparity, however, varied from one federal district to another, with the largest disparity occurring in the East Missouri district where, on average, African Americans were given sentences that were 40% longer than those of Whites (p. 1A). Additionally, the disparity was not due to the imposition of mandatory minimum sentences as the disparity remained even after omitting drug convictions.

Discussion and Conclusion

That mandatory minimum statutes have had an adverse effect on African Americans is corroborated by the literature. Research shows that African Americans are more likely than Whites to be convicted under mandatory minimum provisions and more likely than Whites to be sentenced at or above the indicated mandatory minimum. Much of the disparity is apparently a consequence of the differential treatment accorded crack cocaine offenders.

The disparity between sentences involving crack and powder cocaine has recently been investigated by the U.S. Sentencing Commission. In a 220-page report submitted to Congress in February 1995, the Commission revealed its plans to modify the sentencing guidelines to remedy this disparity (Locy, 1995). Whether the sentencing standards will undergo alterations is unclear, though, as the Justice Department has exhorted Congress to reject the commission's proposal to make the penalty for crack cocaine the same as that for powder cocaine ("Justice Agency Urges," 1995).[9]

Sentencing guidelines research suggests that racial disparities have

been enhanced under the new sentencing structure. Investigators have observed that African Americans are more likely than Whites, under the guidelines, to be sentenced to prison and to receive longer sentences. Overall, African Americans are less likely than Whites to receive a disposition of probation only. They are also less likely than other groups to have their counts reduced or dismissed for certain crimes. Furthermore, since the guidelines have become effective, minority representation in federal court has grown substantially.

Explanations of the inefficiency of sentencing reform to alleviate racial disparity focus on several areas largely concealed from empirical analysis. According to Heaney (1991, 1992), the guidelines have created the possibility of additional sentencing disparity by giving greater power to prosecutors. With judges having carefully circumscribed discretion in sentencing decisions under the new standards, prosecutors now have greater influence on sentencing outcomes. As prosecutors decide who and what to charge, prosecutorial decisions, in effect, establish the appropriate sentencing guideline range. Moreover, prosecutors control the flow of information about the offense that will be used by probation officers in their presentence investigation reports. To the extent that racial bias might enter into prosecutorial decision making, additional disparity is possible.

Another source of disparity involves the decision regarding the court of jurisdiction (Heaney, 1991, 1992). The decision to prosecute in state court or federal court can have important consequences for defendants, particularly in drug cases, because mandatory minimum statutes have influenced the sentencing guidelines in cases prosecuted under federal law. The possibility of more severe sentences in federal court can be readily seen by examining background data from *United States v. Williams* (1990). In this U.S. District Court case, the defendants, who were African American, had been referred to federal court where their crack cocaine distribution carried a sentencing range of 188 to 235 months under the guidelines. In con-

trast, conviction of the same offense by the state would result in a sentence of under 2 years.

Sentencing guidelines are additionally unlikely to eliminate racial disparity because sentence length is tied to the defendant's criminal history and Black defendants are more likely than their White counterparts to have prior criminal records ("Developments in the Law," 1988; Heaney, 1992). Any previous racial bias in enforcement of the law is, therefore, amplified under the new standards.

The investigative and preprosecution practices of law enforcement officials can further lead to hidden sentencing disparities. This is especially evident in the enforcement of drug laws. Because sentence severity increases as the quantity of drugs bought or sold increases, some drug enforcement agents have encouraged their suspects to purchase or sell larger quantities to impose stiffer penalties when they are apprehended (see *United States v. Rosen*, 1991). Another practice leading to a longer sentence is to postpone the arrest until the cumulative amount purchased results in a statutory minimum sentence (Heaney, 1991). Given that drug law enforcement typically focuses on areas of the city where the poor and minorities are concentrated (Mauer, 1991), African Americans are adversely affected by these practices.

A final feature of the new sentencing system that precludes its being an effective deterrent to racial disparity in sentencing is its failure to address racial disparity during the first phase of the sentencing process. Sentencing typically involves two decisions. The first, the in/out decision, involves a decision as to whether the defendant should be incarcerated. If the defendant is to be incarcerated, then another decision must be made regarding the length of the prison term. The guidelines attempt to reduce racial disparity during the second phase of sentencing only. And yet, a review of numerous sentencing studies by Free (1996) found that empirical support for racial bias in sentencing is stronger for the in/out decision than for the decision on sentence length.

In conclusion, neither mandatory minimum sentences nor the

guidelines have been effective in eliminating racial disparity in sentencing in federal court. Much of the disparity can be attributed to drug laws (especially those pertaining to crack cocaine). Although changing the law to make penalties for identical amounts of powder and crack cocaine the same would reduce the disparity, it would not eradicate it because of the greater likelihood of drug enforcement to concentrate on inner-city neighborhoods. Moreover, selective law enforcement at preprosecutorial stages of the criminal justice system has an adverse effect on African Americans by producing criminal records that culminate in longer sentences under the new standards. Therefore, any meaningful attempt to promote equality between African Americans and Whites must address the dual issues of possible preprosecutorial racial bias as well as possible racial bias during sentencing.

Notes

1. For a more thorough discussion of the Sentencing Reform Act of 1984 and the sentencing guidelines that ensued, see Wilkins, Newton, and Steer (1991).
2. Legislation of mandatory minimums at the state level began in 1973 in New York. By 1983, only one state had not passed some mandatory minimum legislation (U.S. Sentencing Commission, 1991b).
3. The minimum prison sentences established by this act for crack cocaine are identical to the minimum prison sentences for persons convicted of selling 100 times that amount of powder cocaine (McDonald & Carlson, 1993).
4. For second and third offenses, the amount of crack cocaine required to trigger the 5-year mandatory minimum sentence declines to 3 grams and 1 gram, respectively (Wallace, 1993, p. 17).
5. In 1993, 44% of the federal caseload involved drug offenses. The next most common offense was fraud, representing only 13% of the federal cases (Miller, 1995, p. 184).
6. Mandatory minimum sentences for drug offenses did not go into effect until October 27, 1986 (Vincent & Hofer, 1994, p. 26).
7. This study has been heavily criticized by Joseph Finley (1993). He notes that the investigators failed to examine such data as quantity of narcotics and the offender's previous criminal record,

which might account for at least some of the reported disparity. Furthermore, a conclusion of selective prosecution in crack cocaine cases at the federal level is considerably weakened by the small number of federal cases involving this drug ($n = 43$).
8. The constitutionality of the sentencing guidelines was questioned by many federal officials until a 1989 Supreme Court decision (*United States v. Mistretta*, 1989) declared the Sentencing Reform Act of 1984 constitutional. Hence, inconsistent application of the sentencing standards was common for several years after the guidelines went into effect.
9. Although rejecting the view that crack cocaine and powder cocaine cases should be identically sentenced, the Justice Department intimated that some adjustment of the structure might be warranted ("Justice Agency Urges," 1995).

References

Alschuler, A. (1991). The failure of sentencing guidelines: A plea for less aggregation. *University of Chicago Law Review, 58*, 901–951.

Berk, R., & Campbell, A. (1993). Preliminary data on race and crack charging practices in Los Angeles. *Federal Sentencing Reporter, 6*, 36–38.

Blumstein, A. (1993). Racial disproportionality of U.S. prison populations revisited. *University of Colorado Law Review, 64*, 743–760.

Developments in the law: Race and the criminal process. (1988). *Harvard Law Review, 101*, 1472–1641.

Finley, J. (1993). Crack charging in Los Angeles: Do statistics tell the whole truth about "selective prosecution?" *Federal Sentencing Reporter, 6*, 113–115.

Frank, L. (1995, September 24). Color of skin affects sentences, study finds. *Wausau Daily Herald*, pp. 1A, 6A.

Free, M. Jr. (1996). *African Americans and the criminal justice system*. New York: Garland.

Heaney, G. (1991). The reality of guidelines sentencing: No end to disparity. *American Criminal Law Review, 28*, 161–232.

Heaney, G. (1992). Revisiting disparity: Debating guidelines sentencing. *American Criminal Law Review, 29*, 771–793.

Johnson, B., Golub, A., & Fagan, J. (1995). Careers in crack, drug use, drug distribution, and nondrug criminality. *Crime & Delinquency, 41*, 275–295.

Justice agency urges Congress to reject cocaine-penalty plan. (1995, April 17). *The Wall Street Journal*, p. A7G.

Karle, T., & Sager, T. (1991). Are the federal sentencing guidelines meeting congressional goals: An empirical and case law analysis. *Emory Law Journal, 40*, 393–444.

Locy, T. (1995, March 1). Panel plans to amend sentencing disparity for crack dealers. *The Washington Post*, p. D3.

Maguire, K., & Pastore, A. (Eds.). (1994). *Sourcebook of criminal justice statistics 1993* (U.S. Department of Justice, Bureau of Justice Statistics). Washington, DC: U.S. Government Printing Office.

Mauer, M. (1991). *Americans behind bars: A comparison of international rates of incarceration*. Washington, DC: The Sentencing Project.

McDonald, D., & Carlson, K. (1993). *Sentencing in the federal courts: Does race matter? The transition to sentencing guidelines, 1986–90 (Summary)* (U.S. Department of Justice, Bureau of Justice Statistics). Washington, DC: U.S. Government Printing Office.

Miethe, T., & Moore, C. (1986). Racial differences in criminal processing: The consequences of model selection on conclusions about differential treatment. *Sociological Quarterly, 27*, 217–237.

Miller, M. (1995). Rehabilitating the federal sentencing guidelines. *Judicature, 78*, 180–188.

Myers, S. Jr. (1985). Statistical tests of discrimination in punishment. *Journal of Quantitative Criminology, I*, 191–218.

Myers, S. Jr. (1993). Racial disparities in sentencing: Can sentencing reforms reduce discrimination in punishment? *University of Colorado Law Review, 64*, 781–808.

Nagel, I., & Schulhofer, S. (1992). A tale of three cities: An empirical study of charging and bargaining practices under the federal sentencing guidelines. *Southern California Law Review, 66*, 501–566.

Schulhofer, S. (1992). Assessing the federal sentencing process: The problem is uniformity, not disparity. *American Criminal Law Review, 29*, 833–873.

State v. Russell, 477 N.W.2d 886 (Minn. 1991).

Tonry, M. (1993). The failure of the U.S. Sentencing Commission's guidelines. *Crime & Delinquency, 39*, 131–149.

Tonry, M. (1995). Twenty years of sentencing reform: Steps forward, steps backward. *Judicature, 78*, 169–172.

U.S. Bureau of the Census. (1992). *Statistical abstract of the United States: 1992* (112th ed.). Washington, DC: U.S. Government Printing Office.

U.S. General Accounting Office. (1992). *Sentencing guidelines: Central questions remain unanswered*. Washington, DC: Author.

U.S. Sentencing Commission. (1991a). *The federal sentencing guidelines: A report on the operation of the guidelines system and short-term impacts on disparity in sentencing, use of incarceration, and prosecutorial discretion and plea bargaining* (Vol. 2). Washington, DC: Author.

U.S. Sentencing Commission. (1991b). *Mandatory minimum penalties in the federal criminal justice system*. Washington, DC: Author.

United States v. Mistretta, 488 U.S. 361 (1989).

United States v. Rosen, 929 F.2d 839 (1st Cir. 1991).

United States v. Williams, 746 F. Supp. 1076 (D. Utah 1990).

Vincent, B., & Hofer, P. (1994). *The consequences of mandatory minimum prison terms: A summary of recent findings.* Washington, DC: Federal Judicial Center.

Wallace, H. (1993). Mandatory minimums and the betrayal of sentencing reform: A legislative Dr. Jekyll and Mr. Hyde. *Federal Probation, 57,* 9–19.

Wilbanks, W. (1987). *The myth of a racist criminal justice system.* Monterey, CA: Brooks/Cole.

Wilkins, W. Jr. (1992). Response to Judge Heaney. *American Criminal Law Review, 29,* 795–821.

Wilkins, W. Jr., Newton, P., & Steer, J. (1991). The Sentencing Reform Act of 1984: A bold approach to the unwarranted sentencing disparity problem. *Criminal Law Forum, 2,* 355–380.

 Article Review Form at end of book.

Is it ethical for blacks to play the race card?

Ethics and Justice:

Playing the Race Card

Florence S. Ferguson

State University of West Georgia

Introduction

Is playing the race card ethical? This issue emerged during the Simpson trial, and it has generated some concerns about the justice system for many Americans. This paper explores the conception of "playing the race card." Ironically, the race card is not a new phenomenon. Historically, it has contributed to the disproportionate number of African-Americans, particularly males who are arrested, convicted, and incarcerated throughout our criminal justice system. Larry Conley, an editor of the *Atlanta Journal Constitution,* published an article in the newspaper after one of his colleagues raised the question "Will the justice system survive after the Simpson trial?"[1] This question became a public concern to many white Americans after Marcia Clark, the lead prosecutor in the trial, publicly accused Johnny Cochran of playing the race card during his closing argument before a predominantly African-American jury. As noted in Conley's article, no one asked, "Will the justice system survive?"after an all-white jury set free white police officers who savagely beat Rodney King. The race card was certainly played in that trial. During the trial,

Paper presented at the 1996 Annual Meeting of the Academy of Criminal Justice Sciences, Las Vegas, Nevada

attorneys for the officers repeatedly played the infamous videotape which showed the police beating King, even as he lay on the ground, emphasizing King's size, his strength, and "his aggressiveness." Their message that King was a hulking black menace was clear and deliberate. To African-Americans, the all-white jury in this case reacted predictably, with one juror explaining after the acquittal of the officers, that King "got what he deserved."

Conley argues that the outrageously unjust verdict did not seem to shake the faith of most white Americans about the American justice system. Further, he argues that there were no indignant calls for immediate judicial reforms throughout the jury system. Why not? Similarly, Conley argues, no one asked, "Will the political system survive?" after Republicans used the blatantly racist Willie Horton advertisements to help secure victory in the 1988 presidential election. This, too, was "playing the race card," as Republicans knowingly and deliberately played to white voters' fear—again, with predictable results. However there were no urgent calls to introduce a bill into Congress to ensure this would never happen again. Finally, let's not forget Susan Smith, or the celebrated case in Boston in which an upper-middle-class white male murdered his pregnant wife. In these criminal cases, the race card backfired on its players. In the first case, Susan Smith accused a black man of kidnaping and murdering her two children. In the second

case, a husband accused a black man of shooting him, and then killing his pregnant wife, in a robbery attempt. These cases are examples of how the "race card" has benefited white Americans. In both cases, these individuals orchestrated these horrendous crimes, then blamed them on African-American males. They were confident that police would believe them and that once a suspect was apprehended, the justice system would punish them. How many similar cases have resulted in the arrest, conviction, and incarceration of innocent African-Americans?

What Is the Race Card?

What is the race card? James Earl Hardy, who published an essay in the *Advocate Magazine* entitled the "River of De-Nile," defines it as such: "With this expression, race is reduced to a game—and I guess we (i.e., African-Americans) are the spades."[2] He continues, saying, "Whites accuse African-Americans of playing the race card whenever whites want to deny that race matters. But if America was conceived on race, and thrives on it, how can it not matter?" What, essentially, is the significance of the "race card" in the Simpson case? First and most important, we have finally recognized that African- and white Americans perceive the justice system in different ways. By complaining about the race card game in the Simpson case, many whites revealed more about themselves than about our system of justice. They showed their complete ingenuousness and/or indifference to the historical injustices suffered by African-Americans. Justice has always meant something different for African-Americans. Charles Grodin, responding to a panel of legal commentators discussing the Simpson trial on his CNBC late-night television show, asked a very important question: "Could it be that white America had its first black experience?" An adage in the African-American community is that blacks go to court looking for justice and that is what they find—"just us." For these African-Americans, the race card means being trumped by a system in which the deck is too often stacked against them.

The literature on sentencing reveals that race, an extralegal factor, usually transcends legal factors (e.g., the seriousness of the offense and prior criminal history) when judges sentence offenders in criminal cases.[3] Statistics substantiate these claims, and here the race card means that the color of one's skin will determine the likelihood of being arrested, convicted, and incarcerated in the criminal justice system. Too often we hear the horror stories of African-American males, who are harassed by police because they merely appeared "suspicious" in a given situation. Similar to the problems posed by one's race is the influence of social economic status. In our system of justice, the poor and powerless are usually treated unjustly. Thus, race and social economic status are reliable predictors of sentence outcomes. Studies reveal that these two factors have led to significantly more unfavorable consequences for African-Americans than for whites who have committed similar offenses and who have similar criminal histories.[4]

A second issue emerging from the Simpson case are the theoretical implications of the victim-offender dyad. The victim-offender dyad is a concept used to predict the outcome of a sentence based on two criteria—the race of the offender and the race of the victim. In cases where the offender is African-American and the victim is white, the outcome of the sentence is usually the most severe, and the severity of punishment decreases when the offender is white

and the victim is African-American. Historically, our system of justice has always devalued the lives of African-Americans. In the Simpson case, many people raised the question: "If Nicole Simpson Brown and Ron Goldman had been African-Americans, would this case have received so much publicity?" If the dyad accurately predicts the outcome of case dispositions, Simpson certainly should have been convicted and sentenced to die for these murders. Instead, he was acquitted, which turned the predictions from the dyad on its head. Was this a case of race or class discrimination? While some believe Simpson bought his freedom with the legal assistance of the "dream team," others contend that his race preceded his social economic status in every instance of this case. This was clearly evident with the racial tension that loomed across this country before, during, and five years after the trial.

If not a race card game, was this a case of jury nullification? Maybe so, and maybe not. It depends on the eyes of the beholder. A jury nullifies the law when it votes its conscience and is engaged in an act of disrespect toward the law. The acquittal supposedly nullifies the law. In place of the law, it is said that the jury interposes its own moral judgment or political preferences.[5] Most African-Americans were satisfied with the verdict the Simpson jury submitted. They also believed that justice had been served because a predominately white jury would have engaged the race of the victims and the race of the defendant in its decision-making process. To them, this would affect their ability to "do justice," and most believed that Simpson would not be given a fair trial. The African-American community did not feel that the Simpson verdict was a case of jury nullification because African-Americans sitting on juries across this nation regularly convict other African-Americans in criminal cases.

Did the Simpson jurors actually follow Cochran's recommendation and nullify the law by voting their conscience, and did they engage in an act of disrespect of the law? In personal media interviews with some jurors, the jurors denied the charge

that they nullified the law by acquitting Simpson. Most jurors said that their decision to acquit Simpson was based on the prosecution's failure to prove its case. Under the law, they felt that they did what they were expected to do as jurors. Following the Simpson verdict, the media called attention to the public criticisms of the Simpson jurors. Criticisms of the Simpsons jurors were harsher than the criticisms of the King jurors. In the King case, a predominately white jury was perceived as "doing justice," even though a videotape displayed the brutal beating of King by white police officers. Conversely, the Simpson jury, in a complicated case based primarily on DNA evidence, was ridiculed. In some instances, the Simpson jurors were judged as being intellectually incapable of deliberating a case of this magnitude. Most white Americans were outraged over the Simpson verdict. They felt that justice was not served. As a result, they accepted Clark's claim that Cochran used the race card to persuade the jury to acquit Simpson.

The race card game is as old as slavery and the inception of institutional racism, which followed after slavery was abolished. Historically, it was a common practice for all-white juries to convict African-Americans for crimes they did not commit. It was also a common practice for judges to impose sentences upon African-Americans for crimes that did not fit the punishment. More important, the constitutional safeguards of the Fourteenth Amendment, which protects its citizens under the laws of equal protection and the due process clause, have never been fully granted to African-Americans. As Marxist theorists would note, the Simpson trial was significant because it "demystified" the true meaning of the race card. That is, it uncovered a game that white America has played for decades. In retrospect, one might agree with Grodin's verbal description that white Americans had their first "black experience" after they failed to accept the reality that a predominantly African-American jury acquitted Simpson. To them, it appeared that the tables of justice were turning. The greatest fear or threat created by the Simpson deliberation was that black juries could change our system of justice by nullifying laws that in the past, may have only protected the legal interests of white Americans. Was this threat really the reason for the racial tension that escalated across this country during the Simpson trial?

Marxist social theory would agree. This theory argues that the best-off people, in any exploitive society, generally find it intolerable to give up great advantages in order to maximize the situation of those who are worse off. The only way they would do this would be by force. They would hold onto their position of power or the advantage, no matter how unjust the situation.[6] The Simpson verdict and the threat of jury nullification by African-Americans may be the reason white Americans reacted in the manner they did. In a society for which a Marxist analysis holds true, the best-off group will not accept an advance toward equality beyond a certain limit as a voluntary expression of their sense of justice.[7] Therefore, the only persons that should be allowed to play the race card are the best-off. The danger in allowing other groups to participate is that the best-off group may eventually be forced to become the disadvantaged group at some point in the game.

Ethical Considerations and the Morality of the Race Card

Kant's theory of ethical formalism best describes the immorality of the race card. In his theory of justice, he defines morality as a universal law of right and wrong.[8] Morality, according to Kant, arises from the fact that humans, as rational beings, impose laws and guidelines of behavior upon themselves. People, as flesh and spirits combined, are in constant dynamic conflict over base desires and morality; only by appealing to higher reason can they do what is right. Kant's theory is premised on the *categorical imperative,* which states that "man must act only according to the maxim whereby one can at the same time will that is should become a universal law." At all times, one is obliged to behave in a manner one would hope all people would follow.

This is an absolute command. In this respect, Kant would argue that people must do what is right, no matter what the outcomes or consequences. If their actions are good, then the outcome is justified, regardless of whether we agreed or disagreed.

On the opposing side is the *hypothetical imperative*. These are commands that designate certain actions to attain certain ends. The person's behavior or actions are contingent on the desired outcome, regardless of one's duty to do what is right. Proponents of the hypothetical imperative argue that doing what is right, no matter what the outcome, may not always be good. For example, Kant uses the example that if someone asks to be hidden from an attacker in close pursuit and then the attacker asks where the potential victim is hiding, it is immoral to lie about it. This seems wrong to many and serves to dissuade people from seeing the value of ethical formalism. However, according to Kant, lying or not lying is not the determining factor in that scenario or in any other. An individual cannot control consequences—only actions—therefore, one must act in a moral fashion without regard to potential consequences. The *hypothetical imperative* allows a person to rationalize his or her actions for the desired outcome, which according to Kant, is immoral. Was the desired outcome based on greed, inequality, power, or wealth? To avoid chaos, Kant would suggest that pure reason demands that one abides by the moral dictates called for by the *categorical imperative.* Ethical formalism is also termed a *deontological* approach because the important determinants for judging whether an act is moral is not its consequences, but the motive or intent of the actor. It is considered an absolutist system. If something is wrong, such as murder, lying, or in the Simpson case, playing the race card, it is wrong all the time.

The prosecution's claim that Johnny Cochran played the race card in the Simpson trial was a falsehood. Was this truly an act of playing the race card? Or was the prosecution trying to vindicate itself in a last attempt to salvage the case? The American Bar Association would uphold Cochran's actions as his legal re-

sponsibility to provide his client with a zealous defense. Kant's theory of ethical formalism would also accept Cochran's actions as moral and in accordance with the rules of procedural justice. These rules were established by rational persons and morally accepted as a universal law. If the Simpson jurors followed the rules of law, then they did what was right. The desired outcome may not have been what some Americans expected. However, the categorical imperative would dictate that these jurors followed the procedures that were established under the Constitution to protect *all* citizens accused of committing a crime. In hindsight, the question that should now be raised is: Was Cochran the one who really played the race card? The race card game did not begin with Cochran's closing argument. It began after Simpson was charged with the murders of Nicole Brown and Ronald Goldman. The victim-offender dyad theorizes that race automatically becomes an issue when the victim of a crime is white and the offender charged with committing the crime is black. Therefore, in his closing argument, Cochran rightfully used the standard of proof, which in a criminal case is "guilt beyond a reasonable doubt." It was appropriate for him to ask the jury to find Simpson "not guilty" if the jurors had any doubt about Simpson committing these crimes.

Marxist theory proposes that white Americans (or the ruling class) practice a considerable amount of self-deception, especially when it is in their best interest to resist the consequences of losing their position as the "best-off." Marx would say that the capacity for self-deception of an exploitive ruling class is practically infinite.[9] The long-term nonmoral interests of a typical member of such a class often sharply conflict with the moral principles that he or she puts forward without conscious hypocrisy. For example, suppose a decision to speed up the pace of work without installing safety equipment will keep profits up at the cost of hundreds of workers' lives. According to Marx, a typical capitalist will use the hypothetical imperative to make the decision that serves the needs of profit, in spite of an appeal to common principles of justice, even if that appeal is backed by the best arguments in the world. Marx contends that the unresponsiveness of members of an exploitive ruling class to arguments conflicting with their class interests is supported by falsehoods—for example, "What's good for business (or what preserves feudal bonds) is good for everyone." The falsehoods are supported by institutions operating in the interests of the ruling class and promoted by everyone in the social circle.

If the deception or falsehood that Marx describes exists in some societies, and if it displays any of the following properties:

> no social arrangement that is acceptable to the best-off class is acceptable to the worst-off,
>
> the best-off class is a ruling class (i.e., one whose interests are served by the major political and ideological institutions), and
>
> the need for wealth and power typical of the best-off class is much more acute than that typical of the rest of society

then there will be no commitment by the best-off to change what is unjust.[10] In the first property, Marx claims that in any society, from the dissolution of primitive communism to the overthrow of capitalism, there is no social contract that the best-off class and the worst-off classes will acquiesce in, except as a result of defeat in class struggle or as a tactical retreat to preserve long-term advantages. The U.S. Constitution is a social contract that governs our lives from the right to bear arms, freedom of speech, religion, and due process of the law. According to Kant's theory, it can also be described as a universal law of right and wrong. Under the Constitution, any violation of these laws is a violation of one's civil rights. The Constitution is supposed to protect *all* citizens in this country from social injustices, not just the "best-off." Kant's position on universalism supports the argument that white Americans should not will anything upon themselves that which they will not will for all. In other words, if the race card is a game White America tolerates, then the game should be tolerated if it is used by other racial groups. No one should complain when the consequences of playing such a game result in an "advantage shift."

The second Marxist feature emphasizes the idea that the best-off class is a ruling class whose deceptive falsehoods and interests are served by all major institutions. Marx and Engels emphasize two aspects of this rule—the repressive and the ideological. In their view, the official instruments of coercion are employed, in almost all crucial instances of class conflict, in favor of the best-off. For example, best-off groups in the United States use the police, the courts, and the media to protect their interests. In most instances, that which should be universal for all becomes self-serving for a few. In addition to institutions of repression, ideological institutions, in the Marxist view, also help to maintain the special status of the best-off class. For example, in the Middle Ages, the Church taught that submission to the dominant social order was an expression of piety. In nineteenth-century England, according to Marx, as class struggles became more intense, academic economists mostly became "hired prize-fighters" of the bourgeoisie,[11] arguing, for example, that abolishing tariffs on grain would immensely enrich workers and that a ten-hour workday would reduce profits to zero.[12] Marx's present-day American example is his argument that the media and the schools foster anti-black racism because they divide those having common interests against those representing the best-off position.

In the Simpson trial, many African-Americans believed that the prosecution became the "hired prize-fighters" of white Americans. Moreover, in an effort to convince the general public that it was not the prosecution that played the race card, Chris Darden, the *only* African-American, was asked to join the prosecution team. Employing Darden on the prosecution team would dispel any claims of racism or social injustice from the defense team and from members of the African-American community. This, however, did not sit well with most African-Americans, who were not deceived by the prosecution's tactics. To them, the race card game is a mundane practice in our criminal justice system. Many African-Americans, familiar with the process, believed that the game began when Simpson was charged with the murders. Many were angry with Darden because they believed that the prosecution did not ask him to join their team until very late in the process. They also believed that Darden was used as a "pawn" to deceive the general public and to give the appearance of fairness during the trial proceedings.

The media were a major catalyst for the racial tension that evolved in this country from Simpson's arrest to his acquittal. They provided twenty-four-hour news coverage of the trial, which dominated local and cable television networks. During the day, some stations canceled popular programs to stay in competition with other stations for viewers. Late-night talk shows took over where the evening news ended, as they engrossed television audiences in day-to-day debates among lawyers, journalists, and the general public. As the racial tension escalated, so did the polarization of black and white America. It became all too obvious that most white Americans wanted a conviction, while most African-Americans wanted an acquittal. On the day the verdict was announced, millions of Americans watched while Simpson was acquitted. This verdict shocked and outraged many white Americans, who experienced a sense of social injustice that is all too common in the African-American community. Conversely, while white Americans stood in disbelief, many African-Americans cheered. White Americans construed the cheering as a disregard for the lives of the two murder victims. What white Americans failed to understand was that the African-American community was not cheering for this reason. They were cheering because they knew it was the prosecution, not Cochran, who had played the race card game and because, ironically, the strategy had backfired.

The Simpson trial was a victory for African-Americans because they have incessantly been the victims of a criminal justice system that has not treated them fairly. To them, with the Simpson verdict, the system finally worked to the advantage of the group that Marx described as the "worst-off." Prior to the verdict, many whites, with the support of the media, arrogantly displayed their confidence that Simpson would be convicted. Justice for them was not premised on Kant's categorical imperative, where justice in this case is based on an adversarial system. Rather, their sense of justice was premised on the hypothetical imperative described by the victim-offender dyad. However, the rules ironically changed in a game that has always brought them desirable results. To them, Simpson, an African-American charged with murdering two white victims, *should* have been convicted, whether he was guilty or not. If white Americans believe they were victims of social injustice, then they have failed to understand how the race card game has unjustly contributed to the disproportionate numbers of African-American males in criminal justice systems across this country. In essence, what the Simpson verdict did was generate a fear that most white Americans would deny—a fear of losing power. If Cochran *did* play the race card, then white Americans experienced the immorality of this game.

Conclusion

Is the race card unethical? It is not only unethical, it is also immoral. The race card is immoral because it is premised on racism and the desire of those in the "best-off" position to oppress those who are "worst-off." It is unethical because African-Americans have been, and continue to be, victims of social injustices in this country. O. J. Simpson is not poor; however, he was an African-American. This supports the thesis that race, not social economic status, can sometimes determine how one is treated by our criminal justice system. Had Simpson appeared before an all-white jury,[13] he certainly would have been convicted and sentenced to die for the murders of Nicole Brown Simpson and Ronald Goldman. This case was significant for several reasons. First and fore-

most, we finally accepted the fact that African- and white Americans have different perceptions of justice in this country. This issue was never seriously considered until the media explicitly revealed how this case divided black and white Americans. The Simpson trial was also significant because it gave white Americans a sense of what it is like to experience a sense of gross injustice. Had the victims not been white, this case would not have received the heightened media attention that began with the freeway chase and continued to the jury's verdict.

Kant's theory of ethical formalism is meaningful to this case because the categorical imperative postulates a system of justice that has procedural rules to ensure that citizens are given a fair trial. If one does what is just, even if the outcome is not what some believe it should be, then the act is moral. The falsehoods that the prosecutors created, in which they accused Cochran of playing the race card, are best described by Marx. Marx would argue that in less-than-just societies, those who are in the "best-off" position believe that they have no duty to help achieve justice, or even to accept advances in this position, especially when it is to their advantage not to do so.[14] The race card game has always given white Americans the advantage in criminal courts when African-Americans are accused of committing crimes against them. However, it backfired on the prosecution in the Simpson trial. In this case, and as history has shown us, the race of the victim and offender matters. White Americans who opposed the handling of the Simpson trial and the jury verdict did so because they could not accept that justice, according to the procedural rules of justice, was served. What was right or moral became irrelevant because they wanted a conviction. It did not matter whether Simpson did or did not murder his victims.

Notes

1. Conley, 1995.
2. Hardy, 1995.
3. Walker et al., 1996; Chiricos and Waldo, 1995; Bridges et al., 1987; Blumstein,

4. Miethe and Moore, 1985; Petersilia, 1983; Kleck, 1981; Unnever et al., 1980.
5. Fletcher, 1988.
6. Miller, 1992, p. 163.
7. Miller, 1992, p. 164.
8. Pollock, 1994, pp.28–30.
9. Miller, 1992, p. 166.
10. Miller, 1992, p. 160.
11. Miller, 1992, pp.160–161 (cf. Karl Marx, *Capital* (Moscow, n.d.) 1, "Preface to the Second German Edition, p. 25).
12. Miller, 1992 p. 160, (cf. Karl Marx, *Capital* (Moscow, n.d.) 1, p. 25 and chapter 9, section 3.
13. Simpson was eventually found guilty in the civil trial that followed; the jury was predominately white.
14. Miller, 1992; p. 159

Bibliography

Blumstein, Alfred. 1982. "On Racial Disproportionality of United States' Prison Populations." *Journal of Criminal Law and Criminology* 73: 1259–81.

Bridges, George S., Robert D. Crutchfield, and Edith E. Simspon. 1987. "Crime, Social Structure and Criminal Punishment: White and Non-White Rates of Imprisonment." *Social Problems* 34: 345–59.

Chiricos, Theodore G., and Gordon Waldo. 1995. "Race and Imprisonment: A Contextual Assessment of the Evidence." In Darnell Hawkins (Ed.), *Ethnicity, Race, and Crime: Perspectives across Time and Place* (New York: State University of New York Press), 281–305.

Conley, Larry. 1995. "Hypocrisy Underlies the Race Card." *Atlanta Journal Constitution,* August 27.

Fletcher, George. 1988. "A Crime of Self-Defense: Bernard Goetz and the Law on Trial 155." In G. Larry Mays and Peter R. Gregware (Eds.), *Courts and Justice: A Reader* (Prospect Heights, Ill: Waveland Press), 58–167.

Free, Marvin D., Jr. 1996. *African Americans and the Criminal Justice System.* New York, NY: Garland Publishing.

Hagan, John, and Kristin Bumiller. 1983. "Making Sense of Sentencing: A Review and Critique of Sentencing Research." In Alfred Blumstein, Jacqueline Cohen, Susan E. Martin, and Michael H. Tonry (Eds.), *Research on Sentencing: The Search for Reform* (Washington, D.C.: National Academy Press), 1–53.

Hardy, James E. 1995. "The River of De-Nile." *The Advocate,* December 26, p. 43.

Kleck, Gary. 1981. "Racial Discrimination in Criminal Sentencing: A Critical Evaluation of the Evidence with Additional Evidence on the Death Penalty." *American Sociological Review* 46: 783–805.

Kemp, Kimberly L., and Roy L. Austin. 1986. "Older and More Recent Evidence on Racial Discrimination in Sentencing." *Journal of Quantitative Criminology* 2: 29–48.

Miethe, Terance D., and Charles A. Moore. 1985. "Socioeconomic Disparties under Determinate Sentencing Systems: A Comparison of Preguideline and Postguideline Practices in Minnesota." *Criminology*, 23: 337–63.

Miller, Richard 1992. "Rawls and Marxism." In James Sterba (Ed.), *Justice: Alternative Political Perspectives* (Belmont, Calif.: Wadsworth) 158–167.

Myers, Martha A., and Susette Talarico. 1986. "The Social Contexts of Racial Discrimination in Sentencing." *Social Problems* 33: 236–51.

Petersilia, Joan. 1983. *Racial Disparities in the Criminal Justice System.* Santa Monica, Calif.: Rand Corporation.

Pollock, Joycelyn M. 1994. *Ethics in Crime and Justice: Dilemmas and Decisions.* Belmont, Calif.: Wadsworth.

Unnever, James D., Charles Frazier, and John C. Henretta. 1980. "Race Differences in Criminal Sentencing." *Sociological Quarterly* 21: 197–207.

Walker, Samuel, Cassia Spohn, and Mirian Delone. 1996. *The Color of Justice: Race, Ethnicity and Crime in America.* Belmont, Calif.: Wadsworth.

 Article Review Form at end of book.

WiseGuide Wrap-Up

- The present jury system discriminates against blacks and their participation as jurors.

- The *Whren* decision may allow law enforcement agents to use traffic codes to abuse Fourth Amendment rights.

- Sentencing guidelines and mandatory minimum statutes are not effective in the reduction of racial disparity in sentencing in federal courts.

R.E.A.L. Sites

This list provides a print preview of typical **Coursewise** R.E.A.L. sites. (There are over 100 such sites at the **Courselinks**™ site.) The danger in printing URLs is that web sites can change overnight. As we went to press, these sites were functional using the URLs provided. If you come across one that isn't, please let us know via email to: webmaster@coursewise.com. Use your Passport to access the most current list of R.E.A.L. sites at the **Courselinks** site.

Site name: U.S. Supreme Court Multimedia Database
URL: http://oyez.nwu.edu/
Why is it R.E.A.L.? This site allows you to search for contemporary and historical Supreme Court cases. In addition, it offers a virtual tour of the U.S. Supreme Court building and a complete listing of the Supreme Court justices. This site should be of particular interest to the individual studying race and crime, since it includes cases that have had an impact on racism in the United States.
Key topics: courts, law, cases, justices, race, crime
Try this: Look for a Supreme Court case that has involved the issue of race.

Site name: United States Sentencing Commission
URL: http://www.ussc.gov/
Why is it R.E.A.L.? This site contains information on today's sentencing practices. It contains federal sentencing statistics and online documents pertaining to various aspects of sentencing practices (i.e., federal sentencing guidelines). This is particularly relevant, since some of these sentencing practices target individuals who belong to certain minority groups.
Key topics: courts, sentencing guidelines, federal sentencing, U.S. Sentencing Commission, State Sentencing Commission
Try this: What is the function of the U.S. Sentencing Commission?

Site name: The Sentencing Project
URL: http://www.sentencingproject.org/
Why is it R.E.A.L.? This site is designed to provide resources and information for those concerned with criminal justice and sentencing issues (including punitive sentencing practices against members of minority groups). It also includes news and information about the National Association of Sentencing Advocates (NASA) and the Campaign for an Effective Crime Policy.
Key topics: courts, sentencing, crime, race, program evaluation, public opinion
Try this: Discuss the effectiveness of deterrence. Assess the crack cocaine sentencing policy.

section 5

Incapacitation: A Color and Class Perspective

 **WiseGuide Intro**

The rich get richer, the poor get prison . . . .
—Jeffrey Reiman

In this section, we present a variety of viewpoints, but the intent is to sensitize you to the realities of sentencing and incapacitation through a race and class perspective.

The sentencing rate for African Americans is the highest in the United States. The evidence comes from almost any examination of the data. Other evidence can be found in the conduct of judges in our nation's courts. Related manifestations of unequal justice can be seen in the sentencing of blacks for crimes against whites, relative to white crimes against blacks.

Some argue that racial disparities stem from higher rates of offending among black people in American society. One inference is that the apparent rates of sentencing may actually be the result of violent crimes committed by black Americans. There are, however, other possibilities, stemming from economic or race-based discrimination. Blacks and the poor are more likely to be detained and are more likely to have been assigned a public defender. And, while public defenders or assigned counsel do not completely disadvantage minority offenders, one might assume that these individuals are mediators—with primary allegiance to the criminal justice bureaucracy and not the offender who is "here today and gone tomorrow." Another concern with regard to the overrepresentation of blacks in prison stems from judicial bias, grounded in stereotypes of black offenders as prone to violence, without marketable skills, and unresponsive to rehabilitation.

On the issue of capital punishment, current statistics suggest that blacks are overrepresented on death row. This phenomenon serves as evidence of racial disparity with regard to blacks accused of capital crimes. The reason for this could be that African Americans are committing a significant number of crimes, resulting in the death penalty. On the other hand, critics respond by maintaining that racial disparity is not the same as racial discrimination. Even in the absence of racial disparity, the question of racial discrimination remains.

There is a large body of literature, for example, illustrating that blacks are more likely to be sentenced to death for crimes against whites than they are for crimes against people of color. This raises questions about prosecutorial discretion. The empirical research reveals a double standard; specifically, blacks are more likely to be charged with capital crimes for offenses against whites. Also, jurors, most of them white, may be more likely to identify with the white victim and to be horrified by the act of aggression directed toward whites by African Americans. It appears that U.S. Supreme Court decisions (e.g., *Gregg v. Georgia*) have not adequately dealt with the misapplication of capital punishment, as it remains arbitrary in application.

Learning Objectives

After studying this section, you will know

- that whites commit most of the violent crimes.

- that the increase of African Americans under correctional supervision is due to the sharp rise of drug-related convictions.

- that the subculture of a Texas prison had a major influence in the life of John William "Bill" King, a white man convicted recently in Texas for dragging a black man to death.

- that the increased enforcement of drug laws has substantially changed the composition of prison populations.

In the early 1990s, The Sentencing Project established empirically what many African Americans already believed to be true—specifically, that one out of four black men between the ages of twenty and twenty-nine is under the correctional umbrella. In other words, one-fourth of the black men in this age cohort are in jail, prison, or some type of community supervision. More recently, The Sentencing Project (1995) released data regarding this finding, showing that the numbers have actually increased. Today, for example, one in three young black men in the age group twenty to twenty-nine is under criminal justice supervision—prison, jail, probation, or parole. This is at an annual cost of over $6 billion. In fact, numbers released by The Sentencing Project reveal that African American women have seen the single largest percentage increase of all demographic groups. It is apparent that the "war on drugs" is one of the biggest reasons for the increased incarceration rates of black women and men. The arrest data show that African Americans and Hispanics constitute 90 percent of all drug offenders sentenced to state prison, despite self-report studies showing that drug use among whites is actually higher. There are several concerns; the punitive penal policy does not portend well for black Americans, or for the African American community. It is speculated that society could easily lose a generation of young blacks through the draconian penal policy, which places imprisonment ahead of education. One of many startling findings from The Sentencing Project is that black men in prison outnumber black men in institutions of higher education.

We are hopeful that you will benefit from this section and think in terms of correctional and societal policy initiatives that will bode well for all involved. Perhaps we can stop the cycle of failure that has been too characteristic of the criminal justice system.

? Questions ?

Reading 21. Compare and contrast the background characteristics of black, white, and Hispanic male federal prison inmates.

Reading 22. Why is it that a third of African American men in their twenties are either incarcerated, on parole, or on probation?

Reading 23. Describe the Aryan Brotherhood of Texas, emphasizing its role in the prison system.

Reading 24. Discuss the effect of the war on drugs on African Americans.

Compare and contrast the background characteristics of black, white, and Hispanic male federal prison inmates.

Differences in the Background and Criminal Justice Characteristics of Young Black, White, and Hispanic Male Federal Prison Inmates

Kevin L. Jackson

Kevin L. Jackson is employed as a Social Science Research Analyst with the Federal Bureau of Prisons in the Office of Research and Evaluation. He is also a magna cum laude graduate of the University of the District of Columbia (UDC) and holds a Master's degree in Urban Policy from UDC.

Research reviews reveal two dominant explanations of race as a factor in disparate imprisonment rates and treatment in the criminal justice system: (a) disparate imprisonment rates are the result of race making a difference and (b) Blacks (people of color) commit not only more crime but also more serious crimes than other groups. In most instances, the hypothesis that race is a significant factor in the existing disproportionate imprisonment rates was either suggested or undeniably supported (Blalock, 1967; Chambliss, 1964;

Christianson, 1981; Davis, 1980; Duster, 1987; Huizinga and Elliot, 1987; Jacobs & Britt, 1979; Joe, 1987; McIntyre, 1993; Quinney, 1980; Welsing, 1991).

However, researchers have argued (Blumstein, 1982; Langan, 1985; Petersilia & Turner, 1988) that the racial disparity in the prison population is due to the seriousness of crimes committed and the offender's prior criminal history, thereby eliminating race as a causal factor and further suggesting that a relationship exists between crime and incarceration rates. But studies that have examined crime and incarceration rates found no significant relationship between a state's crime rate and the percentage of nonwhites in the population, or between its crime rate and incarceration rate (Garofalo, 1979; Nagel, 1977). Instead, these studies found a very strong positive correlation between the racial composition and incarceration rates of states that was too strong to be accounted for by

indirect relationships, like the types of crimes committed.

By simply considering the sums, race can easily be identified as a contributor to the imprisonment rates of Black Americans and particularly young Black Americans. Blacks currently make up 12% of the population of the United States, but 36% of the Federal Prison population. From July 1988 to July 1994, the number of Black federal prison inmates between 18 and 25 years old increased from 1,496 to 6,820 (355%); Hispanics increased from 1,584 to 2,881 (82%); and Whites increased from 1,588 to 2,656 (67%) (Federal Bureau of Prisons, 1994). Although each group experienced a considerable increase in the number of young federal prisoners, the increase for blacks was comparably much higher. Clearly, differences do exist, but in what regard are these offenders different?

This article will provide profiles (descriptive information) of Black, White and Hispanic male inmates

Kevin L. Jackson, *Journal of Black Studies*, Vol. 27, No. 4, March 1997, pp. 494–509. Copyright © 1997 by Sage Publications, Inc. Reprinted by permission of Sage Publications, Inc.

aged 18 to 25 years old housed in the federal correctional system through a reanalysis of the information secured from five areas, as reported in the 1991 Survey of Inmates of Federal Correctional Facilities (SIFCF; Federal Bureau of Prisons (BOP) & U.S. Bureau of the Census). The areas were examined and grouped into two major categories: (a) background and (b) criminal justice characteristics. Socioeconomic, personal, and drug and alcohol use areas were used to determine the background characteristics category. Probation and incarceration history, current sentence and offense, and prison infraction and work assignment areas were used to determine the criminal justice characteristics category.

Prior profiles of inmates focussed primarily on Black and White male offenders housed in state facilities. Black and White inmates were found to be significantly different in terms of personal characteristics, drug use, and probation and incarceration history (French, 1977; Goetting and Howsen, 1983). Other studies found, regardless of race, that inmates have much in common in terms of personality, intellect, behavior, and adjustment to prison; that is, prison rule infractions (Oldroyd & Howell, 1977; White, 1980).

Information about Hispanics was scant. The few studies that did compare Black, White, and Hispanic offenders to ascertain which group received harsher sentences than the other(s) found that when Hispanics and Blacks were the majority of the total population of an area, they experienced similar mistreatment in the criminal justice system with regard to convictions and sentencing (Holmes & Daudistel, 1984; Welch, Gruhl, & Spoon, 1984).

Methods

The subjects of this study were three groups of sentenced federal prison inmates, aged 18 to 25 years old: 274 non-Hispanic Black males, 114 non-Hispanic White males, and 175 Hispanic males. All of these individuals had been randomly selected by statistical sampling from a list of all sentenced inmates in Federal facilities to be voluntarily interviewed for the 1991 SIFCF.

The Bureau of Census, through agreement with BOP, collected and processed the survey data used for the original study. The Bureau of Census also furnished guidelines, including statistical methods, for selecting a stratified random sample of inmates. The BOP, via the methods provided by the Bureau of Census, systematically selected sentenced inmates from each sample prison with expected release dates that were not earlier than the sampling day.

Many items were clustered to make the analyses more efficient. The offense type for which the inmates received the longest sentence was grouped into either a violent (murder, armed robbery, aggravated assault, and weapons offenses) or nonviolent (drug trafficking, possession, and use) category. Work assignments or duties were designed as either skilled or unskilled. Janitorial duties, grounds or maintenance, food preparation, and laundry comprise the unskilled category. UNICOR jobs (prison industries system), repair or construction, and other services (library, stockroom, store, office help, recreation, barber, or beauty shop) comprise the skilled category.

The two statistical techniques used for data analysis were chi-square and analysis of variance (ANOVA). The chi-square test was used to analyze nominal and some ordinal level data. Group means were used in two-way ANOVA procedures, where data were at least interval, to compare the effects of selected variables on the population groups.

Results

Five tables summarize various items for each inmate group from the five areas that were used to provide the profiles for this study. The variables presented in each table are grouped based on the F and χ^2 values produced from the statistical analyses. Narrative, describing the statistically significant results, is provided for each table, followed by profiles for each inmate group in the two major categories for this study.

Background Characteristics

The three inmate groups differed on several items in the area of back-ground (personal and socioeconomic) characteristics as indicated in Table 1. More than half of the Hispanics (58.29%) and Whites (66.67%) had full-time employment before being incarcerated, whereas just more than one-third of the Blacks (37.59%) were employed on a full-time basis. Only 12% of the Hispanics reported that at least some of their annual income came from illegal sources, compared to 25.55% for Blacks and 28.07% for Whites. Another important difference among the inmates involves with whom they lived when growing up. The majority of the White (50.88%) and Hispanic (56.57%) inmates had lived with both parents, but the majority of the Black inmates had lived with just one parent, their mother (48.91%): $\chi^2(2, n = 274$ Blacks; 114 Whites; 175 Hispanics$) = 17.23$, $p < .01$.

Table 2 shows that the White group reported having used drugs (heroin, ice, speed, crack, cocaine, LSD, and marijuana) and alcohol much more extensively than the Black and Hispanic groups, and Table 3 shows that the median annual incomes among the groups also differed. The median annual income of the Black inmates ($6,750) was half that of Whites ($13,500). The median annual income for the Hispanic group ($8,750) was lower than the White group but still higher than that of the Black group. Further, the analysis of variance indicated a significant racial effect: $F(2,470) = 9.57$, $p < .001$. The years of formal schooling (education levels) among the inmates yielded significant differences (see Table 3). The education levels of Black and White inmates were generally the same (means of 11.45 and 11.46, respectively), whereas the mean education level for the Hispanic group was much lower (9.98).

Criminal Justice Characteristics

In the area of probation and incarceration history, several differences were found (see Table 4). The White inmate group ranked first with regard to probation experience (42.98%); the Black group ranked second (31.02%); the Hispanic group ranked third (20.00%). Also in Table 4, significant

Table 1 Chi-Square Results of Background Characteristics of Black, White, and Hispanic Inmates

	Black (n = 274)		White (n = 114)		Hispanic (n = 175)			
Variable	f	%	f	%	f	%	χ^2	df
Had employment	103	37.59	76	66.67	102	58.29	33.48**	2
Some illegal income	70	25.55	32	28.07	21	12.00	14.72**	2
Supported someone	143	52.19	43	37.72	108	61.71	17.44**	4
Married	26	9.49	16	14.04	53	30.29	33.75*	2
Never married	234	85.40	84	73.68	104	59.43	38.50*	2
Lived with								
Mother	134	48.91	38	33.33	54	30.86	17.23*	2
Father	9	3.28	9	7.89	7	4.00	4.15	2
Both parents	87	31.75	58	50.88	99	56.57	30.10*	2
Have children	171	62.41	35	30.70	95	54.29	33.91*	4

*$p < .01$. **$p < .001$.

Table 2 Chi-Square Results of Drug and Alcohol Use Variables for Black, White, and Hispanic Inmates

	Black (n = 274)		White (n = 114)		Hispanic (n = 175)			
Variable	f	%	f	%	f	%	χ^2	df
Drug use								
Heroin	4	1.46	16	14.03	11	6.29	24.85**	2
Ice	5	1.82	26	22.81	6	3.43	61.99**	2
Speed	10	3.65	25	21.93	9	5.14	40.11**	2
Crack	22	8.03	15	13.16	9	5.14	6.03*	2
Cocaine	46	16.79	57	50.00	55	31.43	45.61**	2
LSD	5	1.82	39	34.21	6	3.43	114.29**	2
Marijuana	159	58.03	86	75.44	86	49.14	22.22**	4
Alcohol use	164	59.84	93	81.58	119	68.00	17.93**	6

*$p < .05$. **$p < .01$.

differences were found regarding firearms owned by inmates. The percentage of Whites (63.16%) indicating that they owned firearms prior to incarceration was twice as high as the corresponding figure for Blacks (31.75%) and three times as high as that for Hispanics (20.00%); $\chi^2(2, n = 274$ Blacks; 114 Whites; 175 Hispanics) = 58.66, $p < .01$. Only 12% of the Hispanics reported previous incarcerations as juveniles or adults for crimes other than minor offenses, compared to Blacks (28.83%) and Whites (21.05%).

Although the Hispanic group had noticeably fewer guilty violations and minor offenses (i.e., convictions, sentences, and time served for drunkenness, vagrancy, disorderly conduct, or loitering), the majority of the White and Black inmate groups also reported that they were not found guilty of breaking prison rules (Blacks, 58.76%; White, 65.79%; Hispanic, 78.29%) and had not been convicted, sentenced, or served time for minor offenses (Blacks, 84.67%, White, 74.56%; Hispanics, 90.86%). These findings were expected due to the age and first time offender status of the subjects.

Table 5 shows the White group reported a mean of 3.14 for the number of times they were arrested as juveniles or adults. The corresponding figure for Blacks was 2.56 and 1.61 for Hispanics. The analysis of variance indicated a significant racial effect, $F(2, 550) = 5.02, p < .01$.

White inmates also reported more frequent ownership of firearms. The mean number of firearms owned by White inmates (8.00) was more than twice the mean for Black (3.54) and Hispanic (3.81) inmates.

Profile of Background Characteristics for Black, White and Hispanic Male Federal Prison Inmates

Black inmates are more likely to have:

1. Lived with their mother when growing up
2. Supported others
3. Children and siblings
4. Never been married
5. Completed high school
6. Low incomes
7. At least some of their annual income come from illegal sources
8. Not been employed full-time.

White inmates are more likely to have:

1. Been employed full-time
2. High incomes
3. Completed high school
4. Never been married
5. Lived with both parents when growing up
6. At least some of their annual income come from illegal sources
7. Been users of drugs and alcohol

Table 3 Analysis of Variance Results of Background Characteristics of Black, White, and Hispanic Inmates

	Race of Inmate							
	Black (n = 274)		White (n = 114)		Hispanic (n = 175)			
Variable	X̄	Mdn	X̄	Mdn	X̄	Mdn	F Value	df
Number of children	2.02	2	1.43	1	1.56	1	5.90*	(2,298)
Annual income		6,750		13,500		8,750	9.57**	(2,470)
Number of siblings	4.80		3.30		5.50		15.85**	(2,556)
Highest grade attended	11.45	12	11.46	12	9.98	10.5	27.05**	(2,558)
Mode	12		12		12			

*$p < .01$. **$p < .001$.

Table 4 Chi-Square Results of Criminal Justice Characteristics of Black, White, and Hispanic Inmates

	Race of Inmate							
	Black (n = 274)		White (n = 114)		Hispanic (n = 175)			
Variable	f	%	f	%	f	%	χ²	df
Offense								
Violent	34	12.41	43	37.72	20	11.43	51.67***	2
Nonviolent	205	74.82	42	36.84	138	78.86	65.27***	2
Firearm ownership	87	31.75	72	63.16	35	20.00	58.66**	2
No minor offenses	232	84.67	85	74.56	159	90.86	14.04**	2
Previous incarceration	79	28.83	24	21.05	21	12.00	16.86**	2
Probation experience	85	31.02	49	42.98	35	20.00	23.51***	4
No guilty violations	161	58.76	75	65.79	137	78.29	18.22**	2
Work duties								
Unskilled	110	40.15	34	29.82	75	42.86	5.41	2
Skilled	123	44.90	69	60.53	85	48.57	7.92*	2

*$p < 0.5$. **$p < .01$. ***$p < .001$.

Hispanic inmates are more likely to have:

1. Been employed full-time
2. Been married
3. Lived with both parents when growing up
4. Not completed high school
5. Low incomes
6. Children and siblings
7. Supported others

Profile of Criminal Justice Characteristics for Black, White and Hispanic Male Federal Prison Inmates

Black inmates are more likely to have:

1. Been incarcerated for a nonviolent crime
2. Been found guilty of breaking prison rules

3. Unskilled work assignments
4. Been previously incarcerated

White inmates are more likely to have:

1. Been arrested several times
2. More probation experience
3. Owned more firearms
4. Been incarcerated for a violent crime
5. Skilled work assignments
6. Been found guilty of breaking prison rules

Hispanic inmates are more likely to have:

1. Been incarcerated for a nonviolent crime
2. Not been previously incarcerated
3. Unskilled work assignments
4. Not been found guilty of breaking prison rules

Discussion

The prominent differences among these groups were found in the area of background (personal and socio-economic) characteristics. The lower incomes, less frequent full-time employment, and more frequent reports of illegal sources of income for the Black group was consistent with recent studies on socioeconomic status and contact with the criminal justice system (Duster, 1987; Joe, 1987; Simons & Gray, 1989). These studies concluded that economic inequalities (e.g., lack of employment opportunities, lower incomes, and less wealth) cause this Black youth to view crime and the underground economy as a means of economic survival.

The most potent areas of difference between Blacks and Hispanics were found in the personal characteristics and probation and incarceration histories of the inmates. Specifically, Blacks and Hispanics were different with respect to education levels, previous incarcerations, marital status, and guilty violations. These findings suggest that race may not be the only factor determining the effects on these groups, particularly the Hispanic group.

Analysis of Variance Results of Criminal Justice Characteristics of Black, White, and Hispanic Inmates

	Black (n = 274)		White (n = 114)		Hispanic (n = 175)			
Variable	X	Mdn	X	Mdn	X	Mdn	F Value	df
Current (max1)	9.53	8	8.16	6	7.08	5.5	2.43	(2,211)
Sentence (max2)	15.49	10	15.00	11.5	10.62	10	1.13	(2,740)
Number of firearms owned	3.54	1	8.00	3	3.81	1	5.94**	(2,179)
Juvenile probations	1.19	1	1.55	1	1.24	1	3.69*	(3,141)
Adult probations	1.30	1	1.50	1	1.47	1	.77	(2,161)
Times arrested	2.56	1	3.14	1	1.61	0	5.02**	(2,550)
Age at first arrest	17.10	17	16.55	17	17.70	18	3.41*	(2,355)

$^*p < .05.$ $^{**}p < .01.$

Considering these findings in regard to previous studies, Wilson (1987) suggested that changes in the population age structure and migration flow of Hispanics could possibly cause increasing rates of social problems for this group (e.g., joblessness, crime, out-of-wedlock births, teenage pregnancy, family dissolution, and welfare dependency). Accordingly, Wilson's perspective suggests that as the population for this group grows (and it eventually becomes the largest U.S. minority group), Hispanics are likely to encounter similar experiences as Blacks.

Accordingly, the results of the present study clearly show similarities between these minority groups. Blacks and Hispanics were depended on by others, had more siblings, had lower incomes, and had more of their own children than did Whites. These similar personal characteristics between Black and Hispanic inmates accentuate the economic stress under which both the groups have subsisted.

However, the generally disadvantaged economic conditions of Blacks cannot be explained via education, for the Black group was as educated as the White group. The lower education levels reported by the Hispanic group corroborates findings in another much earlier study that found Hispanics to have completed fewer years of school than Black and White inmates (Oldroyd & Howell, 1977).

The present study also found the White group was arrested more often than the Black and Hispanic groups, which, in turn, suggests that the White group was involved more often in some type of criminal behavior. Further, the White group (37.72%) committed more violent offenses (murder, armed robbery, aggravated assault, and weapons offense) than Black (12.41%) and Hispanic (11.43%) inmates. Nonviolent crimes (drug trafficking and possession or use) were committed predominantly by the Black (74.82%) and Hispanic (78.86%) groups. Moreover, whereas imprisonment was more often the punishment for the Black group for prior offenses (as adults or juveniles), probation was more often the punishment for the White group.

Reasons for the differences in offense types and punishments for offenses among the inmates probably can be traced to the collective opinion of the general public and ultimately to federal drug sentencing policies. If the general public views Blacks—and Hispanics—as being more frequently involved in drug (or criminal) activity, then the law that addresses this issue will target these activities, as well as Blacks and Hispanics, according to Durkheimian theories. These theories hypothesize that laws target unacceptable behaviors and those who participate in the behaviors, based on the general public's perceptions. Thus laws are guided by the collective opinion of the general public (Besnard, 1983).

Prior research findings and the findings of the present study suggest that the views of the general public, which guide the law, are biased toward Blacks—and Hispanics. Studies have found race to be a major issue in mandatory minimum sentencing for drug offenses, contributing to more Blacks and Hispanics being convicted of drug crimes and to longer sentences for these groups (McDonald & Carlson, 1993; Schwarzer, 1992). Other research has shown that a Black person in the United States was found to be four times as likely as a White person to be arrested on drug charges (Meddis, 1993).

Drug and alcohol use findings in the present study were in accordance with prior research in this area but clearly do not fit the general public's perceptions. Whites were found to use drugs and alcohol at a greater rate than Blacks and Hispanics (Wallace & Bachman, 1991). Although drug use among high school students was found to be on the rise, Black students reported the lowest rates of use for virtually all drugs, licit or illicit, in a study by the University of Michigan with the National Institute on Drug Abuse (Bosarge, 1994).

The most obvious similarity between the Black and Hispanic inmate groups are their large samples, that is, disproportionate imprisonment rates in relation to their proportions in the general population. The differential involvement hypothesis states that the disproportionate imprisonment rates stem from differential rates of delinquency involvement. This hypothesis is not supported by the findings in this study. However, the White inmate group, whose imprisonment rate is not at all disproportionate, committed the majority of the serious violent crimes in the study presented here. In addition, studies that found support for the differential hypothesis (Blumstein, 1982; Langan, 1985) noted that the less serious the crime (e.g., drugs and burglary), the greater the amount of disproportionality that must be explained on grounds other than arrests, like race.

No significant differences were found for the maximum sentence lengths among the inmate groups. The sentencing items in the SIFCF were divided into two mutually exclusive categories: inmates who committed only one offense (max1) and inmates who committed more than one offense (max2). To complement the offense data for this study, only the longest sentence received was analyzed for inmates who committed more than one offense.

Conclusions

For 18 out of the 37 analyses conducted (49%), significant differences among Black, White, and Hispanic prisoners become evident. This set of findings suggests that these prisoners differ from one another in terms of background (personal and socioeconomic) characteristics, probation and incarceration history, offense types, and firearm ownership. Significantly fewer Hispanics were previously incarcerated, most Blacks grew up in a one-parent household, and Whites committed a majority of the violent crimes.

For 14 of the 37 analyses conducted (38%), significant differences between nonwhite (Black and Hispanic) and White inmates become evident. This suggests that Black and Hispanic inmates are similar in terms of background characteristics (e.g., income levels and number of children and siblings), drug and alcohol use, offense type, crime characteristics, and work assignments. There were also several areas in which Blacks and Hispanics differed—education levels, marital status, and probation and incarceration histories.

The differences found among the inmates suggest that other secondary causes are possibly operating: socioeconomics, language barriers, the socialization process, child rearing practices, family structure, and values. But no matter how it is discerned, race, or more specifically, the racial perceptions of the general public and discrimination in the criminal justice system, is a major factor in the different outcomes found among the inmate groups in such areas as offense type, employment status, probation experience, arrest history, and drug and alcohol use. Also, the idea that differential incarceration rates stem directly from differential rates of delinquency involvement was rejected by this research effort. To obtain a more in-depth analysis of the key factors contributing to the differences and similarities among the groups, especially the effects of race, future research should include more rigorous statistical tests. Use of different age groups (e.g., 26–33 or 34–41 years old) could help to determine if, as they age, the Black inmates become more violent, and the White inmates become less violent. This study found the White group to be more violent than the Black group. Also, similar studies on female federal prison inmates is essential, as the number of female offenders continues to rise.

It is important to note that the overrepresentation of Black and Hispanic males in the federal prison system may be the result of discrimination at various stages in the judicial process. Ultimately, research is necessary to understand all of the contributing factors that may be operating, as well as their comparative importance, and to discover policies and programs that will effectively reduce incarceration rates, particularly for Blacks. This problem should rise to the top of our national agenda when the public realizes that the constantly expanding number of incarcerated youth is a distinct sign of present social dysfunctions and probable future social turmoil.

References

Besnard, P. (1983). *The sociological domain: The Durkheimians and the founding of sociology.* New York: Cambridge University Press.

Blalock, H. (1967). *Toward a theory of minority group relations.* New York: Capricorn.

Blumstein, A. (1982). On the racial disproportionality of United States' prison populations. *Journal of Criminal Law and Criminology, 73,* 1259–1281.

Bosarge, B. (1994, February 7). Teen drug use increasing. *Crime Control Digest,* p. 3.

Chambliss, W. J. (1964). A sociological analysis of the law of vagrancy. *Social Problems, 12,* 67–77.

Christianson, S. (1981). Our Black prisons. *Crime and Delinquency, 27,* 364–375.

Davis, D. B. (1980). The crime of reform [Review of the book *Conscience and convenience: The asylum and its alternatives in progressive America*]. *New York Review of Books, 27,* 14.

Duster, T. (1987). Crime, youth unemployment, and the Black urban underclass. *Crime and Delinquency, 33,* 300–316.

Federal Bureau of Prisons (BOP). (1994). *Key indicators/strategic support system* [CD-ROM]. Washington, DC: Office of Research and Evaluation (Producer and Distributor).

Federal Bureau of Prisons (BOP) & Bureau of the Census. (1991). *The survey of inmates of federal correctional facilities study* [Survey Data File]. Washington, DC: Federal Bureau of Prisons, Office of Research and Evaluation (Producer and Distributor).

French, W. (1977). An assessment of the Black female prisoner in the South. *Journal of Women in Culture and society, 3,* 483–488.

Garofalo, J. (1979, March). *Social structure and rates of imprisonment: A research note.* Paper presented at the annual meeting of the Academy of Criminal Justice Sciences, Cincinnati, OH.

Goetting, A., & Howsen, R. (1983). Blacks in prison. *Criminal Justice Review, 8,* 21–31.

Holmes, M. D., & Daudistel, H. C. (1984). Ethnicity and justice in the Southwest: The sentencing of Anglo, Black, and Mexican origin defendants. *Social Science Quarterly, 64,* 265–277.

Huizinga, D., & Elliot, D. S. (1987). Juvenile offenders: Prevalence, offender incidence, and arrest rates by race. *Crime and Delinquency, 33,* 206–223.

Jacobs, D., & Britt, D. (1979). Inequality and police use of deadly force: An empirical assessment of a conflict hypothesis. *Social Problems, 26,* 403–412.

Joe, T. (1987). Economic inequality: The picture in black and white. *Crime and Delinquency, 33,* 287–299.

Langan, P. (1985). Racism on trial: New evidence to explain the racial composition of prisons in the United States. *The Journal of Criminal Law and Criminology, 76,* 666–683.

McDonald, D., & Carlson, K. (1993). *Sentencing in the Federal Courts: Does race matter? The transition to sentencing guidelines, 1986–1990.* Washington, DC: U.S. Department of Justice, Office of Justice Programs, Bureau of Justice Statistics.

McIntyre, C.C.L. (1993). *Criminalizing a race: Free Blacks during slavery.* New York: Kayode.

Meddis, S. V. (1993, July 23–25). Is the drug war racist? *USA Today,* pp. 1A–2A.

Nagel, W. G. (1977). On behalf of a moratorium on prison construction. *Crime and Delinquency, 23,* 154–172.

Oldroyd, R. J., & Howell, R. J. (1977). Personality, intellectual, and behavioral differences between Black, Chicano, and White prison inmates in the Utah state prison. *Psychology Reports, 41,* 187–191.

Petersilia, J., & Turner, S. (1988, June). Minorities in prison, discrimination or disparity? *Corrections Today,* pp. 92–94.

Quinney, R. (1980). *Class, state & crime* (2nd ed.). New York: Longman.

Schwarzer, W. W. (1992). Sentencing guidelines and mandatory minimums: Mixing apples and oranges. *Southern California Law Review, 66,* 405–411.

Simons, R. L., & Gray, P. (1989). Perceived blocked opportunity as an explanation of delinquency among lower-class Black males: A research note. *Journal of Research in Crime and Delinquency, 26,* 90–101.

Wallace, J. M., & Bachman, J. G. (1991). Explaining racial/ethnic differences in adolescent drug use: The impact of background and lifestyle. *Social Problems, 38,* 333–354.

Welch, S., Gruhl, J., & Spohn, C. (1984). Dismissal, conviction, and incarceration of Hispanic defendants: A comparison with Anglos and Blacks. *Social Science Quarterly, 65,* 257–264.

Welsing, F. C. (1991). *The Isis papers, the keys to the colors.* Chicago: Third World Press.

White, R. B. (1980). Prediction of adjustment to prisons in a federal correctional population. *Journal of Clinical Psychology, 36,* 1031–1034.

Wilson, W. J. (1987). *The truly disadvantaged: The inner city, the underclass, and public policy.* Chicago: University of Chicago Press.

Article Review Form at end of book.

Why is it that a third of African American men in their twenties are either incarcerated, on parole, or on probation?

A Shocking Look at Blacks and Crime

Are a third of young black men criminals?

Ted Gest

While the trial of O. J. Simpson attracted international attention to the fate of African-Americans in the U.S. judicial system, an even more compelling revelation appeared last week with considerably less fanfare. The Sentencing Project, a Washington-based group that advocates rehabilitation of convicts, reported that nearly 1 in 3 black men in their 20s in America is behind bars or elsewhere in the justice system—up from 25 percent five years ago.

The reality for young blacks may be even worse than the statistics suggest. The report includes only the small fraction of lawbreakers who end up in court, and its focus on men obscures an even more disturbing increase in female convicts. While six times as many black men as women are behind bars or on probation or parole, the percentage of African-American women enmeshed in the legal system nearly doubled in the last five years.

The reaction to the study resembles the racial split in attitudes about Simpson's acquittal. Many whites say the statistics merely reflect that fact that a disproportionate number of criminals are young black men. Many blacks say the numbers are the product of a legal system that is tilted against them in ways ranging from overt racism among police officers and judges to sentencing rules that—intentionally or not—penalize members of minority groups much harder than whites.

Superficially, both views have some merit. More than 60 percent of those arrested for robbery are blacks, for example, although African-Americans account for only 12 percent of the population. This discrepancy is difficult to attribute simply to bias among racist detectives such as Mark Fuhrman. On the other hand, laws like the federal statute that penalizes possession of crack cocaine 100 times more stringently than possession of more-expensive powder cocaine make it appear that blacks are much more dominant in the nation's drug culture than they are.

New research is shattering some stereotypes about race and the drug trafficking that accounts for so many arrests. Conventional wisdom holds that the street-crime plague is almost wholly confined to unemployed inner-city youth. But many working-class blacks are being swept up in the intensified war on drugs, say criminologists James Lynch of American University and William Sabol of the Urban Institute, who have studied enforcement patterns. Discrimination also plays a part. Housing segregation remains so prevalent, says Lynch, that "blacks can move only so far away from pockets of poverty" that tend to be targeted by police.

Unequal Justice?

In 1989, 23 percent of young black males were in prison, in jail, on probation or on parole. Six years later, the proportion has climbed to 32.2 percent.

Black males, ages 20–29, who are in the nation's criminal justice system.

	Number	Share of population
1989	609,690	23.0%
1994	787,692	30.22%

USN&WR: Basic data: The Sentencing Project

Out of Options

Most blacks ensnared in narcotics cases are not hard-core dealers. Two-thirds or more of the participants in drug-sales rings "also work straight jobs and would like to settle down with their families in homes with white picket fences," says criminologist John Hagedorn of the University of Wisconsin at Milwaukee, who has conducted lengthy interviews with Milwaukee gang members over two decades. Many part-time dealers "know that they are poisoning the community and believe it is morally wrong but don't feel that they have an option," he says.

Liberal reformers charge that the rush to imprison street criminals

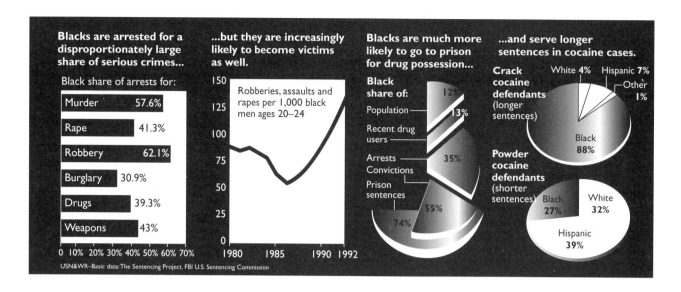

Blacks are arrested for a disproportionately large share of serious crimes...

Black share of arrests for:

Murder	57.6%
Rape	41.3%
Robbery	62.1%
Burglary	30.9%
Drugs	39.3%
Weapons	43%

0 10% 20% 30% 40% 50% 60% 70%

...but they are increasingly likely to become victims as well.

Robberies, assaults and rapes per 1,000 black men ages 20–24

150 125 100 75 50 25 0

1980   1985   1990 1992

USN&WR–Basic data: The Sentencing Project. FBI U.S. Sentencing Commission

Blacks are much more likely to go to prison for drug possession...

Black share of:
Population — 12%
Recent drug users — 13%
Arrests — 35%
Convictions
Prison sentences — 55%
74%

...and serve longer sentences in cocaine cases.

Crack cocaine defendants (longer sentences)
White 4% Hispanic 7%
Other 1%
Black 88%

Powder cocaine defendants (shorter sentences)
Black 27% White 32%
Hispanic 39%

for longer terms is gobbling up resources that should be used to expand drug treatment. That rallying cry resonates among those who work on the front lines with troubled young blacks. The Fortune Society in New York City, which aids 1,500 former convicts each year, needs corporate largess to help it offer education and drug treatment behind prison walls that government doesn't provide. College courses in prison "gave me the self-esteem and motivation to succeed," says Stanley Richards, an ex-convict who now heads Fortune's career programs. He says Congress made the problem worse when it recently denied inmates Pell grants to help finance their educations.

Unfair Penalties?

The Pell cutback is one symbol of the ebbing sympathy in Washington and many states for black lawbreakers. Another is the fight over federal cocaine sentences. The five-year mandatory prison term for possessing 5 grams of crack cocaine (compared with 500 grams of the powder variety) seemed justifiable in 1986 during the crack epidemic that consumed many cities. Many analysts now say the crack penalty is too harsh, especially since blacks account for 88 percent of those charged.

The U.S. Sentencing Commission last spring recommended equalizing the penalties, but the Senate voted in late September to block the plan. The House is moving in the same direction. Last week, Attorney General Janet Reno agreed that the 100-to-1 ratio is unwarranted, but she called for further study. Neither political party wants to act for fear of appearing soft on crime, charges Eric Sterling of the Criminal Justice Policy Foundation, who says that "the issue is being passed along from Congress to the executive branch and back like an empty crack pipe."

The new report on blacks and crime will provoke lots of hand-wringing but probably little constructive action in the corridors of government, where funds are scarce and conservatives dispute the need to choose between prisons and social programs. "It's a false dichotomy," says John Walters, an acting federal "drug czar" in the Bush administration. He says that strong law enforcement and treatment are compatible but "too much money is wasted on inefficient drug treatment" while underlying problems like poor urban schools are ignored. Policy makers of many ideologies could agree on that. But don't expect bold solutions in the coming year of partisan politicking.

Article Review Form at end of book.

Describe the Aryan Brotherhood of Texas, emphasizing its role in the prison system.

Into the Heart of Darkness

A Texas prison's racist subculture spawned the grisly murder in Jasper.

Joseph L. Galloway

With Bruce Selcraig in Austin

A stern-faced jury wasted no time last week deciding that 24-year-old John William "Bill" King should die by lethal injection for his part in the gruesome dragging death of James Byrd Jr., a disabled black man. The swift, certain justice brought a measure of comfort to the quiet east Texas logging town. But even as the last TV lights were turned off, residents were left wondering how their fellow citizen could have become such a monster. King was convicted (two co-defendants, Shawn Berry, 24, and Lawrence Brewer, 31, still face trial) of capital murder in a crime so horrific—chaining Byrd by his ankles to a pickup truck and dragging him 3 miles down a dark country road until his body was literally torn apart—that it repulsed a nation inured to violence. It also raised, once again, the question of what could have bred so much hatred.

At least part of the answer lay buried in the trial's testimony. In the first days, jurors recoiled in horror when they were shown photographs of Byrd's dismembered body. That same day, they seemed almost as stunned by photos of the bizarre tattoos on King's arms and torso: Satanic symbols, Nazi icons, and the silhouette of a black man hanging from a tree. The images combined to paint a grim picture of a ghastly prison subculture—one that morphed during the course of the

trial into something like an unindicted co-conspirator in the case.

Family and friends say King, 5 foot 7 and 140 pounds, was pleasant and quiet—an ordinary guy right up till the moment the prison doors closed on him in 1995 as he began serving an eight-year sentence for burglary. It was another Bill King who emerged two years later, friends say, spouting white supremacist rhetoric, sporting those tattoos, hell-bent on setting up his own racist gang. King's defense lawyer, C. Haden "Sonny" Cribbs, said King was assaulted by black inmates within hours of being transferred into Texas's Beto I Unit, a prison known for its brutality. Though King denied it to him, Cribbs says, he believes his client was raped. Soon after, King turned to a racist white gang for protection. "Our system caused [Bill King's] problem," said defense attorney Brack Jones Jr. Jurors rejected that excuse.

But there's no gainsaying the fact that prison often wreaks profound changes on inmates—very often for the worse. Prisons are toughest on the young nonviolent criminals clapped behind bars under a raft of new laws. In two decades, from 1977 to 1997, the number of inmates in America's prisons soared from 300,024 to 1,244,554. (The number of inmates in Texas ballooned from 22,439 to 140,729 over the same period.)

Waiting for the new arrivals are violent gangs that some experts say have more to do with running the

prisons today than wardens and guards. Within a matter of days, if not hours, an unofficial prison welcome wagon sorts new arrivals into those who will fight, those who will pay extortion cash of up to $60 every two weeks, and those who will be servants or slaves. "You're jumped on by two or three prisoners to see if you'll fight," says a mother from suburban Houston whose son is serving time on cocaine and marijuana charges and recently joined a racist white gang. "If you don't fight, you become someone's girl, until they're tired of you and they sell you to someone else."

The Texas prison system has been under supervision by U.S. District Judge William Wayne Justice since 1980, when he held that the system was unconstitutional for the cruelty it inflicted on inmates. The judge recently concluded a series of hearings and is expected to rule soon on a request to return control of the prisons to the state. A parade of young white male inmates testified that federal control may have done little good: All said they had been beaten, raped, and sold from gang to gang. The state responded that violence in its prisons is a third of the national average.

Texas prison gangs break down along racial lines: white, black, and Hispanic. It was to a small offshoot white supremacist gang calling itself the Confederate Knights of America that King turned for protection after his visit from the Beto welcome wagon. King's lawyer Cribbs says he thinks the Knights probably never had more than 14 members. "It sounds like some wannabes," he says, "who couldn't cut it."

What King wanted to be was a member of the Aryan Brotherhood of Texas, the largest and most violent of the white supremacist gangs in Texas prisons. Some 300 Texas prisoners have been identified as full members of ABT. Dozens of others claim affiliation, but ABT is selective. "I had an ABT recruiter tell me they were not at all pleased that Bill King had claimed membership," says Larry Fitzgerald, spokesman for the Texas Department of Criminal Justice. The King case led prison officials to clamp down on gang members.

In prison, King acquired his ABT-style tatoos and talked with gang members about forming an offshoot. When investigators searched King's apartment, they found hand-written outlines, bylaws, and recruiting letters for what he called the Confederate Knights of America's Texas Rebel Soldiers. He referred to himself and his followers as "a relative handful of Aryans dedicated to fighting on behalf of a world that often fears and hates us."

King took one more thing away from prison with him: an oath sworn by ABT and the other white supremacist gangs that says "blood in, blood out." This is a requirement that you kill or wound someone to get in and a threat that your own blood will be spilled if you ever try to quit. There was testimony at trial that King invoked this code before he and his friends went looking for Byrd, beat him, tied a chain around his legs, and revved up their pickup. Could this be the inevitable outcome of a savage stay in prison? "We all have this need for retribution," says Michael Marcum, a former inmate and prison reform expert with the San Francisco sheriff's department. "But draconian laws do not serve society. They simply create monsters."

The Jasper jurors decided otherwise. Clearly, something went terribly wrong in King's head and heart. But one midnight a few years from now, a technician will strap him to a gurney on death row down in Huntsville. Then he'll drip a fatal dose of drugs into King's veins, and he'll be gone. And we still won't know for sure why King did the terrible thing he did back in Jasper.

 Article Review Form at end of book.

Discuss the effect of the war on drugs on African Americans.

Racial Politics, Racial Disparities, and the War on Crime

Michael Tonry

When discussing the nature and extent of crime in the United States, the emphasis tends to be on Part I offenses (index crimes). In any given year, however, arrests for these crimes comprise only about 20 percent of all arrests; 80 percent of arrests are for Part II offenses. Arrests for Part II offenses largely reflect proactive enforcement efforts in that many of them are first detected by the police rather than being reported to them by citizens; the offenses that are rigorously enforced can vary widely over time and jurisdiction.

Of the Part II offenses, drug abuse violations represents the largest single category, with about 10% of all arrestees in 1996. The "public order" or "victimless" crimes such as drug abuse violations and prostitution are offenses about which the public is ambivalent. Some argue that legally defining such behaviors as crime reflects the government's attempt to legislate morality (see also reading 41). Further, some argue that "overcriminalization" is a problem in our society, that is, we live in a society in which too many types of behaviors are considered criminal. Such behaviors that perhaps should not be defined as criminal, including drug abuse, can have an important impact on the criminal justice system when the enforcement of laws is vigorous.

Such has been true of drugs in the 1980s and 1990s. Although drug laws have been on the books since 1914, social factors have had a tremendous impact on

the increased enforcement of these laws and the resulting rising number of arrests. As Michael Tonry demonstrates in this selection, increased enforcement of drug laws has significantly changed the composition of prison populations. The "War on Drugs" has resulted in increased racial disproportionality in prison populations, due primarily to more rigorous law enforcement and sentencing practices related to drug abuse. Further, these enforcement efforts have resulted in huge increases in the overall prison population (see also reading 40). Central to Tonry's argument is the discussion that the war on drugs is ineffective and disproportionately affects African Americans, both factors that were known about before this policy was pursued.

Racial disparities in arrests, jailing, and imprisonment steadily worsened after 1980 for reasons that have little to do with changes in crime patterns and almost everything to do with two political developments. First, conservative Republicans in national elections "played the race card" by using anticrime slogans (remember Willie Horton?) as a way to appeal to anti-Black sentiments of White voters. Second, conservative politicians of both parties promoted and voted for harsh crime control and drug policies that exacerbated existing racial disparities.

The worsened disparities might have been ethically defensible if they had been based on good faith beliefs that some greater policy good would

thereby have been achieved. Sometimes unwanted side effects of social policy are inevitable. Traffic accidents and fatalities are a price we pay for the convenience of automobiles. Occupational injuries are a price we pay for engaging in the industries in which they occur.

The principal causes of worse racial disparities have been the War on Drugs launched by the Bush and Reagan administrations, characterized by vast increases in arrests and imprisonment of street-level drug dealers, and the continuing movement toward harsher penalties. Policies toward drug offenders are a primary cause of recent increases in jail and prison admissions and populations. Racial disparities among drug offenders are worse than among other offenders. . . .

Crime Reduction Effects of Crime Control Policy

There is no basis for a claim that recent harsh crime control policies or the enforcement strategies of the War on Drugs were based on good faith beliefs that they would achieve their ostensible purposes. In this and other countries, practitioners and scholars have long known that manipulation of penalties has few, if any, effects on crime rates.

Commissions and expert advisory bodies have been commissioned by the federal government repeatedly over the last 30 years to survey

Michael Tonry, *Crime and Delinquency*, Vol. 40, 1994, pp. 363–385. Copyright © 1994 by Sage Publications, Inc. Reprinted by permission of Sage Publications, Inc.

knowledge of the effects of crime control policies, and consistently they have concluded that there is little reason to believe that harsher penalties significantly enhance public safety. In 1967, the President's Commission on Law Enforcement and Administration of Justice observed that crime control efforts can have little effect on crime rates without much larger efforts being directed at crime's underlying social and economic causes. "The Commission . . . has no doubt whatever that the most significant action that can be taken against crime is action designed to eliminate slums and ghettos, to improve education, to provide jobs. . . . We shall not have dealt effectively with crime until we have alleviated the conditions that stimulate it."

In 1978, the National Academy of Sciences Panel on Research on Deterrent and Incapacitative Effects, funded by President Ford's department of justice and asked to examine the available evidence on the crime-reductive effects of sanctions, concluded: "In summary, we cannot assert that the evidence warrants an affirmative conclusion regarding deterrence" (Blumstein, Cohen, and Nagin 1978). Fifteen years later, the National Academy of Sciences Panel on the Understanding and Control of Violent Behavior, created and paid for with funds from the Reagan and Bush administration departments of justice, surveyed knowledge of the effects of harsher penalties on violent crime (Reiss and Roth 1993). A rhetorical question and answer in the panel's final report says it all: "What effect has increasing the prison population had on violent crime? Apparently very little. . . . If tripling the average length of sentence of incarceration per crime [between 1976 and 1989] had a strong preventive effect," reasoned the panel, "then violent crime rates should have declined" (p. 7). They had not.

I mention that the two National Academy of Sciences panels were created and supported by national Republican administrations to demonstrate that skepticism about the crime-preventive effects of harsher punishments is not a fantasy of liberal Democrats. Anyone who has spent much time talking with judges or corrections officials knows that most,

whatever their political affiliations, do not believe that harsher penalties significantly enhance public safety.

Likewise, outside the United States, conservative governments in other English-speaking countries have repudiated claims that harsher penalties significantly improve public safety. . . .

. . . In Brian Mulroney's Canada, the Committee on Justice and the Solicitor General (in American terms, the judiciary committee) proposed in 1993 that Canada shift from an American-style crime control system to a European-style preventive approach. In arguing for the shift in emphasis, the committee observed that "the United States affords a glaring example of the limited effect that criminal justice responses may have on crime. . . . If locking up those who violate the law contributed to safer societies then the United States should be the safest country in the world" (Standing Committee on Justice and the Solicitor General 1993). . . .

There is no better evidentiary base to justify recent drug control policies. . . . There was no reasonable basis for believing recent policies would achieve their ostensible goals. In drug policy jargon, the United States has adopted a prohibitionistic rather than a harm-reduction strategy and has emphasized supply-side over demand-side tactics (Wilson 1990). This strategic choice implies a preference for legal threats and moral denunciation of drug use and users instead of a preference for minimizing net costs and social harms to the general public, the law enforcement system, and drug users. The tactical choice is between a law enforcement emphasis on arrest and punishment of dealers, distributors, and importers, interdiction, and source-country programs or a prevention emphasis on drug treatment, drug-abuse education in schools, and mass media programs aimed at public education. The supply-side bias in recent American policies was exemplified throughout the Bush administration by its insistence that 70% of federal antidrug funds be devoted to law enforcement and only 30 percent to treatment and education (Office of National Drug Control Policy 1990).

It has been a long time since most researchers and practitioners

believed that current knowledge justifies recent American drug control policies. Because the potential income from drug dealing means that willing aspirants are nearly always available to replace arrested street-level dealers, large-scale arrests have repeatedly been shown to have little or no effect on the volume of drug trafficking or on the retail prices of drugs (e.g., Chaiken 1988; Sviridoff, Sadd, Curtis, and Grine 1992). Because the United States has long and porous borders, and because an unachievably large proportion of attempted smuggling would have to be stopped to affect drug prices significantly, interdiction has repeatedly been shown to have little or no effect on volume or prices (Reuter 1988). Because cocaine, heroin, and marijuana can be grown in many parts of the world in which government controls are weak and peasant farmers' incentives are strong, source-country programs have seldom been shown to have significant influence on drug availability or price in the United States (Moore 1990).

The evidence in support of demand-side strategies is far stronger. In December 1993, the President's Commission on Model State Drug Laws, appointed by President Bush, categorically concluded, "Treatment works." That conclusion is echoed by more authoritative surveys of drug treatment evaluations by the U.S. General Accounting Office (1990), the National Institute of Medicine (Gerstein and Jarwood 1990), and in *Crime and Justice* by Anglin and Hser (1990). Because drug use and offending tend to coincide in the lives of drug-using offenders, the most effective and cost effective way to deal with such offenders is to get and keep them in well-run treatment programs.

A sizable literature now also documents the effectiveness of school-based drug education in reducing drug experimentation and use among young people (e.g., Botvin 1990; Ellickson and Bell 1990). Although there is no credible literature that documents the effects of mass media campaigns on drug use, a judge could take judicial notice of their ubiquity. It is not unreasonable to believe that such campaigns have influenced across-the-board declines in drug use in the United States since 1980 (a date, incidentally, that precedes the launch of the War on Drugs by nearly 8 years).

That the preceding summary of our knowledge of the effectiveness of drug control methods is balanced and accurate is shown by the support it receives from leading conservative scholars. Senator-scholar Daniel Patrick Moynihan (1993) has written, "Interdiction and 'drug busts' are probably necessary symbolic acts, but nothing more." James Q. Wilson (1990), for two decades America's leading conservative crime control scholar, observed that "significant reductions in drug abuse will come only from reducing demand for those drugs. . . . The marginal product of further investment in supply reduction is likely to be small" (p. 534). He reports that "I know of no serious law-enforcement official who disagrees with this conclusion. Typically, police officials tell interviewers that they are fighting either a losing war or, at best, a holding action" (p. 534).

Thus a fair-minded survey of existing knowledge provides no grounds for believing that the War on Drugs or the harsh policies exemplified by "three strikes and you're out" laws and evidenced by a tripling in America's prison population since 1980 could achieve their ostensible purposes. . . .

Racial Disparities in Arrests, Jail, and Prison

Racial disparities, especially affecting Blacks, have long bedeviled the criminal justice system. Many hundreds of studies of disparities have been conducted and there is now widespread agreement among researchers about causes. Racial bias and stereotyping no doubt play some role, but they are not the major cause. In the longer term, disparities in jail and prison populations are mainly the result of racial differences in offending patterns. In the shorter term, the worsening disparities since 1980 are not primarily the result of racial differences in offending but were foreseeable effects of the War on Drugs and the movement toward increased use of incarceration. . . .

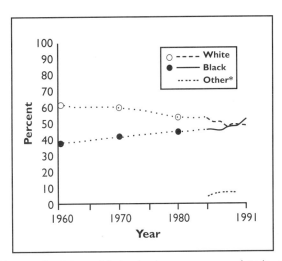

Figure 9.1. Prisoners in state and federal prisons on census date by race, 1961–1991.

Sources: For 1960, 1970, 1980; Cahalan 1986, table 3.31; for 1985–1991: Bureau of Justice Statistics 1993, 1991a 1991b, 1989a, 1989b, 1987.

* = Hispanics in many states, Asians, Native Americans

Figure 9.1, showing the percentages of prison inmates who were Black or White from 1960 to 1991, reveals two trends. First, for as long as prison population data have been compiled, the percentage of inmates who are black has by several times exceeded the percentage of Americans who are Black (10% to 13% during the relevant period). Second, since 1980 the Black percentage among prisoners has increased sharply.

Racial disproportions among prison inmates are inherently undesirable, and considerable energy has been expended on efforts to understand them. In 1982, Blumstein showed that around 80% of the disproportion could be explained on the basis of racial differences in arrest patterns. Of the unexplained 20%, Blumstein argued, some might represent bias and some might reflect racial differences in criminal history or arguably valid case-processing differences. Some years earlier, Hindelang (1976, 1978) had demonstrated that racial patterns in victims' identifications of their assailants closely resembled racial differences in arrests. Some years later, Langan (1985) skipped over the arrest stage altogether and showed that racial patterns in victims' identifications of their assailants explained about 80% of disparities in prison admissions. In

1990, Klein, Petersilia, and Turner showed that, after criminal history and other legitimate differences between cases were taken into account, the offender's race had no independent predictive effect in California on whether he was sent to prison or for how long. There the matter rests. Blumstein (1993a) updated his analysis and reached similar conclusions (with one important exception that is discussed below).

Although racial crime patterns explain a large part of racial imprisonment patterns, they do not explain why the Black percentage rose so rapidly after 1980. Table 9.1 shows Black and White percentages among people arrested for the eight serious FBI Index Crimes at 3-year intervals from 1976 to 1991 and for 1992. Within narrow bands of fluctuation, racial arrest percentages have been stable since 1976. Comparing 1976 with 1992, for example, Black percentages among people arrested for murder, robbery, and burglary were slightly up and Black percentages among those arrested for rape, aggravated assault, and theft were slightly down. Overall, the percentage among those arrested for violent crimes who were Black fell from 47.5% to 44.8%. Because prison sentences have traditionally been imposed on people convicted of violent crimes, Blumstein's and the other analyses suggest that

Table 9.1 Percentage Black and White Arrests for Index I Offenses 1976–1991 (3-year intervals)[a]

	1976		1979		1982		1985		1988		1991		1992	
	White	Black	White	Black	White	Black	White	Black	White	Black	White	Black	White	Black
Murder and nonnegligent manslaughter	45.0	53.5	49.4	47.7	48.8	49.7	50.1	48.4	45.0	53.5	43.4	54.8	43.5	55.1
Forcible rape	51.2	46.6	50.2	47.7	48.7	49.7	52.2	46.5	52.7	45.8	54.8	43.5	55.5	42.8
Robbery	38.9	59.2	41.0	56.9	38.2	60.7	37.4	61.7	36.3	62.6	37.6	61.1	37.7	60.9
Aggravated assault	56.8	41.0	60.9	37.0	59.8	38.8	58.0	40.4	57.6	40.7	60.0	38.3	59.5	38.8
Burglary	69.0	29.2	69.5	28.7	67.0	31.7	69.7	28.9	67.0	31.3	68.8	29.3	67.8	30.4
Larceny-theft	65.7	32.1	67.2	30.2	64.7	33.4	67.2	30.6	65.6	32.2	66.6	30.9	66.2	31.4
Motor vehicle theft	71.1	26.2	70.0	27.2	66.9	31.4	65.8	32.4	58.7	39.5	58.5	39.3	58.4	39.4
Arson	—	—	78.9	19.2	74.0	24.7	75.7	22.8	73.5	25.0	76.7	21.5	76.4	21.9
Violent crime[b]	50.4	47.5	53.7	44.1	51.9	46.7	51.5	47.1	51.7	46.8	53.6	44.8	53.6	44.8
Property crime[c]	67.0	30.9	68.2	29.4	65.5	32.7	67.7	30.3	65.3	32.6	66.4	31.3	65.8	31.8
Total crime index	64.1	33.8	65.3	32.4	62.7	35.6	64.5	33.7	62.4	35.7	63.2	34.6	62.7	35.2

Sources: *Sourcebook of Criminal Justice Statistics.* Various years. Washington, DC: Department of Justice, Bureau of Justice Statistics; FBI 1993, Table 43.

a. Because of rounding, the percentages may not add to total.

b. Violent crimes are offenses of murder, forcible rape, robbery, and aggravated assault.

c. Property crimes are offenses of burglary, larceny-theft, motor vehicle theft, and arson.

the Black percentage among inmates should be flat or declining. That, however, is not what Figure 9.1 shows. Why not?

Part of the answer can be found in prison admissions. Figure 9.2 shows racial percentages among prison admissions from 1960 to 1992. Arrests of Blacks for violent crimes may not have increased since 1980, but the percentage of Blacks among those sent to prison has increased starkly, reaching 54% in 1991 and 1992. Why? The main explanation concerns the War on Drugs.

Table 9.2 shows racial percentages among persons arrested for drug crimes between 1976 and 1992. Blacks today make up about 13% of the U.S. population and, according to National Institute on Drug Abuse (1991) surveys of Americans' drug use, are no more likely than Whites ever to have used most drugs of abuse. Nonetheless, the percentages of Blacks among drug arrestees were in the low 20% range in the late 1970s, climbing to around 30% in the early 1980s and peaking at 42% in 1989. The number of drug arrests of Blacks more than doubled between 1985 and 1989, whereas White drug arrests increased only by 27%. Figure

9.3 shows the stark differences in drug arrest trends by race from 1976 to 1991.

Drug control policies are a major cause of worsening racial disparities in prison. In the federal prisons, for example, 22% of new admissions and 25% of the resident population were drug offenders in 1980. By 1990, 42% of new admissions were drug offenders as in 1992 were 58% of the resident population. In state prisons, 5.7% of inmates in 1979 were drug offenders, a figure that by 1991 had climbed to 21.3% to become the single largest category of prisoners (robbers, burglars, and murderers were next at 14.8 percent, 12.4% and 10.6%, respectively) (Beck et al. 1993).

The effect of drug policies can be seen in prison data from a number of states. . . . In Pennsylvania, Clark (1992) reports, Black male prison admissions for drug crimes grew four times faster (up 1,613%) between 1980 and 1990 than did White male admissions (up 477%). In California, according to Zimring and Hawkins (1994), the number of males in prison for drug crimes grew 15 fold between 1980 and 1990 and "there were more people in prison in California for

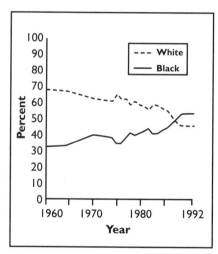

Figure 9.2. Admissions to federal and state prisons by race, 1960–1992.

Sources: Langan 1991; Gilliard 1992; Perkins 1992, 1993; Perkins and Gilliard 1992.

Note: Hispanics are included in Black and White populations.

drug offenses in 1991 than there were for *all* offenses at the end of 1979" (p. 89; emphasis in original).

Why, if Blacks in their lives are no more likely than Whites to use illicit drugs, are Blacks so much more likely to be arrested and imprisoned? One possible answer, which is almost

Table 9.2 U.S. Drug Arrests by Race, 1976–1992

Year	Total Violations	White	White %	Black	Black %
1976	475,209	366,081	77	103,615	22
1977	565,371	434,471	77	122,594	22
1978	592,168	462,728	78	127,277	21
1979	516,142	396,065	77	112,748	22
1980	531,953	401,979	76	125,607	24
1981	584,776	432,556	74	146,858	25
1982	562,390	400,683	71	156,369	28
1983	615,081	423,151	69	185,601	30
1984	560,729	392,904	70	162,979	29
1985	700,009	482,486	69	210,298	30
1986	688,815	463,457	67	219,159	32
1987	809,157	511,278	63	291,177	36
1988	844,300	503,125	60	334,015	40
1989	1,074,345	613,800	57	452,574	42
1990	860,016	503,315	59	349,965	41
1991	763,340	443,596	58	312,997	41
1992	919,561	546,430	59	364,546	40

Sources: FBI 1993, Table 43; *Sourcebook of Criminal Justice Statistics—1978–1992.*
Various tables. Washington, DC: U.S. Department of Justice, Bureau of Justice Statistics.

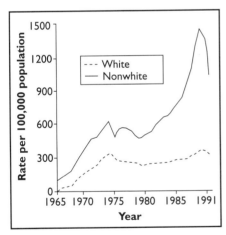

Figure 9.3. Arrest rates for drug offenses by race, 1965–1991.

Source: Blumstein 1993b.

certainly wrong, is that Blacks are proportionately more likely to sell drugs. We have no representative surveys of drug dealers and so cannot with confidence paint demographic pictures. However, there is little reason to suspect that drug crimes are more interracial than are most other crimes. In addition, the

considerations that make arrests of Black dealers relatively easy make arrests of White dealers relatively hard.

Drug arrests are easier to make in socially disorganized inner-city minority areas than in working or middle-class urban or suburban areas for a number of reasons. First, although drug sales in working or middle-class areas are likely to take place indoors and in private spaces where they are difficult to observe, drug sales in poor minority areas are likely to take place outdoors in streets, alleys, or abandoned buildings, or indoors in public places like bars. Second, although working or middle-class drug dealers in stable areas are unlikely to sell drugs to undercover strangers, dealers in disorganized areas have little choice but to sell to strangers and new acquaintances. These differences mean that it is easier for police to make arrests and undercover purchases in urban minority areas than elsewhere. Because arrests are fungible for purposes of both the individual officer's personnel file and the department's year-to-year statistical comparisons, more easy arrests look better than

fewer hard ones. And because, as ethnographic studies of drug trafficking make clear (Fagan 1993; Padilla 1992), arrested drug dealers in disadvantaged urban minority communities are generally replaced within days, there is a nearly inexhaustible potential supply of young minority Americans to be arrested.

There is another reason why the War on Drugs worsened racial disparities in the justice system. Penalties for drug crimes were steadily made harsher since the mid-1980s. In particular, purveyors of crack cocaine, a drug used primarily by poor urban Blacks and Hispanics, are punished far more severely than are purveyors of powder cocaine, a pharmacologically indistinguishable drug used primarily by middle-class Whites. The most notorious disparity occurs under federal law which equates 1 gram of crack with 100 grams of powder. As a result, the average prison sentence served by Black federal prisoners is 40% longer than the average sentence for Whites (McDonald and Carlson 1993). Although the Minnesota Supreme Court and two federal district courts have struck down the 100-to-1 rule as a denial of constitutional equal protection to Blacks, at the time of writing, every federal court of appeals that had considered the question had upheld the provision.

The people who launched the drug wars knew all these things—that the enemy troops would mostly be young minority males, that an emphasis on supply-side antidrug strategies, particularly use of mass arrests, would disproportionately ensnare young minority males, that the 100-to-1 rule would disproportionately affect Blacks, and that there was no valid basis for believing that any of these things would reduce drug availability or prices.

Likewise, as the first section showed, there was no basis for a good faith belief that the harsher crime control policies of recent years—more and longer mandatory minimum sentences, tougher and more rigid sentencing guidelines, and three-strikes-and-you're-out laws—would reduce crime rates, and there was a good basis for predicting that they would disproportionately damage Blacks. If Blacks are more likely than Whites to be arrested, especially for drug crimes, the greater harshness of toughened penalties will disproportionately be borne by Blacks. Because much crime is intraracial, concern for Black victims might justify harsher treatment of Black offenders if there were any reason to believe that harsher penalties would reduce crime rates. Unfortunately, as the conservative national governments of Margaret Thatcher and Brian Mulroney and reports of National Academy of Sciences Panels funded by the administrations of Republican Presidents Ford, Reagan, and Bush all agree, there is no reason to believe that harsher penalties significantly reduce crime rates.

Justifying the Unjustifiable

There is no valid policy justification for the harsh drug and crime control policies of the Reagan and Bush administrations, and for their adverse differential effect on Blacks. The justification, such as it is, is entirely political. Crime is an emotional subject

and visceral appeals by politicians to people's fears and resentments are difficult to counter.

It is easy to seize the low ground in political debates about crime policy. When one candidate campaigns with pictures of clanging prison gates and grief-stricken relatives of a rape or murder victim, and with disingenuous promises that newer, tougher policies will work, it is difficult for an opponent to explain that crime is a complicated problem, that real solutions must be long term, and that simplistic toughness does not reduce crime rates. This is why, as a result, candidates often compete to establish which is tougher in his views about crime. It is also why less conservative candidates often try to preempt their more conservative opponents by adopting a tough stance early in the campaign. Finally, it is why political pundits congratulate President Clinton on his acumen in proposing federal crime legislation as or more harsh than his opponents. . . .

Conservative Republican politicians have, since the late 1960s, used welfare, especially Aid to Families with Dependent Children, and crime as symbolic issues to appeal to anti-Black sentiments and resentments of White voters, as Thomas and Mary Edsall's *Chain Reaction: The Impact of Race, Rights, and Taxes on American Politics* (1991) makes clear. The Edsalls provide a history, since the mid-1960s, of "a conservative politics that had the effect of polarizing the electorate along racial lines." Anyone who observed Ronald Reagan's portrayal in several campaigns of Linda Evans, a Black Chicago woman, as the "welfare queen" or George Bush's use of Black murderer Willie Horton to caricature Michael Dukakis's criminal justice policies knows of what the Edsalls write. . . .

Public discourse about criminal justice issues has been debased by the cynicism that made Willie Horton a major participant in the 1988 presidential election. That cynicism has made it difficult to discuss or develop sensible public policies, and that cynicism explains why conservative politicians have been able year after year successfully to propose

ever harsher penalties and crime control and drug policies that no informed person believes can achieve their ostensible goals.

Three final points, arguments that apologists for current policies sometimes make, warrant mention. First, it is sometimes said to be unfair to blame national Republican administrations for the failures and disparate impacts of recent crime control policies. This ignores the efforts of the Reagan and Bush administrations to encourage and, through federal mandates and funding restrictions, to coerce states to follow the federal lead. Attorney General William Barr (e.g., 1992) made the most aggressive efforts to compel state adoption of tougher criminal justice policies, and the Bush administration's final proposed crime bills restricted eligibility for federal funds to states that, like the federal government, abolished parole release and adopted sentencing standards no less severe than those in the federal sentencing guidelines. In any case, as the Edsalls' book makes clear, the use of crime control issues (among others including welfare reform and affirmative action) to elicit anti-Black sentiments from White voters has long been a stratagem of both state and federal Republican politicians.

Second, sometimes it is argued that political leaders have merely followed the public will; voters are outraged by crime and want tougher policies (Dilulio 1991). This is a half-truth that gets the causal order backwards. Various measures of public sentiment, including both representative surveys like Gallup and Harris polls and work with focus groups, have for many years consistently shown that the public is of two minds about crime (Roberts 1992). First, people are frustrated and want offenders to be punished. Second, people believe that social adversity, poverty, and a troubled home life are the principal causes of crime, and they believe government should work to rehabilitate offenders. A number of surveys have found that respondents who would oppose a tax increase to pay for more prisons would support a tax increase to pay for rehabilitative programs. These findings of voter ambivalence about crime should not be surprising. Most people have complicated views about complicated problems. For example, most judges and corrections officials have the same ambivalent feelings about offenders that the general public has. Conservative politicians have seized upon public support of punishment and ignored public support of rehabilitation and public recognition that crime presents complex, not easy, challenges. By presenting crime control issues only in emotional, stereotyped ways, conservative politicians have raised its salience as a political issue but made it impossible for their opponents to respond other than in the same stereotyped ways.

Third, sometimes it is argued that disparate impacts on Black offenders are no problem and that, because much crime is intraracial, failure to adopt tough policies would disserve the interests of Black victims. As former Attorney General Barr (1992) put it, perhaps in ill-chosen words, "the benefits of increased incarceration would be enjoyed disproportionately by Black Americans" (p. 17). This argument also is based on a half-truth. No one wants to live in unsafe neighborhoods or to be victimized by crime, and in a crisis, people who need help will seek it from the police, the public agency of last resort. Requesting help in a crisis and supporting harsh policies with racially disparate effects are not the same thing. The relevant distinction is between acute and chronic problems. A substantial body of public opinion research (e.g., National Opinion Research Center surveys conducted throughout the 1980s summarized in Wood 1990) shows that Blacks far more than Whites support establishment of more generous social welfare policies, full employment programs, and increased social spending. The congressional Black and Hispanic caucuses have consistently opposed bills calling for tougher sanctions and supported bills calling for increased spending on social programs aimed at improving conditions that cause crime. Thus, in claiming to be concerned about Black victims, conservative politicians are responding to natural human calls for help in a crisis while ignoring evidence that Black citizens would rather have government support efforts to ameliorate the chronic social conditions that cause crime and thereby make calls for help in a crisis less necessary.

The evidence on the effectiveness of recent crime control and drug abuse policies, as the first section demonstrated, cannot justify their racially disparate effects on Blacks, nor, as this section demonstrates, can the claims that such policies merely manifest the peoples' will or respect the interests of Black victims. All that is left is politics of the ugliest kind. The War on Drugs and the set of harsh crime control policies in which it was enmeshed were adopted to achieve political, not policy, objectives, and it is the adoption for political purposes of policies with foreseeable disparate impacts, the use of disadvantaged Black Americans as means to the achievement of White politicians' electoral ends, that must in the end be justified. It cannot.

References

Anglin, M. Douglas and Yih-Ing Hser. 1990. "Treatment of Drug Abuse." In *Drugs and Crime*, edited by M. Tonry and J. Q. Wilson. Chicago: University of Chicago Press.

Austin, James and Aaron David McVey. 1989. *The Impact of the War on Drugs*. San Francisco: National Council on Crime and Delinquency.

Barr, William P. 1992. "The Case for More Incarceration." Washington, DC: U.S. Department of Justice, Office of Policy Development.

Beck, Allen et al. 1993. *Survey of State Prison Inmates, 1991*. Washington, DC: Bureau of Justice Statistics.

Blumstein, Alfred. 1982. "On the Racial Disproportionality of United States' Prison Populations." *Journal of Criminal Law and Criminology*, 73:1259–81.

———. 1993a. "Racial Disporportionality of U.S. Prison Populations Revisited." *University of Colorado Law Review*, 64:743–60.

———. 1993b. "Making Rationality Relevant—The American Society of Criminology 1992 Presidential Address." *Criminology*, 31:1–16.

Blumstein, Alfred, Jacqueline Cohen, and Daniel Nagin. 1978. *Deterrence and Incapacitation*. Report of the National Academy of Sciences Panel on Research on Deterrent and Incapacitation Effects. Washington, DC: National Academy Press.

Botvin, Gilbert J. 1990. "Substance Abuse Prevention: Theory, Practice, and Effectiveness." In *Drugs and Crime*, edited by M. Tonry and J. Q. Wilson. Chicago: University of Chicago Press.

Bureau of Justice Statistics. 1987. *Correctional Populations in the United States, 1985*. Washington, DC: U.S. Department of Justice, Bureau of Justice Statistics.

———. 1989a. *Correctional Populations in the United States, 1987*. Washington, DC: U.S. Department of Justice, Bureau of Justice Statistics.

———. 1989b. *Correctional Populations in the United States, 1986*. Washington, DC: U.S. Department of Justice, Bureau of Justice Statistics.

———. 1991a. *Correctional Populations in the United States, 1989*. Washington, DC: U.S. Department of Justice, Bureau of Justice Statistics.

———. 1991b. *Correctional Populations in the United States, 1988*. Washington, DC: U.S. Department of Justice, Bureau of Justice Statistics.

———. 1993. *Correctional Populations in the United States, 1991*. Washington, DC: U.S. Department of Justice, Bureau of Justice Statistics.

Cahalan, Margaret Wemer. 1986. *Historical Corrections Statistics in the United States, 1850–1984*. Washington, DC: U.S. Department of Justice, Bureau of Justice Statistics.

Canadian Sentencing Commission. 1987. *Sentencing Reform: A Canadian Approach*. Ottawa: Canadian Government Publishing Centre.

Chaiken, Marcia, ed. 1988. *Street Level Enforcement: Examining the Issues*. Washington, DC: U.S. Government Printing Office.

Clark, Stover. 1992. "Pennsylvania Corrections in Context." *Overcrowded Times*, 3:45.

Clarke, Stevens H. 1992. "North Carolina Prisons Growing." *Overcrowded Times* 3:1, 11–13.

Dilulio, John J. 1991. *No Escape: The Future of American Corrections*. New York: Basic Books.

Edsall, Thomas and Mary Edsall. 1991. *Chain Reaction: The Impact of Race, Rights, and Taxes on American Politics*. New York: Norton.

Ellickson, Phyllis L. and Robert M. Bell. 1990. *Prospects for Preventing Drug Use Among Young Adolescents*. Santa Monica, CA: RAND.

Fagan, Jeffrey. 1993. "The Political Economy of Drug Dealing Among Urban Gangs." In *Drugs and the Community*, edited by R. C. Davis, A. J. Lurigio, and D. P. Rosenbaum. Springfield, IL: Charles C. Thomas.

Federal Bureau of Investigation. 1993. *Uniform Crime Reports for the United States—1992*. Washington, DC: U.S. Government Printing Office.

Gerstein, Dean R. and Henrik J. Jarwood, eds. 1990. *Treating Drug Problems*. Report of the Committee for Substance Abuse

Coverage Study, Division of Health Care Services, National Institute of Medicine. Washington, DC: National Academy Press.

Gilliard, Darrell K. 1992. *National Corrections Reporting Program, 1987*. Washington, DC: U.S. Department of Justice, Bureau of Justice Statistics.

Hindelang, Michael. 1976. *Criminal Victimization in Eight American Cities: A Descriptive Analysis of Common Theft and Assault*. Washington, DC: Law Enforcement Assistance Administration.

———. 1978. "Race and Involvement in Common Law Personal Crimes." *American Sociological Review*, 43:93–108.

Home Office. 1990. *Protecting the Public*. London: H. M. Stationery Office.

Klein, Stephen, Joan Petersilia, and Susan Turner. 1990. "Race and Imprisonment Decisions in California." *Science*, 247:812–16.

Langan, Patrick A. 1985. "Racism on Trial: New Evidence to Explain the Racial Composition of Prisons in the United States." *Journal of Criminal Law and Criminology*, 76:666–83.

———. 1991. *Race of Persons Admitted to State and Federal Institutions, 1926–86*. Washington, DC: U.S. Department of Justice, Bureau of Justice Statistics.

McDonald, Douglas and Ken Carlson. 1993. *Sentencing in the Federal Courts: Does Race Matter?* Washington, DC: U.S. Department of Justice, Bureau of Justice Statistics.

Moore, Mark H. 1990. "Supply Reduction and Drug Law Enforcement." In *Drugs and Crime*, edited by M. Tonry and J. Q. Wilson. Chicago: University of Chicago Press.

Moynihan, Daniel Patrick. 1993. "Iatrogenic Government Social Policy and Drug Research." *American Scholar*, 62:351–62.

National Institute on Drug Abuse. 1991. *National Household Survey on Drug Abuse: Population Estimates 1990*. Washington, DC: U.S. Government Printing Office.

Office of National Drug Control Policy. 1990. *National Drug Control Strategy*, January 1990. Washington, DC: Author.

Padilla, Felix. 1992. *The Gang as an American Enterprise*. New Brunswick, NJ: Rutgers University Press.

Perkins, Craig. 1992. *National Corrections Reporting Program, 1989*. Washington, DC: U.S. Department of Justice, Bureau of Justice Statistics.

———. 1993. *National Corrections Reporting Program, 1990*. Washington, DC: U.S. Department of Justice, Bureau of Justice Statistics.

Perkins, Craig and Darrell K. Gilliard. 1992. *National Corrections Reporting Program, 1988*. Washington, DC: U.S. Department of Justice, Bureau of Justice Statistics.

President's Commission on Law Enforcement and Administration of Justice. 1967. *The Challenge of Crime in a Free Society*. Washington, DC: U.S. Government Printing Office.

President's Commission on Model State Drug Laws. 1993. *Final Report*. Washington, DC: U.S. Government Printing Office.

Reiss, Albert J., Jr. and Jeffrey Roth. 1993. *Understanding and Controlling Violence. Report of the National Academy of Sciences Panel on the Understanding and Control of Violence*. Washington, DC: National Academy Press.

Reuter, Peter. 1988. "Can the Borders Be Sealed?" *Public Interest*, 92:51–65.

Roberts, Julian V. 1992. "Public Opinion, Crime, and Criminal Justice." In *Crime and Justice: A Review of Research*, vol. 16, edited by M. Tonry. Chicago: University of Chicago Press.

Sourcebook of Criminal Justice Statistics. 1978–1992. Washington, DC: Department of Justice, Bureau of Justice Statistics.

Standing Committee on Justice and the Solicitor General. 1993. *Crime Prevention in Canada: Toward a National Strategy*. Ottawa: Canada Communication Group.

Sviridoff, Michele, Susan Sadd, Richard Curtis, and Randolph Grine. 1992. *The Neighborhood Effects of Street-Level Drug Enforcement*. New York: Vera Institute of Justice.

Tonry, Michael. 1994. *Malign Neglect: Race, Crime, and Punishment in America*. New York: Oxford University Press.

U.S. General Accounting Office. 1990. *Drug Abuse: Research on Treatment May Not Address Current Needs*. Washington, DC: U.S. General Accounting Office.

Wilson, James Q. 1990. "Drugs and Crime." In *Drugs and Crime*, edited by M. Tonry and J. Q. Wilson. Chicago: University of Chicago Press.

Wood, Floris W. 1990. *An American Profile: Opinions and Behavior 1972–1989*. New York: Gale Research.

Zimring, Franklin E. and Gordon Hawkins. 1994. "The Growth of Imprisonment in California." *British Journal of Criminology* 34:83–95.

 Article Review Form at end of book.

WiseGuide Wrap-Up

- Whites commit most of the violent crimes.

- The increase in African American men under correctional supervision is due mostly to the rise of drug-related convictions.

- The increased enforcement of drug laws has substantially changed the makeup of the prison population.

R.E.A.L. Sites

This list provides a print preview of typical **Coursewise** R.E.A.L. sites. (There are over 100 such sites at the **Courselinks**™ site.) The danger in printing URLs is that web sites can change overnight. As we went to press, these sites were functional using the URLs provided. If you come across one that isn't, please let us know via email to: webmaster@coursewise.com. Use your Passport to access the most current list of R.E.A.L. sites at the **Courselinks** site.

Site name: The American Correctional Association

URL: http://www.corrections.com/aca/

Why is it R.E.A.L.? This site provides information on various aspects of corrections in the United States. It is a good source of information on recent correctional practices, conference and employment information, and services online.

Key topics: corrections, juvenile offenders, violence, management, criminal justice, training

Try this: Discuss the contributions made by the Violent Crime Control and Law Enforcement Act of 1995.

Site name: The American Jail Association

URL: http://www.corrections.com/aja/

Why is it R.E.A.L.? This site contains a wide variety of information on jails. Specifically, it offers information on the practices, organization, and policies of jails in the United States. Of particular interest are the statistics mentioned in this site, as they suggest that minorities are overrepresented in the jail system.

Key topics: corrections, jails, training, prisons, organization, management

Try this: What do the Bureau of Justice Statistics data suggest about the traditional assumptions that form policy issues affecting jails?

Site name: National Criminal Justice Reference Service

URL: http://www.ncjrs.org/corrhome.htm

Why is it R.E.A.L.? This site offers a series of articles that cover numerous aspects of correctional practices in the United States. These range from boot camps to the death penalty. Of special interest are the articles concerning the census of correctional facilities. These include information regarding the overrepresentation of minorities in the correctional system.

Key topics: corrections, capital punishment, boot camps, drug offenders, mental illness, HIV, shock incarceration

Try this: What are the characteristics of prison inmates? Have most incarcerated offenders experienced some type of childhood abuse or neglect?

---

section

6

After studying this section, you will know

- that some convicted death row inmates are being released due to exculpatory evidence discovered after they have been found guilty in a court of law.

- that high school dropouts have the highest homicide risk of all educational groups.

- that there are different levels of concern about crime among blacks, Asians, and whites in certain areas of Great Britain.

- that personal vulnerability is the strongest determining factor of fear of crime among the black elderly.

- that nonwhite males who are urban residents and live in low-income households may not be the most victimized group.

The Face of Victims: A Racial Analysis

WiseGuide Intro

In this section, we discuss and raise issues specific to African Americans as victims. There is a tendency to think that African Americans are primarily predators, but, as will be made clear, the victimization rates for African Americans are high. In fact, victimization studies reveal that, with respect to violent crimes, blacks experience higher rates of victimization than their white counterparts. And, despite the influences of the popular press and newspaper headlines, the real truth is that blacks are more likely to be victims of homicide and robbery. These high rates of victimization also correlate with high rates of offending, and they affirm that most crimes are largely an intraracial phenomenon. One perspective is that whites' fear of blacks may be overexaggerated, given the intraracial nature of most crimes, especially violent crimes.

Another issue worth mentioning surrounds the living conditions of blacks relative to those of whites. It could be that living in high-density, highly heterogeneous neighborhoods also contributes to high rates of victimization. Living in public housing units that do not take into consideration the importance of personal space may contribute to high rates of offending and the resulting high rates of victimization.

In a sense, black Americans are victimized in other ways as well. Black neighborhoods fall victim to high levels of suspicion and police patrols. The net result may be that suspicious behavior by black men and women results in harassment or an arrest that otherwise would not have taken place. In addition, the phrase "black-on-black" crime creates the impression that crime is largely race-specific. As we have made clear elsewhere in this reader, one interpretation is that crime among black people is routine, and the urgency to address this issue is lessened. Crime may be viewed as indigenous to the black community, whereas the recent shootings (and bomb threats) in suburban schools have stimulated interest and calls for action in Washington. The last time black victims saw this type of urgency was in the mid-1960s.

Some evidence suggests that African American youth are at great risk for acts of violence and victimization. In fact, some insurance companies in New York City sell life insurance policies to the parents of African American teenagers. The policies may be used to cover anticipated funeral expenses for African American youth living at risk in our nation's largest cities.

Other areas of victimization can be found, once more, in our sentencing policies, especially the crack cocaine versus powder cocaine dilemma. In this case, blacks are criminalized and victimized for less use of crack cocaine than their white counterparts, who report greater usage of powder cocaine, a deadlier substance. Black Americans, especially black females, have fallen victims to the war on drugs. The use of crack cocaine by African American females has been met primarily with criminal justice sanctions. The intended or unintended effect of concerns about drug use in black communities, some would argue, has actually resulted in more victimization. At a higher level, black academics report varying degrees of exclusion—most books and articles about race and crime are written by white academics. Exclusion of black researchers in major projects related to race and crime results in old paradigms that preserve the status quo. An argument can be made that links the patterns of exclusion to the marginalization of black academics and the continuing victimization of poor people and visible minorities, as few new policy initiatives emerge.

In concluding, we are hopeful that the issues raised here will generate thoughts about the broader issues related to rates of victimization for blacks. The remaining articles in this section range from vignettes about the realities of victimization in America, those wrongly accused by the system, to cogent empirically based articles on the criminal victimization of black Americans. You are encouraged to think critically about many of the points made in each article. It is clear that African American men and women are not only "just" offenders; they are victims as well.

? ? Questions ? ?

Reading 25. Briefly discuss the saga of four jailed Chicago men cleared of murder charges by a professor and three female students.

Reading 26. Discuss the homicide trends in California between 1970 and 1993, emphasizing the homicide risk differentials by ethnicity, sex, and age.

Reading 27. Compare and contrast the different responses to crime given by blacks, Asians,

and whites in a crime survey implemented in Leeds in 1987.

Reading 28. Does the fear of crime among the black elderly affect their lifestyle?

Reading 29. Discuss the validity of the widely held belief that males, high school dropouts, residents of large cities, and people over the age of thirty-five are the most likely to be victimized.

Briefly discuss the saga of four jailed Chicago men cleared of murder charges by a professor and three female students.

Extra Credit

The saga of four jailed Chicago men cleared of murder charges by a crusading professor and three female students made great copy. Far less attention was paid to the question of how the men could have been convicted and why they had to languish in prison for nearly two decades.

Alicia C. Shepard

It's a crisp, spring Chicago morning and a close friend is explaining how to file an income tax extension to Dennis Williams, who at age 40 is paying taxes for the first time. Williams strongly believes he shouldn't have to pay the government a dime after all of the grief and loneliness authorities have inflicted on him. For nearly half of his life Williams lived in a cell the size of a small bathroom, sleeping on a slab of steel, sentenced to die for a crime he didn't commit.

Williams has never married. Never had children. Never held a full time job. Has no pension, no health benefits, no work history to convince potential employers he's worth hiring. No nothing, in his opinion. "They took everything away from me that constitutes the human experience," he says. "If someone offered me a million dollars to become a lawyer, I'd choose to work on a garbage truck instead. That's what I think of our legal system."

A year ago charges were dropped against Williams and three other black men convicted in 1978 of raping and killing a young white woman and murdering her fiancé after a tenacious Northwestern University journalism professor and three of his students finally forced the state to admit it had botched the case. Eager to round up suspects in the highly publicized black-on-white murder, law enforcement authorities had quickly arrested and convicted

the wrong men—even though evidence existed then that four other men may have committed the crime.

On July 2, 1996, Williams, Kenneth Adams, Verneal Jimerson and William Rainge were freed. After 18 years they finally had the opportunity to recoup the lives they'd lost behind bars.

"Seeing the guys walk into the courtroom on the day they were officially released was so exciting," says Stephanie Goldstein, one of the students who helped clear them. "I'd only seen them in little rooms inside of prison. Seeing them walk in with their attorneys and then walk out was thrilling."

So, at first, was all the media attention focused on then-Northwestern seniors Goldstein, Stacey Delo and Laura Sullivan, then 22. It was an irresistible angle. Three young, white, upper-middle-class students venture into a rough Southside Chicago neighborhood to try to unearth evidence that four black men—two of whom were on death row—had not committed the horrific double murder. Stories about the students appeared in *People* magazine, *Glamour,* the *National Enquirer,* the *New York Times,* the *Los Angeles Times.* Oprah Winfrey showcased them on national television.

> "Chasing down the cops takes a lot of work," says WGN anchor Larry Potash. "A news department has to flush out the cops, but they don't necessarily have the resources and the time, particularly in a city like Chicago, where there's so much going on. But, yeah, the media is at fault for not pursuing the cops and prosecutors."

The storyline shifted dramatically when Walt Disney Co. came calling with a million-dollar offer for movie rights. Media attention quickly turned to the petty bickering about who deserved credit for the men's release, who was and who wasn't getting money, and the fact that the professor was no longer speaking to his former students because he felt they shouldn't profit at the men's expense.

But what failed to draw the serious attention of the local and national media, with a few exceptions, was the more important and significant story: How was it that four innocent African Americans could have been wrongly incarcerated for 18 years? Why didn't local detectives investigate a solid tip in 1978 that nearly two decades later led to the four men who actually raped Carol Schmal and shot her and Larry Lionberg in the head?

It's another example of how journalists sometimes focus their attention on the sexy, easy-to-report story while ignoring far more significant issues. It took little effort to zero in on the three students and their professor and to portray them as heroes, then shift to the bitterness that followed when money entered the picture. Examining the more

Reprinted by permission of *American Journalism Review.*

complex and painstaking question of how something like this could have happened would have proven far more difficult.

"I don't fault reporters for educating the public on how these guys got out of prison," Goldstein says. "But no one took the story to the next level, which is really looking into what happened and why they spent so long in prison."

The professor, David Protess, 50, agrees. "I find it very tragic that the energy devoted to this case has been to focus on the media's definition of newsworthy, the students and movie deals," he says, "instead of the larger story: How could the authorities have done this? Where were the reporters on this story and many other stories where they could have played the kind of role that we played?"

WGN anchor Larry Potash, who has reported sporadically on the case, says there are just too many crime stories in Chicago and not enough time. "Chasing down the cops takes a lot of work," he says. "A news department has to flush out the cops, but they don't necessarily have the resources and time, particularly in a city like Chicago, where there's so much going on. But, yeah, the media is at fault for not pursuing the cops and prosecutors."

Stephanie Goldstein signed up for a course in investigative reporting in the winter semester of 1996. She planned to go to law school, but was intrigued by Protess' course. She had heard how he and five students at Northwestern's Medill School of Journalism had helped free David Dowaliby in 1992 after he had been sentenced to 45 years in prison for murdering his 7-year-old step-daugher. One student, Carl Ganter, now a photojournalist, was instrumental in finding the girl's uncle, who confessed to Protess and his partner, journalist Rob Warden. The story, based on a book by Protess and Warden, became a TV miniseries in January starring Shannen Doherty.

During the first class, Protess outlined four death penalty cases in which he felt the wrong men might have been convicted. He explained what kind of investigating would be required and how much work and travel would be involved. The

Dennis Williams case, he indicated, would be very time-consuming.

At the second class, after giving the students time to think, Protess asked the students to choose the case that most interested them. Sullivan and Delo gravitated to the Williams case. Goldstein initially picked another one but quickly moved to join the students who chose the Williams case. She's still not sure why she changed her mind.

"I was drawn to [the case] because of the age of the people involved, both those convicted and the victims," says Stacey Delo, who now produces educational videos in St. Louis. "Also, two white people died, and four black men were convicted in a hasty manner."

These were the facts presented to the students in stacks of files: After 2:30 a.m. on May 11, 1978, Schmal, 23, and Lionberg, 29, were kidnapped at gunpoint at a gas station where Lionberg worked in a suburb just south of Chicago. They were driven to an abandoned townhouse in a poor area of Chicago known as Ford Heights, where Schmal was repeatedly raped and then shot twice in the head. Lionberg was taken out back, shot in the head and left to die.

Later that day, Williams, 21, Jimerson, 26, Rainge, 20, and Adams, 20, were arrested after a man living across from the abandoned townhouse called police, saying he had seen Williams and Adams near where the bodies were discovered. It was later proven that he had in fact seen both men, but much earlier in the evening. Jimerson was also in the crowd that gathered after the murder, and was arrested after retrieving his sunglasses from Williams' car. Rainge was implicated by Paula Gray, Adams' girlfriend.

While both men insisted they were innocent, they were nonetheless convicted that fall, largely on the testimony of Gray, who had a long history of mental instability. None of the men had violent pasts, although Williams served time briefly for a property crime. Gray soon recanted, claiming police had badgered her into incriminating the four men. She was convicted of perjury and being an accomplice to the murder and sentenced to 50 years in prison.

What was never investigated in 1978 was information from an infor-

mant named Marvin Simpson, who lived in the neighborhood where the killings occurred. Six days after the murder, Simpson provided officers from the East Chicago Heights police department and the Cook County sheriff's office information implicating four other men in the crime. "The police seemed like they were interested in what I was saying," Simpson later told the students, but "I never heard from the police again." (In April one of the men Simpson named was convicted of murdering Schmal and Lionberg, marking the first time in Illinois history that a wrongful murder conviction was reversed and someone else was successfully prosecuted for the same crime.)

Chicago's newspapers and TV news operations also didn't show much interest in the 1978 case. The press accepted the version of law enforcement authorities. "The media assumed what the authorities were telling them was true when the four men were initially arrested," Delo says, "and they didn't do any probing."

Williams can testify to that. "The media at the time of our arrest didn't want to hear anything I had to say," Williams says. "The first person to listen was Rob Warden from the *Chicago Lawyer*." Williams learned of the legal magazine, which Warden started in 1978, from another prisoner. Both were impressed by its critical coverage of the criminal justice system. Williams wrote a letter, and Warden followed up.

In July 1982, Warden and reporter Margaret Roberts wrote a long story for *Chicago Lawyer* detailing flaws in the case against Williams and in his legal defense. After the article appeared, Williams and Rainge, who shared a lawyer, had their convictions overturned because of poor legal representation. "I became persuaded early on that [Williams] didn't do it because the prosecutor offered deals to the other defendants to testify against Dennis," says Warden. "None of the defendants would do it. That just rarely happens unless they are innocent."

Gray changed her story again after the state offered to let her out of prison if she testified against Williams and Rainge. She did and also implicated Jimerson. The three were convicted, and Williams and

Jimerson were sentenced to die in the electric chair.

The students were intrigued by the case. Protess "definitely thought they were innocent," recalls Laura Sullivan, now a reporter at the *Baltimore Sun.* "I definitely thought they were guilty until we met Paula Gray. I came around very quickly. But everything has a real spin with Protess. It's always focused in one direction, for good and for bad."

Protess, a Medill professor since 1981, says he always approaches death penalty investigations objectively. But once he becomes convinced that an innocent man has been condemned to die, he becomes a zealot, jettisoning any pretense of objectivity. He and Warden are a different breed of journalist. They enjoy being called muckrakers or crusaders. They get emotionally involved in their stories. "Basically, we are two annoying guys who cause trouble," Protess says.

Not surprisingly, they are sometimes criticized for getting too involved in a case, for acting more like defense attorneys than journalists. "I go a little further than investigative reporters," says Protess. "Once I feel I've reached a firm conclusion that someone is innocent, I can't think of something I wouldn't do to help them except break the law."

Warden, who once reported for the late *Chicago Daily News,* established a reputation as a hard-hitting investigative reporter for *Chicago Lawyer.* Protess, now a tenured professor at Northwestern, spent five years as research director for the Better Government Association, a citizen watchdog group, and he also wrote for *Chicago Lawyer.*

"Rob Warden is so far ahead that he often doesn't get credit," Protess says. "Rob lays the groundwork for the rest of us." Of the nine death row cases since 1977 in which defendants ultimately were exonerated, Warden had written stories questioning the evidence in six of them.

Not surprisingly, Protess and Warden have attracted a lot of media attention. "The downside of what I do," Protess says, "is it makes me a celebrity. It's a fine line between being a source on a story you think is of public importance and being a celebrity who gets credit for the results even if you don't deserve it. I

get death threats now, and my personal life is always being investigated to discredit me."

"Say what you will about Dave Protess, but he's one of the good guys," says Eric Zorn, a *Chicago Tribune* columnist who has written about Protess' crusades. "He's worked very hard to get innocent people out of jail."

Protess turns his investigative reporting classes into workshops for uncovering miscarriages of justice. He uses smart, high-energy students to do the legwork many reporters don't have time for, at the same time giving them real-life reporting experience. "I want to train the students to think of their profession in broad terms," Protess says, "and not be afraid to shed their objectivity and get their hands dirty."

Ten of his students tried desperately for six months to help death row inmate Girvies Davis escape the Illinois electric chair in 1995. They did not succeed. Hours before his death, Davis asked Protess to look into the plight of his prison friend Dennis Williams.

"I was grieving. I was hurt bad by [Davis'] death," Protess says. "I had to honor the wishes of a dead man."

After looking into the Williams case, Protess decided to get his students involved. "The first thing we did was read about the case," recalls Goldstein, who now books guests for CNN. Then they interviewed Paula Gray, who said that police had coerced her into testifying against the men who came to be known as the Ford Heights Four by keeping her in a motel room for two days until she relented. The trio also spent time at the Capital Resource Center, where lawyers working on the case had a room full of old files. The students pulled many documents and photocopied them, not knowing what they had.

One night, around 12:30 a.m, an exhausted Goldstein at last found a file that looked promising. Protess had been pressing the women to find a police interview that had taken place in a Chicago Hospital after the mur-

ders. That's all Protess knew. "Here, maybe this will get Dave off our backs," said Goldstein, tossing a file to Delo.

It was the "street file," so called because its contents came from a police interview on the "street." It held the names and details informant Marvin Simpson had given police 18 years earlier when he was in the hospital with a back injury. It has been reported repeatedly that the students "discovered" this file, when in fact it had been part of a post-conviction motion filed by one of Williams' lawyers. "The state knew about the street file," says Goldstein, "and they chose not to do anything with it."

It remains unclear why the defense didn't do more with the file. Williams' lawyer, John Greenlees, told Chicago Magazine, "We'd tracked down the people on the list [of suspects mentioned by Simpson] but they wouldn't talk to us." Why it was never investigated is a story the Chicago media have yet to explore.

John Carpenter, a *Chicago Sun-Times* reporter, wrote several stories about the case last summer. "My observation was it was fairly cut-and-dried what went wrong," says Carpenter, explaining why he didn't pursue it. "Mainly that Paula Gray testified against them falsely. But the police obviously ignoring the street file was significant. What you would find in this case is a combination of shoddy police work based on their willingness to accept Paula Gray's testimony."

Carpenter may be right, but that story hasn't been done. Sullivan recently learned why police had relied on Gray. "There was some negligence by the police, but I don't know if it was as malicious as we thought," she says. "The police found Carol Schmal's boots in Gray's closet. She had bought them from Ira Johnson two days after the crime. So they had some reason to directly correlate her to the crime. It was an atrocious mistake to make, and the police should have checked out the Simpson lead,

The three journalism students had played a crucial role in clearing the Ford Heights Four, but many others—investigator Rene Brown, death penalty lawyer John Greenlees and other members of the defense team—also worked hard to win their release.

but I don't think their intention was to consciously disregard the truth."

Protess and the students later got retired East Chicago Heights Lt. George Nance, who had interviewed Simpson, to admit in an affidavit that his department had never followed up on the information.

Among the names mentioned in the file were brothers Ira and Dennis Johnson. Dennis Johnson died of a drug overdose, but Ira was in prison for murder. Chicago private investigator Rene Brown, hired by Protess last year for $2,000, shared information he had on the Johnson brothers and helped the students make contacts in Ford Heights, where they obtained much of their evidence.

They visited Ira Johnson in prison and also met "Red" Robinson, with the help of investigator Brown. In response to their questions, Robinson confessed to participating in the crime to the students, and implicated Ira Johnson. Johnson then admitted to Protess and later to Delo and Sullivan that he killed Lionberg and that his brother Dennis murdered Schmal. "I seen Dennis rape her," Ira Johnson said on tape to Protess. "I shot the guy in the head."

Protess says that the youth and gender of the students helped elicit the confessions. "The confessions came because Ira Johnson agreed to see my students because they were women," he says. "He then sent them love letters through me at Northwestern. My view was this was a situation that had to be dealt with professionally. I didn't want my students to be in danger." So Protess also interviewed Ira Johnson in prison.

But confessions and ignored evidence might not be enough, Protess feared. So he enlisted the help of the media.

Protess contacted *Tribune* columnist Zorn and Doug Longhini, at the time senior producer of the investigative unit at WMAQ, two journalists he knew and trusted. "With the Ford Heights Four, I've never been shy about saying I took information and documents from Protess and re-reported the things that struck me as relevant," Zorn says. "I'd always do the re-reporting, but they'd do the legwork. I trust Dave."

In 1996, Zorn wrote a series of columns about the Ford Heights Four case, and WMAQ, NBC's local affiliate, aired nearly 40 stories on it. Protess was the spark, says Dave Savini, a WMAQ investigative reporter who covered the story. "People like us and Eric Zorn kept the flame burning by doing our jobs," says Savini. "That created a sense of public pressure, and the guys eventually got out."

The story of what was happening with the Ford Heights Four was largely ignored until DNA testing last June showed the original defendants could not have been involved. Then it was a top story on the local news and radio stations and prominently played in the *Sun-Times* and *Tribune*. But the vindication of the Ford Heights Four wasn't the only element of the saga that attracted major attention. So, too, did the notion that they'd been cleared by journalism students.

Newsday ran a story trumpeting the successful class project, as did the *Chicago Sun-Times*, and *Chicago Tribune* columnist Clarence Page also played up that angle. The *New York Times'* Don Terry wrote a front page article focusing on the extraordinary miscarriage of justice. But the headline on his story mentioned both aspects of the saga, saying that innocent men had been freed, "Thanks to Students and DNA."

The students had played a crucial role, but many others—investigator Rene Brown, death penalty lawyer Greenlees, staffers at the government-funded Capital Resource Center and the team of high-priced lawyers Protess assembled shortly before the men were freed—also worked hard to win their release. But it was Protess and the students who received the most attention, although they protested that they shouldn't have. "I know that we consciously made efforts in interviews to say to reporters that they needed to talk to the legal team," Goldstein says. "We tried over and over to say this was a joint effort. . . . But using us was the easy angle, the cliché angle."

Nonetheless, when Hollywood discovered the case, it was Protess and the students who found their answering machines jammed with messages from producers.

Hollywood was offering big money for exclusive rights. Disney promised to pay seven figures (it won't say exactly how much) for a book and movie deal. The students, Protess (who says he hopes Harrison Ford will play him) and the four freed men were offered a total of about $400,000 for their life stories. Not much, if anything, was offered to those who had worked in the shadows for years, such as Brown or Greenlees.

Bad feelings ensued. Brown aired his gripes to the *Chicago Reader*, the city's alternative newspaper, ripping into Protess. Protess didn't believe the students should get anything; he felt all money should go to the four men and promised to donate his share. As it stands now, the rights to the stories of the four men and three women will be divided five ways—four shares to the men, one to be split by the three students.

Protess and the students now refuse to talk about the money squabble. However, the students took umbrage when Protess told them after graduation, "Your Nancy Drew story is over." Protess says he feared the women would take money that he felt belonged to the men. "We felt like we didn't have any choice in the movie thing," Laura Sullivan told *Chicago Magazine*. "Protess sold us as a group and signed on without even conferring with us in any way on what was best for us—or if we even wanted to make a movie."

The students say they aren't interested in the money as much as they are concerned about how they will be portrayed. "Instead of celebrating, the important characters in this script—the freed men, the professor, his students and the others—are squabbling over who should get credit, who should profit from the Hollywood payday and how events should be portrayed in the upcoming movie," wrote *Chicago Magazine*'s Jonathan Eig. "Some players have even accused the professor of nurturing the heroic myth because he craved the fame of the big screen. For such an admirable good deed, there are an awful lot of bad feelings."

Each of the four men who were cleared has received $21,000 up front. Protess and Warden are writing a book about the case, and all parties are working with California screen-writer Brian Ross on a screenplay.

Chicago Magazine and the *Chicago Reader* wrote extensively about the bitterness engendered by the dispute over money, and the *Tribune*'s Zorn wrote a column detailing the unfortunate intersection of money and good intentions. "They were a storybook team," Zorn wrote. "Stephanie Goldstein, a future law student . . . , was the brains. . . . , Stacey Delo, an aspiring documentary filmmaker . . . , was the heart. And Laura Sullivan . . . was the guts; the tough-talking cynic who wouldn't be intimidated by the underclass milieu in which this story was still hidden."

That kind of coverage makes Protess and Warden—and even the students—furious. The students, each agree, were part of the story but not *the* story. "What I find troubling is not so much the effort to exploit the minor differences among people who tried to make a difference," says Protess, "but that journalists turned their back on these guys for 18 years. Journalists were part of the problem. They created the environment initially in which a rush to judgment could occur. And they turned their back on the letters of these men sent to journalists begging them to take a look at their cause."

Few news organizations have examined in depth how the criminal justice system could have performed so badly—with the exception of WMAQ. Doug Longhini, the station's producer at the time, Savini and reporter Tracy Haynes all worked on the story, exposing the existence of the "street file," airing Ira Johnson's confession and showing Robinson on camera saying he was there at the time of the murders and still remembers the sound of the gunshots.

"If the other media in this town put in as much effort as us and Eric, you might have seen more pressure put on the sheriff's department and former prosecutors," says Savini. "It's great the men are free. But once the men were free, it seemed to take pressure off of the criminal justice system."

Chicago Reader columnist Michael Miner admits the question of what went wrong "probably would have been a good thing to write about." Instead, he focused on who was upset about not receiving credit. "I won't say anything I wrote got down to the bedrock issues in this case, which is about right and wrong, not credit," he says.

Says Steve Huntley, the *Chicago Sun-Times'* metro editor at the time of the story, "I'm not sure it's known what went wrong with this case." But, adds Huntley, now the paper's editorial page editor, "We have so many stories and demands on our staff. . . . We cannot investigate every story that perhaps warrants investigation."

A year after the government's case unraveled, there is no grand jury investigation of the Cook County authorities involved in the wrongful conviction of the four men. In December, Zorn called for the appointment of a special prosecutor. But Zorn also blames the media for failing to follow up. "We know to a fair degree of certainty that no one, including myself, has really pushed this," he says. "We don't often uncover or advance the cause of miscarriages of justice."

Tribune Metro Editor Paul Weingarten adds, "It certainly is not my attitude that the men are out so now no one cares what went wrong. We are still looking into it. Newspapers can get distracted. But this is still a tremendous miscarriage of justice that needs to be examined completely. I'm hoping I can put a little heat on it."

Williams is especially angry at the local media. When they interview him, he says, they never mention the depth of his anger toward Chicago law enforcement. The former police and prosecutors have just as much to answer for as the actual killers, Williams says. "There's no excuse for not punishing them. But all the reporters for mainstream papers like the *Sun-Times* and *Tribune* don't quote me about what I say about the prosecutors. They allowed murderers to roam the streets for 18 years. Who

knows what else these men did in those 18 years."

It is known that in 1991, Ira Johnson was convicted of murdering Cherry Wilder, 31, a crime her parents now blame on the police.

Since Illinois brought back the death penalty in 1977, nine men on death row have been exonerated. "You have to sort out which ones of these kind of cases are worth investigating," says Protess. "Part of the problem is so few people are willing to investigate them."

Warden agrees. "What's wrong is that nobody listens to the guy who said he never did it," he says. "If a reporter got a tip that Alderman X is stealing money, they'd investigate it. But if someone says, 'I've been wrongfully convicted of a capital offense,' nobody listens."

Protess continues the conversation. "In an era of celebrity journalism it's more attractive to prove someone in power did something than someone poor and not in power didn't do it. When you think about how tragically easy it was for us, all it took was someone to care enough to go down to Ford Heights and talk to the right people. Reporters don't do that anymore."

The problem, of course, is that reporters get hundreds of letters from prisoners claiming to be falsely accused. How do you determine which case is worth a second look?

Despite the complexity, reporters shouldn't simply toss prisoners' pleading letters into the trash. There is a way to weed out time-wasting cases and find the nuggets that could lead to important stories.

Dennis Williams, who wrote well over 60 letters to members of the press during his incarceration, has this advice: "You don't have to believe every letter you get," he says. "Ask them to send you some evidence that can confirm what the person is claiming. I sent Rob Warden police reports, excerpts from the trial transcripts."

And, he adds, "I dealt with logic. A person just doesn't go from stealing a piece of candy from a store to murder."

> **"In an era of celebrity journalism,"** says Northwestern University journalism professor David Protess, **"it's more attractive to prove someone in power did something than someone poor and not in power didn't do it."**

 Article Review Form at end of book.

Discuss the homicide trends in California between 1970 and 1993, emphasizing the homicide risk differentials by ethnicity, sex, and age.

Trends in California Homicide, 1970 to 1993

Lawrence D. Chu, M.S., and Susan B. Sorenson, Ph.D.

Los Angeles, California

Homicide is an increasing public health concern in the United States. It perennially ranks among the ten leading causes of death, and rates have been increasing since 1960 even as death rates from other causes have decreased.[1-5] The United States leads industrialized nations with the highest homicide numbers and rates; among 15- to 24-year-olds, the U.S. homicide rate is more than four times the next highest rate.[6] The increased number of homicides and other intentional injuries is so alarming that violence was declared a public health emergency in 1992.[7]

Sex, race or ethnicity, and age have been associated with homicide risk, and firearms have been identified as a major external cause of homicide.[8-12] The highest homicide rates in the nation generally occur in men, African Americans, and 15- to 34-year-olds; in fact, homicide is the leading cause of death for young African-American men and women.[13] Geographic comparisons of homicide show high rates in the South and West and lowest rates occurring in the North and Northeast.[14,15]

California is of particular interest because it has one of the highest rates in the United States, accounting for nearly one of every six homicides in the nation.[16] From 1986 to 1988, California reported homicide rates for young white men and young Africa-American men to be 92% and 67%, respectively, above the nation's average. Studying an ethnically diverse population such as California's will expand the knowledge about the homicide risk in groups about whom we know relatively little, specifically, Hispanics and Asians. Data on homicide trends and patterns in California will be useful in developing future studies targeting other risk factors and expanding our knowledge of homicide risk.

Methods

Study Population

The study population comprised the 69,621 persons who died of homicide in California from 1970 through 1993. California residents who died outside the state were excluded. Death certificate data were obtained through the California Master Mortality Data Tapes made available by the California Department of Health Services. Homicide deaths were identified using the eighth and ninth revisions of the *International Classification of Diseases* (ICD-8, ICD-9) external cause-of-death codes.[17,18]

Abbreviations Used in Text
CI = confidence interval
ICD = *International Classification of Diseases*
RR = relative risk

Variables of Interest

The variables of interest from the death certificate data included sex, race, ethnicity, age, and education level of the victim and the method of homicide as identified through the ICD external-cause-of-death codes. Referent groups were established for each of the demographic variables for comparison and for calculating the relative risk.

Race and ethnicity were classified into four groups: non–Hispanic white, African American, Hispanic, and Asian and other based on three death certificate variables: race, Hispanic origin, and Spanish surname. Race categories on death certificates included black, white, Asian, American Indian, and other. California death certificates consistently used a Hispanic identifier beginning in 1987, which precluded the identification of Hispanics, a substantial portion of California's population[19] for much of the study period. For this reason, a Spanish surname file of 12,497 names from the U.S. Bureau of the Census was compared with decedents' last names

"Trends in California Homicide, 1970 to 1993," Lawrence D. Chu and Susan B. Sorenson. *The Western Journal of Medicine*, Vol. 165, No. 3, September 1996. Reprinted by permission.

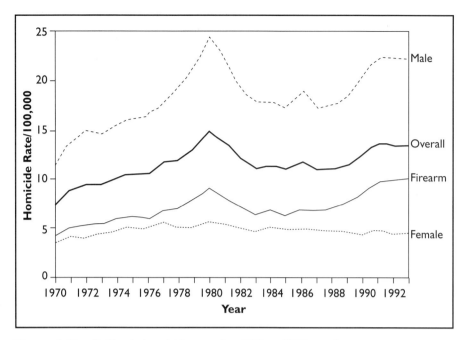

Figure 1. The California homicide rates for 1970 to 1993 are shown.

to identify Hispanic homicide victims.[20] An additional 2,064 surnames were added to the list to identify those who were missed by the original surname file but who were thought to be of Spanish descent (for example, hyphenated names such as Lopez-Garcia). African Americans and Asians were excluded from the surname linkage to reduce possible misclassification. Four ethnic-racial groups were created: black, white, Hispanic, and Asian or other.* Because of the relative stability of their homicide rate, non–Hispanic whites were used as the referent group for comparisons by ethnicity.

Age was categorized into ten groups: 0 to 4 years, 5 to 14 years, 15 to 19 years, 20 to 24 years, 25 to 34 years, 35 to 44 years, 45 to 54 years, 55 to 64 years, 65 to 74 years, and 75 years or older. Because most homicide victims are teenagers and young adults, the 15- to 24-year age group was divided into two 5-year age groups. The 35- to 44-year age group was used as a referent because the annual average homicide rate of that group closely parallels the annual overall homicide rate; it has one of the most stable homicide rates; it can

*Population projections—that is, denominator data—for Native Americans were not available until 1990. Thus, an "Asian and other" group was used in the analyses.

be regarded as a transition period between youth and middle age and would highlight differential risks between the two; and better comparisons to youth homicide can be made with this group (than with, for example, 65- to 74-year-olds) because of the proximity in age.

Five categories of educational attainment were established for homicide victims aged 25 years or older: eighth grade or less, high school dropouts (grades 9 to 11), high school graduates (grade 12), some college (1 to 3 years), and college graduates (≥4 years of college). Denominator data for education status were obtained from the annual Current Population Surveys from the California Department of Finance and included persons aged 25 years or older only. Data on education level were available on death certificates starting in 1989, so relative risks were calculated for the 1989 to 1993 period. High school graduates were used as a referent group because of the relative stability of their homicide rates and because it was the modal education level.

The external cause of homicide (ICD E-codes) was separated into firearm or explosive (965), cutting or stabbing (966), and other (960 to 964, 967 to 969). Firearm and explosive homicides were treated as one category until 1976, when they were as-

signed separate categories. The number of homicides due to explosives is negligible compared with the number of firearm homicides; explosives consistently accounted for less than 0.5% of all firearm and explosive homicides after 1976.

Temporal variations in homicide frequency were examined by month and season: winter (January through March), spring (April through June), summer (July through September), and fall (October through December).

Denominator data for sex, race or ethnicity, age, and education level were based on estimates provided by the California Department of Finance.

Statistical Analysis

Frequencies were tabulated to compare homicide methods across time and to assess seasonal variations. Homicide rates per 100,000 persons and relative risks (RR; and their 95% confidence intervals [CI] were calculated to examine homicide risk by sex, race and ethnicity, age, and education. Five time periods—1970 to 1974, 1975 to 1979, 1980 to 1984, 1985 to 1989, and 1990 to 1993—were used to facilitate comparisons across time.

Results

California's 1993 homicide rate of 13.4 per 100,000 is an 81% increase from the 1970 rate of 7.4, but is less than the 1980 peak of 14.8. The nation's homicide rate follows a similar trend observed in California data: increasing during the 1970s, peaking in 1980, decreasing in the early 1980s, and increasing again after 1985. California and US homicide rates by sex, race and ethnicity, and age groups also are relatively similar.

Homicide rates are higher among men than women, and the gender disparity is growing (Figure 1). The 1993 male homicide rate of 22.1 per 100,000 is 1.9 times the 1970 rate of 11.5 per 100,000. Although the annual rate change was relatively small, the 1993 female homicide rate was 1.3 times the 1970 rate, increasing from 3.6 to 4.7 per 100,000. The rate increase was not consistent; as can be seen in Figure 1, rates increased throughout the 1970s, decreased in the early 1980s, and increased rela-

Figure 2. The California homicide rates by race or ethnicity—African American, Hispanic, Asian or other, and non-Hispanic white—for 1970 to 1993 are shown.

tively steadily to the end of the study period.

As shown in Figure 2, homicide rates differ substantially by ethnic group, and the difference between non–Hispanic whites and the three minority groups is also growing. African-American homicide rates are consistently higher than those of other groups; the 1993 rate of 57.7 per 100,000 is 1.6 times the 1970 rate of 36.4 per 100,000. Non–Hispanic whites had a 1.2 times increase in homicide rates from 1970 to 1993 (from 5.0 to 5.9 per 100,000). Hispanic homicide rates rose 2.5 times (from 7.7 to 19.4 per 100,000), and homicide rates for Asians and others increased 1.7 times (from 4.5 to 7.6 per 100,000) from the 1970 rate during the same period. Thus, the greatest change in homicide rates by ethnicity is in two traditionally understudied groups, Hispanics and Asians.

The greatest increase in homicide rates was not for a certain sex or a specific ethnic group but for youth. Homicide rates for 15- to 19-year-olds increased 4.0-fold from 8.4 to 33.7 per 100,000 from 1970 to 1993 (Figure 3). The 5- to 14-year-old group had the second largest increase—3.2 times from 0.76 to 2.4 per 100,000—followed by 20- to 24-year-olds with a 2.6 times increase of 13.7 to 35.3 per 100,000. While the youth homicide rate climbed, the risk remained relatively stable or dropped for other age groups.

Changing patterns of relative risk are documented in Table 1. Whereas men consistently had significantly higher homicide rates than women, their risk relative to women increased from 3.27 in 1970 to 1974 to 4.70 in 1990 to 1993. African Americans and Hispanics are at a substantially higher risk than non-Hispanic whites. Moreover, the differential increased over time, ending with a 9.00-fold risk for African Americans and a 3.26-fold risk for Hispanics in 1990 to 1993. Asians and others had lower relative risks during the early time periods (0.96, 0.71, 0.72, 0.86), indicating a protective factor until 1990 to 1993, when the relative risk changed direction and rose to 1.17, a statistically significant difference.

A pronounced change is noted for the 15- to 19-year age group. From 1970 to 1984, the risk of homicide for 15- to 19-year-olds was not significantly different from that for 35- to 44-year-olds. In the latter half of the 1980s, their relative risk increased substantially to a 2.26-fold risk in 1990 to 1993. Across each of the five time periods, 20- to 24-year-olds had the highest risk, and 5- to 14-year-olds had the lowest risk relative to the 35- to 44-year age group. The 20- to 24-year and 25- to 34-year age groups have consistently high relative risks for homicide, ending with a 2.41- and 1.50-fold risk of homicide, respectively, in 1990 to 1993. Persons younger than 15 years and older than 44 years were consistently at a lower risk of homicide than 35- to 44-year-olds.

For persons aged 25 and older during 1989 to 1993 (the years for which education level information is available), high school dropouts had a 1.63 (95% CI = 1.46, 1.83) times

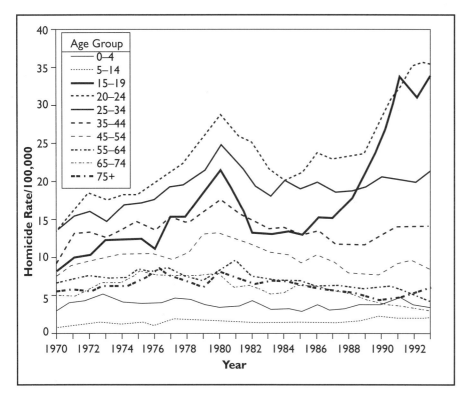

Figure 3. The California homicide rates by age groups for 1970 to 1993 are shown.

greater risk than high school graduates of being a homicide victim (data not tabled). Those with an eighth grade education or less did not differ significantly from those with a high school diploma (RR = 1.07; 95% CI = 0.95, 1.20). In comparison, persons with some college or who are college graduates have a substantially lower risk (RR = 0.44, 95% CI = 0.39, 0.50; and, RR = 0.23, 95% CI = 0.19, 0.27, respectively) of being a homicide victim.

As shown in Figure 1, the firearm homicide rate parallels the overall homicide rate, which can be explained by the large proportion of homicides involving firearms (see Figure 4). Firearms and explosives consistently accounted for about 60% of all homicides from 1970 until the mid–1980s, when the percentage began to climb. The percentage of homicides due to cuttings and stabbings dropped from 20% to 11%, and other methods have dropped from 24% to 14% of all homicides. In 1993, firearms and explosives accounted for 75% of all homicides.

Temporal variations (data not tabled) indicate that most homicides occur in the summer months (July through September), with the most

homicides occurring in August. The average annual percentage of homicides adjusted by month varied from a low of 8.2% in February to a high of 8.9% in July and 9.1% in August. No significant seasonal differences were detected across the time periods, aside from the overall increase in the number of homicides each year.

Discussion

California data from 1970 to 1993 document a growing disparity in traditional patterns of homicide risk and a substantial shift in others. Homicide risk differences are increasing between men and women and between persons of color and non–Hispanic whites. Two traditionally understudied population groups illustrate this trend well: Hispanics are at a consistently higher risk of homicide than non–Hispanic whites, whereas Asians and others were at a lower or similar risk until the 1990s, when their risk of homicide became significantly greater than that of non–Hispanic whites. African Americans are at an extremely high risk of homicide, a fact that has been widely documented and is corrobo-

rated herein. Thus, minority group status is associated with higher homicide rates, albeit not uniformly higher.

Young people are at a dramatically increasing risk of homicide. If existing trends continue, 15- to 19-year-olds will soon overtake 20- to 24-year-olds as the leading category in age-specific homicide rates. This is due, in no small part, to the fact that the homicide rate for 15- to 19-year-olds has more than quadrupled since 1970. Moreover, the homicide rate for persons aged 45 or older has remained stable or decreased. Thus, there is a pronounced trend toward younger victims of homicide.

High school dropouts are at the highest risk of homicide among all education groups. Persons with eight or fewer years of schooling are at a risk similar to that of high school graduates. By contrast, persons with some college or a college degree are at a substantially lower risk of homicide. Given that the education level was added recently to death certificate forms, the association between educational level and homicide risk is just beginning to be explored.[21]

Firearms play a central role in homicide; three of every four homicides in California in 1993 were committed with a firearm. Firearm homicide risk is even higher for youth: in the same year, 90% of the murdered 15- to 19-year-olds in California were killed with a gun. The increase in the number of firearm homicides has been related to an increase in firearm sales,[12] and keeping a gun in the home has been associated with an increased risk of in-home homicide.[10] This is a disturbing outcome of the ease of obtaining a firearm in the United States, where "buying a handgun is as easy as buying a toothbrush,"[22(p.1375)] Firearm deaths currently are the leading cause of injury death in California, surpassing even motor vehicle crashes; this change is mostly a result of an increase in the number of firearm deaths rather than a decrease in motor vehicle fatalities.[23]

A few cautions about these data should be noted. Because of the unique minority population distribution of California and the traditionally more violent aspect of the western United States,[15] these results

Table I Relative Risks for California Homicides, 1970 to 1993*

Variable	1970 to 1993	1970 to 1974	1975 to 1979	1980 to 1984	1985 to 1989	1990 to 1993
Sex[†]						
Male	**3.83** (3.50, 4.19)	**3.28** (2.94, 3.65)	**3.51** (3.20, 3.85)	**3.87** (3.54, 4.23)	**3.67** (3.37, 4.00)	**4.71** (4.34, 5.10)
Race and Ethnicity[‡]						
African American	**7.26** (6.63, 7.94)	**7.33** (6.61, 8.12)	**6.17** (5.62, 6.77)	**6.42** (5.88, 7.01)	**7.64** (7.00, 8.34)	**9.01** (8.29, 9.79)
Hispanic	**2.55** (2.33, 2.79)	**1.96** (1.72, 2.23)	**2.43** (2.21, 2.67)	**2.48** (2.27, 2.70)	**2.27** (2.08, 2.48)	**3.26** (3.02, 3.53)
Asian and other	0.89 (0.73, 1.08)	0.96 (0.71, 1.30)	**0.71** 0.56, 0.92)	**0.72** (0.59, 0.89)	0.86 (0.72, 1.02)	**1.17** (1.02, 1.36)
Age, yr[§]						
0 to 4	**0.28** (0.22, 0.36)	**0.35** (0.27, 0.45)	**0.28** (0.22, 0.37)	**0.24** (0.19, 0.31)	**0.28** (0.22, 0.36)	**0.29** (0.24, 0.36)
5 to 14	**0.12** (0.09, 0.15)	**0.09** (0.07, 0.13)	**0.11** (0.08, 0.14)	**0.11** (0.08, 0.14)	**0.12** (0.09, 0.16)	**0.17** (0.13, 0.20)
15 to 19	**1.26** (1.10, 1.45)	0.87 (0.73, 1.04)	0.98 (0.85, 1.14)	1.05 (0.91, 1.21)	**1.34** (1.17, 1.54)	**2.26** (2.03, 2.52)
20 to 24	**1.75** (1.55, 1.98)	**1.38** (1.18, 1.61)	**1.47** (1.29, 1.68)	**1.61** (1.42, 1.82)	**1.88** (1.66, 2.12)	**2.42** (2.18, 2.68)
25 to 34	**1.42** (1.27, 1.59)	**1.25** (1.08, 1.45)	**1.29** (1.14, 1.47)	**1.39** (1.24, 1.55)	**1.55** (1.39, 1.73)	**1.50** (1.36, 1.64)
45 to 54	**0.73** (0.62, 0.85)	**0.76** (0.64, 0.91)	**0.740** (0.63, 0.87)	**0.77** (0.66, 0.89)	**0.73** (0.63, 0.86)	**0.63** (0.55, 0.73)
55 to 64	**0.52** (0.43, 0.63)	**0.59** (0.48, 0.73)	**0.54** (0.45, 0.65)	**0.52** (0.44, 0.62)	**0.51** (0.42, 0.62)	**0.43** (0.36, 0.52)
65 to 74	**0.42** (0.34, 0.53)	**0.48** (0.36, 0.62)	**0.51** (0.41, 0.64)	**0.41** (0.33, 0.51)	**0.44** (0.35, 0.55)	**0.29** (0.23, 0.37)
≥75	**0.45** (0.34, 0.58)	**0.48** (0.35, 0.66)	**0.48** (0.36, 0.62)	**0.48** (0.37, 0.61)	**0.47** (0.37, 0.61)	**0.34** (0.26, 0.44)

*Relative risks in bold-faced type are statistically significant at $P < .05$.

[†]Referent = female

[‡]Referent = non-Hispanic white.

[§]Referent = 35- to 44-year-olds.

may not generalize to other states or to the nation. Second, education data are relevant for persons aged 25 or older; therefore, associations between education and homicide risk are not valid for the bulk of homicide victims—15- to 24-year-olds—who are excluded from education analyses. Third, although we expect the numbers to be low, there may be some misclassification of Hispanics using the Spanish surname list when non–Hispanic women change their last names when they marry Hispanic men. Fourth, the Asian and other group contains Native Americans who have extremely high

homicide rates,[24] which may strongly influence the overall Asian-and-other homicide rate. Last, homicide rates may be affected by the substantial increase in California's foreign-born population in the 1980s, a group that appears to be at a higher risk of homicide.[25]

Conclusion

Homicide is a growing problem among the populations traditionally served by public health agencies. Persons of color are at a substantially higher risk than non–Hispanic

whites, and the differences between the groups are growing. Of particular concern is the rapidly escalating homicide risk for 15- to 19-year-olds and an accompanying increase among 20- to 24-year-olds. Furthermore, using recently available education data, these findings indicate that high school dropouts have the highest homicide risk of all educational groups. And, relative to that of women, men's risk of homicide is growing. In essence, even as we assess the role of previously undocumented factors such as education, long-established discrepancies in homicide risk are expanding.

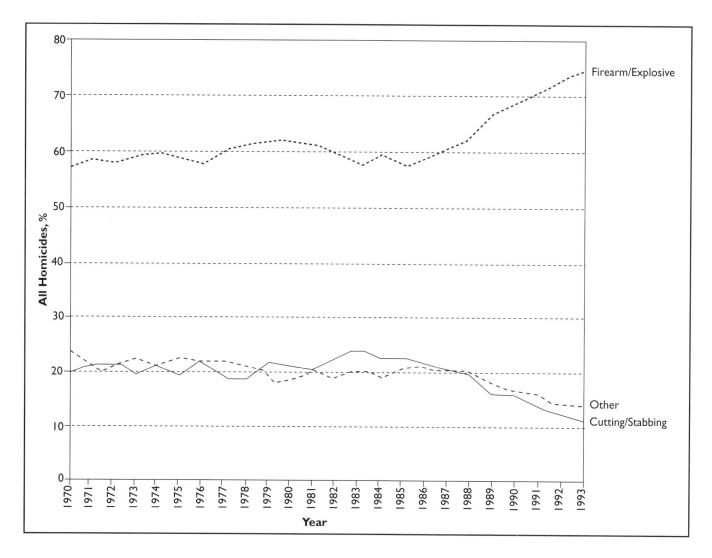

Figure 4. The graph shows percentages of the methods of homicide—firearms or explosives, cutting or stabbing, or other—for 1970 to 1993.

Law enforcement efforts are crucial but singularly insufficient in reducing violence perpetration and victimization. Although the Centers for Disease Control and Prevention has exercised considerable leadership in the field, many state and local health departments still do not define violence and injury prevention as part of their mission. Public health departments need to develop the capacity to be an effective partner in collaborative interagency efforts to meet the thriving public health challenge of homicide.

Acknowledgment: Haikang Shen, Ph.D. provided assistance, and Diana Tisnado and Raymond Rios helped construct the supplemental Spanish surname list.

References

1. Baker SP, O'Neill B, Ginsburg MJ, Li G: *The Injury Fact Book.* New York, NY, Oxford University Press, 1992
2. Klebba AJ: Homicide trends in the United States, 1900–1974. *Public Health Rep* 1975; 90:195–204
3. Martinez-Schnell B, Waxweiler RJ: Increases in premature mortality due to homicide—United States, 1968–1985. *Violence Vict* 1989; 4:287–293
4. Centers for Disease Control and Prevention (CDC): Mortality trends and leading causes of death among adolescents and young adults—United States, 1979–1988. *MMWR Morb Mortal Wkly Rep* 1993; 42:459–462
5. Seltzer F: Trend in mortality from violent deaths: Suicide and homicide, United States, 1960–1991. *Stat Bull Metrop Insur Co* 1994; 75:10–18
6. Fingerhut LA, Kleinman JC: International and interstate comparisons of homicide among young males. *JAMA* 1990; 263:3292–3295
7. Koop CE, Lundberg GB: Violence in America: A public health emergency—Time to bite the bullet back (Editorial). *JAMA* 1992; 267:3075–3076
8. Hammett M, Powell KE, O'Carroll PW, Clanton ST: Homicide surveillance—United States, 1979–1988. *MMWR CDC Surveill Summ* 1992; 41:1–33
9. Kellermann AL, Mercy JA: Men, women, and murder: Gender-specific differences in rates of fatal violence and victimization. *J Trauma* 1992; 33:1–5
10. Kellermann AL, Rivara FP, Rushforth NB, et al: Gun ownership as a risk factor for homicide in the home. *N Engl J Med* 1993; 329:1084–1091
11. Onwuachi-Saunders D, Hawkins DF: Black-white differences in injury—Race or social class? *Ann Epidemiol* 1993; 3:150–153
12. Wintemute GJ: Firearms as a cause of death in the United States, 1920–1982. *J Trauma* 1987; 27:532–536

13. Kochanek KD, Hudson BL: Advance report of final mortality statistics, 1992 [Hyattsville, Md. National Center for Health Statistics]. *Monthly Vital Stat Rep.* March 22, 1995; 43(suppl 6): Table 8

14. Nisbett RE: Violence and US regional culture. *Am Psychol* 1993; 48:441–449

15. O'Carroll PW, Mercy JA: Regional variation in homicide rates: Why is the West so violent? *Violence Vict* 1989; 4:17–25

16. Fujitani L: Homicide deaths by race/ethnicity, age, and sex. California, 1992. Sacramento, Calif., Health and Welfare Agency, Dept of Health Services, Center for Health Statistics, 1994

17. International Classification of Disease. *Manual of the International Statistical Classification of Diseases, Injuries, and Causes of Death*, 8th revision. Geneva, Switzerland, World Health Organization, 1969

18. International Classification of Disease. *Manual of the International Statistical Classification of Diseases, Injuries, and Causes of Death*, 9th revision. Geneva, Switzerland, World Health Organization, 1977

19. *Statistical Abstracts of the United States.* 114th edition. U.S. Dept of Commerce, Bureau of the Census, 1994

20. Census of Population and Housing, Spanish Surname List [machine-readable data file] prepared by the Bureau of the Census. U.S. Dept of Commerce, Census Bureau [producer and distributor], 1980

21. Christenson BA, Johnson NE: Educational inequality in adult mortality: An assessment with death certificate data from Michigan. *Demography* 1995; 32:215–229

22. As easy as buying a toothbrush (Editorial). *Lancet* 1993; 341:1375–1376

23. Wintemute GJ: Motor vehicles or firearms: Which takes a heavier toll? (Letter) *JAMA* 1993; 269:2213

24. *Trends in Indian Health—1994.* U.S. Dept of Health and Human Services, Indian Health Service, 1994

25. Sorenson SB, Shen H: Immigrants and homicide risk.California, 1970–1992. *Am J Public Health* 1996; 86:97–100

 Article Review Form at end of book.

Compare and contrast the different responses to crime given by blacks, Asians, and whites in a crime survey implemented in Leeds in 1987.

Measuring Concern about Crime:

Some Inter-Racial Comparisons

Monica A. Walker

Centre for Criminological and Legal Research, University of Sheffield.

Several victim surveys of the general population in certain areas of Great Britain have been carried out over the last few years. The impact of crime on people's lives has also been incorporated to some extent, mainly in the form of a question about "fear of crime." This has been operationalized by a question such as "do you think it is safe to go out alone in this area at night?" The limitations of this simple question have been realized (see for example, Maxfield 1984). It only relates to reaction to a single situation, which may, in any case, not be relevant to some people's experience. Other types of concern about crime have been investigated in some surveys, such as whether people worry about being burgled, and whether crime is a problem in the area in which they live.

A study in the United States (Lewis and Salem 1986) compared ten areas which differed considerably on many socio-economic variables and also the crime rate. They found that areas with social deprivation and higher crime rates tended to have higher scores on "fear of crime." Since areas of social deprivation tend

to have higher offender rates (Baldwin and Bottoms 1976) and non-whites tend to be socially deprived and live in these areas, it would not be expected that, taken over larger areas, whites and non-whites would have the same fear and general concern about crime. Surveys in this country which have compared ethnic groups have mainly been of large areas in which there is considerable variation in social class and other socio-economic variables. The British Crime Survey was carried out in the whole of England and Wales, and Box *et al.* (1988), in their analysis of survey data, examined "fear" in relation to several variables, including a white/non-white dichotomy. Surveys of London boroughs (with populations of over 300,000) have also reported on this variable (Hammersmith and Fulham by Painter *et al.* 1989 and two surveys in Islington by Jones *et al.* 1986 and Crawford *et al.* 1989). A survey in the whole of London by the Policy Studies Institute (Smith 1983), which was mainly concerned with attitudes to the police, also compared ethnic groups on "fear of crime." In none of these studies were adequate controls made in the design or analysis to enable comparisons to be made between ethnic groups living in similar conditions.

The study reported here[1] was carried out in Leeds in 1987, and incorporated a survey in which the sampling scheme enabled comparisons to be made between blacks, Asians, and whites *living in the same small areas* (enumeration districts (EDs)) who would therefore be living in roughly the same circumstances as each other. Differences between them are therefore more likely to be due to ethnicity *per se,* rather than differences in the environment. The areas sampled were those where most of the non-whites in Leeds lived and tended to be socially deprived, so the results cannot be extrapolated to all areas (see Table 1). Besides this, only males aged 16–35 were included in the main questionnaire, since females and older men were thought to be less likely to have had experience of crime. Their attitudes to the police have been reported elsewhere (Jefferson and Walker 1993); here the results of analysing three measures of "concern about crime" labelled "fear," "worries," and "problems" are reported.

Comparisons with other surveys addressing these topics are difficult to make because their results are seldom presented broken down by age and sex. In addition, in other studies blacks and Asians have sometimes been combined as "non-white,"

Table 1 Socio-Economic Characteristics of Survey Areas

%	Survey Areas >10% Non-white	Other Areas <10% Non-white	All[a]
Social class 1,2	8.7	14.2	12.4
Social class 4,5	37.2	28.4	31.3
Unemployed	18.2	10.8	13.2
Overcrowding[b]	2.5	0.6	1.2
Privately rented	23.9	13.1	16.6
No. of EDS	212	436	648

Source: 1981 census.

[a] "All" excludes outer wards of Leeds. These were excluded from the main study as they contained so few non-whites that arrest rates could not be calculated satisfactorily.

[b] "Overcrowding" means percentage of households with over 1.5 persons per room.

which is shown here not to be justified since there were clear differences between them. However, extrapolation from the Leeds survey to other towns should only be undertaken with care, since the experiences of Asian and blacks (and of course, whites) may well differ in other parts of the country.

Full details of the survey are given in the Main Report (Walker *et al.* 1990). Jefferson and Walker (1992) give an overview of the research.

The Leeds Survey

The sample was selected from EDs (which contain about 150 houses), estimated to have over 10 per cent households which were non-white.[2] These areas contained over 50 per cent of blacks and Asians, but only 6 per cent of the whites in the city, and clearly the sample could not be regarded as representative of the whole city. The areas included in the survey, compared with the rest of Leeds, had fewer in Social Classes 1 and 2; more in Social Classes 4 and 5; more people unemployed; more overcrowding, and more households which were privately rented. These data (from the 1981 census) show that non-whites tend to live in areas which are socially deprived—see Table 1. EDs were stratified into five groups as follows: A contained EDs with over 50 per cent non-white households, B contained 33–50 per cent, C contained 20–33 per cent, D contained 15–20 per cent, and E contained 10–15 per cent non-white. A

random sample of households was selected from EDs in A, and an interview was requested if there was a male aged 10–35 (one aged under 16 and one aged 16 or over, if possible). Households selected in B were asked "are there any men/boys of West Indian, African, or Asian descent?" and if the answer was "yes" an interview was requested in the appropriate age group and the ethnic origin stated by the respondent was recorded. If the answer was "no," only one in three households were asked for an interview. In stratum C all non-white but only one in five white households were asked for an interview; in strata D and E the sampling fraction was one in eight.

The response rate overall was 77 per cent and did not differ significantly between ethnic groups. The number of black men aged 16–35 interviewed as 171; there were 199 Asian men and 271 white men, totalling 641. Altogether 225 boys were interviewed; their results are presented in the Main Report (Walker *et al.* 1990) and will not be discussed here.

Fear of Crime

Respondents were asked: "How safe do you feel walking about in this area after dark on your own?" The percentages giving the answers "very safe," "fairly safe," "a bit unsafe" and "very unsafe" are given in Table 2. Those saying "a bit unsafe" or "very unsafe" will be referred to simply as feeling unsafe and it can be seen that more Asians felt unsafe (at 31 per

cent), next were whites (21 per cent) and fewest blacks (10 per cent): the three races all differing significantly. If we look at the proportions feeling "very safe," the figures are Asians 23 per cent, whites 35 per cent, and blacks 54 per cent, showing the same trend but even bigger differences. The four answers were scored, for the purposes of analysis, as 1, 2, 3, 4 (the score being labelled Fear or F) and as would be expected, the mean F scores differed significantly, Asians being highest and blacks lowest.

The relationship with age was explored and only for Asians was it found that more older men (those ages 31–35) felt unsafe than younger men; for the other groups there was no correlation with age. It should be remembered that, unlike other studies, the highest age here was only 35, so we know nothing about those aged over 35. Maxfield (1984), for example, found that those aged over 35 were more likely to feel unsafe.

The number of times people went out the previous week was examined in relation to "fear." The correlation was not significant for any race group, unlike Maxfield's finding that those who tended to go out more tended to feel unsafe. The Leeds study incorporated a question on victimization, and found significantly fewer blacks had been victims in the preceding 12 months (blacks 23 per cent, Asians 37 per cent, whites 42 per cent). Fear was correlated with the number of times people had been victimized only for blacks (for burglary <.05) and Asians (for car theft <.05), so victimization, in general, does not appear to have affected fear in the street.

In an examination of data from the 1984 British Crime Survey, Box *et al.* (1988) found that the percentage feeling unsafe among all non-whites was similar to that for whites in inner-city areas (for which our areas would qualify), but no breakdown was given by age and sex, and all non-whites were taken together, so satisfactory comparisons cannot be made.

The wording of the question in the PSI study was slightly different. Respondents were asked, first, if there were risks to women going out alone after dark. They were then asked if they sometimes worried for themselves (the figures being blacks 28 per cent, Asians 52 per cent, and

Table 2 Fear of Crime

	Percentages		
	Black	**Asian**	**White**
Very safe[a]	54	23	35
Fairly safe	36	46	44
A bit unsafe	8	21	15
Very unsafe	2	10	6
n = 100%	167	198	271
F score[b]	1.6	2.2	1.9

[a]Answers to: "How safe do you feel walking about in this area after dark on your own?"

[b]F = Fear; for scoring see text. Asians are significantly higher than whites and blacks (p<0.05).

Differences between any 2 ethnic groups of 10 or more in the percentages are significant at p < 0.05 or higher.

whites 48 per cent) (Smith 1983: 32). This study indicated that blacks felt less afraid than whites and Asians, and this was true for all age groups. Smith (p. 33) suggests this is because blacks "may wish to deny that a serious problem exists because their own group is held responsible for the problem," but this is clearly hypothetical.

The other London studies, in Islington and Hammersmith, had rather different results. The Islington study (Jones *et al.* 1986) found about 50 per cent "feeling worried" about going out alone, with no significant differences between races, and this figure seems remarkably high compared with other studies; the explanation of these findings is not clear. The Hammersmith report does not give the percentages of respondents who themselves felt unsafe going out alone after dark, but gives the percentages of blacks and whites who felt it was risky for several specified groups to go out on their own after dark. For each group blacks had higher percentages than whites thinking it was risky. For example 13 per cent of blacks thought black people were at risk and only 6 per cent of whites thought this (Painter *et al.*, Table 61). There is no indication that in Hammersmith or in Islington blacks were less afraid than other racial groups, as we found in Leeds, and as Smith (1983) found for the whole of London. There is a possibility that respondents do not interpret feeling "unsafe" about going out alone after

dark as the same as being "worried" about it and that might account for differences in the results. This will be explored in the next section.

Worries about Crime

A second indication of people's concern about crime was obtained from their answers to the question: "How much do you yourself worry about the possibility of (a) your home being broken into and something stolen (burglary); (b) being mugged or robbed (robbery); (c) having your home or property damaged by vandals (vandalism); or (d) being insulted or bothered by strangers (being insulted or bothered may be unpleasant but are, of course, not necessarily offences)?"

Comparisons between races showed, again, that Asians differed from blacks and whites, with higher percentages worried about each item. However, in this case blacks and whites did not differ significantly. Table 3 shows the percentages saying "quite a bit" or "a lot" for each item. In particular about two-thirds of Asians worried about burglary and only half of blacks and whites; twice as many Asians (36 per cent) worried about robbery as did blacks and whites (about 18 per cent). On the whole people who worried about one offence tended to worry about the other offences and the answers referring to different offences were significantly correlated (the average correlation within race being about 0.5). This justified the calculation of

an overall worries score (W)[3] from the individual scores for the three offences. Worry about insults from strangers was also significantly higher for Asians, and correlated highly with worries score (W).

Comparing our results with those of others, the Islington study gave figures ranging from 15.5 per cent (worried about attacks by strangers) to 26.6 per cent (for burglary). The Hammersmith study reported that considerably more Asians (about 73 per cent) worried about burglary and property damage than did whites and blacks (averaging 63 per cent for burglary and 53 per cent for damage), who did not differ. These differences and similarities are consistent with those found in Leeds (see Table 3).

Correlations of worries with age were not significant except for a slight tendency, among blacks, for older people to worry more about burglary and *less* about insults from strangers than the other groups. Maxfield (1984) found (using British Crime Survey data, which covers the whole of England and Wales) an increase in the percentage of males with a "big worry about crime" with age, which is not confirmed in the current study. His figures increased from about 2 per cent at age 16 to 10 per cent at age 35—considerably fewer than in Leeds. The London studies did not give results in relation to age.

Correlations of worries with actual victimization in our study were not significant for blacks or whites; for Asians there was a low (just significant) correlation (r = 0.19), those having been victims of more offences tending to be more worried.

Relationship between Worries and Fear

Were those who worried about being a victim of an offence the same as those who felt unsafe in the area at night? It is perhaps surprising to find that the correlations of "fear" with worry about *robbery* are about the same as those with worry about *burglary* and (for Asians and whites) with worry about *vandalism* (see Table 4, first three columns). It might be expected that fear in the streets would only be associated with worry

Table 3 Worries about Crime

% Who Worry[a]	Black	Asian	White
Burglary[a]	50	66	52
Robbery[a]	19	36	18
Vandalism[a]	41	60	36
Insults from strangers[a]	15	33[b]	12
Mean of first three	37	54	35
W score[c]	6.5	7.7	6.7

[a]Percentage saying they worry quite a bit or a lot about being victims.

[b]Offences with significant differences.

[c]W = Worries' for scoring see text. Asians are significantly higher than whites and blacks (p<0.05).

Differences between any 2 ethnic groups of 10 or more in the percentages are significant at p<0.05 or higher.

Table 4 Fear Related to Worries

Worries about:	Correlation[a] Fear Score (F) with Worries Score (W)			% A Bit or Very Unsafe[b]					
	Black	Asian	White	Black		Asian		White	
				High[c]	Low[c]	High	Low	High	Low
Burglary	0.23	0.28	0.28	14	4	37	19	28	13
Robbery	0.22	0.29	0.37	19	7	44	23	43	16
Vandalism	(0.16)	0.23	0.40	13	6	36	24	30	16
Insults	(0.02)	0.19	0.22	8	9	41	26	29	19

[a] Correlations are significant at p<0.05 or more except those in parentheses.

[b] For interpretation see text.

[c] High = worried quite a bit or a lot. Low = worried not much or not at all.

about being robbed, rather than worry about burglary or vandalism. Correlations were low (of the order of 0.3), but in the main significant.

Table 4 illustrates the meaning of these correlations by also showing that the percentages feeling very or a bit unsafe tend to be higher for those having high as compared with low values of "worry." For example, of those Asians who say they worry about being a victim of burglary quite a bit or a lot, 37 per cent feel a bit very unsafe while only 19 per cent of those who do not worry about being a victim of burglary do so.

The low correlations between fear on the street and worry about robbery suggest the questions addressed are to some extent tapping *different* types of concern. On the other hand the fact that there are many *significant* correlations between the fear and the worry scores for *each* of the three offences (in the main of the order of 0.3 for Asians and whites) suggests there is a diffuse feeling of "concern" about being a victim of any of the three types of crime.

Crime As an Area Problem

Another approach to respondents' concern about crime was to ask them whether they thought certain features (including crime) were a problem in the area they lived in. This is a less personal concern and invokes a more general perception of the area. The items were in four main groups:

these are briefly described as relating to (1) crime; (2) attacks on women; (3) people (incivility); and (4) civic problems. They were intermingled in the questionnaire. Those related to crime were: "crime," "burglary," "robbery," and "vandalism." There were two items referring to women: "sex attacks on women" and "women being pestered" (which is unpleasant but not necessarily an offence). The other items (3) and (4), are described in the following section. Possible answers were "a big problem," "a slight problem," and "not really a problem." The percentages in the first and last categories are given in Table 5, where it can be seen that the ethnic groups differed significantly on only three items. First, in relation to "burglary," fewer blacks thought it a big problem: 38 per cent compared with an average of 51 per cent for Asians and whites, who did not differ significantly. For the two items involving women as victims (assaults and pestering women), significantly more whites thought these a problem: about a quarter compared with about 12 per cent for blacks and Asians. This is consistent with Smith (1983) who found considerably more whites thought so (42 per cent) than did blacks (24 per cent) or Asians (30 per cent) (the statement was "risks to women are serious"). He also found, as did we, that Asians and blacks did not differ. These groups included men and women respondents, and all ages, so no direct comparison is possible. Older people and women tended to have higher percentages. This was one of the few variables, in the Leeds survey, where blacks and Asians did not differ. It is possible that Asian women go out less than black or white women, and therefore the men do not regard them as being at risk.

The average inter-correlations between the four crime scores were fairly high, being over 0.5 for each ethnic group, and an overall crime problem score (P) was calculated.[4] The two items referring to women had correlations (within races) of over 0.7 and were scored together as S. P (crime) was fairly highly correlated with S (problems for women), the correlations averaging 0.47 for the three ethnic groups. The overall

Table 5 Crime a Problem in Area						
	% A Big Problem			**% Not Really a Problem**		
	Black	**Asian**	**White**	**Black**	**Asian**	**White**
"Crime"	38	46	44	23	26	25
Burglary[a]	38	50	52	25	18	16
Vandalism	36	42	44	24	28	25
Robbery	25	26	24	51	47	48
Mean of last three (Crime problems)	33	39	40	33	31	30
P score[a,b]	3.9	4.3	4.3			
Sex assaults[a]	9	1	23	77	65	53
Women pestered (not a crime)	14	13	25	67	62	45
S score[a,b]	0.7	0.8	1.1			

[a] Significant differences between ethnic groups (p<0.05 or higher).

[b] P = Problems, S = Sex attacks, for scoring see text.

Differences between any 2 ethnic groups of 10 or more in the percentages are significant at p<0.05 or higher.

scores on crime problems (P) showed whites and Asians as having slightly and significantly higher scores respectively (<0.05), while for "problems for women" the difference between whites and the rest was more highly significant (<0.01). On average about a third of blacks and about 10 per cent of whites and Asians thought the crime items a big problem, but the proportion saying these items were "not really a problem" did not differ significantly, averaging just under one third.

Neither age nor number of times people went out were significantly correlated with these two problem scores. However, for Asians and for whites the number of times people had been a victim of an offence was significantly correlated with the problem score (P) (r = 0.29 and r = 0.19 respectively), those who had been victims of an offence, perhaps not surprisingly, tending to regard crime as a problem.

The report on the Islington study does not give full details of the different ethnic groups' perception of specific offences as a problem. However, for "crime" generally, the percentages thinking it a big problem are given by sex, age group, and race (Jones et al., Table 23). For men aged 16–24 only 18.9 per cent of Asians thought so, compared with 31 per

cent of whites and 35.7 per cent of blacks (for those aged 25–44 the figures are slightly higher for whites and Asians but lower for blacks). These figures are quite the opposite from those in the Leeds study, where blacks had the *lowest* problem scores.

In the Hammersmith and Fulham study (Painter et al. 1989), figures are not given by age group and sex, so they cannot be compared directly. Here Asians had figures *similar* to those of blacks, and both had a higher proportion than whites thinking vandalism and crime generally "a big problem" (36 per cent thinking so, compared with 26 per cent of whites). This is at variance with their finding that Asians had considerably more saying they worried quite a bit or a lot about burglary and vandalism (nearly 75 per cent or three quarters compared with about 58 per cent of the rest). Without knowing more about the characteristics of the Asians and the populations involved it is difficult to interpret these very diverse results.

Crime Problems and Fear

The relationships between fear and regarding offences as a problem are shown by the correlation coefficients in Table 6 (first three columns). The correlations between "fear" and re-

garding robbery as a problem are significant but perhaps surprisingly low (averaging 0.30); correlations with burglary are of about the same magnitude. The correlations of fear and regarding vandalism as an area problem were significant for Asians and whites (0.28), but were not significant for blacks.

Crime Problems and Worries

The correlations between problems and worries for the individual offence types—burglary, robbery, and vandalism—are also shown in Table 6. While those for the same offences (underlined in the table) are undoubtedly significant, they were not as high as would be expected if they were tapping the same type of concern. The average correlation (over the three ethnic groups) between the worry score and problem score for burglary was 0.37, and that for robbery 0.31. For the vandalism items blacks had a correlation of only 0.19, significantly lower than that of Asians (0.41), whites having a value of 0.31. Several of the correlations between regarding an offence as a problem and worrying about a *different* offence were also significant. In particular Asians and blacks had correlations of 0.47 and 0.41 respectively between "burglary a problem" and "worrying about vandalism"; this is perhaps not surprising as both are attacks on the home. On the other hand, considering that blacks had over a third (36 per cent) thinking vandalism a big problem and 41 per cent saying they worried about vandalism, the low correlation (0.19) with "worries" scores (bottom line) is puzzling.

Overall, it is clear that the three measures of concern: "fear" of attack, "worries" about different offences, and regarding different offences as "problems" in the area are all intercorrelated, if not highly.

Correlations between *overall* scores for the four measures "fear" (F), "offences a problem" (P), "problems for attacks on women" (S), and "worries about offences" (W) are shown in Table 7. The only non-significant one is for blacks, between fear and attacks on women being a problem. (It should be borne in mind that the sample was for males only.) Twelve of the 18 coefficients in the

Table 6 Correlation of "Crime Problems" with "Fear" and "Worries"

					Worries about							
	Fear			Burglary			Robbery			Vandalism		
Problems	Bl	As	Wh	Bl	As	Wh	Bl	As	Wh	Bl	As	Wh
Burglary	0.24	0.23	0.32	0.42	0.34	0.33	0.22	(0.15)	(0.13)	0.41	0.47	0.19
Robbery	0.23	0.30	0.37	(0.12)	0.27	0.22	0.28	0.34	0.30	(0.17)	0.40	0.24
Vandalism	(0.15)	0.28	0.28	(0.16)	0.23	0.23	(0.11)	(0.15)	0.17	0.19	0.41	0.31

Figures in parentheses are not significant.

Underlined figures are those expected to be high, as they relate to same offence.

Table 7 Correlations between Overall Scores for Fear, Worries, and Problems

	Black	Asian	White
F. W	0.24	0.33	0.40
F. P	0.21	0.35	0.28
F. S	(0.08)	0.26	0.23
P.W	0.36	0.49	0.37
W. S	0.26	0.37	0.32
P. S	0.45	0.52	0.48

P = crime problems score.

W = worries about crime score (for scoring see text).

S = attacks on women score.

F = fear score.

table are between 0.32 and 0.52 indicating that *within* each race group the scores were to some extent, but by no means entirely, measuring the same concept. For each pair of variables the correlations were lower for blacks, perhaps indicating a slightly less generalized concern, and a consequence of their mean scores on each measure tending to be lower than the rest.

General Area Problems

As already mentioned in the Leeds survey the question on problems in the area included general topics intermingled with those related to crime discussed above. They have been divided into two main groups. The first group, named "people problems," had four items and consisted of "race relations," "general unfriendliness," "rowdiness among teenagers," and "fights and disturbances." The score obtained from this group was labelled PP. The second was named "civic problems" (CP).

There were five items consisting of housing, schools, public transport, street lighting, and play space. (These groups are similar to, but not identical with, those of Box *et al* (1988) named "Incivilities," "Cohesion," and "Housing conditions.") There were three additional items relating to unemployment, lorry noise, and "activities for young people." The percentages thinking each item "a big problem" or "not really a problem" are given in Table 8.

Differences between ethnic groups were small. In the PP group there were no differences between races except that fewer whites and more blacks thought race relations were "not really a problem" and blacks had a lower problem score (PP)[5] (but not significantly lower). On the CP items significantly more whites than Asians thought housing a big problem but the overall scores (CP) were almost the same. The correlation between PP and CP scores were blacks 0.52, Asians 0.47, and whites 0.27, and it is apparent that

people had general feelings of satisfaction or dissatisfaction about problems in their areas, although this was true to a lesser extent for whites. The fact that the ethnic groups did not differ significantly on the overall scores may be a consequence of the samples being taken from the same areas. Painter, in contrast, found in Hammersmith and Fulham that more blacks than whites found nearly every one of 19 items a big problem, but it is not clear if they lived in the same areas as the whites. Jones *et al.* (Islington survey) did not give details for ethnic groups.

Relationship between Area Problems and Concern about Crime

The correlation between the area problem scores PP and CP with each of the four measures of concern about crime are shown in Table 9. The "fear" score was significantly correlated with PP (people problems) for all three races, but the correlation was low for blacks (blacks r = 0.19, Asians r = 0.31, whites r = 0.27). The correlation between fear (F) and crime problems (CP) was only significant for Asians (r = 0.29).

Worry about crime items was significantly correlated with PP (people problems) for all three ethnic groups, the average of the three correlations being r = 0.30. Correlations with CP (civic problems), however, are again considerably lower, being less than 0.22, but are just as significant.

However, the problem scores for crime (P) and attacks on women (S) were consistently and fairly highly correlated with the area problem scores (CP and PP), straight averages from correlations being 0.45 (blacks) 0.45 (Asians) and 0.45 (whites). This is of considerable interest because it suggests concern about crime as a problem is part of a general pattern of perception of problems in the area.

Summary and Conclusions

The survey reported here differed from many other similar surveys in that it was restricted to areas of Leeds

Table 8 Area Problems

	% A Big Problem			% Not Really a Problem		
	Black	**Asian**	**White**	**Black**	**Asian**	**White**
People problems:						
Race relations[a]	14	15	20	64	61	53
General unfriendliness	10	7	10	71	68	67
Rowdiness by teenagers[a]	25	29	26	45	35	38
Fights and disturbances	14	19	14	62	47	58
Mean %	16	18	18	60	53	54
PP score	0.1	0.5	0.5			
Civic problems:						
Poor housing[a]	58	53	65	16	24	24
Poor schools	34	30	33	40	39	39
Public transport	14	12	15	74	67	66
Street lighting	12	7	11	72	72	70
Play space	44	45	52	28	26	21
Mean %	32	29	35	46	46	44
CP score	1.0	0.9	1.0			
Other items:						
Unemployment	76	68	70	8	8	8
Lorry noise	14	17	14	67	62	65
Activities for young	57	49	54	18	21	20

[a]Significant differences between some groups.

Differences between any 2 ethnic groups of 10 or more in the percentages are significant at p<0.05 or higher.

Table 9 Correlations between Area Problems and Concern about Crime

	Black	**Asian**	**White**
PP.F	0.19	0.31	0.27
PP.W	0.37	0.27	0.27
PP.P	0.62	0.57	0.56
PP.S	0.45	0.53	0.38
CP.F	(0.12)	0.29	(0.10)
CP.W	0.19	0.17	0.21
CP.P	0.52	0.44	0.41
CP.S	0.22	0.32	0.44
CP.PP	0.52	0.48	0.27

PP = people problems score.

P = crime problems score.

W = crime worries score.

CP = civic problems score.

S = attacks on women score.

F = fear score.

All correlations are significant (p<0.05 or higher) except those in parentheses.

where over 10 per cent of the people were estimated to be non-white; these contained over half the Asian and black population of Leeds but only 6 per cent of the white population. This had the advantage that comparisons between those of different ethnic origin were between those having roughly the same living conditions, although there were some differences in their socio-economic status, which have been described in the Main Report (Walker *et al.* 1990). Useful comparisons cannot be made with the results of other surveys which covered large areas, and where the non-whites would be more likely than whites to be living in socially deprived areas. It was interesting to find, however, that none of our measures was correlated with the percentage of non-whites in the areas included in the survey. This varied from 10 per cent to 60 per cent.

The respondents of the main survey were all males aged 16 to 35, which is another reason why it is difficult to compare the results with other surveys, where breakdowns by sex and age, in relation to ethnic origin, are often not given. Besides this, sometimes Asians and blacks are taken together as non-white, and differences between them have not been presented.

"Concern about crime" has been examined here in three different ways, and while the results of sample surveys can only give indications of underlying reactions to crime, those presented here suggest that the subject is a complex one. The three measures, which we have named "fear," "worries," and "problems," were in the main, significantly correlated with each other *within* each race group, so to some extent they were measuring the same thing. But, insofar as the correlations were small, it is clear that all three are measuring slightly different concepts and these should all be examined separately.

Differences and similarities between the three ethnic groups are a further indication that the three measures should be examined separately. For, while blacks are evidently less fearful than whites about walking on the streets at night (Table 2), they did not appear to worry about crime any less than whites (Table 3). With regard to problems, more whites than blacks thought burglary a problem (in spite of living in the same areas), and that attacks on women were a problem (the reaction of women to this question would be of considerable interest). About the same proportion (a quarter) thought robbery a problem.

Asians tended to differ from both blacks and whites on both "fear" (having considerably more who were fearful) and on "worries" (with more who worried a lot). This ties up with their reaction to the police (Jefferson and Walker 1993), which was generally favourable, and their believing there were not sufficient police around. On the other hand, they did not differ from whites in regarding crime a problem, the figures were fairly high, with, on average, about 40 per cent thinking this was the case (Table 4). Significantly fewer Asians than whites thought attacks on women a problem, (possibly because Asian women are unlikely to go out on their own).

Perception of particular features as being problems in the area did not differ greatly between ethnic groups. Under 20 per cent regarded what we called "people problems" (see Table 8) as being big problems, and about a third, on average "civic problems." It was interesting to find

that there were mainly significant correlations between these measures and the three measures of "concern" (Table 9). This suggests that "crime" is one of a constellation of factors which people regard as part of life's problems.

Overall, it is clear that just one measure of "concern about crime" is inadequate. It is also clear that deconstructive work on the meanings of the terms used, for the different ethnic groups, could be usefully undertaken.

Notes

1. This was part of a research project entitled "Ethnic minorities, Young People and the Criminal Justice System", funded by the Economic and Social Research Council, Ref. E 06250023.
2. The 1981 Census included a question on place of birth and EDs were selected in which the head of household was born in the New Commonwealth or Pakistan.
3. The answers coded were "not at all" (scored 1); "quite a bit" (scored 2) and "a lot" (scored 3) ("don't know" was also scored 1).
4. For the analysis these were scored as: a large problem = 3; a slight problem = 2; not really a problem = 1.
5. Scoring: big problem = 3, not really a problem = 1; other = 2.

References

Baldwin, J., and Bottoms, A. E. (1976), *The Urban Criminal: A Study in Sheffield*. London: Tavistock.

Box, S., Hale, C., and Glen, A. (1988), "Explaining Fear of Crime," *British Journal of Criminology*: 28: 340–56.

Crawford, A., Jones, T., Woodhouse, T., & Young, J. (1989), *Second Islington Crime Survey*. Middlesex Polytechnic.

Hough, M., and Mayhew, P. (1983), *The British Crime Survey: First Report* Home Office Research Study, No. 76, London: HMSO.

Jefferson, T., and Walker, M. A. (1992), "Ethnic Minorities and the Criminal Justice System," *Criminal Law Review*, February, 83–95.

—— (1993), "Attitudes to the Police of the Ethnic Minorities in a Provincial City," *British Journal of Criminology*, 33/2: 251–66.

Jones, T., Maclean, B., and Young, J. (1986), *The Islington Crime Survey*. Aldershot: Gower.

Lewis, D. A., and Salem, G. (1986), *Fear of Crime, Incivility and the Production of a Social Problem*. New Brunswick, NJ: Oxford: Transaction Books.

Maxfield, M. G. (1984), *Fear of Crime in England and Wales*. Home Office Research Study, No. 78. London: HMSO.

Painter, K., Lee, J., Woodhouse, T., and Young, J. (1989), *Hammersmith and Fulham Crime and Policing Survey*. Middlesex Polytechnic, Centre for Criminology.

Smith, D. (1983), *A Survey of Londoners: Police and People in London 1*. London: Policy Studies Institute.

Walker, M. A., Jefferson, T., and Seneviratne, M. (1990), *Ethnic Minorities, Young People and the Criminal Justice System*. Main Report, Centre for Criminological and Legal Research, University of Sheffield.

Article Review Form at end of book.

Does the fear of crime among the black elderly affect their lifestyle?

Fear of Crime among Black Elderly

Janice Joseph

Janice Joseph is an associate professor in the Criminal Justice at Richard Stockton College of New Jersey. Other research interests include violence against women, women and criminal justice youth violence, juvenile delinquency, gangs, and minorities and criminal justice.

Many studies show that fear of crime among the elderly is a serious problem (Clark, Ekblom, & Mayhew, 1985; Eve & Eve, 1984; Ollenburger, 1981; Ortega & Myles, 1987). Most of the studies also suggest that fear of crime has serious psychological, physical, and financial consequences for the elderly (Garafalo, 1981; Jayewardene, Juliani, & Talbot, 1983; Yin, 1985). Although several studies have focused on the fear of crime among the elderly, few have analyzed fear of crime within the person-environment context. As a consequence, the causes of fear of crime remain unclear. Rather than viewing fear of crime as a consequence of victimization, fear of crime should be viewed within a more general context of person-environment, which reflects the interaction between the person and the environment. Such a context places fear of crime in a broader and more analytic perspective. Moreover, although the Black elderly represent the largest minority group among the aged (U.S. Census Bureau, 1992), information on the fear of crime among elderly Blacks is sparse because the Black el-

derly are underrepresented in most of the studies on fear of crime. Therefore, it is difficult to evaluate the representative nature and relevance of the data collected with regard to Black seniors.

The purpose of this study is to examine the nature, extent, and causes of the fear of crime among Black seniors by focusing on the environmental factors, perceptions of vulnerability, vicarious victimization, and personal victimization.

Review of Literature on Fear of Crime

Data from over 20 years of research have consistently shown that the elderly are less likely to be victimized than younger persons (Bureau of Justice Statistics, 1983, 1991, 1992a, 1992b; Cook, Skogan, Cook, & Antunes, 1978; Ennis, 1967; Reiss, 1967).

In 1991 the elderly comprised 14% of the population. The data also showed that certain groups of elderly experienced higher rates of victimization. Elderly males experienced a higher rate of victimization than elderly females. Elderly females, however, were more likely to be victims of personal larceny with contact, such as purse snatching. Those who were either separated or divorced had the highest rates of victimization for all types of crimes compared to other marital categories. Elderly residents in cities, compared to either

suburban or rural elderly, experienced the highest rates of victimization of crime. Blacks were more likely than Whites to be victims of crime. In general, research shows that elderly men, minorities, urbanites, and the unmarried are more likely to be victimized than their counterparts.

Despite the low victimization rate, the elderly have the highest fear of crime because of perceived vulnerability. Research has shown that the elderly express the greatest fear of crime of all age groups (Bureau of Justice Statistics, 1992b; Braungart et al., 1980; Cook et al., 1978; Erskine, 1974; Garafalo, 1981; Linquist & Duke, 1982; Ollenburger, 1981; Yin, 1982). Fear of crime is highest among elderly females, elderly African Americans, low socioeconomic-status elderly, and urban dwellers (Braungart et al. 1980; Brillon, 1987; Erskine, 1974; Lee, 1982a, 1982b, 1983; Toseland, 1982; Yin, 1980, 1985).

The relationship between age, victimization, and fear of crime is, therefore, paradoxical because the high fear of crime in the elderly is disproportionate to their risk of victimization. What then accounts for this paradoxical situation of lowest rate of victimization and highest fear of crime among the elderly? Hindelang, Gottfredson, and Garafalo (1978) and Lawton, Nahemow, Yaffe, and Feldman (1976) argue that lifestyle is an important factor in victimization. Certain people are more vulnerable to victimization because of their lifestyles. Most

Janice Joseph, *Journal of Black Studies*, Vol. 27, No. 5, May 1997, pp. 698–717. Copyright © 1997 Sage Publications, Inc. Reprinted by permission of Sage Publications, Inc.

personal crimes occur in public (streets, parks); therefore, those who frequent these places are more vulnerable to victimization. Because the elderly are less likely than younger persons to visit such places, they are less exposed to the risk of being victimized. In addition, the fact that the elderly are at home more often than younger persons reduces the risk of household victimization, in that occupancy of a house tends to deter burglars. Many of the elderly live alone and often stay home after dark. The elderly, therefore, do not have lifestyles that expose them to household and personal victimization as do young people.

The fear of crime among the elderly is related to several factors. Yin (1985) suggested that personal and environmental factors are relevant to the fear of crime. The personal factors include perceptions of vulnerability, personal victimization, and environmental factors. Perceptions of vulnerability refer to the perceptions one has of being victimized. Environmental factors include two dimensions: (a) the physical dimension, such as abandoned buildings, population density, and quality of housing, and (b) the social dimension, such as economic status and the composition of the population. There are two types of victimization: vicarious victimization, which refers to the knowledge one has of others who have been victimized, and personal victimization, which refers to the actual victimization experienced by the individual.

Elderly Blacks

The research on elderly Blacks is very sparse. According to Richardson (1992), African Americans represent the largest minority group in the United States (12%) and approximately 8% of African Americans were 65 years and older in 1980. By the year 2000, the African American elderly population is expected to increase by 46%, compared with an increase of 23% for Whites (Jackson, 1988).

Research has shown that elderly Blacks are in a disadvantaged position relative to Whites. They are poorer (Markides & Mindel, 1987; Minkler & Stone, 1985), their education is lower (Husaini, Moore, & Castor, 1991), their life expectancy is shorter (Atchley, 1988), and they are more at risk for institutional placement than their White counterparts (Husaini et al., 1991).

Elderly Blacks rarely use community-based elderly facilities (Carlton-LaNey, 1991; Richardson, 1992; Spence & Atherton, 1991). Black seniors fail to use these services because they are either unaware of their existence, are not involved in the planning and implementation, feel embarrassed about seeking public service, or are skeptical about these services because they often lack cultural programming for Blacks (Carlton-LaNey, 1991; Dancy, 1980; Husaini et al., 1991; Maldonado, 1982; Richardson, 1992; Wallace, 1990). Rather than use these services, elderly Blacks rely on informal networks such as the family and the church for support and assistance (Nye, 1993; Ralston, 1983; Spence & Atherton, 1991; Taylor, 1985).

Elderly Blacks were also more likely than elderly Whites to be victims of crime. This was particularly true for violent crimes, personal theft, and household crimes in 1992 (Bureau of Justice Statistics, 1992b). The victimization of Blacks is largely related to location. Black elderly are almost twice as likely as Whites to reside in central cities where crimes tend to be highest. Furthermore, because of their generally low incomes (they are the poorest of all Americans), they are also more concentrated in poorer areas than Whites (Alston, 1986).

Wiltz (1982) in his study on elderly Blacks found that the fear of crime was an integral part of their daily lives. Seven percent of the respondents were victimized at least once, and of these, 68% had suffered loss of property as a result of burglaries, robbery, and fraud. The victims of crimes were likely to be male, residing in public housing facilities, and living alone. Wiltz's study also revealed that those who were victimized had a higher fear of crime compared with those who were not victims.

Methodology

Sample

The data for this study were collected by means of an interview schedule from a sample of 119 Black seniors 65 and over, living in Atlantic City. The interviews were conducted in senior citizen centers, recreation centers, and homes of the respondents.

The sample consisted of 53% males and 47% females. The modal age range was 70 years (40%). Forty-one percent had incomes between $5,000 and $9,999, and only 2% had incomes over $20,000. Sixty-six percent of the sample were widowed, 12% were married, 11% were single, and 11% were divorced or separated. Eighty-two percent were retired, 86% lived on their own, 2% lived in a nursing home, 4% lived with relatives, and 8% lived elsewhere. Sixty-six percent had completed or had some secondary education, 26% had elementary education, and 8% had completed or had some college education.

Measures of Variables

Environmental factors were measured on a 10-item index that included the assessment of safety around the neighborhood, assessment of the safety of certain areas just outside the neighborhood, perceived safety of the home and public transportation, and physical as well as social conditions of the neighborhood.

Perception of vulnerability was measured on a four-item index. The indicators included gender, age, race, perceptions of being a victim of crime, and perceptions of physical effects, if victimized.

Vicarious victimization was measured on a five-item index, which examined the knowledge one has of others who have been victimized and the effects this knowledge has on the individual.

Personal victimization was measured on a five-item index, which examined personal experiences of being a victim of crime including the victimization, place of crime, whether alone or not at the time of the incident, fearfulness because of victimization, and the effects of the victimization.

Fear of crime was measured on two dimensions. One was concrete fear of crime, which included the fear of four major crimes: assault, robbery, burglary, and murder. The second dimension was formless fear of some vague threat to one's security, which included fear of being alone, fear of strangers, fear of going outside, and fear for personal safety.

General Results

Neighborhood Factors

The perception of safety in one's surroundings is a basis for one's subjective definition of fear of crime and victimization. Respondents were asked a series of questions concerning their perceptions of safety in various places in their environment. As would be expected, people felt safer in their homes than walking either in the neighborhood or just outside the neighborhood at night. These results are shown in Table 1.

Gubrium (1974) suggests that a homogeneous neighborhood should make a difference in the fear of crime. The majority of the respondents (80%) lived in an age-homogeneous environment. Seventy-six percent considered their neighborhoods "bad" neighborhoods, and only 24% felt that their neighborhoods were safe. Eighty-eight percent of those who felt that their neighborhoods were bad felt this way because of the high crime rate in those neighborhoods. Seventy-one percent felt that their neighborhoods were not well kept, and 81% felt that there were social problems in their neighborhoods. The mean scores are shown in Table 1.

Perception of Vulnerability

Seventy-seven percent of respondents reported being vulnerable to crime because of age. When asked about their vulnerability to crime because of gender, only 41% stated that they felt vulnerable because of their gender. Of those who felt that they were vulnerable because of gender, 92% did so because they felt that they were easy prey for criminals. They were also asked whether they felt that they would be badly hurt if they were victimized. Seventy-five percent believed that they would be seriously hurt if they were victimized.

Victimization

The respondents were also asked if they knew of anyone personally who had been a victim of crime (vicarious victimization). Fifty-one percent reported knowing someone who was a victim of crime within the 12 months prior to the research, and of these, 72% said that this knowledge had made them fearful. Of those who knew of someone who was victimized, 63% said that they were of the same gender and 62% said that they were of the same age.

Only 27% of the respondents had been victims of crime in the 12-month period prior to the research. Of these, 44% were victims of assault, 36% of robbery, and 20% of burglary. Fifty-two percent of these took place in the home, and 48% outside the home; 56% of the victims were alone. Of those who were victimized, only 15% had become fearful because of the victimization. Of those who were victimized in the home, 80% were victimized by relatives. Fifty-six percent of the victims said that the victimization affected them psychologically, 28% said financially, and 16% physically. However, only 30% of those who were victims of crimes reported it to the police.

Fear of Crime

The respondents were also asked which crime they feared the most, if any. Eighty-three percent of the respondents reported being fearful of personal crimes, 8% said property crimes, and 9% no crimes at all.

Table 1 shows that the mean scores for the items measuring formless fear are higher than those measuring concrete fear. These elderly seem to be more prone to formless fear, perhaps because of their low socioeconomic status and personal isolation, which in turn engender insecurity. Overall, 70% of the respondents had a high fear of crime.

Effects of Fear of Crime

The extent to which the fear of crime had a "chilling effect" on lifestyle was examined. Reynolds and Byth (1976) argued that the fear of crime affects the daily routine of people and creates stress and anxiety. Lawton et al. (1976) and Butler (1975) also argued that because of fear of crime, the elderly restrict their activi-

ties outside the home. Sixty-seven percent of respondents limited their activities, and 73% said that they avoided going out at night because of fear of crime. In short, the term "prisoners of fear of crime" does seem to accurately describe the elderly in our study.

Security Precautions Taken

Besides attempting to document whether fear of crime limited activities, the study also examined how respondents coped with an environment that they perceived to be dangerous. Only 70% said that they had taken precautions, and of these, 49% used more caution, 29% had installed locks, 17% owned a weapon, and 5% owned a dog. Interestingly, only 61% of those who were victimized took precautions against further crimes.

Looking at the rank order of measures taken, those elderly who did take precautions relied primarily on increased caution. None of the respondents indicated that he or she had purchased burglar alarms or expensive electronic devices. This may be attributed to the low socioeconomic status of the respondents (the average income of respondents was between $5,000 and $9,999).

Interestingly, of those who did not take any precautions, 48% said that they did not think that they would be victimized, 37% said that they did not want to think about it, 7% said that they did not know what to do, and 7% said that there was good security in their buildings.

Causes of Fear of Crime

The results show that there was a strong significant relationship between perceptions of vulnerability and fear of crime (beta = .30, $p < .01$), whereas the relationship between environmental factors and fear of crime was weak (beta = .19, $p < .05$). Vicarious and personal victimization fear of crime were not related to fear of crime. These results are shown in Table 2.

Personal vulnerability explained 11% of the variance in the dependent variable, environmental factors explained 4%, whereas vicarious and personal victimization contributed nothing to the variance. The variables, together, explained 16% of the variance.

Table 1 | Mean Score of Variables

Perceptions of neighborhood

Safe from crime in neighborhood	2.7
Afraid to walk in certain areas of neighborhood at night	1.2
Neighborhood bad	1.3
Neighborhood safe	1.6
Safe to walk just outside neighborhood	1.8
Likely someone walking around neighborhood will be a victim of crime	3.0
Safe in house	1.2
Safe in public transportation	1.7
Neighborhood well kept	1.3
Know neighbors well	1.3

Personal vulnerability

Vulnerable because of age	1.5
Vulnerable because of gender	1.2
Vulnerable because of race	1.2
Hurt badly if victimized	1.3
Perceptions of being victimized	2.2

Victimization

Vicarious victimization

Know personally of victim of crime	1.5
Knowledge makes you fearful	1.2
Victim same age	1.4
Victim same gender	1.3
Victim same race	1.7

Personal victimization

Victim of crime personally	1.7
Place of crime	1.7
Alone at time of incident	1.3
Fearful because of personal victimization	1.4
Effects of victimization	1.9

Types of fears

Concrete fear

Fearful of burglary	1.9
Fearful of assault	1.3
Fearful of robbery	1.6
Fearful of murder	1.9

Formless fear

Fearful of being alone	2.1
Fearful of stranger in neighborhood	2.0
Fearful of going outside	2.7
Fearful of one's personal safety	2.0

Note: Higher score indicates feeling of less safety or higher fear.

Gender Differences

The data in Table 3 indicate that there is a significant difference between the males and females with regard to their perception of vulnerability because of their gender and age. Females had a higher perception than males of vulnerability because of age, whereas males had a slightly higher feeling than females that they were vulnerable because of their gender. Fifty-three percent of the males and 44% of the females reported knowing of someone who was victimized. Thirty-one percent of the males and 23% of the females were victimized personally. Of those victimized, 90% of the females compared with 40% of the males had become fearful after the victimization; significant at $r = -.50, p < .01$. More males than females (70% versus 30%, respectively, of those victimized) were alone when the incident occurred with a significance of $r = .43, p < .01$. In addition, males were significantly more likely than females to be fearful of murder. These results are shown in Table 3. Overall, 77% of the males and 76% of the females expressed a high fear of crime.

Males expressed a higher perception of vulnerability than females; 73% of the males did so, compared to 49% of the females ($F = 21.64, p < .001$). This particular result is contrary to research showing that females have higher perceptions of vulnerability than males do (Brillon, 1987; Lee, 1983; Yin, 1980, 1985). There was a weak significant difference between environmental factors and gender with $r = .20, p < .05$. There were no significant differences between males and females with regard to vicarious victimization and personal victimization.

The data in Table 4 indicate that perceptions of vulnerability and environmental factors were related to the fear of crime for the males, whereas only perceptions of vulnerability were related to the fear of crime for females. These factors explained 38% of the variance for males and 22% for females. Overall, the results indicate that these factors were related more to the fear of crime for the males than for the females.

There are two possibilities for these results. The first possibility could be related to this sample; more males than females reported residing in bad neighborhoods ($F = 12.83, p < .001$). Consequently, they may experience higher feelings of vulnerability than the females in this sample. The second possibility could be related to the fact that Black males have the highest rate of victimization of any group in the United States. For example, victimization statistics for 1991 indicate that Black males were victims of violent crimes at the rate of 61 per 1,000 persons, compared with a White male rate of 38, a Black female rate of 31, and a White female rate of 22. In addition, the murder rate for Black males was 52 per 1,000 in 1991, compared with a White male rate of 8, a Black female rate of 12, and a White female rate of 3. Assault rate was 41 per 1,000 for Black males; for White males, 31; for Black females, 22; and for White females, 18. The pattern is similar for robbery:

Table 2 Mean Scores and Multiple Regression of All Variables

Variables	Feaofcri	
	Mean Scores	Multiple Regression Beta
Vicarvic	5.1	.13
Environ	5.3	.19*
Pervulne	6.6	.30**
Pervictm	3.4	.13
R		.40
R²		.16

Note: Vicarvic = vicarious victimization, Environ = environmental peril, Pervulne = personal vulnerability, Pervictm = personal victimization, Feaofcri = fear of crime

*Significant at .05 level. **Significant at .01 level.

Black males were victimized at a rate of 20 per 1,000 in 1991; White males at 6, Black females at 8, and White females at 3 (Bureau of Justice Statistics, 1992b). Given these realities, it is understandable why the Black males in this study would have a higher perception of vulnerability than Black females.

Public Policy Implications

The fact that the elderly express a high fear of crime suggests that special efforts should be made to assist the elderly. Unfortunately, there are very few policies specifically designed for the elderly.

Atlantic City has several crime prevention programs that include Neighborhood Watch, Project Identification, Crime Prevention Lectures, and Holiday and Vacation Tips. In addition, the Crime Prevention Unit of the Atlantic City Police Department conducts security surveys, crime prevention lectures, and drug awareness seminars (Atlantic City Police Department, 1982). However, only 59% of the respondents were able to identify one of these programs, 10% identified two programs, and 31% could not identify any of these programs. There needs to be a greater awareness of these programs by the elderly in the city.

The data showed that many of the respondents had low incomes and, therefore, many (76%) lived in neighborhoods that they perceived as bad because of crime. Their lack of financial resources may have prevented them from finding accommodation in safer neighborhoods. Many of the buildings where the study took place lacked proper security systems, and nonresidents gained easy access to these buildings. Moving the elderly from their neighborhoods is not feasible. What is necessary is to make their defensible space more secure. This would entail providing entrances, hallways, and stairways with surveillance devices for easy detection of crime. Designs of these buildings should include fewer floors, entrances that serve only a small number of units, and other features to discourage outsiders from entering.

Even if the defensible space is improved, the elderly need to protect their individual apartments or homes by "hardening the targets," making victimization more difficult. This can be done through the installation of locks, window bars, alarms, and other electronic devices. The study showed that some elderly did take precautions against crimes, but many of the devices used were not very sophisticated. Given the low incomes of the elderly in this study, effectively protecting their homes may be financially prohibitive for them. Moreover, studies have shown that low socio-economic-status Black senior citizens use few "target-hardening" devices. For those seniors who cannot afford to properly protect their homes from crimes, money should be provided by the city, county, or state to assist them in this endeavor.

The elderly face victimization on the streets as well. Forty-eight percent of those victimized in this study were victimized on the streets.

The elderly need to be informed about the dangers that threaten them. Efforts should be made to warn the elderly about the crimes to which they could fall prey and to inform them on how to protect themselves. Public campaigns could be launched to inform the elderly of their role in fighting crime. By educating the elderly in crime prevention strategies, it might be possible to reduce the incidence of victimization and fear of crime. The police, and other practitioners in Atlantic City and elsewhere, could inform the elderly on how to avoid street crimes and should encourage the elderly to take precautions to make themselves more defensible while on the streets.

A significant way to reduce vulnerability of the elderly while outside their homes is strengthening their social network. This would include "buddy systems" and "volunteer escorts," which provide peer support and protection for the elderly.

Comradery among neighbors, developed through such programs as Neighborhood Watch, Block Watch, Crime Watch, and Defensible Space Programs, can lessen some of their fears. The elderly should also be fully informed of the presence of these programs in their community. Involvement in community action preventive strategies is an effective way of making them feel useful as well as allaying their fear of crime, which is often exaggerated in relation to their risk of being victimized.

The extent of elderly abuse in the home in the Black population is unknown, but 80% of those victimized in the home were victimized by family members. There have been very few initiatives taken to prevent elderly abuse. The most significant effort to date is the implementation of legislation, in 43 states as of 1990, mandatorily requiring individuals to report elderly abuse. There are, however, some problems with this legislation. The meaning of the legislation is not very clear; it does not include psychological and emotional abuse, and it violates both doctor-patient confidentiality and the civil rights of the elderly. Even if this legislation assists in preventing elderly abuse, more needs to be done by providing better programs to assist those who take care of the elderly, especially family members.

Table 3 Mean Score of Variables by Race and Gender

	Gender		
	Male	**Female**	**F-value**
Perceptions of neighborhood			
Safe from crime in neighborhood	3.10	3.00	.25
Afraid to walk in certain areas of neighborhood at night	2.33	1.81	6.24*
Neighborhood bad	1.43	1.12	12.83
Neighborhood safe	1.67	1.63	.706
Safe to walk just outside neighborhood	1.20	1.19	.07
Likely someone walking around neighborhood will be a victim of crime	1.54	1.70	1.04
Safe in house	1.95	1.72	1.81
Safe in public transportation	1.63	1.79	1.61
Neighborhood well kept	1.41	1.26	2.63
Know neighbors well	1.31	1.37	.35
Personal vulnerability			
Vulnerable because of gender	1.88	1.28	51.57**
Vulnerable because of age	1.12	1.33	6.30**
Vulnerable because of race	1.27	1.18	.91
Perceptions of being victimized	2.25	2.19	.18
Hurt badly if victimized	1.29	1.20	.80
Victimization			
Vicarious victimization			
Know personally of victim of crime	1.43	1.56	1.31
Knowledge makes you fearful	1.25	1.31	.16
Victim same age	1.41	1.47	.19
Victim same gender	1.44	1.26	1.56
Victim same race	1.57	2.11	1.83
Personal victimization			
Victim of crime personally	1.69	1.73	.72
Place of crime	1.60	1.90	1.18
Alone at time of incident	1.27	1.70	5.14**
Fearful because of personal victimization	1.63	1.10	7.67**
Effects of victimization	1.73	2.10	1.89
Fear of crime			
Concrete fear			
Fearful of burglary	1.66	1.56	1.31
Fearful of assault	1.27	1.39	1.58
Fearful of robbery	1.20	1.16	.30
Fearful of murder	2.08	1.65	6.14**
Formless fear			
Fearful of being alone	2.06	2.07	.01
Fearful of stranger in neighborhood	2.01	1.95	.05
Fearful of going outside	1.95	1.85	.26
Fearful of one's personal safety	1.95	2.00	.06

Note: Higher score indicates feeling of less safety or higher fear.

*Significant at .05 level. **Significant at .01 level.

Many minorities, such as Blacks, often depend on informal networks to deal with problems, but such networks may not be effective if adequate resources are not available. Increasing the services for primary caregivers for the Black elderly might remedy the problem of abuse. Such programs include respite care, day care, and home care programs. If elderly abuse increases because of the lack of services, the Black elderly would be more vulnerable to abuse, because there appears to be fewer social services in Black communities.

The most significant policy is for politicians to eliminate crime at its source. Although changing one's lifestyle can reduce crime, it is, however, necessary for politicians and policy makers to examine the root causes of crimes. Once those causes have been identified, societal changes can be the focus. It is undeniably true that changing society is more difficult than changing the lifestyles of the elderly. However, if significant changes in the rates and pattern of criminal victimization do not occur, then changing one's lifestyle and protecting one's home will not prevent crimes. Societal changes should focus on providing more economic and educational opportunities for individuals, especially for the youth. It also necessitates providing better living conditions for disadvantaged groups of individuals. In general, it may mean the restructuring of our society.

Although these recommendations can be useful, they have to be implemented very carefully. For example, crime prevention programs should not intensify anxiety about victimization. Programs that are intended to increase protection and safety should not sensitize these elderly about the problem to the point where they become more frightened. In addition, policies of this nature are designed to establish a safe place without creating an exclusive fortress for the elderly by separating them from the rest of the community.

Summary

The findings illustrate that personal vulnerability was the strongest determinant factor of fear of crime, whereas environmental factors showed a weak relationship with fear of crime. The results in the study also suggest that fear of crime did affect behavioral elements of the lifestyle of this sample by limiting their activities.

It is important to note the gender differences with regard to the major variables. The data on vulnerability to crime revealed that males expressed higher perceptions of vulnerability than did females (Table 4). In addition, 83% of the males and

Table 4 Mean Scores and Multiple Correlation of All Variables by Gender

| | Feaofcri | | | | |
| | Mean Scores | | | Multiple Regression Beta | |
Variables	Male	Female	F-Value	Male	Female
Vicarvic	5.11	5.05	.04	.01	.07
Environ	3.47	3.28	3.58*	.32*	.22*
Pervulne	5.77	4.79	21.79***	.44**	.32**
Pervictm	6.73	6.30	.55	.21	.38*
R				.61	.46
R²				.38	.22

Note: Vicarvic = vicarious victimization, Environ = environmental peril, Pervulne = personal vulnerability, Pervictm = personal victimization, Feaofcri = fear of crime.

*Significant at .05 level. **Significant at .01 level. ***Significant at .001 level.

70% of the females had a high fear of crime. These two latter results are inconsistent with previous research.

Future research needs to explore the extent, nature, and frequency of victimization among the Black elderly, especially elderly abuse. Studies should focus on the differences in fear of victimization from different crimes for the Black elderly. It is important for future research to distinguish between fear of violent crimes and fear of property crimes. Future research also needs to explain fear of crime with regard to the individual's perception of risk of victimization and vulnerability to crime.

Most research on the elderly has no gerontological focus for there is no specific reference and study to the impact of the aging process in many of the studies. Future research should also focus on the relationship between ageism and fear of crime especially among minorities. This may necessitate combining sociological and criminological concepts, theories, and methods with those of gerontology.

References

Alston, L. (1986). *Crime and older Americans.* Springfield, IL: Charles C Thomas.

Atchley, R. (1988). *Social forces and aging* (5th ed.). Belmont, CA: Wadsworth.

Atlantic City Police Department. (1982). *Atlantic City Police Community Police Relations and Crime Prevention Unit.* Atlantic City, NJ: Atlantic City Police Benevolence Association.

Braungart, M., Braungart, R., & Hover, W. (1990). Age, sex and social factors in fear of crime. *Sociological Focus, 13*(1), 55–66.

Braungart, M., Hoyer, W., & Braungart, R. (1979). Fear of crime and the elderly. In A. P. Goldstein, W. J. Hoyer, & P. J. Monti (Eds.), *Police and the elderly.* New York: Pergamon.

Braungart, M., Braungart, R. & Hoyer, W. J. (1980). Age, sex, and social factors in fear of crime. *Sociological Focus, 13*(1) 55–66.

Brillon, Y. (1987). *Victimization and fear among the elderly.* Toronto: Butterworth.

Bureau of Justice Statistics. (1983). *Criminal victimization in United States, 1982.* Washington,DC: U.S. Government Printing Office.

Bureau of Justice Statistics. (1991). *Black victims.* Washington, DC: U.S. Government Printing Office.

Bureau of Justice Statistics. (1992a). *Criminal victimization in United States, 1991.* Washington, DC: U.S. Government Printing Office.

Bureau of Justice Statistics. (1992b). *Elderly victims.* Washington, DC: U.S. Government Printing Office.

Bureau of Justice Statistics. (1993). *Criminal victimization in United States, 1992.* Washington, DC: U.S. Government Printing Office.

Butler, R. (1975). *Why survive? Being old in America.* New York: Harper & Row.

Carlton-LaNey, I. (1991). Some considerations of the rural elderly Blacks' underuse of social services. *Journal of Gerontological Social Work, 16,* 3–15.

Carter, K., & Beaulieu, L. (1984). *Rural crime in Florida: Victimization study of the rural nonfarm population.* Mississippi State, MS: Southern Development Center.

Clark, R. P., Ekblom, H. M., & Mayhew, P. (1985). Elderly victims of crime and exposure to risk. *The Howard Journal, 24,* 1–10.

Clemente, F., & Kleiman, M. B. (1976). Fear of crime among the aged. *The Gerontologist, 16,* 207–210.

Clemente, F., & Kleiman, M. B. (1977). Fear of crime in the United States: A multivariate analysis. *Social Forces, 56,* 519–531.

Cohen, L., & Cantor, D. (1981). Residential burglary in United States: Lifestyle and demographic factors associated with the probability of victimization. *Journal of Research in Crime and Delinquency, 18,* 113–127.

Cook, F., Skogan, W., Cook, T., & Antunes, G. (1978). Criminal victimization of the elderly: The physical and economic consequences. *The Gerontologist, 18,* 338–349.

Dancy, J. (1980). *The Black elderly: A guide for practitioners.* Ann Arbor: Institute of Gerontology, University of Michigan/Wayne State University.

Downing, R. A., & Copeland, E. J. (1980). Services for Black elderly: National or local problems? *Journal of Gerontological Social Work, 2,* 289–303.

Ennis, P. H. (1967). *Criminal victimization in United States: A report of a national survey.* Washington, DC: U.S. Government Printing Office.

Erskine, H. (1974). The polls: Fear of violence and crime. *Public Opinion Quarterly, 38,* 131–145.

Eve, S. B. (1985). Criminal victimization and fear of crime among the noninstitutionalized elderly in the United States: A critique of the empirical research literature. *Victimology, 10,* 397–408.

Eve, S. B., & Eve, R. A. (1984). The effects of powerlessness, fear of social change, and social integration on fear of crime among the elderly. *Victimology, 9,* 290–295.

Garafalo, J. (1981). The fear of crime: Causes and consequences. *Journal of Criminal Law and Criminology, 72,* 839–857.

Garafalo, J., & Laub, J. (1979). The fear of crime: Broadening our perspective. *Victimology, 3,* 242–253.

Gordon, M. T., Riger, S., Bailly, R., & Heath, L. (1980). Crime, women and the quality of urban life. *SIGNS: Journal of Women in Culture and Society, 5,* S144–S160.

Gubrium, J. (1974). Victimization in old age: Available evidence and three hypotheses. *Crime and Delinquency, 20,* 245–250.

Hindelang, M. (1976). *Criminal victimization in eight American cities.* Cambridge, MA: Ballinger.

Hindelang, M., Gottfredson, M., & Garafalo, J. (1978). *Victims of personal crimes.* Cambridge, MA: Ballinger.

Husaini, B. A., Moore, S., & Castor, R. S. (1991). Social and psychological well being of Black elderly living in high-rises for the elderly. *Journal of Gerontological Social Work, 16,* 57–77.

Jackson, J. (1988). *The Black American elderly.* New York: Springer.

Janson, P., & Ryder, L. L. (1983). Crime and the elderly: The relationship between risk and fear. *The Gerontologist, 23*(2), 207–212.

Jayewardene, T. J., Juliani, T. J., & Talbot, C. K. (1983). The elderly as victims of crime (Crime Victims, Working Paper No. 5). Research and Statistics Division, Policy Planning and Development Branch, Department of Justice, Canada.

Lawton, M. P., Nahemow, L, Yaffe, S., & Feldman, S. (1976). Psychological aspects of crime and fear of crime. In J. Goldsmith & S. S. Goldsmith (Eds.), *Crime and the elderly*. Lexington, MA: Lexington.

Lawton, M. P., & Yaffe, S. (1980). Victimization and fear of crime in elderly public housing tenants. *Journal of Gerontology, 35,* 768–779.

Lee, G. (1982a). Sex differences in fear of crime among the older people. *Research on Aging, 4,* 284–298.

Lee, G. (1982b). Residential location and fear of crime among the elderly. *Rural Sociology, 47,* 655–669.

Lee, G. (1983). Social integration and fear of crime among older persons. *Journal of Gerontology, 38,* 745–750.

Lee, N., & Coulander, M. (1982). Fear of crime among the elderly: The role of crime prevention programs. *The Gerontologist, 22,* 388–392.

Lejeune, R., & Alex, N. (1973). On being mugged: The event and its aftermath. *Urban Life and Culture, 2,* 259–287.

Linquist, J., & Duke, J. M. (1982). The elderly at risk: Explaining the fear of crime paradox. *Criminology, 20,* 115–126.

Liska, A., Lawrence, J. L., & Sanchirico, A. (1982). Fear of crime as a social fact. *Social Forces, 60,* 760–770.

Lotz, R. (1979). Public anxiety about crime. *Pacific Sociological Review, 22,* 241–254.

Maldonado, D. (1982). Prevention among the minority elderly. In S. O. Miller, G. Neal, & C. Scott (Eds.), *Primary prevention approaches to the development of mental health services for ethnic minorities: A challenge to social work education and practice*. New York: Council on Social Work Education.

Markides, K., & Mindel, C. (1987). *Aging and ethnicity*. Newbury Park, CA: Sage.

Midwest Research Institute. (1977). *Crime against the elderly: Patterns and prevention*. Kansas City, KS: Midwest Research Institute Norton.

Minkler, M., & Stone, R. (1985). The feminization of poverty and older women. *Gerontologist, 25,* 351–357.

Nye, W. P. (1993). Amazing grace: Religion and identity among elderly Black individuals. *International Journal and Human Development, 36,* 103–114.

Ollenburger, J. C. (1981). Criminal victimization and fear of crime. *Research on Aging, 3,* 101–118.

Ortega, S. T., & Myles, J. L. (1987). Race and gender effects on fear of crime: An interactive model with age. *Criminology, 25,* 133–152.

Pollack, L., & Patterson, A. (1980). Territoriality and fear of crime in elderly and nonelderly homeowners. *Journal of Social Psychology, 111,* 119–129.

Ralston, P. A. (1983). Senior center utilization by Black elderly adults: Social attitudinal and knowledge correlates. *Journal of Gerontology, 39,* 224–229.

Reiss, A. (1967). *Studies in law and law enforcement in major metropolitan areas*. Washington, DC: U.S. Government Printing Office.

Reynolds, P., & Byth, D. (1976). *Occurrence, reaction to and perception of victimization in an urban setting: Analysis of a survey in the twin cities region*. Unpublished monograph, University of Minnesota, Minneapolis.

Richardson, V. (1992). Service use among urban African American elderly people. *Social Work, 37,* 47–54.

Sacco, V. (1982). The effects of mass media on perceptions of crime: A reanalysis of the issues. *Pacific Sociological Review, 25,* 475–493.

Spence, S. A., & Atherton, C. R. (1991). The Black and the social service delivery system: A study of factors influencing the use of community-based services. *Journal of Gerontological Social Work, 16,* 19–32.

Spence, S. A., & Maxfield, M. (1981). *Coping with crime: Individual and neighborhood reactions*. Beverly Hills, CA: Sage.

Stafford, M., & Galle, O. R. (1984). Victimization rates, exposure to risk and fear of crime. *Criminology, 22,* 173–185.

Taylor, R., & Hale, M. (1986). Testing alternative models of fear of crime. *Journal of Criminal Law and Criminology, 77,* 151–189.

Taylor, R. J. (1985). The extended family as a source of support for Black elderly. *The Gerontologist, 25,* 488–495.

Teski, M. (1981). Environment, crime and the elderly. In D. Lester (Ed.), *The elderly victim of crime*. Springfield, IL: Charles C Thomas.

Toseland, R. W. (1982). Fear of crime: Who is most vulnerable? *Journal of Criminal Justice, 10,* 199–209.

U.S. Census Bureau. (1992). *Census population*. Washington, DC: U.S. Government Printing Office.

Wallace, S. (1990). Race versus class in the health care of African-American elderly. *Social Problems, 37,* 517–533.

Wiltz, C. J. (1982). Fear of crime, criminal victimization and elderly Blacks. *Phylon, 43,* 283–294.

Yin, P. T. (1980). Fear of crime among the elderly: Some issues and suggestions. *Social Problems, 27,* 492–504.

Yin, P. T. (1982). Fear of crime among the elderly. *Social Problems, 30,* 240–245.

Yin, P. T. (1985). *Victimization and the aged*. Springfield, IL: Charles C Thomas.

Article Review Form at end of book.

Discuss the validity of the widely held belief that males, high school dropouts, residents of large cities, and people over the age of thirty-five are the most likely to be victimized.

Criminal Victimization among Black Americans

Keith D. Parker

Keith D. Parker is currently an Assistant Professor at the University of Nebraska—Lincoln. His research interests include criminology, race and ethnicity, and stratification.

For decades, criminal victimization has been an important subject of investigation for social and behavioral scientists. This importance is the result, in part, of the uneven distribution of actual victimization (Karmen, 1984, p. 50). Studies of criminal victimization show that males were victimized more than women, except for cases of rape and purse snatching; young persons, especially teenagers and adults in their early twenties, were the targets of criminal attack much more often than older people; divorced or separated people and those who had never married experienced far greater troubles than married couples or widowed persons; Black people were victimized more than Whites or members of other minority groups, except for crimes of theft; households with family incomes less than $7,500 were burdened much more often by burglary than households in higher income categories; city dwellers were the targets of criminal attack much more often than those living in suburban or rural areas; and suburban resi-

dents were victimized more often than residents of rural areas (Bureau of Justice Statistics, 1986b). These findings do not necessarily indicate that victimization falls evenly among Blacks or other groups. They do suggest, however, that individuals and/or families unable to escape high crime areas too often fall prey to the criminal elements which, in increasing numbers, stalk the residents of these areas (Bureau of Justice Statistics, 1982, pp. 4–16; Reiman, 1979, p. 140).

The primary purpose of this article is to investigate the occurrence of criminal victimization among Black Americans. Many studies indicate that non-Whites and racial/ethnic minorities in general are most adversely affected by crime (Bureau of Justice Statistics, 1982, pp. 4–16; Silberman, 1980, pp. 159–169; Wilbanks, 1985, p. 117). The problem is generally conceded to be a phenomenon in metropolitan areas of the United States (Wiltz, 1982, p. 283).

The axiom that criminal victimization is a greater problem for urban than rural residents is not without merit. Many studies have found that victimization experience varies directly with community size or population density (Burdge, Kelly, Schweitzer, Keasler, & Russelman, 1979; Bureau of Justice Statistics, 1981, p. 13, 1985, p. 3,

1986a, p. 4; Curtis, 1975; Dahlin et al., 1981; Fischer, 1975, p. 1328; Harries, 1974). However, much of the existing research has used national, regional, or state data and has focused on comparisons involving a variety of community attributes (e.g., metro and nonmetro or urban and rural classifications) and interracial differences (e.g., Black and White or White and non-White). Few studies have focused on the intraracial attributes of individuals as potentially important factors influencing variations in criminal victimization. In particular, there is little beyond anecdotal observations to suggest that within each racial or ethnic population, certain categories of people face greater dangers than others. Two exceptions ("Black on Black," 1979; "When Brother," 1985) present evidence suggestive of greater victimization among certain groups. These findings, however, only pertain to crimes reported to the police and underestimate the true crime picture.

The strategy employed in the present study will allow us to focus on those variables most often included in studies of victimization. In general, the variables include sex, age, socioeconomic status, marital status, and size of community. Keying on these variables will maintain continuity with previous work and, at the same time, investigate the

Keith D. Parker, *Journal of Black Studies*, Vol. 22, No. 2, December 1991, pp. 186–195. Copyright © 1991 by Sage Publications, Inc. Reprinted by permission of Sage Publications, Inc.

supposition that criminal victimization hits certain groups of Black Americans harder than others.

In this article, variation in victimization experience according to the independent variables is assessed by using complex measures of both variables. We, therefore, hypothesize that victimization experience will differ as a result of gender, age, education, marital status, dwelling type, residential location, and household composition. In order to examine fully the effect of these variables on victimization, recalled victimization experience and/or the victimization of family members are employed as control variables in the analysis that follows.

Methods

The Sample

The data for this analysis were obtained from a simple random sample of 3,414 residents of Mississippi who were registered as licensed drivers and lived in the state in the spring of 1983. The sampling procedure involved mailing each individual a self-administered questionnaire, a cover letter explaining the purpose of the survey, and a stamped, self-addressed envelope in which he or she could return the completed instrument. Two subsequent mailings were made to those individuals who had not returned the completed instrument. After adjusting the sample for those who had died, moved out of the state, had an undeliverable address, or stated their race other than Black, 402 eligible respondents remained.

Measurement

The primary dependent variable, victimization experience, was measured by asking each respondent, were you, or any number of your household, the victim of a crime during 1982 (e.g., violent crimes such as assault and murder, theft, threats, or vandalism)? Responses to all questions were scored as *1* (no) or *2* (yes).

Residential location was given by a 6-point continuum ranging from farm and rural nonfarm to cities of over 50,000. The cutoff points separating intermediate categories included towns of less than 2,500

population, cities with populations between 2,500 to 9,999, and cities of 10,000 to 49,999.

The other variables were straightforward. Age was broken down into six groups: under 18 years of age, 18 to 24, 25 to 34, 35 to 44, 45 to 64, and 65 and over. Marital status was coded as not married and married. Dwelling type was coded as single family house and multiple family units. Household composition was coded as living alone and two or more individuals residing in the same dwelling. Education was coded as less than high school, high school graduate, and greater than high school. In addition, sex was included as a natural dichotomy; coded as female and male.

Statistical Procedures

Simple bivariate distributions were calculated to yield some idea of the relationship between the dependent and independent variables. Because of the dichotomous nature of the dependent variable(s) and the nominal or ordinal nature of the predictor variables, simple bivariate analysis was employed to examine the respondents' patterns of response to key variables. Similarly, a regression analysis was used which specifies sex, age, educational level, marital status, residence, dwelling type, and household composition as determinants of victimization experience.

Results

Before turning to the possible relationships between dependent and independent variables, it is useful as well as interesting to examine selected sociodemographic characteristics of respondents and their patterns of response to key variables. The data in Table 1, based solely on the responses of those who returned questionnaires, indicate that at least half of the respondents were the victim of some type of crime in 1982. The only exceptions were persons aged 45 and over and individuals residing on farms. In general, the data suggest that younger people, high school graduates, and those people not married were victimized more than their respective counterparts.

Table 2 shows the selected sociodemographic characteristics of re-

Table 1	Percentage Distribution of Victimized Respondents
Category	**% Victimized**[a]
Sex	
Male	56.0
Female	65.2
Age	
< 18	73.3
18–24	68.3
25–34	66.4
35–44	51.9
45–64	46.7
65+	42.9
Education	
< High school	52.7
High school	72.2
> High school	65.2
Marital status	
Married	54.0
Not married	67.0
Community size	
Farm	47.4
Rural nonfarm	56.3
Town < 2,500	60.0
2,500–9,999	71.0
10,000–49,999	64.0
50,000+	61.9
Dwelling type	
Single family	60.2
Multiple family	60.0
Household composition	
Alone	50.0
Two or more	61.0

[a]Percentage not victimized is, in each case, 100 minus the percentage victimized.

spondents and their patterns of response to the four general categories of crime. The data reveal that about half of the respondents were victims of theft in 1982. Although respondents differed very little in their patterns of response to crimes of vandalism and threats, being young and the resident of a large city seem to contribute to victimization experience. For crimes of violence, however, certain sociodemographic characteristics such as age, education, residence, and household composition appear to be important factors influencing victimization.

The results of the regression analysis are reported in Table 3. The findings are presented, first, for the combined victimization experience (e.g., vandalism + theft + threats + vi-

Category	% Victimized by Specific Type of Crime[a]			
	Violent Crimes	Theft	Threats	Vandalism
Sex				
Male	16.6	49.2	13.5	15.1
Female	18.6	58.1	9.0	16.4
Age				
< 18	26.7	63.3	20.0	17.2
18–24	19.0	58.3	9.9	16.0
25–34	16.7	61.3	10.2	20.8
35–44	11.3	47.3	13.0	13.2
45–64	20.0	36.7	6.7	13.3
65+	16.7	41.4	13.3	3.7
Education				
< High school	19.8	45.3	12.7	12.6
High school	16.7	66.7	11.1	16.9
> High school	15.5	58.9	9.1	19.3
Marital status				
Married	15.7	48.1	8.9	15.8
Not married	19.1	59.8	12.9	15.5
Community size				
Farm	10.0	39.5	5.0	8.3
Rural nonfarm	18.3	51.9	11.5	12.7
Town < 2,500	14.3	52.7	5.4	9.3
2,500–9,999	16.4	64.5	12.9	16.4
10,000–49,999	21.1	56.8	11.8	16.4
50,000+	23.8	54.8	16.3	32.5
Dwelling type				
Single family	17.5	54.3	11.2	15.3
Multiple family	17.3	49.7	11.1	16.9
Household composition				
Alone	8.0	52.0	3.8	25.9
Two or more	18.2	54.2	11.7	14.9

[a]Percentage not victimized is, of course, 100 minus percentage victimized.

olent crimes = victimization in 1982) and, second, separately for violent crimes, theft, threats, and vandalism. The data show that for overall victimization, sex is clearly the strongest determinant (beta = .172), followed by age (.114). Females and younger people were the targets of criminal victimization much more often than their counterparts. Household composition, marital status, residence, dwelling type, and education do not effect victimization.

When looking at the four general victimization categories, one finds that age (.131) and residence (.106) are significant predictors of crimes of violence. Younger people and residents of large cities were victimized more than older people and residents of small towns. Further inspection of the data indicates that sex (.159) is a significant determinant of theft victimization. As with overall victimization, females experienced more crimes of theft than males. For the act of threat, age is the strongest determinant (.109), followed by residence (.103) and sex (.086). Younger people, residents of larger cities, and males were threatened more than older people, residents of small towns, and females. The strongest determinants of vandalism are sex (.186) and marital status (.092). Females and married couples were vandalized more than others.

Summary and Conclusions

The results of this analysis provide the basis for several observations which both substantiate and contradict earlier research findings. As noted previously, most of the contemporary literature on victimization asserts that males, non-Whites, urban residents, low income families or households, and younger people experienced far greater victimization than others. However, the findings reported here (see Table 1) call into question such assertions.

The data indicate that targets of criminal victimization in 1982 were more likely to be females than males, high school graduates than high school dropouts, residents of mid-size towns (e.g., 2,500 to 9,999 population) than large cities, people under the age of 35 than those over age 35, and individuals living in the household with others than those living alone.

The findings of this study suggest that the burden of victimization falls unevenly, hitting certain groups of people harder than others. In particular, females and young people faced more incidents of victimization than their counterparts. Substantively, these findings suggest that studies reporting higher rates of victimization among Blacks, especially those describing Blacks as a monolithic group, should be reevaluated. A comprehensive explanation of the effects of individual characteristics on victimization must not only entail careful consideration of between-group attributes, but within-group characteristics.

The findings of the effects of selected sociodemographic characteristics on the effects of violent crimes, theft, threats, and vandalism are less impressive. The data show that about half of the respondents were victims of theft in 1982 (see Table 2). Only about 15% had been vandalized in that year. Only 11% had been threatened, but 17% reported they had been victims of violent crimes. The failure to detect

Table 3 Regression of Victimization, Violent Crimes, Theft, Threats, and Vandalism with Independent Variables

	Victimization	Violent Crimes	Theft	Threats	Vandalism
Household composition	.048	.062	−.046	.072	.063
Marital status	−.064	−.044	−.078	−.018	.092*
Sex	.171***	.023	.158***	.085*	.186***
Age	.114**	.131**	.054	.109**	.071
Residence	.056	.108**	.007	.104**	.055
Dwelling type	−.041	−.063	−.012	−.065	.012
Education	.045	.022	−.011	.039	.058

*$p < .10$; **$p < .05$; ***$p < .01$.

significant effects of selected sociodemographic characteristics on threats, vandalism, and violent crimes could, of course, reflect the rural composition of the population base. Moreover, it could reflect methodological limitations of the analysis. Nevertheless, these findings suggest that criminal victimization is not a racial problem. They indicate that certain individuals are victimized more often than others. The analysis presented in Table 3 shows that

1. Sex and age are significantly related to overall criminal victimization.

2. Residence and dwelling type are significantly related to violent crimes.

3. Sex is significantly related to theft.

4. Sex, age, and residence are significantly related to threats.

5. Marital status and sex are significantly related to vandalism.

Data such as these demonstrate that victimization is not an exclusively urban or Black problem. In fact, in some respects, victimization may be more of a problem for young people, females, and residents of mid-size cities than for Blacks or urban residents. The social and behavioral scientists concerned about the quality of life in America cannot afford to dismiss criminal victimization as an urban issue or as an exclusive problem for Black Americans. Hence, future research should investigate the possibility that the antecedents of victimization are individual characteristics (e.g., age, sex, marital status) and the attributes of specific communities (e.g., urban, rural, community's experience with rapid growth, length of residence) rather than race.

References

Black on Black crime. (1979, August) *Ebony* Special Issue.

Burdge, R. J., Kelly, R. M., Schweitzer, H. J., Keasler, L., & Russelman, A. (1979). *Crime victimization in Illinois: The citizen's perspective.* Urbana: University of Illinois Press.

Bureau of Justice Statistics. (1981). *Violent crime in the United States.* Washington, DC: U.S. Department of Justice.

Bureau of Justice Statistics. (1982). *Criminal victimization in the United States, 1980.* Washington, DC: U.S. Department of Justice.

Bureau of Justice Statistics. (1985). *Households touched by crime, 1984.* Washington, DC: U.S. Department of Justice.

Bureau of Justice Statistics. (1986a). *Criminal victimization in the United States, 1984.* Washington, DC: U.S. Department of Justice.

Bureau of Justice Statistics. (1986b). *Households touched by crime, 1985.* Washington, DC: U.S. Department of Justice.

Curtis, L. (1975). *Violence, race, and culture.* Lexington, MA: D. C. Heath.

Dahlin, D. C., Roche, M. R., Spaker, D., Rumbols, J., Swenson, D., LaPierre, R., Wise, S., & Orr, R. (1981). *Crime prevention in South Dakota.* Vermillion: University of South Dakota Press.

Fischer, C. (1975). Toward a subcultural theory of urbanism. *Journal of Sociology, 80*(6), 1319–1341.

Harries, K. D. (1974). *The geography of crime and justice.* New York: McGraw-Hill.

Karmen, A. (1984). Crime victims: An introduction to victimology. Monterey, CA: Brooks/Cole.

Reiman, J. H. (1979). *The rich get richer and the poor get prison: Ideology, class, and criminal justice.* New York: Wiley.

Silberman, C. E. (1980). *Criminal violence, criminal justice.* New York: Vintage.

When brother kills brother. (1985, September 16). *Time,* pp. 32–35.

Wilbanks, W. (1985). Is violent crime intraracial? *Crime & Delinquency, 31*(1), 117–128.

Wiltz, C. J. (1982). Fear of crime, criminal victimization and elderly Blacks. *Phylon, 43*(4), 283–294.

Article Review Form at end of book.

WiseGuide Wrap-Up

- Some individuals sentenced to death row are released by the introduction of new exculpatory evidence.

- High school dropouts have the highest homicide risk of all educational groups.

- Personal vulnerability has been found to be the strongest determinant factor of fear of crime among the black elderly.

R.E.A.L. Sites

This list provides a print preview of typical **Coursewise** R.E.A.L. sites. (There are over 100 such sites at the **Courselinks**™ site.) The danger in printing URLs is that web sites can change overnight. As we went to press, these sites were functional using the URLs provided. If you come across one that isn't, please let us know via email to: webmaster@coursewise.com. Use your Passport to access the most current list of R.E.A.L. sites at the **Courselinks** site.

Site name: African Reparations Movement

URL: http://the.arc.co.uk/arm/home.html

Why is it R.E.A.L.? This site offers information pertinent to the struggle for reparations for the harm done to Africa and the African diaspora through enslavement, colonization, and racism. It contains articles covering topics that range from hijacked African treasures to slavery.

Key topics: African Americans, slavery, racism, Africa, global order, reparations

Try this: Explain why some argue that the underdevelopment and poverty that affect ghetto conditions in which many African Americans live in the United States and elsewhere are not the result of laziness, incompetence, or corruption of Blacks.

Site name: National Institute of Justice

URL: http://www.ojp.usdoj.gov/nij/victdocs.htm

Why is it R.E.A.L.? This site contains information on victims of crime. Specifically, it allows you to read the existing victimology-related literature online. Topics discussed include the rights of crime victims, stalking, the victimization of immigrants, and batterer programs.

Key topics: victimization, victims' rights, stalking, women, violence, immigrants, child sexual molestation

Try this: What is the common sentence given to persons convicted of child sexual abuse? What is the percentage of crime victims who, once notified of their right to make an impact statement at sentencing, do so?

Site name: Office for Victims of Crime

URL: http://www.ojp.usdoj.gov/ovc/

Why is it R.E.A.L.? This site offers information pertaining to the victims of crime. It also contains a comprehensive list of links and addresses of various crime victims' organizations, as well as a number of publications on crime victims.

Key topics: victimization, victims of violence, sexual abuse, victim assistance, victims' rights, fraud victims

Try this: Discuss the three objectives of victim activism.

Index

Note: Names and page numbers in **bold** type indicate authors and their articles; page numbers in *italics* indicate illustrations; page numbers followed by *t* indicate tables; page numbers followed by *n* indicate notes.

D

Darden, Chris, 115, 136
data collection, 117–18
death penalty. *See* capital punishment
del Carmen, Alejandro, 3
Delo, Stacey, 164, 165
demagogic messages, 57
demand-side tactics, 154–55
differential involvement hypothesis, 146–47
differential punishment
    among federal prison inmates, 146–47
    basis for, 90–95
    in mandatory minimum sentences, 97,
        126, 128, 150, 158
    and the race card, 134
    and selective prosecution, 109
discrimination. *See* economic
    discrimination; racial discrimination
disorderly conduct arrests, 38t
disparate impact theory, 41–42, 43–45
disparate treatment theory, 41
DNA testing, 81
dogs, for drug detection, 113, 114, 116
Dred Scott v. Sanford, 86
driving, in American culture, 111
drug abuse
    among federal prison inmates, 143,
        144t, 146
    arrests by race for, 38t
    effective control of, 153–55
    and victimization, 162–63
drug control policies, racial bias in, 155–59.
    See also mandatory minimum sentences
drug education, 154–55
drug offenses
    incarceration rates for, 156
    mandatory minimum sentences for,
        125–26, 128, 130
    racial discrimination in penalties for,
        90, 91–95, 141, 156–58
drug-sniffing dogs, 113, 114, 116
drug trafficking
    and joblessness, 55, 149
    traffic stops for, 107, 108, 112–14
drug treatment, 154–55
drunken driving arrests, 38t
drunkenness, 38t
Dugan, Brian, 81, 82
Dukakis, Michael, 9

E

Eagle County Sheriff's Department, 114
Earned Income Tax Credit, 58
economic change, 56
economic disadvantage
    as cause of crime, 48–49, 50–51
    and racial antagonism, 52–59
economic discrimination
    and black crime, 3–4, 64–65, 69, 75–76
    impact on minority jury representation,
        101–2

education
    among federal prison inmates, 143, 145t
    as crime prevention measure, 4, 5
    and homicide rates, 171–72
elder abuse, 186, 188–89
elderly African-Americans, fear of crime
    among, 184–90
embezzlement arrests, 38t
employment, among federal prison
    inmates, 143, 144t
employment discrimination, 40–45
epidemics, of hate crimes, 13–21
equal employment opportunity, 40–45
Equal Protection Clause violations.
    See Fourteenth Amendment
equipment violations, 111
ethical formalism, 135, 137
ethnic groups, assimilation of, 74
ethnicity, 10, 44t. *See also* race
ethnic neighborhoods, 53
evolution, 63
execution. *See* capital punishment
exigency, 88, 89
Explanations of Criminal Behavior
    web site, 77
external vs. internal causation, 73–76

F

false confessions, 81
family life
    effects of unemployment on, 55
    impact on crime, 60–61
FBI hate crime data, 18
fear of crime
    among African-Americans, 184–90
    in Leeds survey, 176–83
federal prisons, racial profile of inmates
    in, 142–47
feminists, and hate crime "epidemic," 14, 22n
Ferguson, Florence S., 133
Fifteenth Amendment, 86, 89n
firearms
    and homicide rates, 172
    ownership by race, 144, 145t
Ford Heights Four, 164–68
forgery arrests, 38t
formless fear of crime, 186, 187t
The Fortune Society, 150
Fourteenth Amendment
    drug law violations of, 91, 92
    proving discrimination under, 93–94
    Supreme Court weakening of, 86
    text of, 89n
Fourth Amendment protections, erosion of,
    87, 88, 89n, 107–19
fraud arrests, 38t
Free, Marvin D. Jr., 125
free enterprise zones, 49
free-floating anger, 4
Fukurai, Hiroshi, 99

G

gambling arrests, 38t
gangs, in prisons, 151–52
Gauger, Gary, 80–82
gays and lesbians, and hate crime
    "epidemic," 14, 15, 18
gender
    and fear of crime, 187–88, 189–90
    and homicide rates, 170–71
gender bias, and hate crimes, 21n
genetics
    as early explanation for crime, 7
    and racial differences in crime rates,
        60–63, 72, 75
gerrymandering, 103
Gest, Ted, 149
Goetz, Bernhard, 15
Goldstein, Stephanie, 164, 165, 166
government, differing views of, 50–51
Gray, Paula, 165, 166
Griggs v. Duke Power Company, 40–41
Gyamerah, Jacquelyn, 90

H

Harris, David A., 107
Harris, Ryan, 81
hate crimes
    data about, 17–20
    history and, 20–21
    reasons for recognizing, 78
    support for epidemic view of, 13–17
Hate Crimes: Confronting Violence Against
    Lesbians and Gay Men, 15
Hate Crime Statistics Act, 18
Hawkins, Darnell F., 71
Hawkins, Steven, 83
head perimeter, 63
Henry, Jessica S., 13
Hernandez, Alejandro, 81
Herndon, Angelo, 91
Hispanics
    California homicide trends among,
        171, 173t
    classifying, 9, 38
    competition with African-Americans,
        54, 56
    and discriminatory traffic stops, 107–19
    in police departments, 43t
    profile among federal prison inmates,
        145–46
    scarcity in criminological studies, 33
homicides
    among African-Americans, 8, 64, 71–76,
        169, 171, 173t
    arrests by race for, 38t
    and capital punishment, 80–82, 102, 164,
        165–66
    data about, 23n
    news stories about, 26
    trends in California, 169–74
Horton, Willie, 9, 37, 39

Howard Beach incident, 16, 22–23*n*
hypothetical imperative, 135

I

Illinois State Police, 113–14
incarceration rates
    among African-Americans, 9, 125, 141,
        149–50, 155–58
    increases in, 8–9
    inmate characteristics and, 142–47
index offenses
    arrests by race for, 38*t*, 155–56
    as minority of total crimes, 10, 11*n*, 153
    percentage of white vs. black
        perpetrators of, 35, 37, 38*t*
individual perspectives, 6, 7
Innocence Project, 81
integration, 4, 50, 51
intelligence, and race, 62, 63
internal vs. external causation, 73–76
interracial marriage, 37
intimidation, 18
inventory searches, 124*n*

J

Jackson, Kevin L., 142
Jacobs, James B., 13
jails, web sites about, 161
Jews, hostility against, 17, 21
judges, racial discrimination by, 102–3
judicial activism, 97
juries, bias in selecting, 99–104
jury nullification, 134
justice system
    biased use of death penalty by, 67, 109
        (*see also* capital punishment)
    differential punishment in
        (*see* differential punishment)
    and discriminatory traffic stops, 107–19
    effects of sentencing reform on, 125–31
    federal prison inmate racial profiles,
        142–47
    proving discrimination in, 93
    and the race card, 133–37
    racial bias in jury selection, 99–104
    racial inequities in, 4–5, 10
    studies of, 7–8
    web sites about, 139
    wrongful convictions by, 80–82, 164–68

K

Kant, Immanuel, 135
King, John William, 151–52
King, Rodney, 133
Klanwatch, 17–18
Know Nothing Party, 21
Korgen, Kathleen O., 33
Krooth, Richard, 99
Ku Klux Klan, 20

L

LaFree, Gary, 6
larceny theft arrests, 38*t*
law enforcement, employment
    discrimination in, 40–45. *See also* police
lawyers, court-appointed, 81, 140
Leeds survey, 176–83
legal system. *See* justice system
Lest We Forget: White Hate Crimes, 15
Lionberg, Larry, 164, 165
liquor law violations, 38*t*
Long, Breckenridge, 21
Long Walk, 20
lynching, 20, 66

M

mandatory minimum sentences
    development of, 125–26
    racial bias in, 97, 127–28, 130, 150, 158
marijuana laws, 94–95
Marxist theory, 134, 135–36
Maryland State Police, 112–13
Maryland v. Buie, 88
materialism, 67–68
McCleskey, Warren, 94, 109
McCleskey v. Kemp, 94, 109
McDonnell Douglas v. Green, 41
media. *See* news media
migration, 74, 101–2
Miranda v. Arizona, 88
mixed race classifications, 33–34
moral decline, 50–51
moral turpitude, 93, 94
mortality rates, among African-American
    males, 67
motor vehicle theft arrests, 38*t*
multiculturalism, web sites about, 47
murders. *See* homicides
mutual assent, 87

N

National Crime Survey, 8, 9
National Criminal Justice Reference Service
    web site, 161
National Gay and Lesbian Task Force, 14
National Institute of Justice web site, 196
National Multicultural Institute web site, 47
National Union for Social Justice, 21
Native Americans, hate crimes against, 20
nativism, 20–21
Navajos, atrocities against, 20
Negro courts, 91
neighborhood problems, and fear of crime,
    181–82, 186, 187*t*
New Federalism, 52–53
new poverty neighborhoods, 56–57
news media
    coverage in Ford Heights Four case,
        164–65, 166, 167–68
    coverage of Simpson trial, 136

factors in crime story coverage by, 25–31
    reporting of hate crimes by, 14–15, 17, 18
    role in images of crime, 1
Newton, Huey, 103

O

Odell, Patricia M., 33
Office for Victims of Crime web site, 196
Omnibus Anti-Drug Abuse Act, 126
"one drop" rule, 9–10, 33
overcriminalization, 153

P

Parker, Keith D., 192
PBS Online Newshour Race Relations
    web site, 47
Pell grants, 150
penalties, effect on crime rates, 153–54
peremptory challenges, 101
personal victimization, 185, 187, 189*t*
Pinkney, Alphonso, 15
Plessy v. Ferguson, 87
police
    black suspicion of, 4, 85
    brutality against African-Americans,
        66–67
    discriminatory traffic stops by, 107–19
    formal policies for, 117
    hate crime data of, 18
    lying by, 81
    minority representation among, 43*t*
    racial harassment by, 37
    Supreme Court decisions affecting,
        85–86, 87–89
    view of death penalty, 83
policies, for police agencies, 117
politicians
    and hate crime "epidemic," 16–17
    influence on racial tensions, 57,
        58–59, 158
Polk, O. Elmer, 40
popular culture, violence in, 65–68
poverty
    in black urban neighborhoods, 54–57
    as factor in black crime rates, 68, 69
    and homicide, 75
prejudice, 18–19
prima facie cases, 41, 45*t*
prisons
    effect on inmates, 151–52
    federal inmate characteristics, 142–47
    private, 78
    web sites about, 161
    See also incarceration rates
private prisons, 78
probation, 129–30
problem neighborhoods, 181–82, 186, 187*t*
property crime arrests, 38*t*
prosecutors, sentencing power of, 127, 130
prostate cancer, 61
prostitution arrests, 38*t*

U.S. Supreme Court. *See* Supreme Court
U.S. Supreme Court multimedia database
    web site, 139

V

vagrancy arrests, 38*t*
vandalism
    arrests by race for, 38*t*
    victimization data for, 194
    worries about, 178–81
vicarious victimization, 185, 187, 189*t*
vice arrests, 38*t*
victim-offender dyad, 134
victims
    data about, 8, 17–18, 192–95
    elderly, 184
    influence on media crime coverage,
        26, 29, 30
    race of, 51, 64, 134, 162
    web sites about, 196
violence
    in American culture, 65–68
    genetic theories of, 75
    subcultural theory of, 74–75
Violence Against Women Act (1994), 16
violent crime
    among African-Americans, 64–69, 71–76,
        169, 171, 173*t*
    arrests by race for, 38*t*

association with blacks, 7, 36
and crack cocaine, 128
effect of harsh penalties on, 154
explanations for, 4, 55, 65–68, 71–76
growing concern about, 48
homicide trends in California, 169–74
media emphasis on, 25
race of victims, 162
victimization data for, 194
See also hate crimes
Vogel, Bob, 112
Volusia County Sheriff's Department, 112
voting rights, 86
vulnerability, perceptions of, 185, 186,
    187–88

W

Walker, Monica A., 176
Wall Street Journal/NBC News poll results,
    50–51
Warden, Rob, 165, 166
Wards Cove Packing v. Antonio, 41, 42, 44
war, glamorization of, 68
war on drugs, 153–59
Wayte v. U.S., 88
weapons offenses, 37*t*
white collar crimes, 10

whites
    California homicide trends among, 171
    concern about crime among, 177–83
    early repression by, 20–21, 65–67
    opinions on causes of crime, 50–51
    percentage of index crimes committed
        by, 35, 37, 38*t*
    profile among federal prison inmates,
        144, 145, 146
    in urban areas, 53
Whitfield, Jhenita, 114
Whren v. United States, 107–19
Wilkins, Robert, 112–13, 115
Williams, Dennis, 164, 165–66, 168
Wilson, William Julius, 52
Wilson v. Arkansas, 88
women, perceived risks for, 179
women's groups, and hate crime
    "epidemic," 14, 22*n*
"would have" rule, 107, 108, 109
wrongful convictions, 80–82, 164–68

Y

youth homicide, 171, 172

Z

Zorn, Eric, 167

Putting It in *Perspectives*
-Review Form-

Your name:_____   Date: _____

Reading title: _____

Summarize: Provide a one-sentence summary of this reading: _____

_____

_____

_____

Follow the Thinking: How does the author back the main premise of the reading? Are the facts/opinions appropriately supported by research or available data? Is the author's thinking logical?

_____

_____

_____

_____

_____

Develop a Context (answer one or both questions): How does this reading contrast or compliment your professor's lecture treatment of the subject matter? How does this reading compare to your textbook's coverage?

_____

_____

_____

_____

_____

_____

Question Authority: Explain why you agree/disagree with the author's main premise.

_____

_____

_____

_____

_____

_____

COPY ME! Copy this form as needed. This form is also available at http://www.coursewise.com
Click on: *Perspectives*.